# DRAWN FROM NATURE
## The Flowering of Irish Botanical Art

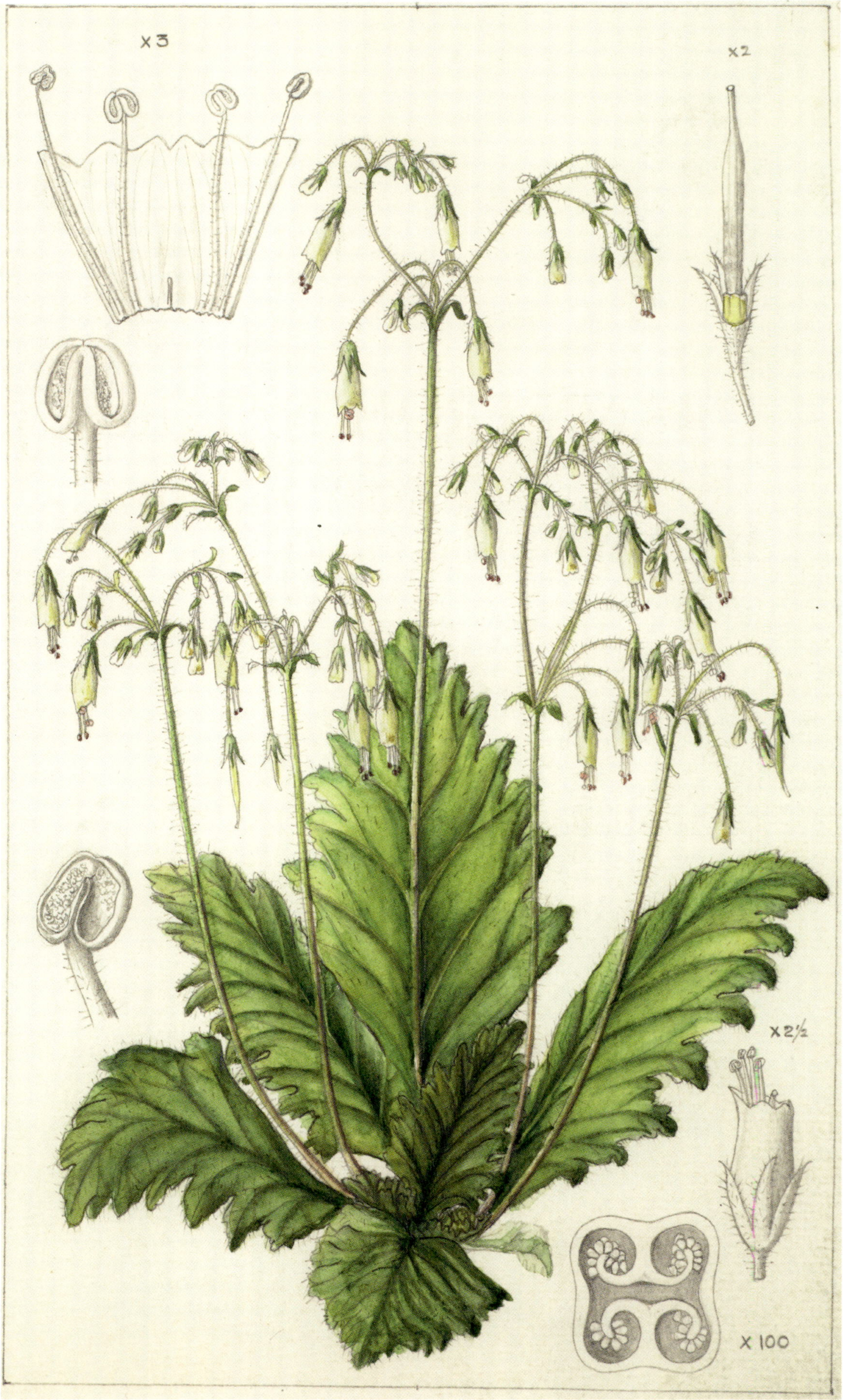
x 3
x 2
x 2½
x 100

# DRAWN FROM NATURE
## The Flowering of Irish Botanical Art

**by**
**Patricia Butler**

**with Foreword by**
**Dr Shirley Sherwood, OBE**

ACC ART BOOKS

8721

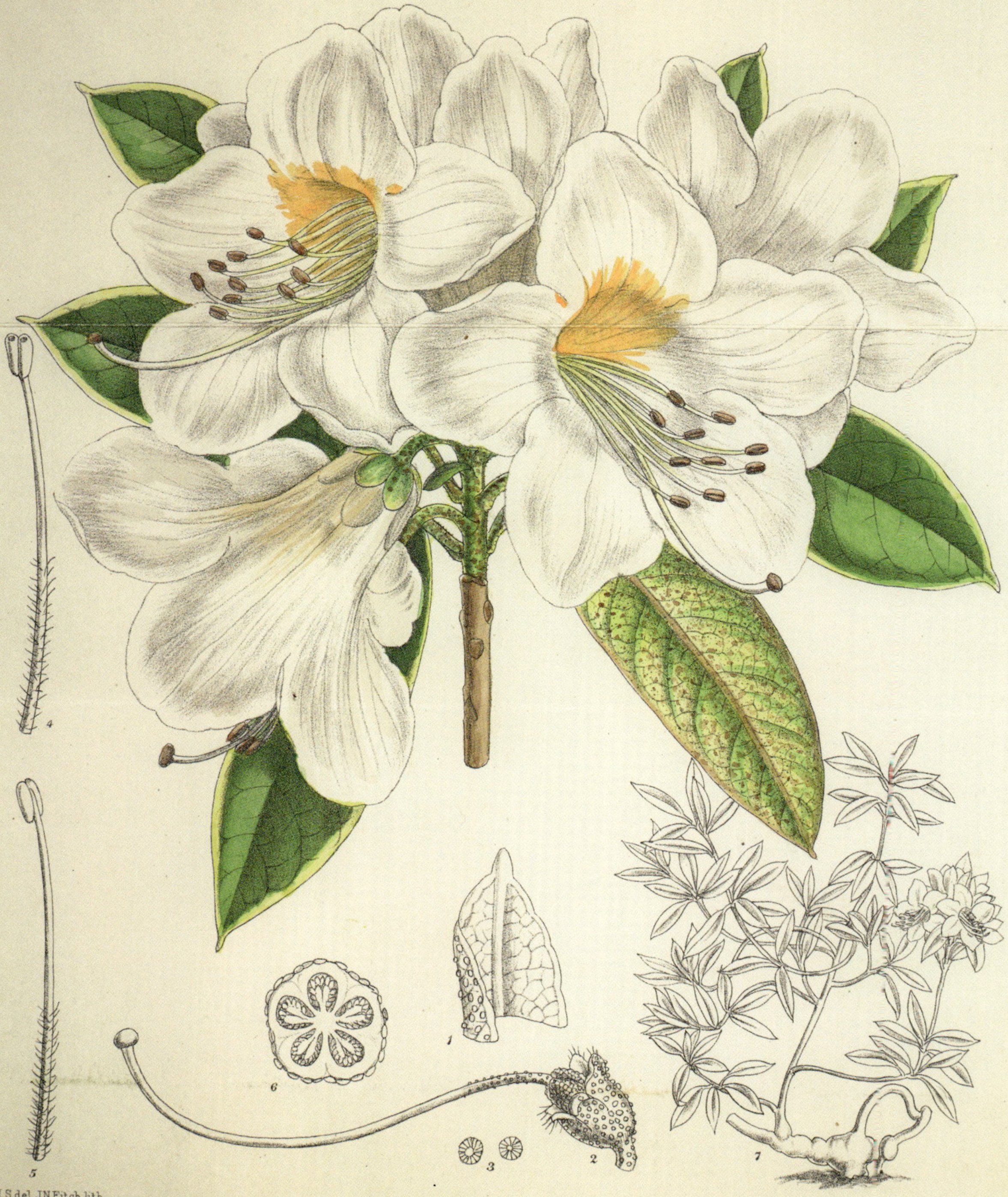


M.S.del. J.N.Fitch lith.

Vincent Brooks, Day & Son Ltd imp

L. Reeve & Cº London.

# Contents

# Foreword

I have had many trips to Ireland and until recently wondered why botanical art tended to be a somewhat forgotten part of Irish heritage. Irish botanical artists seemed to have no local platform and no society on which to exhibit and support their contribution not only to botany but to art in general.

All this changed in March 2014 when the Irish Society of Botanical Artists (ISBA) was founded with the outstanding support and encouragement from the Director and staff of the National Botanic Gardens, Glasnevin, Dublin. I was delighted to open their first exhibition based on the Irish alphabet where I met many of the country's devoted and original botanical artists.

Today, ISBA is providing much needed encouragement and support for botanical artists throughout Ireland. There have been some excellent publications produced by the Society and group meetings, lectures, exhibitions and demonstrations are proving to be an ideal platform through which artists can join together in order to exchange ideas and offer support to one another. This has resulted in a number of contemporary Irish botanical artists' work being represented in both national and international collections around the world including my own gallery, The Shirley Sherwood Gallery of Botanical Art, RBG, Kew, London which is devoted entirely to botanical art.

This book, based to some degree on Patricia Butler's exhibition *Drawn from Nature. Irish Botanical Art* held at the National Gallery of Ireland, Dublin (March–August 2020) is the first real attempt to chart the history of Irish botanical illustration from around 1730 to the present. I am sure it will succeed in providing encouragement and recognition for Irish botanical artists both at home and abroad and above all, draw attention to the splendid body of work held in both private and public collections. Botanical art is alive and well in Ireland and I would like to think this book will help to increase the reader's interest in this flourishing field.

Dr Shirley Sherwood, OBE

*Dr Sherwood has always been interested in plants as well as the arts. She trained as a botanist at the University of Oxford and was awarded her DPhil working with a team which discovered the important drug, Tagamet.*

*She began the Shirley Sherwood Collection in 1990 and this now includes over 1,000 paintings and drawings, representing the work of more than 300 contemporary artists from 36 countries around the world. Dr Sherwood has exhibited her collection in many prestigious locations including the Smithsonian Institution, Washington, the Ashmolean Museum, Oxford, the Marciana Library, Venice, the Real Jardín Botánico, Madrid and in Tokyo and Sydney, Australia. Author of six books and many articles relating to botanical art, Dr Sherwood has served as an honorary trustee of the American Society of Botanical Artists and on the Board of the Smithsonian Institution. She was awarded the Veitch Memorial Medal by the RHS and received an OBE for services to botanical art.*

*Recently, she completed a retrospective publication relating to her 30 years of collecting which accompanied a major exhibition in the Shirley Sherwood Gallery.*

# Preface

The tradition of botanical painting is one of the most skilled and captivating forms of expression. A delight in picturing plants, particularly flowering plants, and recording them for posterity has been a consistent source of inspiration for the botanical artist.

In contrast with Britain, Ireland does not appear to have had a strict, continuous history in the field of botanical illustration. Instead, vital contributions were made in a number of wide-ranging areas, beginning with early botanical exploration and collecting in 17th-century Ireland, together with recordings by 18th-century Irish botanical illustrators.

*Drawn from Nature: The Flowering of Irish Botanical Art*, based on an exhibition held at the National Gallery of Ireland entitled *Drawn from Nature. Irish Botanical Art* (March–August 2020), the author being invited to act as guest curator, explores distinguished contributions made by Irish artists down through the centuries.

Their work, expressed in a wide variety of fascinating areas included the field of design (see Chapter 5: A Designer of Distinction), ordnance survey work in 19th-century Ireland (Chapter 7: A Recorder of Life) and women's vital contributions but lack of public recognition in the field of plant exploration and illustration (Chapter 8: The Fair Discoverers). Also included in this publication are a selection of illustrated floras which began to place on record the well-known plants of the day together with those of the keen, amateur botanical artist.

Research and access to both public and private collections have been made available largely through the generosity of their owners or custodians. For the first time, unknown examples of the work of Irish botanical illustrators, both past and present, are appearing in print.

The backgrounds, motivations and methods of the artists discussed in this book are diverse, yet all were and indeed are today connected by a shared desire to observe, record and advance our knowledge of the natural world – botanical artists demonstrating how they have triumphed in bringing the plant to life.

Patricia Butler
Summer 2023

# Chapter 1
# Botanical Exploration in Ireland c.1600–c.1800

*When England and France had their provincial Floras, the Botany of* [Ireland] *was as much known as that of an island in the Pacific*[1]

Ireland was relatively isolated in the 17th and eighteenth centuries due to a number of factors, geographical, social, economic and intellectual. As a result, botanical exploration and recording were somewhat restricted and largely the preserve of enthusiastic individuals, many of whom had no opportunity to train as full-time professional horticulturists; nor, indeed, were they full-time academics.

Philip O'Sullivan Beare (c.1590–1636) was one such early enthusiast. Soldier, writer and exile, his vigorous defence of Ireland's fame against her malicious representation propounded by 12th-century writer Giraldus Cambrensis (in *Topographia Hibernica*) may be found in O'Sullivan's publication *Zoilomastix* (1625–1626),[2] in which the author (while an exile living in Spain) provides an early seventeenth-century manuscript account of the Irish flora (including grasses, fruit-bearing trees and herbs), together with a general account of the natural history of Ireland. Although O'Sullivan did not set out to attempt a description of the flora and fauna of this entire island, he did succeed in recording Irish plants in a systematic manner, each one being noted in Latin, Greek, Spanish and Irish, together with a commentary. It is thought he 'consulted at least one botanical work, the two-volume *Historia generale des plantes* [*sic*] (1615) by the French botanist and physician, Jacques Dalechamps (1513–1588)'.[3]

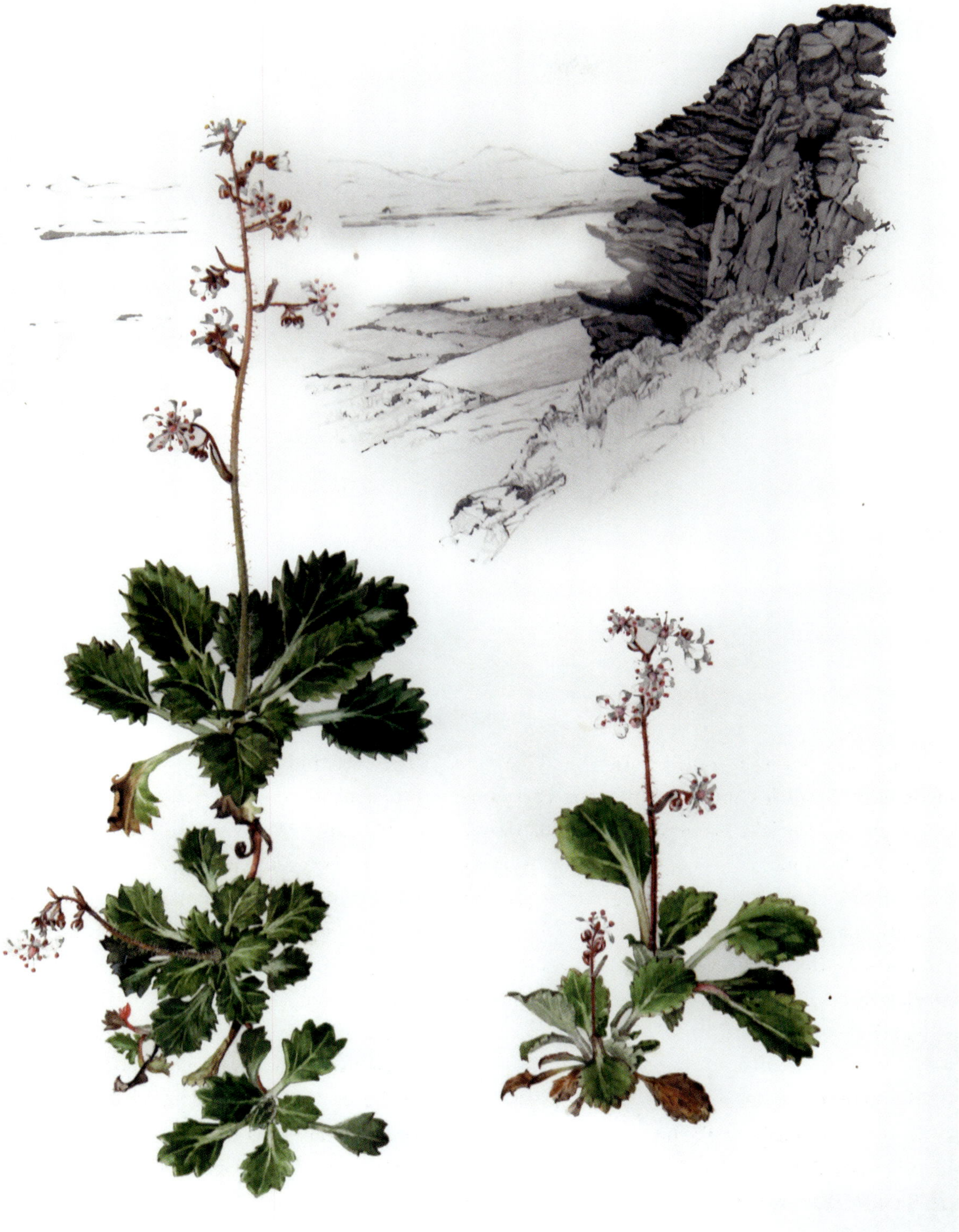

Fig. 1. *Saxifraga spathularis*, St Patrick's cabbage
Watercolour and pencil by Wendy F. Walsh
[© Estate of Wendy Walsh. Private collection. Reproduced by kind permission]

O'Sullivan may also have derived much of his awareness of the natural world from his own Munster childhood spent on Dursey Island, Co. Cork. The O'Sullivan Beare family settled in the Beara peninsula having come from South Tipperary in the early 13th century. O'Sullivan was born on Dursey Island c.1590. Among the plants O'Sullivan mentions in *Zoilomastix* is the sunflower:

> *We consider the sunflower well worth remembering because it is a wonder which even on a cloudy day moves itself around to the various aspects of the sun shining on the world, looking attentively at the star, its cup completely expanded as though captured by love of it; by night indeed as if affected by the desire for light, it covers over its flower, which be either white or yellow by again contracting its cup.*[4]

The second half of the 17th century witnessed one of the earliest to botanise in Ireland, antiquarian Edward Llwyd (Lhuyd) (1660–1709), born in Loppington, Shropshire, and recognised today as a pioneer of Welsh botany. Keeper of the Ashmolean Museum, Oxford (1690), he paid at least two visits to Ireland, recording several species new to both Britain and Ireland, including *Potentilla fruticosa*, *Saxifraga spathularis* and *Adiantum capillus-veneris*. Regarded as an excellent field naturalist, Llwyd was highly respected by his contemporaries and elected a Fellow of the Royal Society in 1708. The rare alpine plant the Snowdon lily was named in his honour: *Lloydia serotina* (now known as *Gagea serotina*).[5]

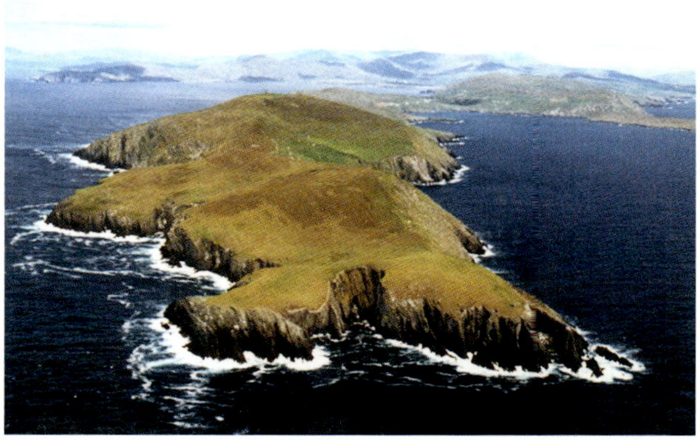

Fig. 2. Dursey Island, Co. Cork, southerly vista
[Aerial photograph by Daphne Pochin Mould. Reproduced by kind permission of the Trustees of Muckross House, Co. Kerry]

William Sherard (1659–1728), an influential figure in English botany of the late 17th and early 18th centuries, and a generous benefactor,[6] collected plants not only in Greece and Asia Minor, but also spent around three years in Ireland (1690–1693). Acting as tutor to the children of horticulturist, Sir Arthur Rawdon (1662–1695),[7] and while living on Rawdon's estate, Moira, Co. Down, Sherard availed of the opportunity to explore Ulster and its flora. His Irish plant records were later to be published by the father of English natural history, the Reverend John Ray (1627–1705).[8]

The first known systematic, scientific study of the Irish flora was initiated by another member of the church, the Reverend Richard Heaton (1601–1666), today acknowledged as Ireland's first known botanist, 'a man of competent skill in Botanicks and an honest person...'[9] Heaton's localised Irish plant

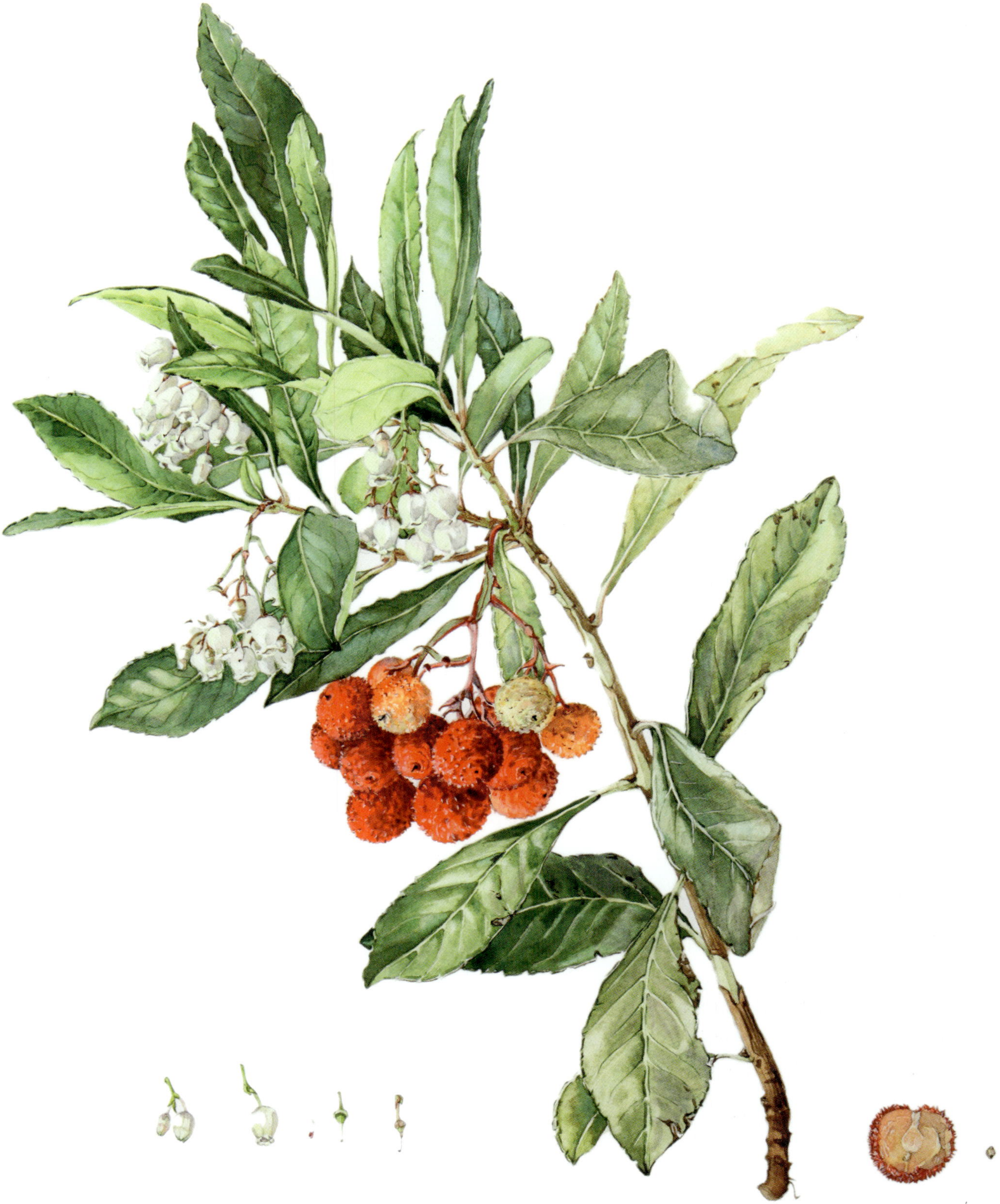

Fig. 3. *Arbutus unedo*, strawberry tree
Watercolour by Wendy F. Walsh
[© Estate of Wendy Walsh. Private collection. Reproduced by kind permission]

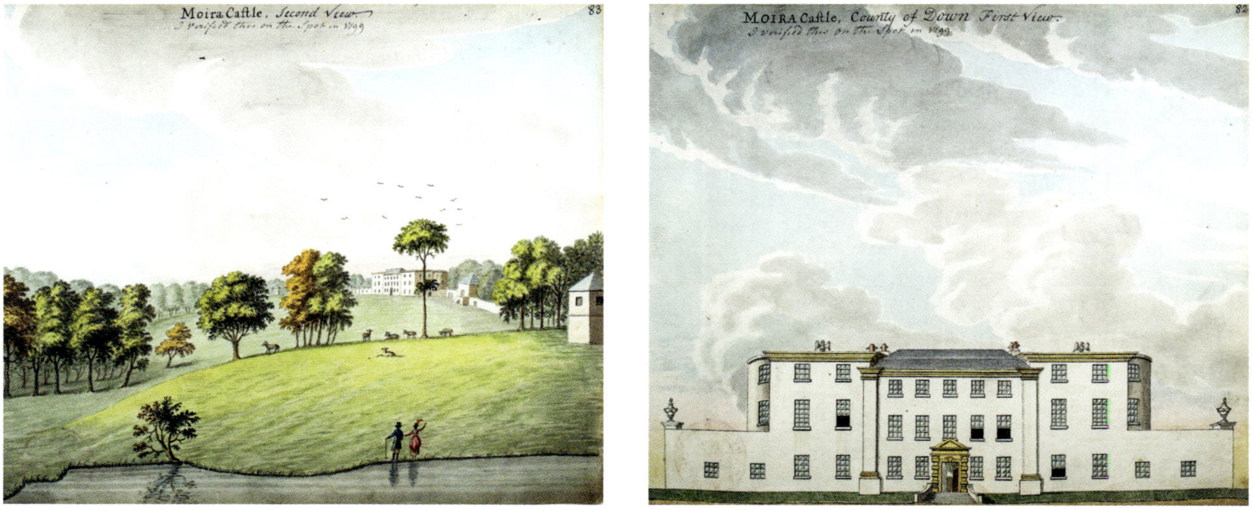


Fig. 4. Views of Moira Castle, Co. Down
[By permission of the Royal Irish Academy. © RIA]

records were made known as early as 1640. This was the first published record of native Irish plants and appeared in John Parkinson's (1567–1650) *Theatrum Botanicum* (1640).[10] Included were the strawberry tree (*Arbutus unedo*) found in 'the West part of Ireland', together with *Drosera anglica*, the great sundew that Heaton had collected from the Bog of Allen.[11] Lavishly illustrated with woodcuts and copperplate engravings, and including a portrait of the author, this substantial and influential herbal contained no botanical illustrations by Irish artists.

Ten years later, the situation had not changed. Heaton's native Irish-plant records[12] were revealed in physician William How's (1778–1841) English flora, *Phytologia Britannica* (1650),[13] which contains some of the earliest printed records of localised Irish plants, e.g., *Gentiana verna* (the spring gentian) and a native evergreen, the common *Juniperus repens* (now known as *Juniperus horizontalis*, the creeping juniper) collected by the Reverend Richard Heaton.

The exploration, study and portrayal of native Irish plants in early 18th-century Ireland were not only the work of keen and enthusiastic individuals but were also undertaken by members of the short-lived Dublin Physico-Historical Society of Ireland formed on 14 April 1744.[14] Its primary purpose was to carry out a county-by-county survey of Ireland and to promote an exploration of the country's natural history. Following its inception, Isaac Butler (1689/1690?–1755)[15] who described himself as a

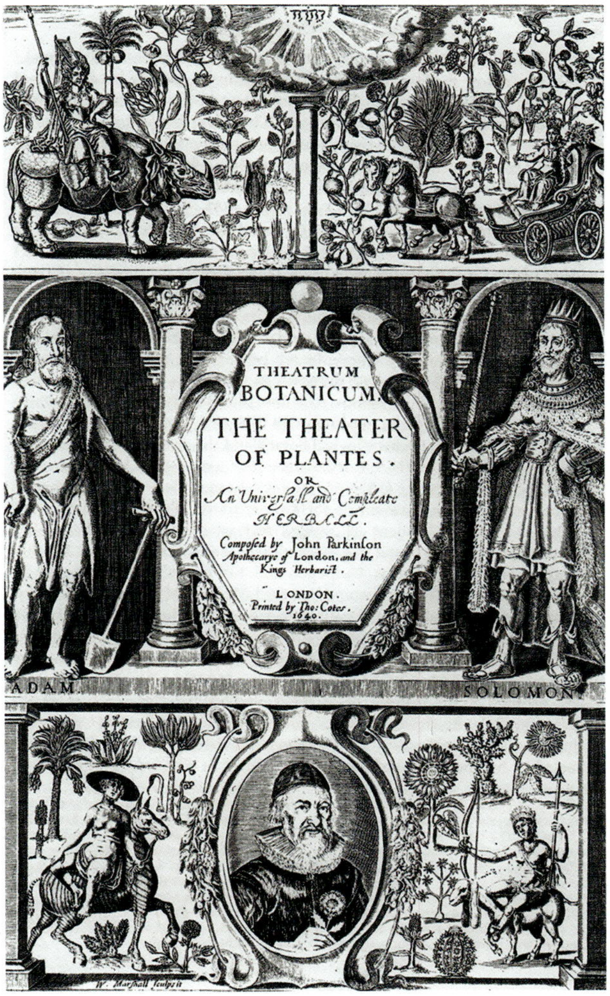


Fig. 5. Title page from Parkinson's *Theatrum Botanicum: The Theater of Plantes* (1640)
[Private collection. Reproduced by kind permission]

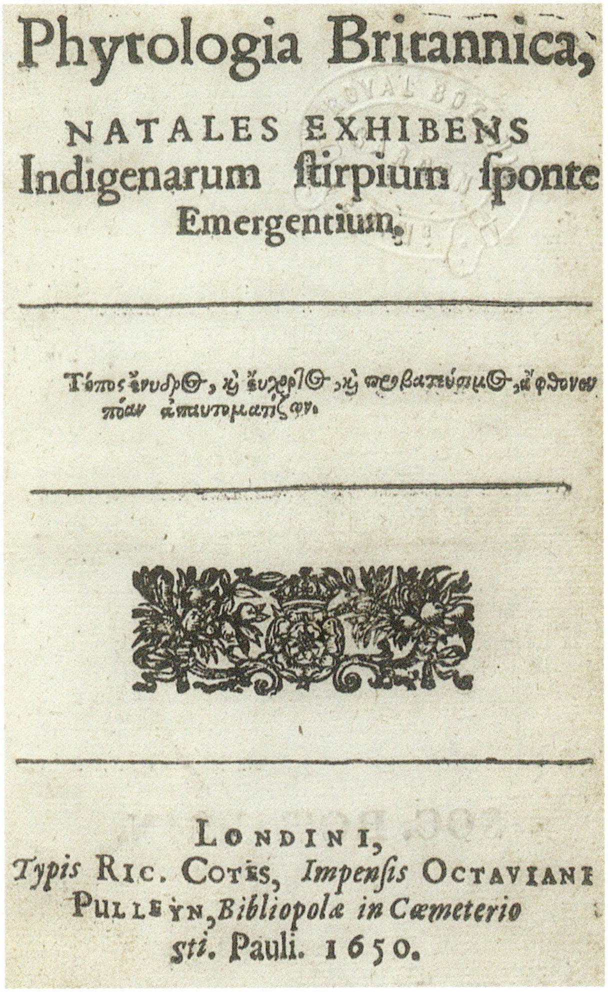

Phytologia Britannica,
NATALES EXHIBENS
Indigenarum stirpium sponte
Emergentium.

Τόπος ἔνυδρος, καὶ εὔχερος, καὶ περιβατεύσιμος, ἄφθονον
πόαν ἀπαυτοματίζων.

LONDINI,
*Typis* RIC. COTES, *Impensis* OCTAVIANI
PULLEYN, *Bibliopolæ in Cœmeterio*
*sti.* Pauli. 1650.

Fig. 6. Title page from *Phytologia Britannica* (1650)
[© Royal Botanic Gardens, Kew]

'student of astronomy and botany...and well skilled in the occult', was employed by a founder member of the Society and co-ordinator of surveys, Quaker physician Dr John Rutty (1697–1775).[16] Butler was requested to carry out, on behalf of the Society, field work relating to both botanical and geological specimens that would form part of a series of surveys. In May 1745, he undertook a survey of Dublin. However, it

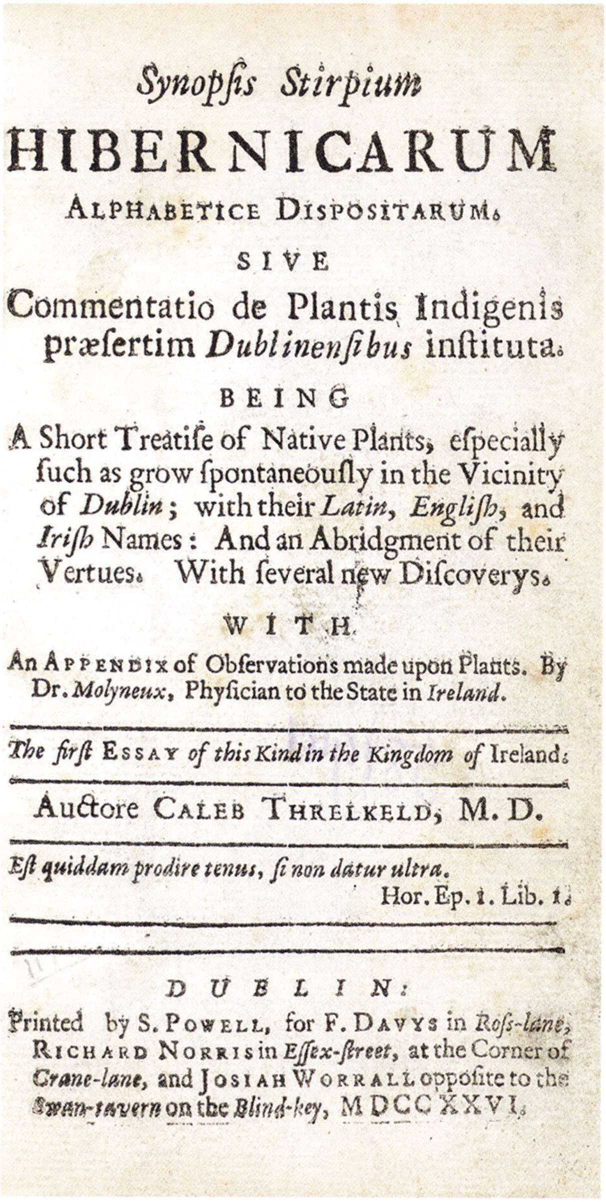

*Synopsis Stirpium*

HIBERNICARUM

ALPHABETICE DISPOSITARUM.

SIVE

Commentatio de Plantis Indigenis præsertim *Dublinensibus* instituta.

BEING

A Short Treatise of Native Plants, especially such as grow spontaneously in the Vicinity of *Dublin*; with their *Latin*, *English*, and *Irish* Names: And an Abridgment of their Vertues. With several new Discoverys.

WITH

An APPENDIX of Observations made upon Plants. By Dr. *Molyneux*, Physician to the State in *Ireland*.

*The first* ESSAY *of this Kind in the Kingdom of* Ireland.

Auctore CALEB THRELKELD, M.D.

*Est quiddam prodire tenus, si non datur ultra.*
Hor. Ep. 1. Lib. 1.

*DUBLIN:*

Printed by S. POWELL, for F. DAVYS in *Ross-lane*, RICHARD NORRIS in *Essex-street*, at the Corner of *Crane-lane*, and JOSIAH WORRALL opposite to the *Swan-tavern* on the *Blind-key*, MDCCXXVI.

Fig. 7. Title page from Caleb Threlkeld's *Synopsis Stirpium Hibernicarum* (1726)
[Courtesy, National Library of Ireland]

was not until 1772 that the two-volume work entitled *An Essay Towards a Natural History of the County of Dublin* (1772)[17] was finally published, not by the Society, which had survived for a mere eight years, but by the DS (later RDS). This was the first county natural history in Ireland. Relying on contributions from Butler, which were acknowledged, including all the plants he had observed, Rutty was cited as the author. This publication, which discussed a wide range of subjects, including Dublin's vegetation, soil, climate, fossils, minerals, animals and population, had received financial funding from the Royal College of Physicians of Ireland (£30) and enjoyed the support of 350 subscribers. In relation to Irish botany, it was a major contribution and included 28 species new to the known flora of Dublin, together with a unique account of Irish plants considered suitable for dyeing purposes.[18]

Following the Reverend Richard Heaton's death in 1666, there would appear to have been no immediate successor specialising in the field of Irish botanical studies. The latter had reached a low ebb, that is until the publication of Caleb Threlkeld's (1676–1728)[19] *Synopsis Stirpium Hibernicarum* (1726),[20] the first published catalogue of Irish plants. A graduate of Edinburgh University (1713), Threlkeld practised medicine in Dublin and made a study of Irish botany and, for around 12 years, spent his time collecting and recording plants in and around the city. His Irish flora, 'regarded as a first essay at a county Dublin flora no less than the earliest attempt to provide a general catalogue of Irish plants' (Colgan),[21] drew

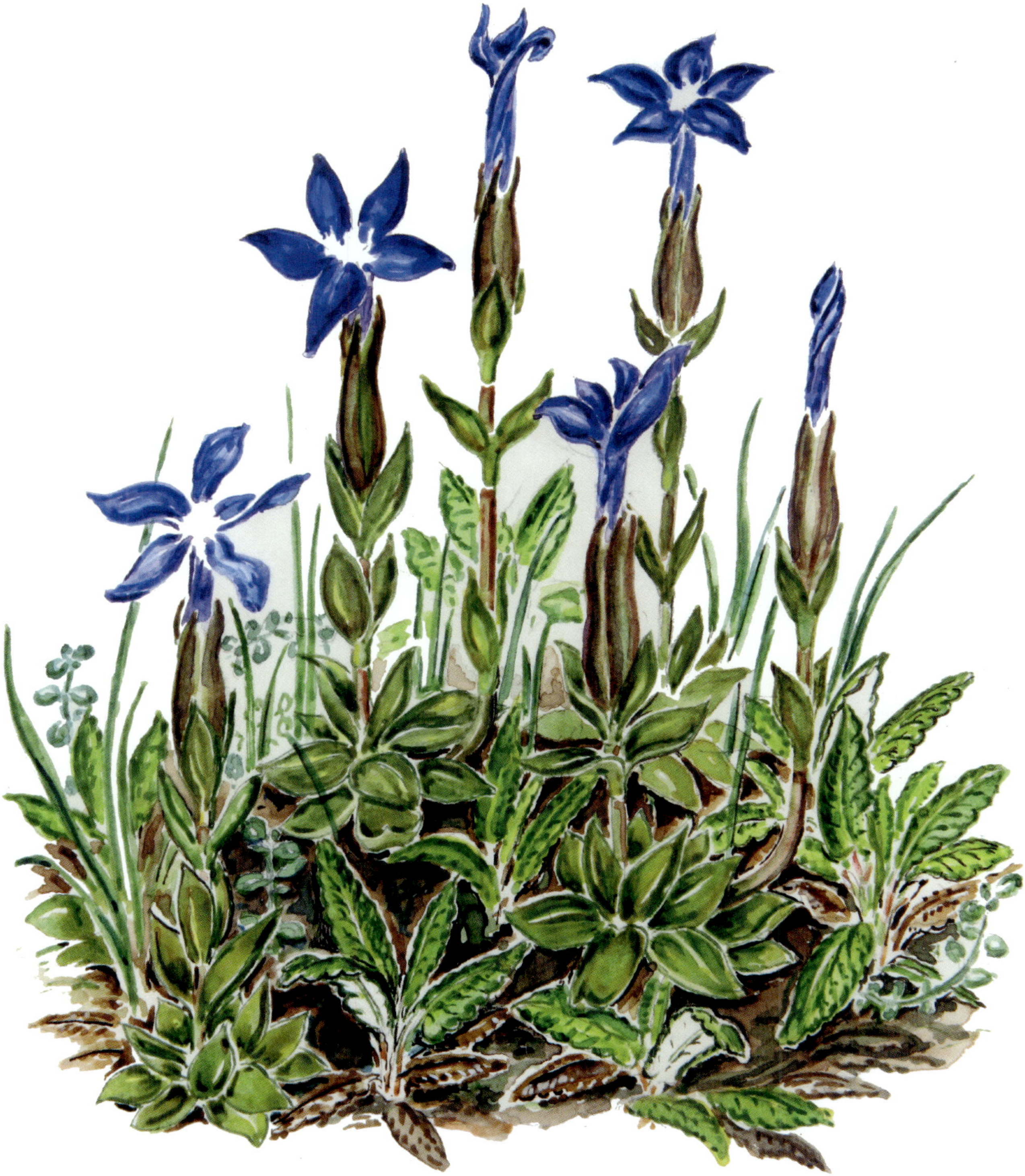

Fig. 8. *Gentiana verna*, spring gentian
Watercolour by Wendy F. Walsh
[© Estate of Wendy Walsh. Private collection. Reproduced by kind permission]

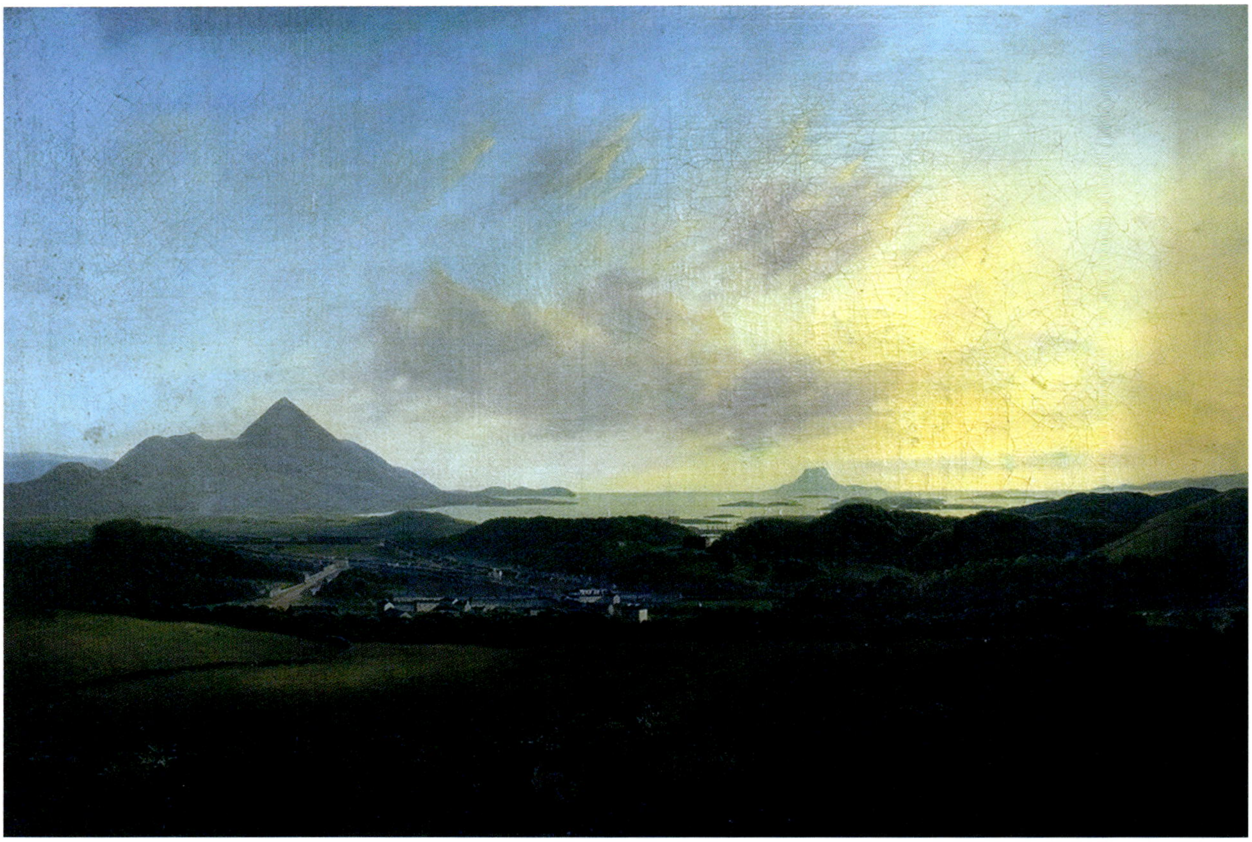

Fig. 9. View of Westport and Croagh Patrick, Co. Mayo
[Reproduced by kind permission of Westport House, Westport Estate, Co. Mayo, Republic of Ireland]

on a number of principal sources for research: (a) plant records (eight) contributed by Heaton; (b) Threlkeld's own observations – plants found in the Dublin region only, together with observations submitted by his correspondents and drawn from different parts of the island; (c) Irish plant records (around 40 species) received from botanist William Sherard (qv);[22] (d) descriptions of a number of plants by distinguished English botanist the Reverend John Ray (qv), which were believed to contain certain therapeutic properties.[23]

Threlkeld arranged the plant list (around 530) in alphabetical order providing their Latin name,

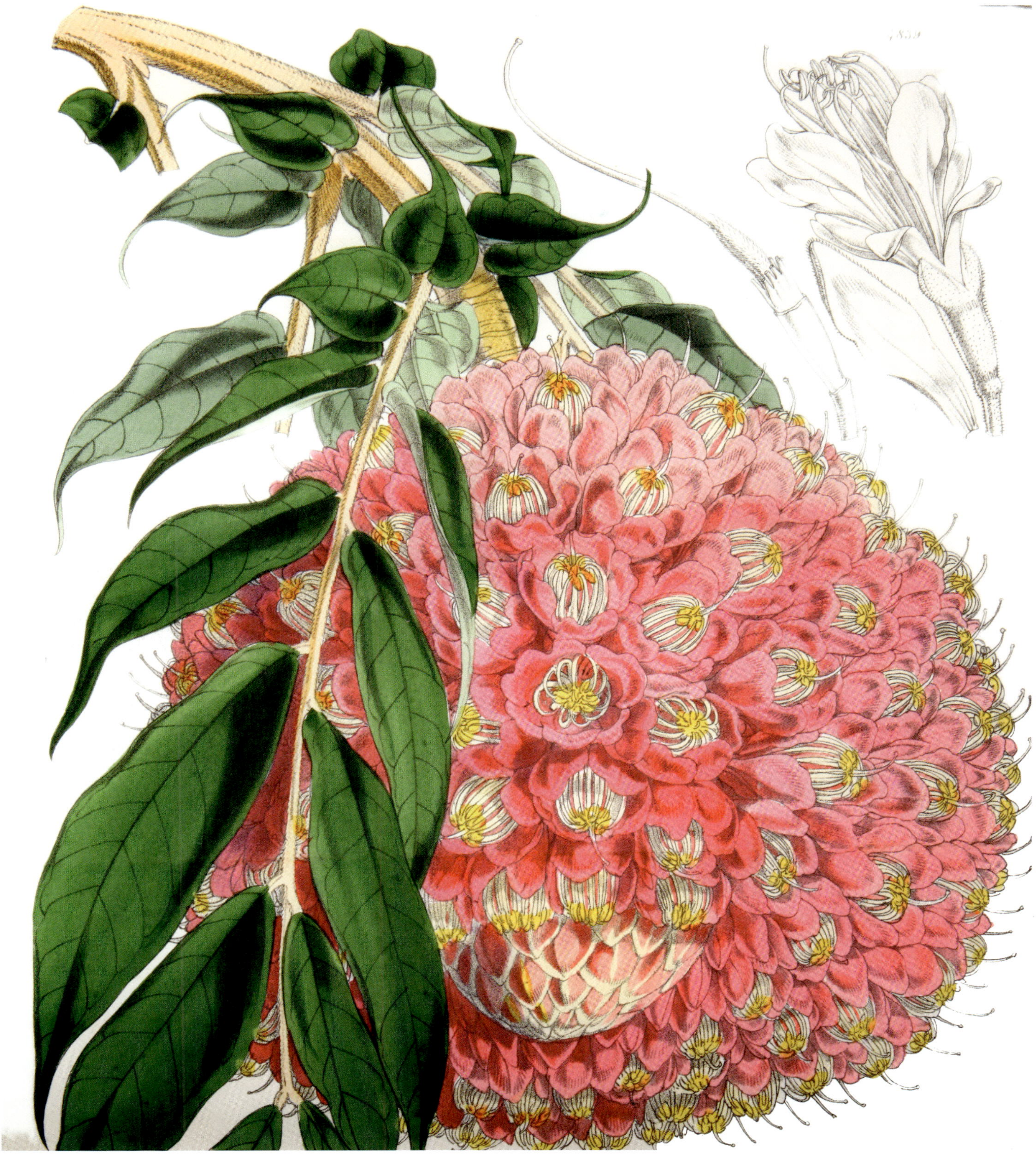

Fig. 10. *Brownea grandiceps*, commonly known as the rose of Venezuela
Colour lithograph by W.H. Fitch (1817–1892) for *Curtis's Botanical Magazine*, vol. 81, tab. 4839
[Courtesy, National Botanic Gardens, Glasnevin, Dublin]

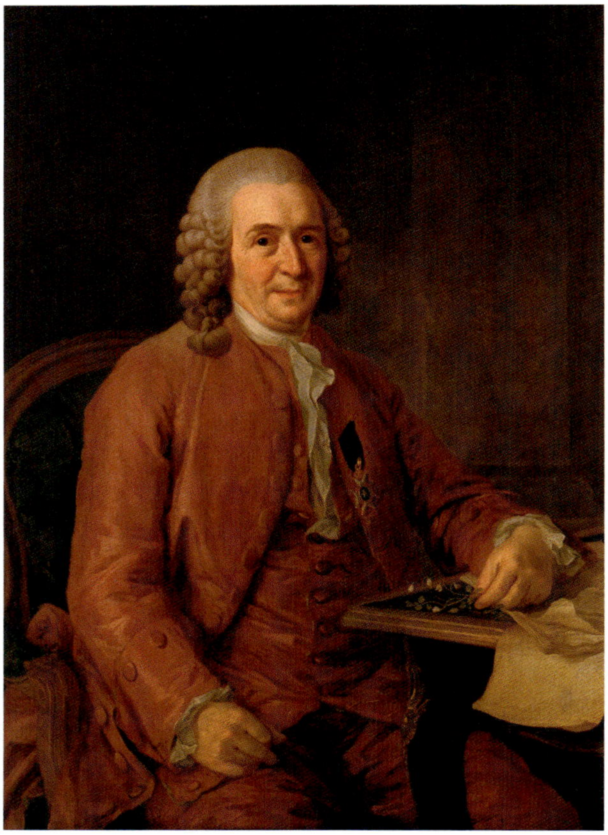

Fig. 11. Carl Linnaeus [Carl von Linné] (1707–1778)
[The Linnean Society, Burlington House, London]

followed by their English and Irish names. This was the first real attempt to chart, record and publish an Irish flora, although it should be stated that it did not cover the flora of the entire island. Plants listed included the yellow flag iris, *Iris palustris* (*Iris lutea*) and the yellow water iris, *Iris pseudacorus*, together with the common cowslip, *Primula veris*. It was not illustrated.

An Irish botanist, influenced by Caleb Threlkeld, and one of the earliest to research but not publish a post-Linnaean floristic work relating to Irish plants, was Dr Patrick Browne (c.1720–1790). Described by Robert Lloyd Praeger (1865–1953)[24] as 'one of the pioneers in Irish natural history',[25] Browne was born in Woodstock, a townland close to Claremorris, Co. Mayo, the fourth son of Edward Browne, 'a gentleman of respectable family and handsome estate'.[26] Browne is perhaps best remembered today as the author of one of the most significant natural history books of the mid-18th century – *The Civil and Natural History of Jamaica* (1756),[27] illustrated by Georg Dionysius Ehret (1708–1770).[28] When published, it received high praise from the author's contemporary, the distinguished and influential Swedish naturalist, Carl Linnaeus (1707–1778).[29] Today, several species and subspecies of plants native to the Americas have been named after this distinguished Co. Mayo botanist, *Brownea grandiceps* (see Figure 10) being but one example.

Browne studied physic (medicine) and botany in Paris but received his degree in medicine from the University of Rheims. He continued his postdoctoral studies at Leiden, matriculating on 21 February 1743. He then moved to London and practised medicine largely at St Thomas' Hospital.

While living in Jamaica and studying the natural history of the island, Browne corresponded with Carl Linnaeus. The latter's influence is seen in Browne's *The Civil and Natural History of Jamaica*, which not

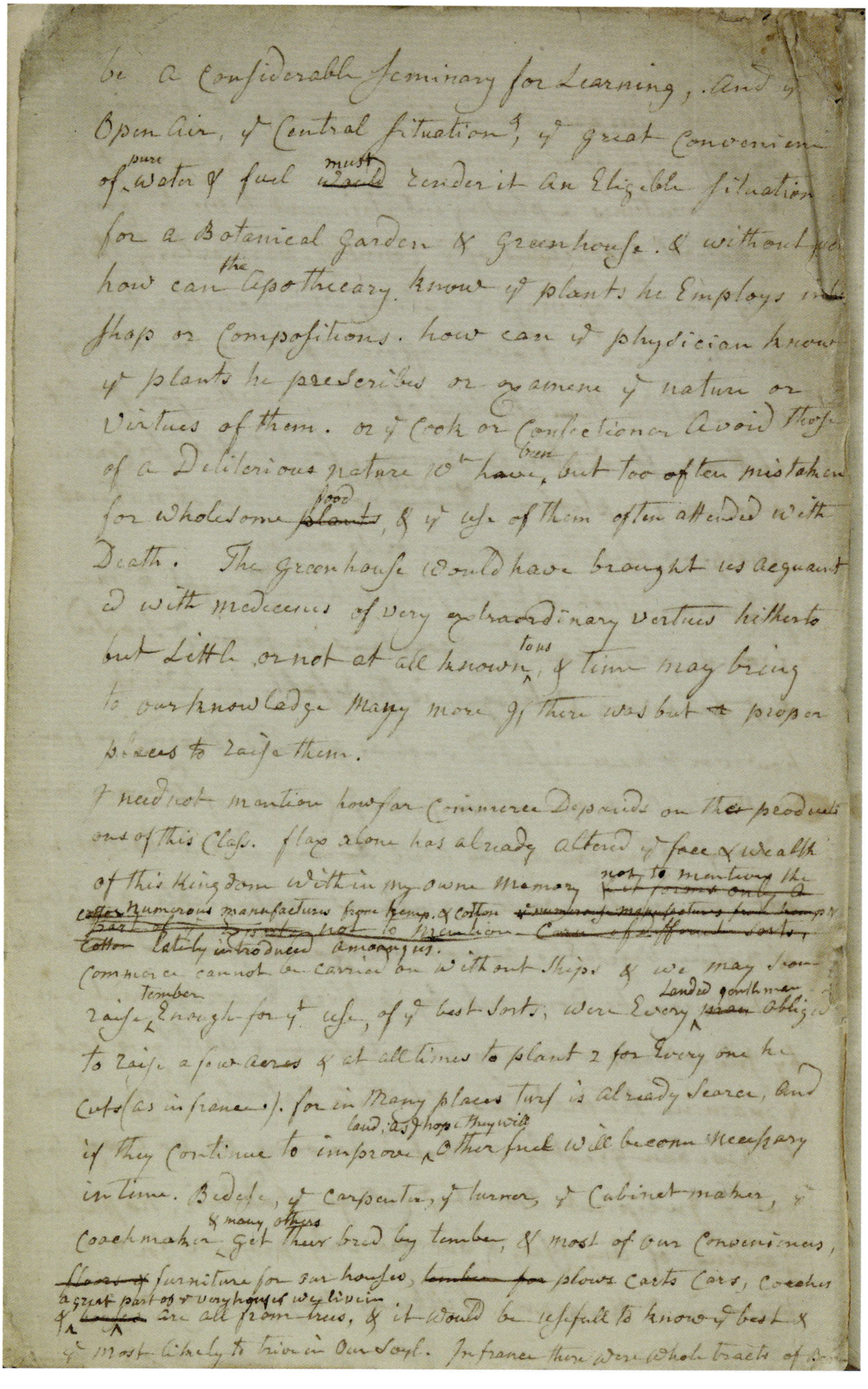

be a Considerable Seminary for Learning, And ye
Open Air, ye Central situation, ye great Convenienc[e]
of pure water & fuel must ~~would~~ render it an Eligible situation
for a Botanical Garden & Greenhouse. & without [?]
how can the Apothecary know ye plants he Employs in
shop or Compositions. how can ye physician know
ye plants he prescribes or examine ye nature or
Virtues of them. or ye Cook or Confectioner avoid those
of a Deliterious nature wch ~~have~~ been, but too often mistaken
for wholesome food ~~plants~~, & ye use of them often attended with
Death. The Greenhouse would have brought us acquaint
ed with medecines of very extraordinary vertues hitherto
but Little, or not at all known tous, & time may bring
to our knowledge Many more if there was but ~~a~~ proper
places to raise them.
I need not mention how far Commerce Depends on the products
ons of this Class. flax alone has already altered ye face & wealth
of this Kingdom within my owne Memory not to mention the
~~cotton~~ Numerous manufactures from hemp & Cotton ~~[illegible]~~
~~[illegible] not to mention [illegible]~~
~~Cotton~~ lately introduced amongst us.
Commerce cannot be carried on without Ships & we may soon
raise timber Enough for ye use, of ye best Sorts, were Every Landed gentleman ~~man~~ Obliged
to raise a few acres & at all times to plant 2 for Every one he
Cuts (as in France). for in Many places turf is already Scarce, and
if they Continue to improve land; as I hope they will Other fuel Will become Necessary
in time. Besides, ye Carpenter, ye turner, ye Cabinet maker, ye
Coachmaker & many others get their bread by timber, & most of our Conveniences,
~~[illegible]~~ furniture for our houses, ~~timber for~~ plows Carts Cars, Coaches
& a great part of ye very houses we live in ~~[illegible]~~ are all from trees, & it would be usefull to know ye best &
ye most likely to thrive in Our Soyl. In France there were whole tracts of [...]

Fig. 12. A page from Patrick Browne's *Fasciculus Plantarum Hiberniae* (1788)
[The Linnean Society, Burlington House, London]

only contained new names relating to 104 genera but was also noteworthy because it employed Linnaeus's sexual system.[29]

Following his return to Ireland in 1770, where he settled on the family's estate at Ballinrobe, Co. Mayo, Browne began compiling a manuscript that was never published, relating to the plants of counties Mayo and Galway, *Fasciculus Plantarum Hiberniae* (1788).[31] It included a substantial number of localities for plants that grow easily in a peat soil. His handwritten manuscript was, as he freely acknowledged, influenced by Caleb Threlkeld, John K'Eogh's (c.1681–1754)[32] *Botanalogia Universalis Hibernica*, or, a *General Irish Herbal* (1735) and Rutty's *An Essay Towards a Natural History of the County of Dublin* (1772) qv. Written in Latin, English and Irish, the book classifies and describes several hundred plants according to the Linnaean system. In his manuscript (1788), it is interesting to note that Browne puts forward the idea of forming a botanic garden in Dublin, six years before the actual establishment of the RBG Glasnevin (now known as the NBG Glasnevin), Dublin.[33]

As we have seen, the earliest known manuscript flora (Irish; 30 August 1788) to carry Linnaean names was compiled by Dr Patrick Browne but left unpublished at the time of his death. Several years later, in 1794, Dr Walter Wade's (c.1740–1825)[34] Dublin catalogue[35] was published by the DS and introduced the Linnaean system into Irish botany, employing as it did binary (Linnaean) names.

By 1800, only one Irish flora (qv) had been published, together with Walter Wade's 1794 Dublin catalogue (qv), and county lists were few and far between. Perhaps Dr Mitchell's remark: 'When England and France had their provincial Floras, the Botany of [Ireland] was as much known as that of an island in the Pacific' carried, sadly, more than a ring of truth.

Fig. 13. *Cladium mariscus* (*Cladium chinense*), great fen sedge
Watercolour by Wendy F. Walsh
[© Estate of Wendy Walsh. Private collection. Reproduced by kind permission]

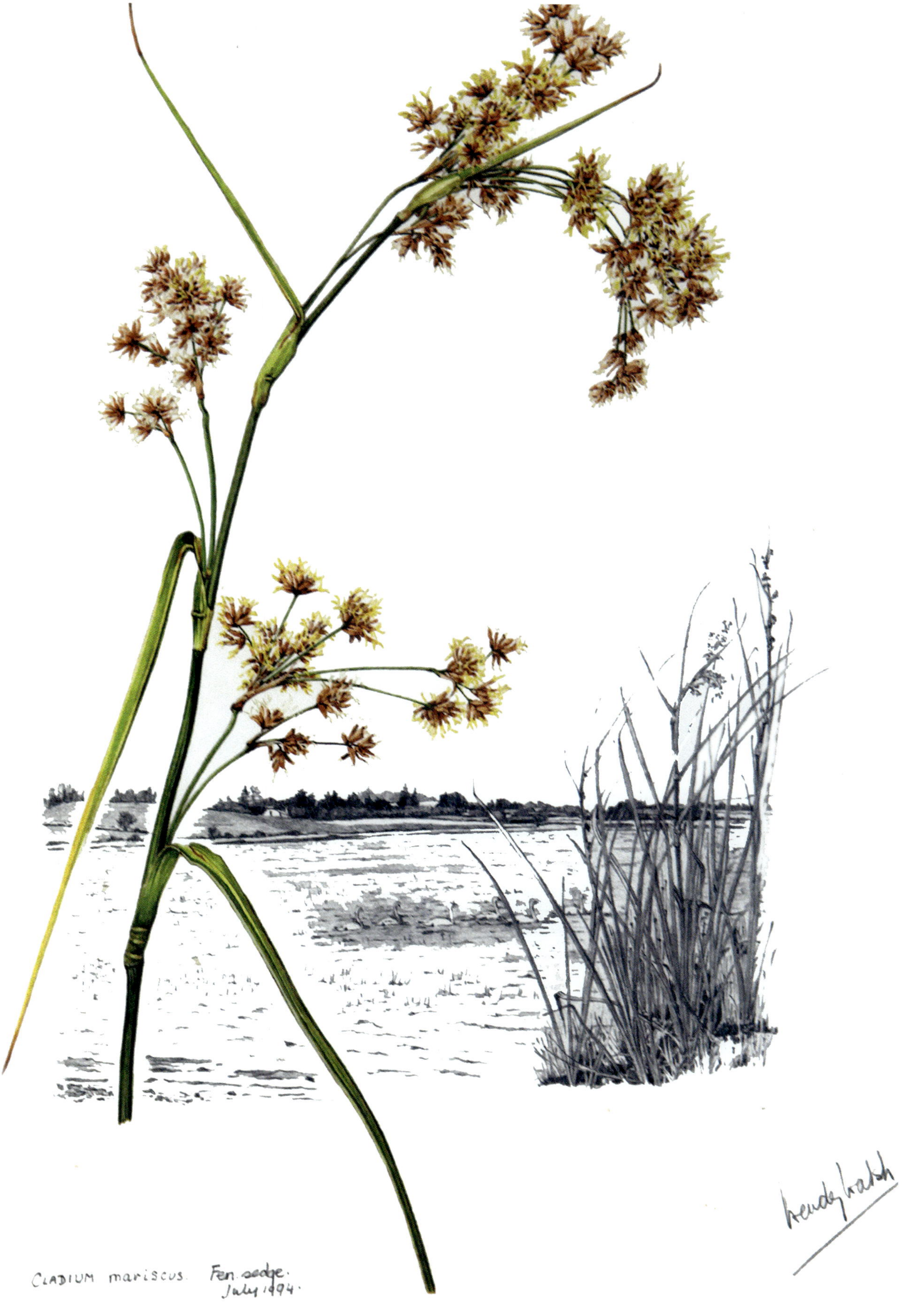
CLADIUM mariscus. Fen sedge.
July 1994.

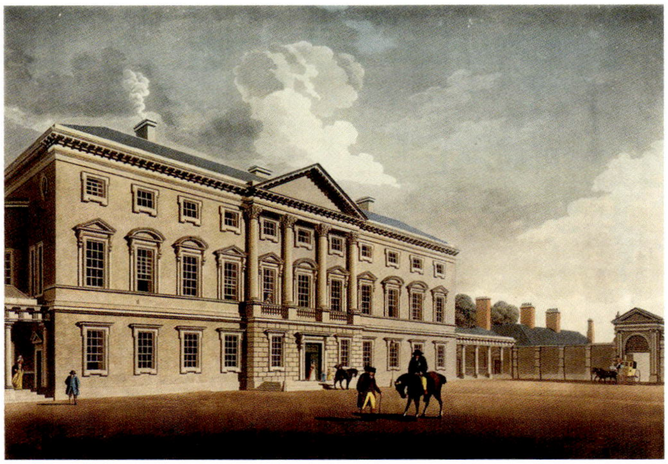

# Chapter 2
# Botanical Illustration c.1720–1820

The Dublin Society (DS) was founded on 25 June 1731, when a number of 'reformers' met in the rooms of the Philosophical Society, Trinity College, Dublin anxious to 'improve husbandry, manufactures, and other useful arts'. On 1 July of that same year 'sciences' was added to their list of intentions.

Members were determined to raise the standards of agricultural practice throughout the counties of Ireland. The 14 founding members, all from similar Anglo-Irish backgrounds and armed with a determination and vision to tackle the problems of the country, immediately began to publish a number of booklets/pamphlets relating to the growing and cultivation of saffron, hemp, flax, hops and other agricultural subjects of interest. In the majority of these publications, botanical illustration was to play a vital role.

(Above) Fig. 14. Leinster House, Kildare Street, Dublin, headquarters of the RDS from 1818 for over 100 years. [Courtesy, National Library of Ireland]

One of the earliest known botanical portraits by an Irish artist, James Gwim (or Gwin) (1700–1769)

– a small, competent, hand-coloured print of *Potentilla anglica* or trailing tormentil – appeared in the Society's pamphlet relating to tanning written by founder member, William Maple (d.1762).[1] Here, Gwim portrays, in a highly accurate and lively way, the minute botanical details of this plant, essential in tanning processes, the roots being used to produce a dye for reddening leather.

Frequently described as an 'eccentric man',[2] this artist/engraver and portraitist was born in Co. Kildare. He began his career as a coach-painter, eventually going to Dublin, where he was employed by publisher George Grierson, D'Olier Street. A fine portraitist,[3] Gwim contributed to such works as Milton's *Paradise Lost* and several Dublin-based publications.

However, he would appear to have been a somewhat volatile character and perhaps difficult to employ. Around 1755, he travelled to London. There, he joined the famous Battersea enamel factory already established at York House, which specialised in producing small objects – delicately coloured copper-based enamel plaques, snuffboxes and labels. According to Sir John Gilbert:

> *Some of his drawings were very neat and imposing...he got his livelihood by designs for the lids of snuff-boxes, which he did for a manufactory at Battersea, under the direction of Sir Stephen Theodore Jansen.*[4]

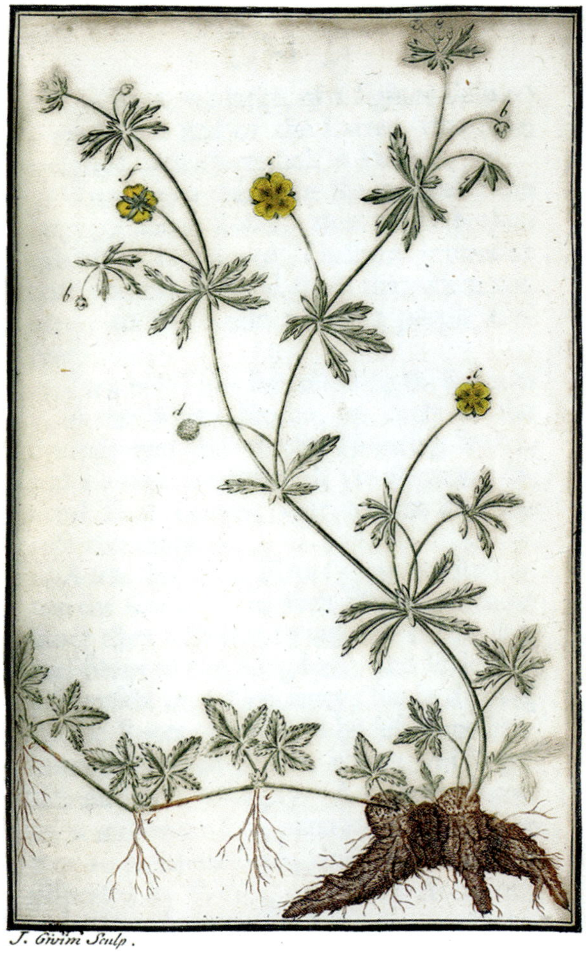


Fig. 15. *Potentilla anglica*, trailing tormentil
Engraving by James Gwim (Gwin), 1732
[Courtesy, National Library of Ireland]

The factory was run by a partnership of three: Messrs Jansen (d.1777), Delamain(e) (fl.c.1752–1757) and Brooks (fl.1730–1756). Henry Delamain(e) and John Brooks were both Irish. Henry Delamain(e), a potter who had worked in Dublin and had introduced coal-

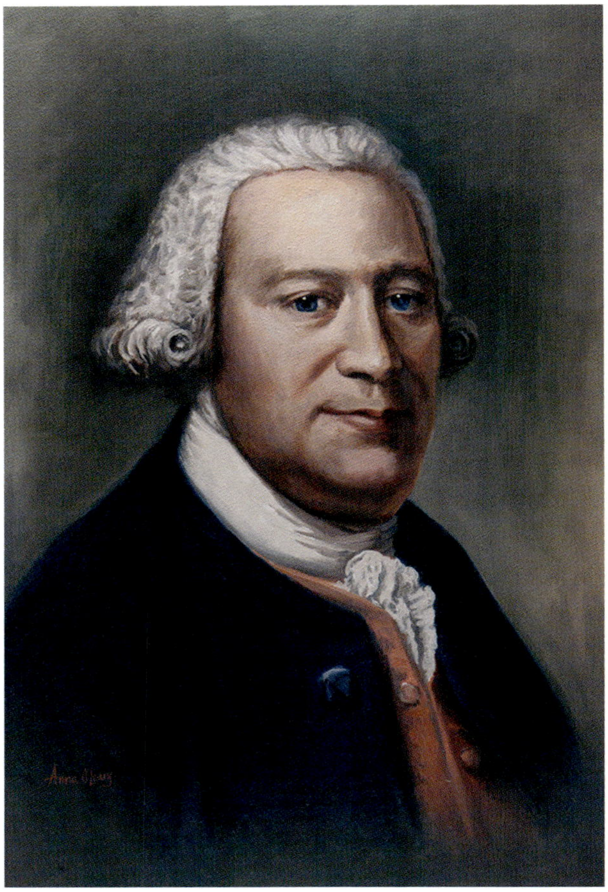

Fig. 16. Dr Walter Wade c.1740–1825
[Courtesy, National Botanic Gardens, Glasnevin, Dublin]

firing into the delftware industry, was in charge of the kilns. John Brooks[5] was a well-known engraver and mezzotinter in Dublin and the manager responsible for providing the expertise and knowledge required to carry out the process of transfer-printing.[6] The third member of the trio, Sir Stephen Theodore Jansen, was a wealthy city merchant who supplied the capital. Gwim was responsible for the majority of the designs on enamel that are attributable to the French engraver Simon François Ravenet (1706–1774).[7] The artist would appear to have concentrated on the historical, mythological and allegorical subjects relating to Ravenet's work, as demonstrated by a Battersea enamel plaque that carried the inscription on verso: 'Drawn by Gwim, engraved by Ravenet for ye Battersea Manuf'rs under Sir S. Theodore Janssen...'[8]

Due to dissension amongst the three partners, the factory lasted only three years (1753–1756), but within that short period gained a high reputation which has endured to this day. Gwim continued to live in London following the closure of the factory and, as far as is known, did not return to Ireland. He died on 26 April 1769.

Born in Dublin, surgeon, physician and self-taught botanist Walter Wade, MD, FRS, ALS (c.1740–1825), combined his medical career with botany.[9] Wade was one of the earliest to stimulate an interest in this area in Ireland, and his publications were to add considerably to the knowledge and distribution of Irish plants. Elected an Honorary Member of the DS in 1792, two years later, he presented his lists of native Irish plants relating to Co. Dublin to the Society, which were published by them in 1794.[10] Writing in Latin, English and Irish, Wade employed, for the first time in Irish (published) botany, the Linnaean system and nomenclature identifying each plant in its habitat and adding many species

(Opposite) Fig. 17. *Salix acutifolia*, Caspian osier or Siberian violet-willow
Copperplate engraving by James Ford (fl.1778–1812) after Daniel Richardson (1783–1830)
[Courtesy, National Library of Ireland]

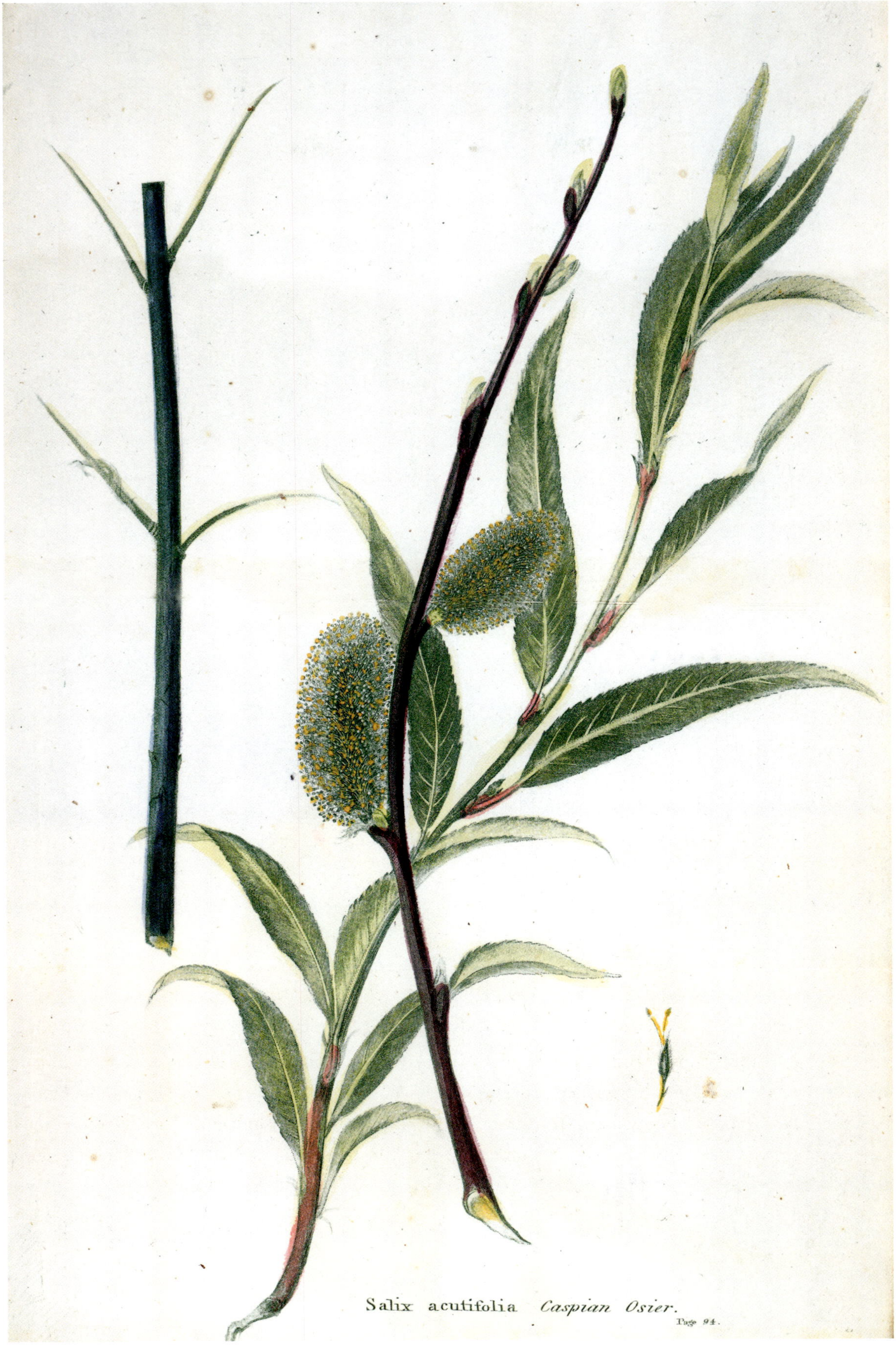

Salix acutifolia *Caspian Osier.*

Page 84.

not previously recorded. His published manuscript also identified 41 species of grasses, together with information relating to their economic, agricultural and other uses.

As can be seen from the native Irish plant list that he presented to the DS, Wade was interested in native Irish grasses and is believed to be among the first-known Irish botanists to study them in detail. His notes were published by the Society in 1808 – *Sketch of Lectures on Meadow and Pasture Grasses* (1808).[11]

His essay on *Salices: Or an Essay towards a General History of Sallows, Willows & Osiers*[12] published three years later and supported by the DS, is considered to be his most substantial work and carried, as its frontispiece, a copperplate engraving by James Ford (fl.1778–1812), hand-coloured in sepia wash, *Salix acutifolia*, after an original by 'Richardson Dubl' (see Figure 17). Artist, Daniel Richardson (fl.1783–1830) was a still-life painter who had exhibited at the Royal Academy. He remained in Dublin for 10 years contributing to the Society of Artists before returning to London. According to Strickland, Richardson enjoyed:

> *some reputation in Dublin as an artist; his pictures which seem to have been eagerly bought by collectors are said to have been rich in colour and well painted.*[13]

Unlike Richardson, Ford did receive an academic art training in Dublin. Entering the DS Drawing Schools in 1772, the following year he was awarded a prize for design and pattern-drawing. Employed by the Society, he began his career as an engraver and in 1778 was awarded a prize of 10 guineas 'for his improvement in the art of engraving'.[14] Involved with the Society in illustrating its County Surveys, Ford's Dublin scenes, now in the NGI, are an important recording of the city at the turn of the 19th century.[15]

Wade's study of Irish grasses (see above) also interested John White (c.1760–1837), who was appointed as an under gardener at Glasnevin in 1796. A native of Co. Louth, and familiar with the Irish language, he was married with a young family and may have received some practical training before joining the staff of Glasnevin.

The same year that Wade's essay on Irish grasses appeared also saw the publication of White's essay by the DS.[16] This contained descriptions relating to all known native Irish grasses, Irish names and habitats being supplied. This is one of the earliest Irish botanical monographs to be illustrated and carried hand-coloured copperplate engravings of two species: *Alopecurus pratensis* and *Poa trivialis* (see Figure 21).

The Society was equally determined to improve standards in relation to design in Ireland. Subjects in which pupils applied their skills in the art of drawing flowers included interior decoration, wallpapers, porcelain, coach panels and textiles. All of these would have involved the drawing of patterns, primarily in the late Rococo tradition, using plants and flowers.

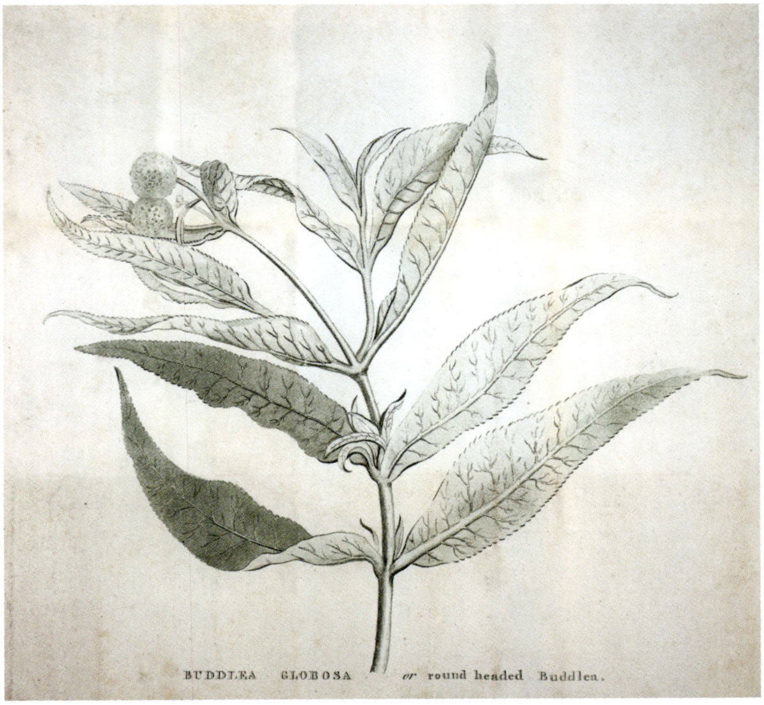


Fig. 18. *Buddleja globosa*, round-headed buddleia
Engraving by an unknown artist
[Courtesy, National Library of Ireland]

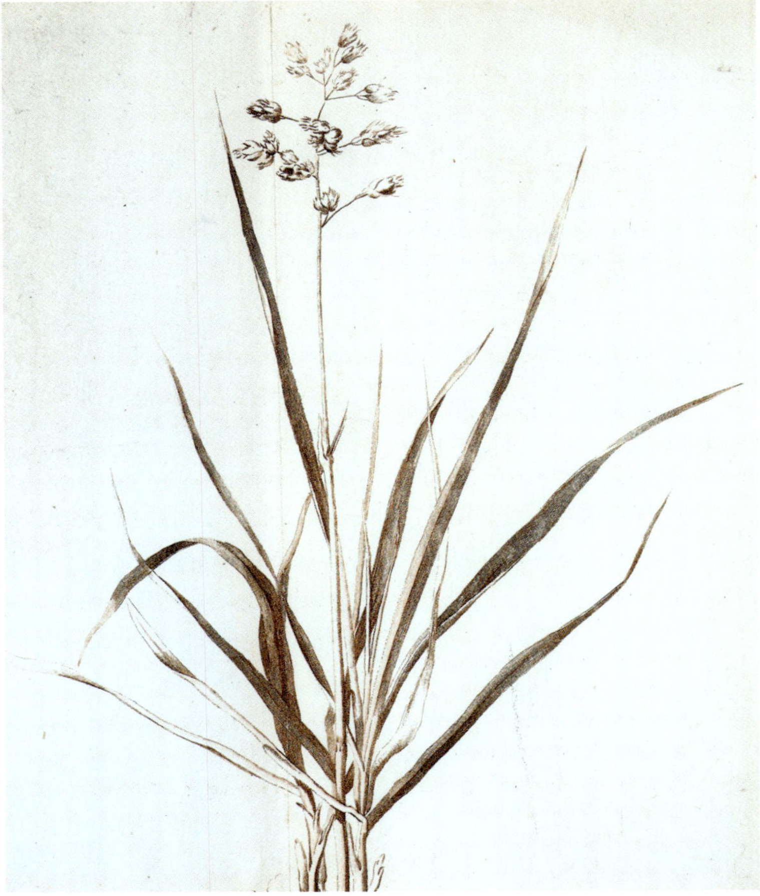

Fig. 19. *Holcus odoratus* (*Anthoxanthum nitens*), sweet grass
Engraving by an unknown artist
[Courtesy, National Library of Ireland]

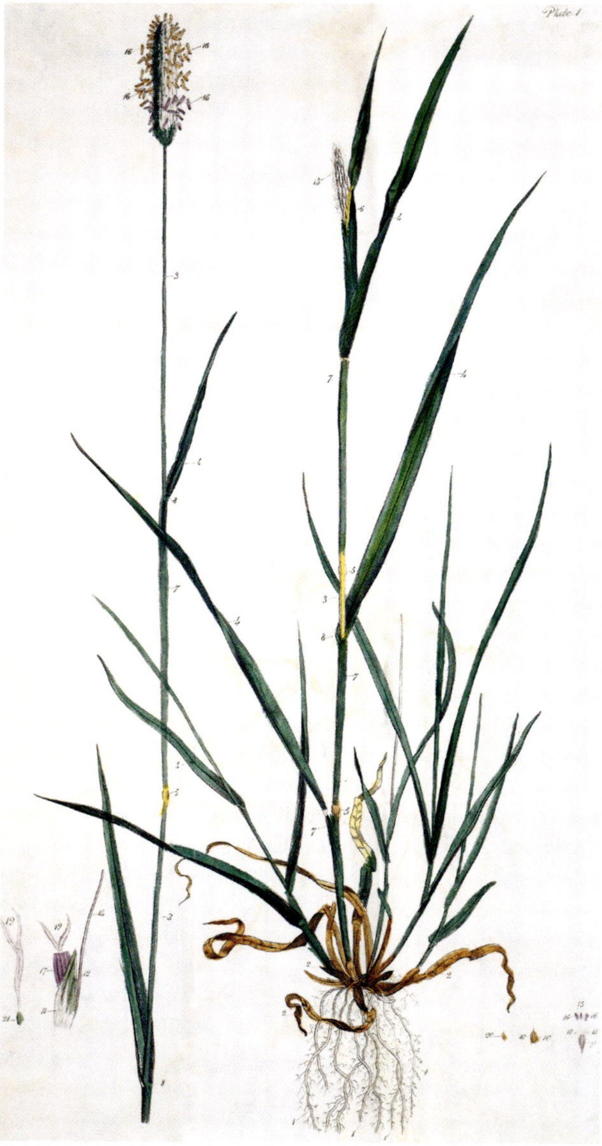

Fig. 20. *Alopecurus pratensis*, meadow fox-tail
Engraving by Patrick Maguire (fl.1790–1820) from John White *An Essay on the Indigenous Grasses of Ireland* (Dublin: Graisberry & Campbell for the DS, 1808), plate 1
[Courtesy, National Library of Ireland]

In 1777, the duties of the Society's Master of the School of Ornament and Drawing, James Mannin (d.June 1779)[17] were defined as 'twenty-five pounds per Annum for two years to teach two boys... his Art of drawing Foliages'. Later, the duties were outlined in more detail: 'to instruct in the Art of Drawing Ornaments in Foliages, Flowers and Scrolls, and Patterns and Designs proper for the several manufacturers'. When Henry Brocas, Senior (1762–1837) was appointed to the post on 14 August 1800, the Society began to award prizes for the drawings of trees and flowers. Samuel Frederick Brocas (c.1792–1847), who was taught by his father (c.1801–1804), was awarded a medal for flower painting in 1801.[18]

An example of botanical work executed by Henry Brocas, Senior may be found in the Reverend George Vaughan Sampson's *A Memoir, Explanatory of the Chart and Survey of the County of London-Derry, Ireland* (London: G. & W. Nicol, 1814) which carried an accurate, workman-like full botanical portrait (engraving hand-coloured in watercolour) of the marsh grass of Parnassus, *Parnassia palustris* (see Figure 25).

A year after its foundation, the DS carried out a series of experiments connected with agriculture, including the culture of flax. *An Account of Saffron: The Manner of Its Culture and Saving for Use* (1732)[19] contained several engravings, the author stating with confidence that saffron (*Crocus sativus*) produced in Ireland was 'superior in every quality, to that of other countries'.[20] This publication came from the press of Aaron Rhames, Dublin who, in 1731, had been appointed first printer to the Society.

(Opposite) Fig. 21. *Poa trivialis*, rough meadow grass
Engraving by Patrick Maguire (fl.1790–1820)
[Courtesy, National Library of Ireland]

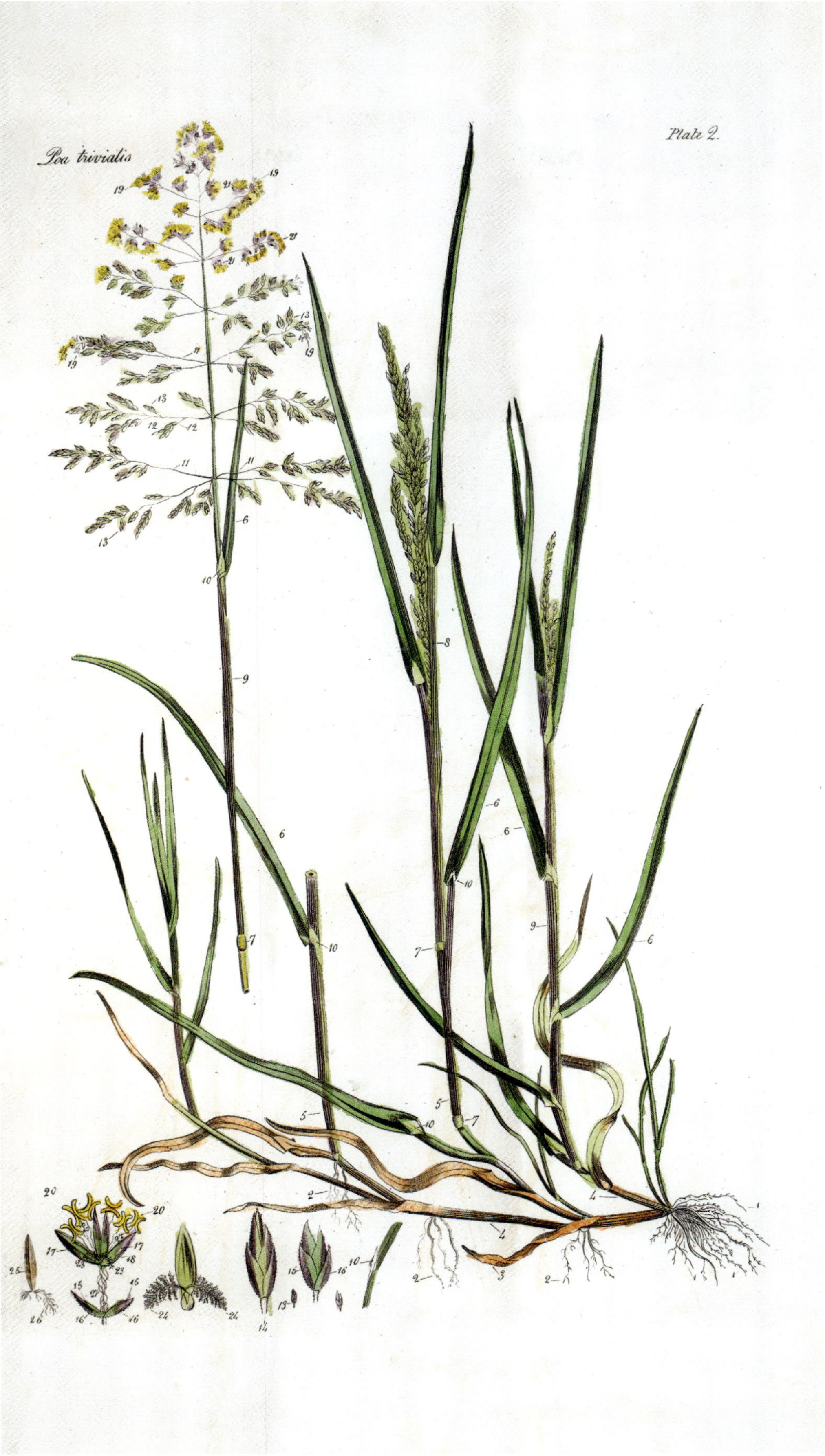
Poa trivialis
Plate 2.

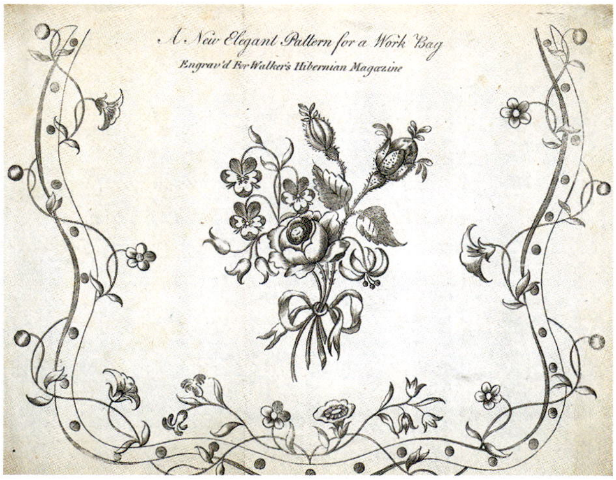


Fig. 22. Design for a work bag
Engraving by Henry Brocas, Senior (c.1762–1837)
[Courtesy, National Library of Ireland]

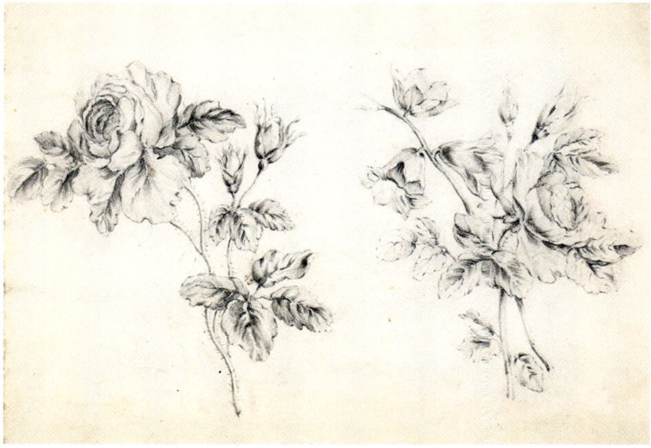

Fig. 23. Botanical studies
Pencil drawing by Samuel F. Brocas (c.1792–1847)
[Courtesy, National Library of Ireland]

The DS did much to encourage the planting of trees. As early as 1741, it was announced that premiums were to be offered for the greatest number of fruit and timber trees raised by nurserymen.[21] In 1794, *A Practical Treatise on Planting: And the Management of Woods and Coppices* was published.[22] The author, Samuel Hayes (c.1743–1795) of Avondale, Co. Wicklow, a member of the RIA, was also a keen and active member of the Committee of Agriculture, in the DS.

The work, produced by William Sleater who had replaced Aaron Rhames as printer to the Society, appeared on good-quality paper and contained a number of charming vignettes. These ranged from how to move a mature tree to a delightful portrait of the 'Great Ash of Leinster' by the Dublin-born engraver and artist, William Esdall (c.1750–1795).[23]

Son of James Esdall (d.1755), a Dublin printer publisher and bookseller, William Esdall was a student at the DS Drawing Schools in 1767. From the early 1770s, he began to contribute engravings to a variety of printed books, mainly in the form of title pages, vignettes, tailpieces and other ornaments. A regular contributor to the *Hibernian Magazine* and *Exshaw's London Magazine*, in 1777 he was admitted to the Guild of Saint Luke. Throughout the second half of the 18th century, Esdall's attractive copperplate engravings were a familiar sight in magazines and books published in Ireland.

As the 19th century progressed, the practice of botanical illustration in Ireland became more commonplace, with less interest being demonstrated in beautifully illustrated flower books (*florilegia*) and

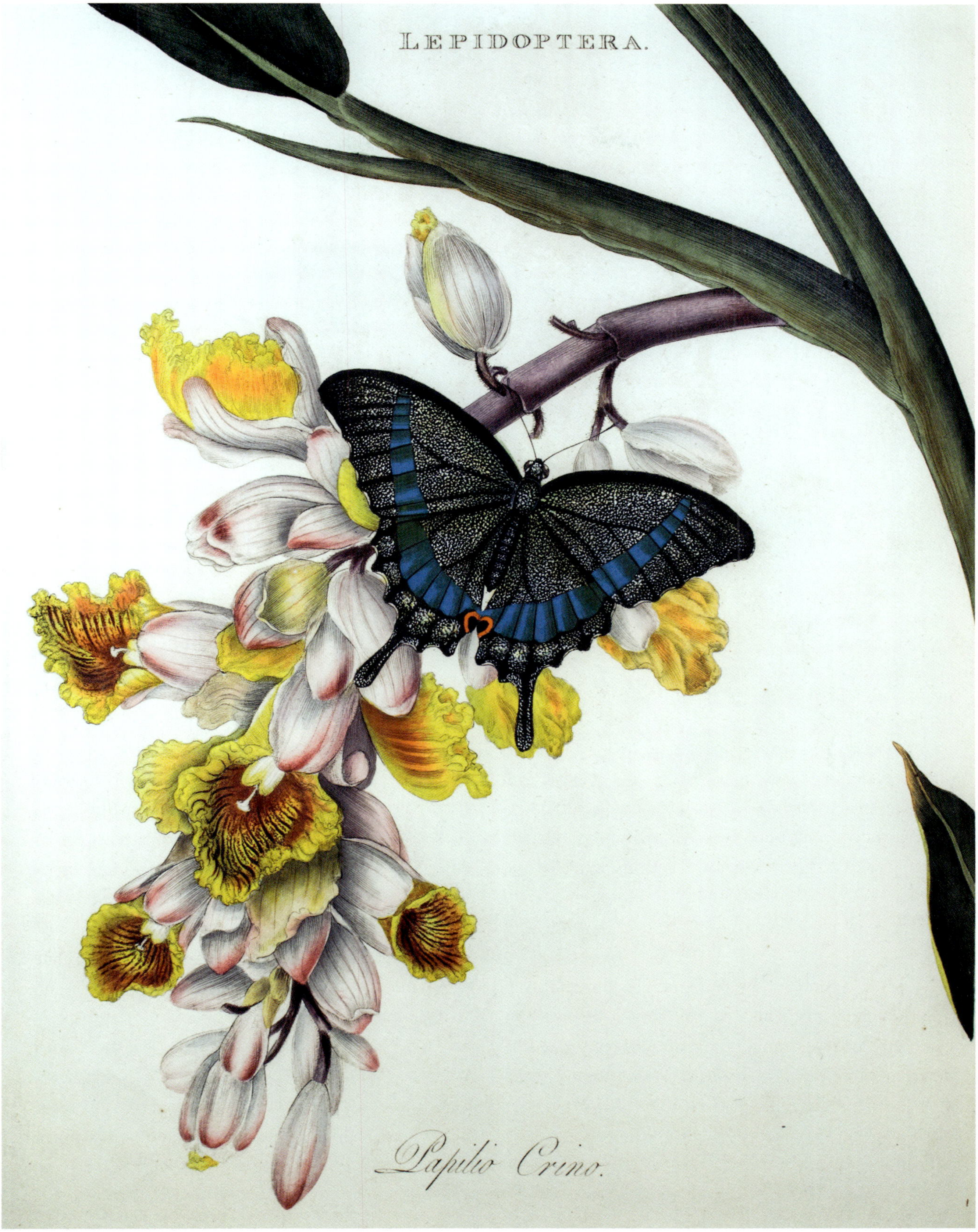


Fig. 24. *Papilio crino* and *Renealmia exaltata* (*Renealmia alpinia*), shell ginger
By Edward Donovan (1768–1837)
[By permission of the Royal Irish Academy. © RIA]

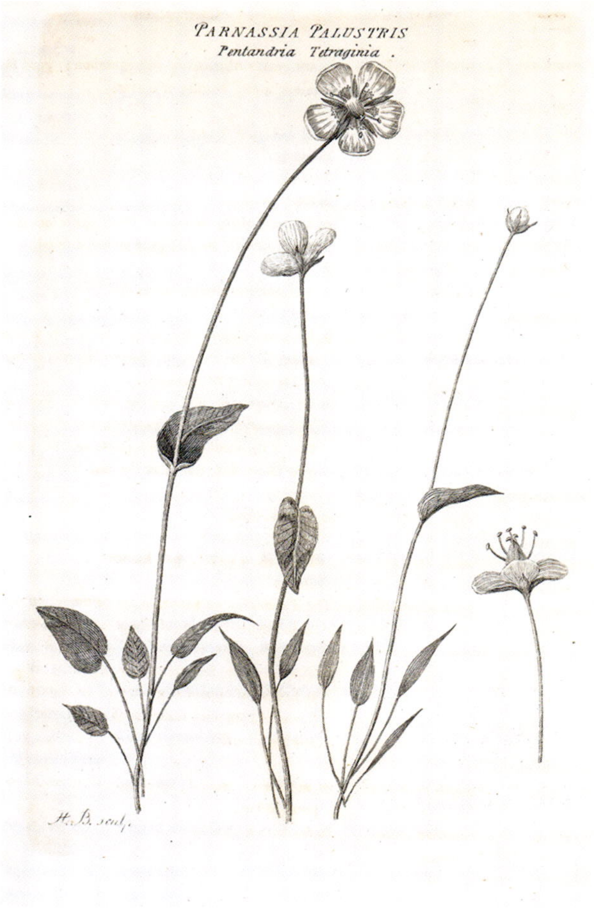


Fig. 25. *Parnassia palustris*, marsh grass of Parnassus
Engraving by Henry Brocas, Senior (c.1762–1837)
[Courtesy, National Library of Ireland]

more in publications relating to botany and zoology. As exotics from around the world were discovered and introduced, amateur naturalists, ranging from wealthy travellers on the Grand Tour to members of the clergy, together with keen scientists, were anxious to promote the understanding of these specimens. The demand for natural history publications, created to promote these introductions, often included hand-coloured engraved illustrations accompanied by a text of varying degrees of scientific value and held a wide appeal.

Cork-born, Edward Donovan (1768–1837) was acutely aware of the public's interest and curiosity in the natural world. A keen collector of natural history specimens, an author, naturalist, illustrator,[24] and the owner of a natural history museum (London), he collected specimens and information from personal excursions around the British Isles. He also purchased 'items' at natural history auctions relating, in particular, to voyages of exploration, which provided him with material for his publications.

Donovan was also fortunate to have access, as a Fellow of the LS and the Wernerian Natural History Society,[25] to outstanding collections that provided him with further information relating to insects, shells, fish and plants. In each of his publications, Donovan not only undertook to write the text, but also illustrated his work preparing the handsome hand-coloured copperplate engravings. Exotic plants featured in his early publications, such as the short-lived *The Botanical Review, or the Beauties of Flora* (London, 1789–1790) which contained descriptions and figures of the 'most beautiful foreign plants'. At an early stage, it was discontinued possibly because it failed to compete with William Curtis's better and more popular periodical, begun in 1787 under the title *The Botanical magazine, or, Flower garden displayed* (see Chapter 6, p.90).

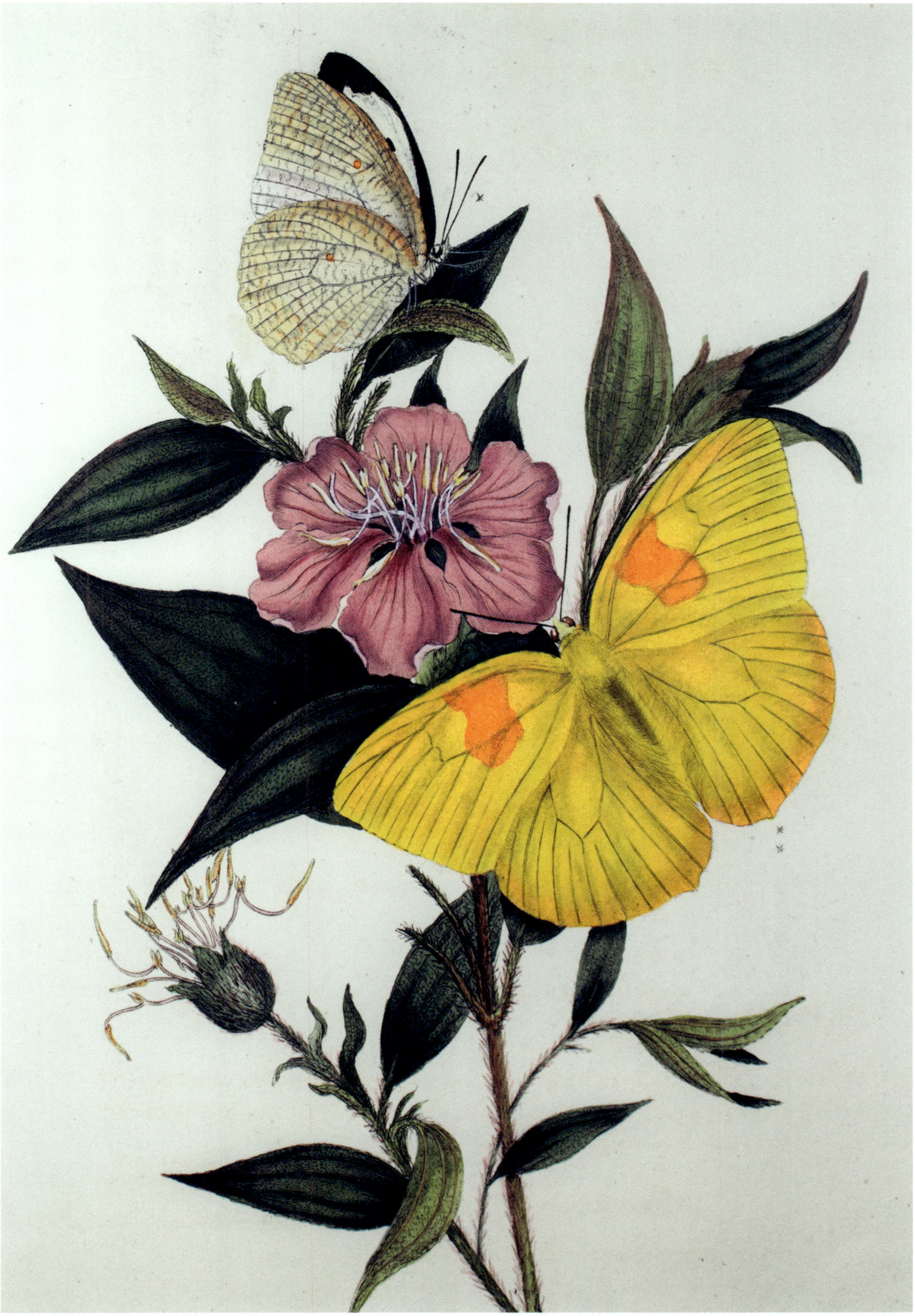

Fig. 26. *Appias phoebe*, albratross or puffin butterfly (above) and *Phoebis philea*, orange-barred sulphur butterfly (below)
By Edward Donovan (1768–1837)
[By permission of the Royal Irish Academy. © RIA]

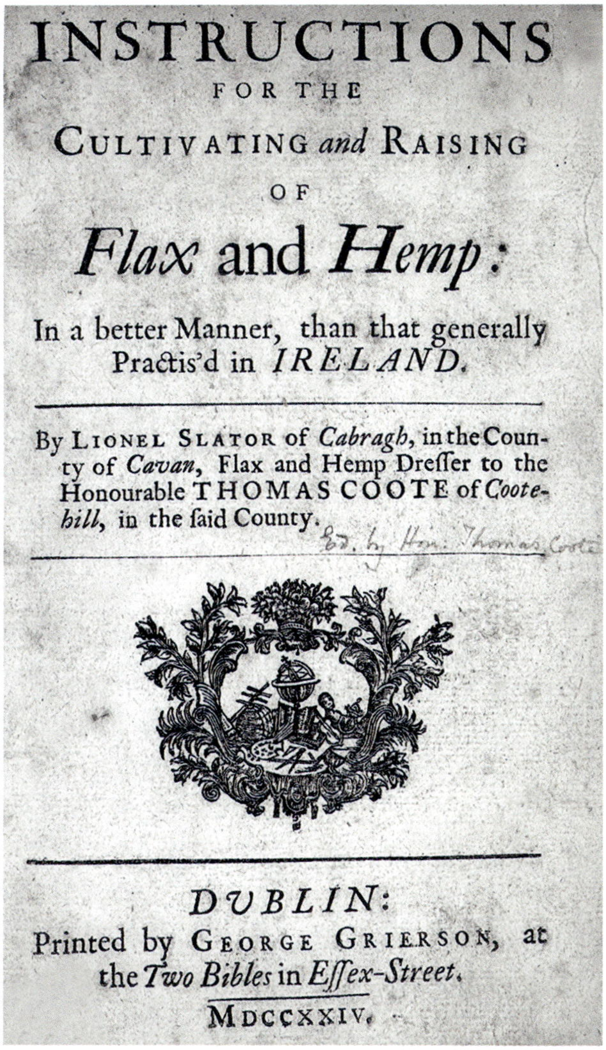

INSTRUCTIONS
FOR THE
CULTIVATING *and* RAISING
OF
*Flax* and *Hemp*:
In a better Manner, than that generally
Practis'd in *IRELAND*.

By LIONEL SLATOR of *Cabragh*, in the County of *Cavan*, Flax and Hemp Dreſſer to the Honourable THOMAS COOTE of *Cootehill*, in the ſaid County.

Ed. by Hon. Thomas Coote

*DUBLIN*:
Printed by GEORGE GRIERSON, at the *Two Bibles* in *Eſſex-Street*.
MDCCXXIV.

Fig. 27. Plate from *Instructions for the Cultivating and Raising of Flax and Hemp* by Lionel Slator (Dublin: George Grierson, 1724)
[Courtesy, National Library of Ireland]

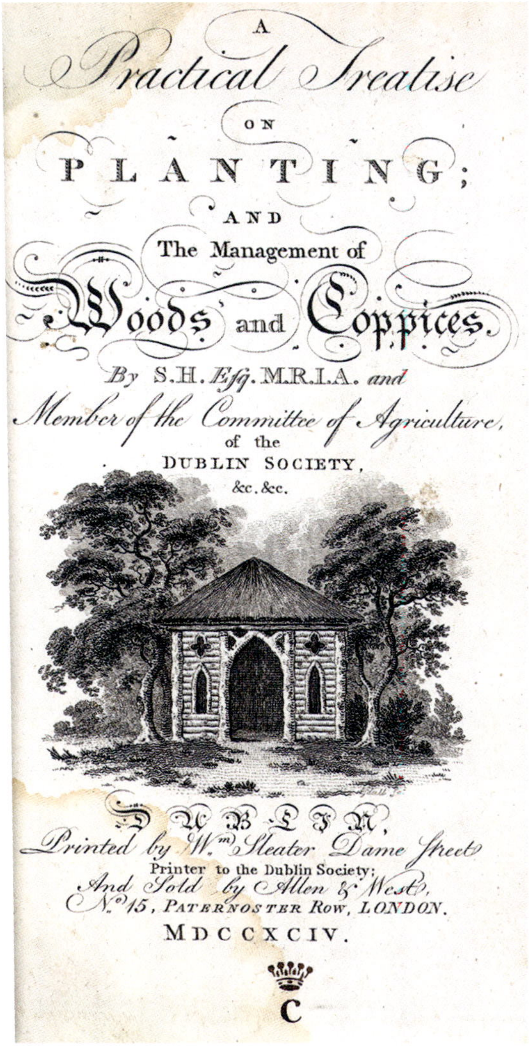

A
*Practical Treatise*
ON
PLANTING;
AND
The Management of
Woods and Coppices.
*By* S.H. *Esq.* M.R.I.A. *and*
*Member of the Committee of Agriculture,*
of the
DUBLIN SOCIETY,
&c. &c.

DUBLIN,
*Printed by W.m Sleater Dame ſtreet*
Printer to the Dublin Society;
*And Sold by Allen & West,*
*N.o 15*, *PATERNOSTER ROW*, *LONDON*.
MDCCXCIV.
C

Fig. 28. Frontispiece from *A Practical Treatise on Planting and the Management of Woods and Coppices* by Samuel Hayes
Engraved by William Esdall
[Courtesy, National Library of Ireland]

Speculation, than the Improvement of the Planter, I shall take no Notice of it. he says, he tried the Spicket Roots, but never could produce a Single flower, from any of them.

Mortimer, Laurence, Bradley, & some others have given very general & imperfect Directions, such as are in no wise, worth Notice.

Not only from the Report of others, but from repeated Trials of the Safron, I have raised, & the several little Parcells I have purchased from Others; the Safron produced by this Country, is superiour in every Quality, to that of other Countries. and was I to ascertain the Proportion, I would Say, 1 oz of Irish Safron, is equall to 1 oz½ of English, 3 oz of french, & 4 or 5 oz.s of Spanish.

A little Experience, arising from Curiosity, would lead me to choose a sandy loose Soil, such is most agreable to all Bulbous Roots, and if not naturally so, I would rather manure with Sea Sand, than Dung.

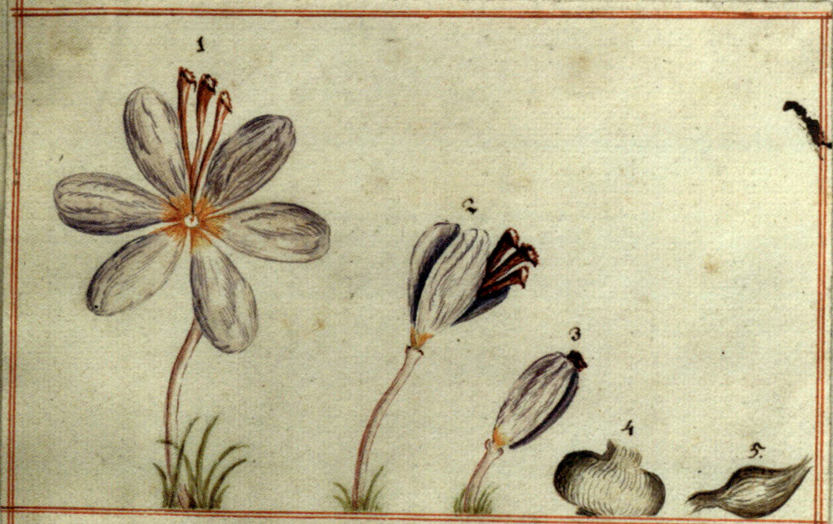


1, A Saffron flower too much blown, the Chives decaying, 2, a flower in full state, 3 a flower scarce ripe, 4, an eligible Root, 5, a Spicket, one never to be planted.

The best Time for gathering, in respect to the flowers, is before they are fully open, that in the Scheme markt 2, is in the fullest State, No 3 is rather too soon, but I would recomend the gathering of it, for fear before the Succeeding Morning, it be too ripe, for the Sun, in 3 or 4 hours, will much decay the Chives, in such Manner as is endeavour'd to be exprest by the flower markt. 1.

The Number of Chives, in each flower is generally 3, often 4, & sometimes, tho but very seldom, you will meet with 5, in a flower.

Rather than question the Veracity of the Dr. Acct. I wd. impute some Disagreements between his Acct. & my Observations, to our Soil, and

Fig. 29. From the Register of the DS minutes (1731–1736) dated 20 January 1731/32, p. 42
[Courtesy, RDS Library & Archives]

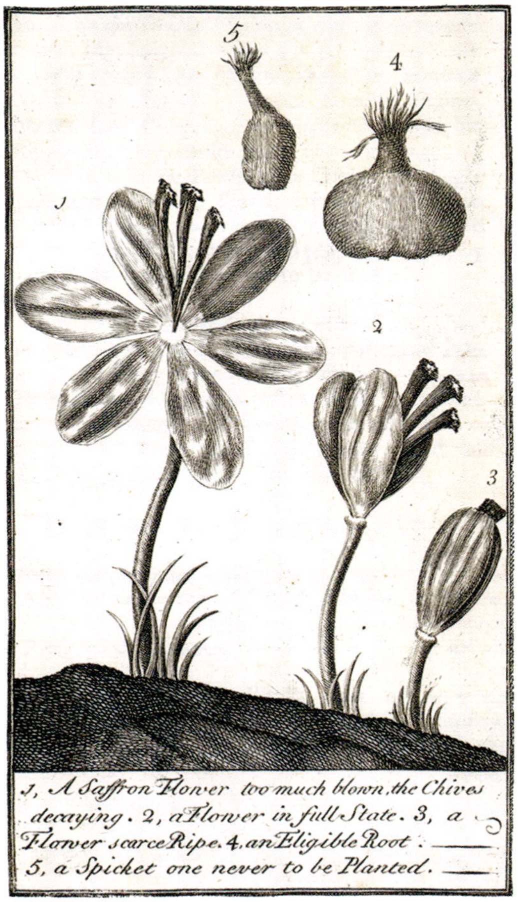


Fig. 30. 'A saffron flower too much blown, the chives decaying...'
Engraving by unknown artist
[Courtesy, National Library of Ireland]

In common with much of Edward Donovan's work, *An Epitome of the Natural History of the Insects of China* (1798)[26] reveals colours lavishly applied, frequently described as 'gems of colour'. The artist often applied thick paints, burnished highlights, metallic paints and albumen over glazes, the latter to cover his own hand-coloured copperplate engravings.

This work contains a portrait of the rare butterfly, *Papilio crino* accompanied by the plant, shell ginger – *Renealmia exaltata* (*Renealmia alpinia*). The author explains that the plate was painted from a unique specimen in the collection of private collector, Dru Drury, and 'on that authority', the author concludes, 'is a native of Cochin in China and Ceylon'. He stresses that the plant *Renealmia exaltata* is painted from the 'nursery plants of Messrs Grimwoods and Wykes, Kensington'.[27] It would appear that Donovan did not travel to China himself but obtained information from fellow Irishman Sir George Leonard Staunton (1737–1801), of Cargin, Co. Galway, an employee of the East India Company and a botanist. Staunton travelled extensively in China and made natural history collections and observations which, in turn, he conveyed to naturalists in England.

Sheer extravagance coupled with booksellers behaving in an unscrupulous manner caused Edward Donovan's financial ruin. The fortune he had spent on his museum,[28] together with, in many cases, non-payment for his work from publishers and booksellers, resulted in penury. He died on 1 February 1837 at John Street, Kennington Road, London leaving his large family destitute.

# Chapter 3
# Early Illustrated Floras

Prior to around 1900, a published 'flora' was defined as a comprehensive, itemised description of the plants of a specific geographical region. As outlined in Chapter 2, botanists had begun in the 18th century to place on record the well-known plants of the day – Threlkeld's *Synopsis Stirpium Hibernicarum*, a catalogue of Irish plants for the layman (October 1726; qv) and Rutty's *An Essay Towards a Natural History of the County of Dublin* (1772; qv). The whole area of botany, including scientific illustration, began to reach new heights with the work of Linnaeus (qv), whose binomial system of naming plants, the Linnaean system, was introduced in the late 1700s and continues to be used today. Although the binomial system remains unchanged, the classification of plants has been updated, which has resulted in name changes for species.

The earliest known manuscript flora (Irish; 1788) to carry Linnaean names was compiled by Dr Patrick Browne (qv) and was not illustrated. To date, it has not been published. Several years later, Dr Walter Wade's (qv) Dublin catalogue,[1] published by the DS in 1794, introduced the Linnaean system into Irish botany, employing, as it did, binary (Linnaean) names.

A flurry of botanical activity in the early years of the 19th century added substantially to the existing knowledge of the Irish flora and provided botanical studies with a natural framework within which to work. The baseline floras and lists were in place and further research would serve to refine that framework.

Botanical illustrator Dublin-born William Kilburn (qv)[2] made a vital contribution to scientific botany and illustration in the closing years of the 18th

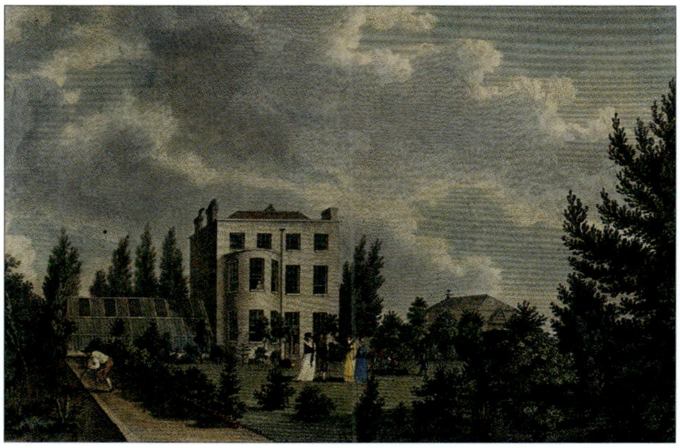

Fig. 31. John Coakley Lettsom's house: south view of Grove Hill, Camberwell, Surrey. Coloured line engraving by Thomas Medland (1765–1833), after George Samuel (fl.1785–1823), 1817
[British Museum Wellcome Collection]

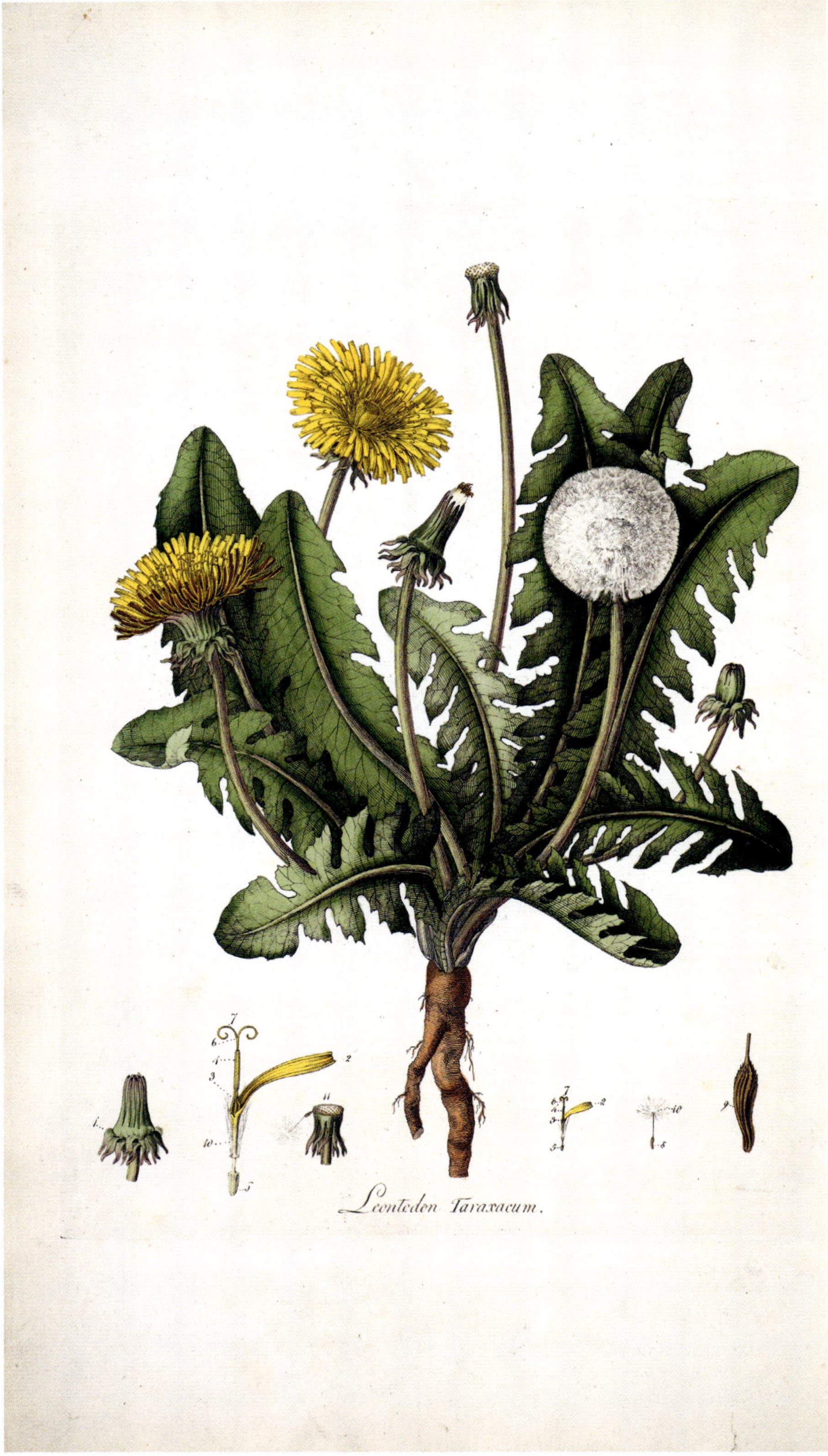


Fig. 32. *Leontodon taraxacum* (*Taraxacum officinale*), dandelion
Copperplate engraving, hand-coloured from an original watercolour drawn for *Flora Londinensis*
by William Kilburn
[Courtesy, National Library of Ireland]

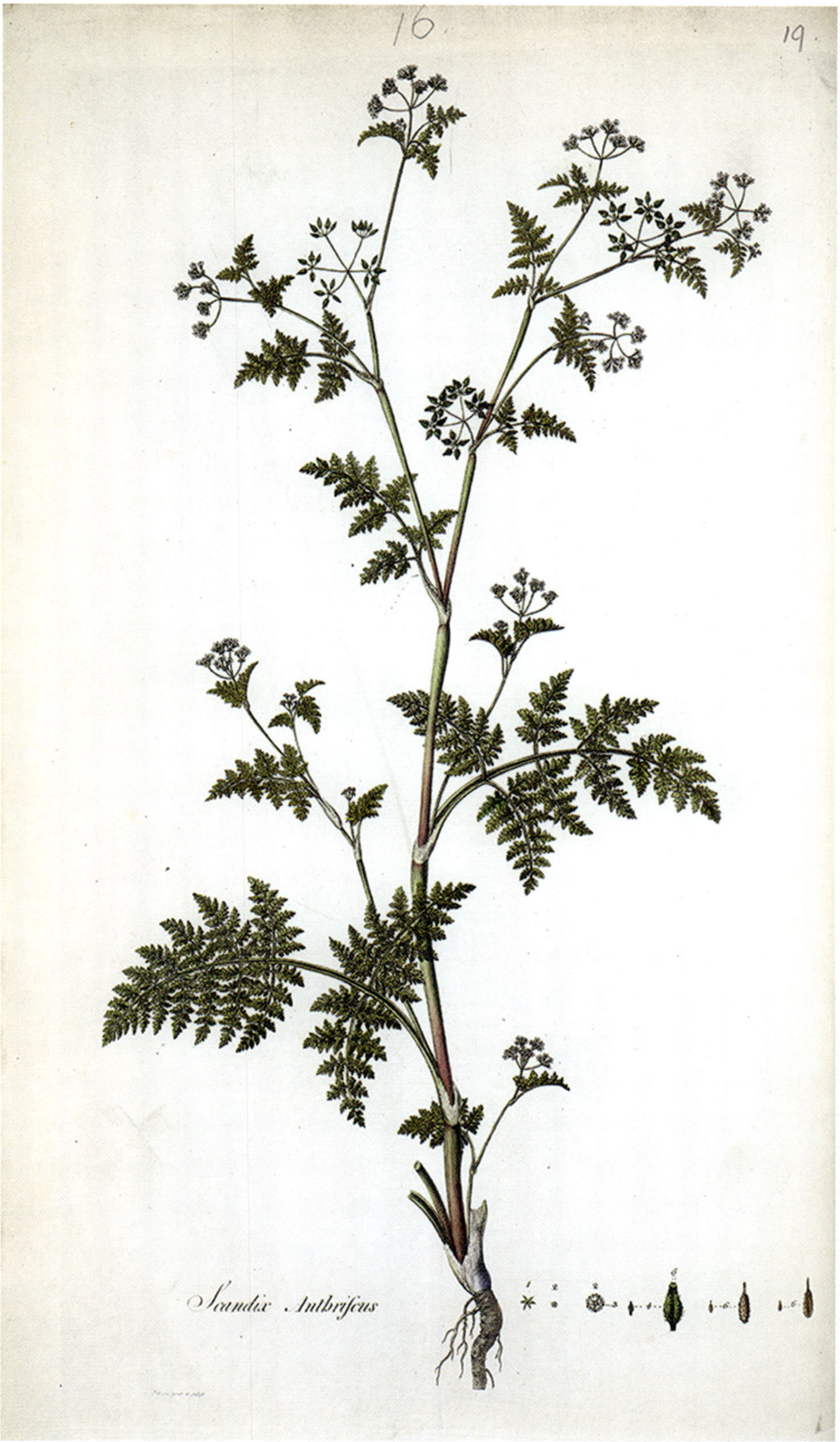


Fig. 33. *Scandix anthriscus* (*Anthriscus caucalis*), bur chervil
Copperplate engraving, hand coloured from an original watercolour drawing for *Flora Londinensis*
by William Kilburn
[Courtesy, National Library of Ireland]

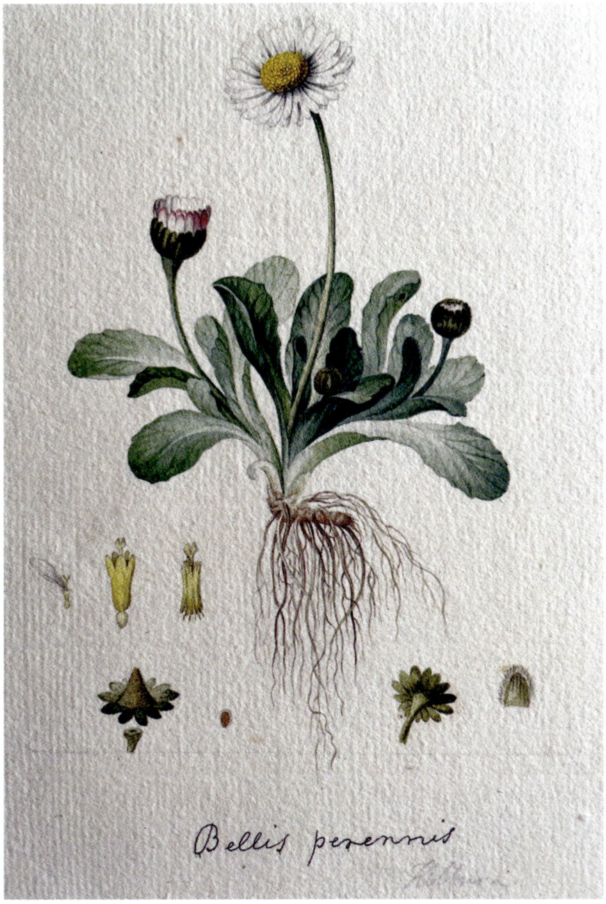


Fig. 34. *Bellis perennis*, common or English daisy
Watercolour and pencil drawing by William Kilburn, inscribed
'*Bellis perennis Kilburn*'
[Private collection. Reproduced by kind permission]

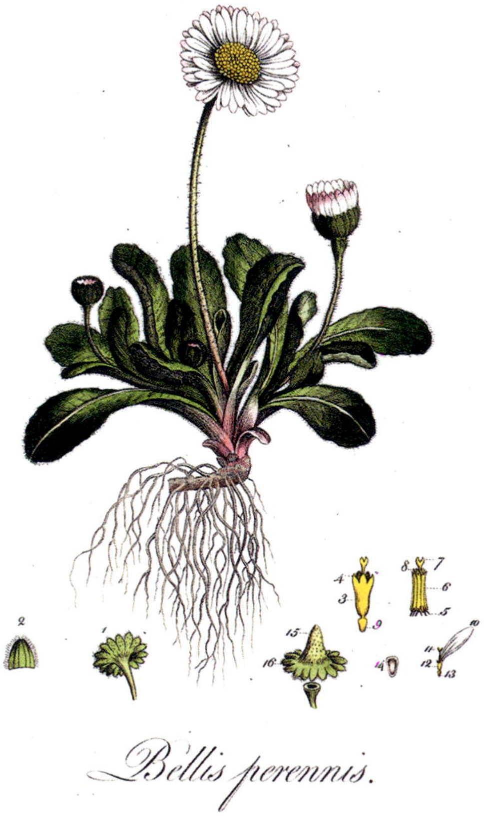


Fig. 35. *Bellis perennis*, common or English daisy
Copperplate engraving by William Kilburn
[Courtesy, National Library of Ireland]

century, contributing the majority of plates (around 28)[3] found in volume 1 to naturalist and botanist William Curtis's (qv) well-known *Flora Londinensis*.[4] The flora was originally published as numbered instalments, 72 of these appearing from May 1775, and continuing until 1798.[5]

Curtis aimed to record and figure all plants growing wild within a 10-mile radius of the city of London and then to publish a continuation to extend to all indigenous plants found in the British Isles. The project was never completed. The first volume is dedicated to John Stuart, 3rd Earl of Bute (1713–1792), a distinguished botanist and patron of the arts from whom Curtis received support. The second is dedicated to Dr John Coakley Lettsom (1744–1815), owner of a distinguished library and a botanic garden arranged on the Linnaean system, which was located at Grove Hill, Camberwell, London.

The majority of botanical portraits, hand-coloured copperplate engravings found in volume 1, are signed by Irish artist, William Kilburn, born Capel Street, Dublin, 1745, who is considered to be the principal contributor. Others included English botanical artists, naturalists and engravers, James Sowerby, ALS, FLS[6] (1757–1822) and Sydenham Teast Edwards, FLS (1768–1819).

Kilburn's plant portraits are depicted life-size on good-quality paper and, in the case of larger plants, represent only a part. They demonstrate the artist's firm understanding of plant structure, superb sense of draughtsmanship, and close attention to detail. Several are signed in full or carry his initials. Detail and love of accuracy are made clear in Kilburn's portraits of *Leontodon taraxacum* (*Taraxacum officinale*, dandelion) and *Scandix anthriscus* (*Anthriscus caucalis*, bur chervil), both are illustrated here (see Figures 32 and 33). It is interesting to note that it is more than likely the artist used a camera obscura to help draw these plant portraits, sketching with Indian ink before the hand-colouring was applied.[7]

It is also likely that *Curtis's Flora Londinensis* provided the format for Dr Walter Wade's (qv) proposed publication, an illustrated flora, *Floræ Dublinensis Specimen* (1789). In 1787, Wade sought support by advertising in the *Dublin Chronicle*[8] for subscribers, to enable him to publish his flora of Dublin. In a series of advertisements, he promised that the work would be confined to plants growing within the Dublin area and would contain descriptions and illustrations. It was to be issued in parts, each part containing five to eight plates with accompanying letterpress. Latin, English and Irish names were to be provided.

Due to lack of subscriptions and financial support, *Floræ Dublinensis Specimen* was never published.

> *At his own expense he had sample sheets printed on which the engraving and its letterpress survive. Dr. Wade's Flora Dublinensis was intended to rival the famous Flora Londinensis being published by William Curtis.*[9]

A single, unsigned, uncoloured proof-sheet, a superb engraving, *Hyoscyamus niger* (common henbane), is all that has survived and is illustrated here (see Figure 36, page 42).

The promotion of *Floræ Dublinensis Specimen* by Wade helped to establish him as a prominent Irish botanist, and also provided him with an opportunity to give lectures from his home on Capel Street, Dublin. Wade was appointed professor and lecturer in botany by the DS in 1796 (–1825), which gave him the opportunity to lecture on such subjects as diet, medicine, the rural economy, meadow, pasture and artificial grasses.

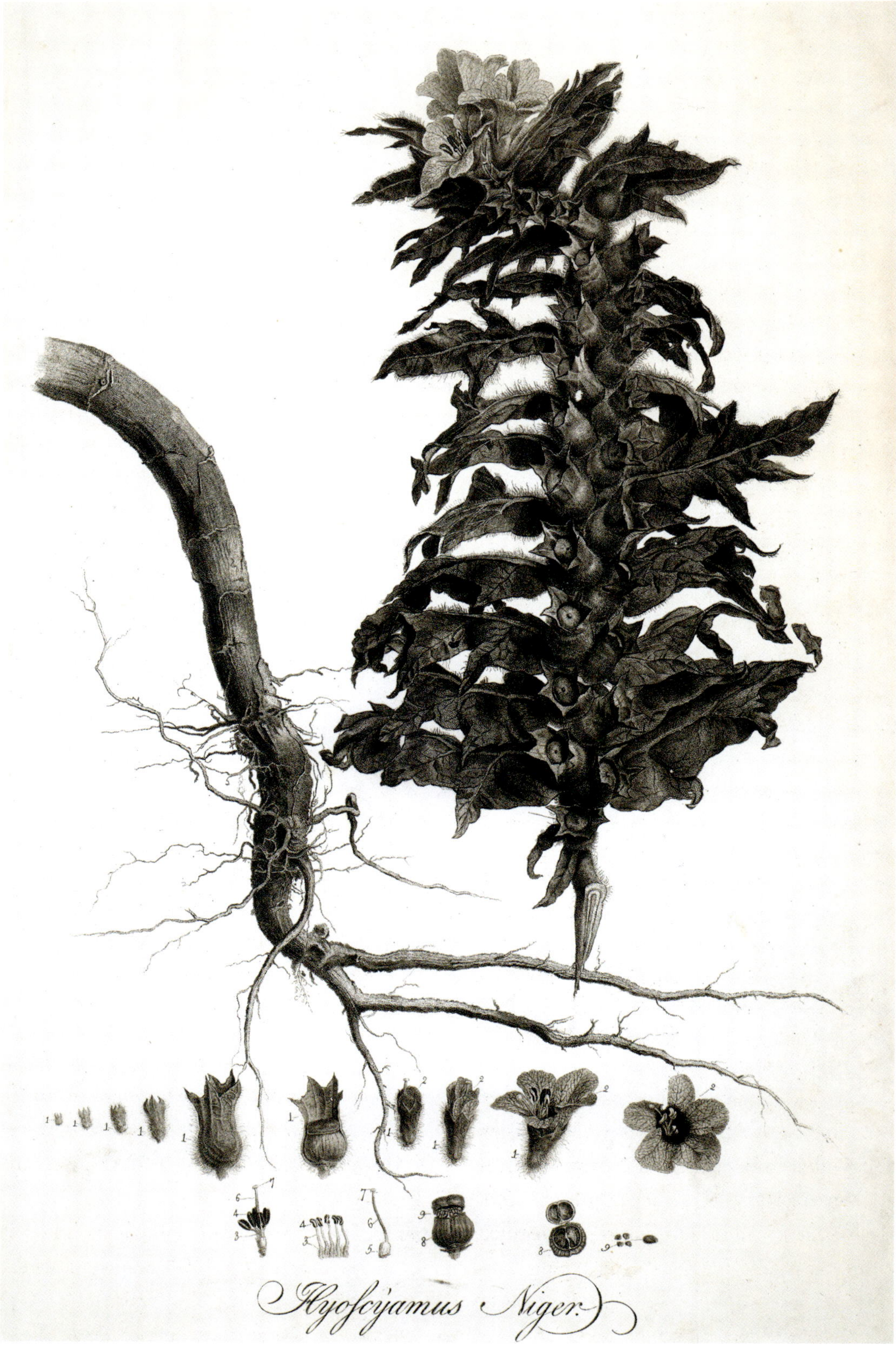


Fig. 36. *Hyoscyamus niger*, common henbane from *Floræ Dublinensis Specimen* by Walter Wade, c.1789
Copperplate engraving
[Courtesy, National Library of Ireland]

As far back as 1790, Wade had submitted a petition to the Irish House of Commons for the establishment of a botanic garden in Dublin, encouraged by the Speaker of the House, John Foster (1740–1828). In the same year, the Dublin Society Act was passed providing the Society with £300 towards establishing the RBG Glasnevin (later BG Glasnevin), Dublin. It took a further four years before 16 Irish acres and the sum of £2,200 were made available to the DS, to enable it to acquire land at Glasnevin.[10] Figure 41 shows a view of the gardens from the east bank of the River Tolka. The school shown on the left was nicknamed the 'Ink Pot'. In the far distance, in the centre is the Octagon House. Wade was invited to undertake the layout of the gardens, an invitation he had no hesitation in accepting, and he and John Underwood (fl.1780s–1834), acting as Superintendent, set about designing and planting.

Responsible for acquiring rare and interesting plants, together with seed for the newly secured site, Wade travelled extensively to well-known nurseries and gardens in England. In 1800, the gardens opened to the public, the largest publicly supported botanic garden in Europe.

Walter Wade, an enthusiastic and hard-working Irish botanist, was to add considerably to the knowledge and distribution of Irish plants. His expeditions to Connemara resulted in his being the first to discover (1801) the American pipewort, *Eriocaulon aquaticum*. A coloured engraving of a rare moss *Buxbaumia aphylla*, found near Killarney, appeared in his work *Plantae Rariores in Hibernia Inventae*, published three years later.[11] An associate of the Linnean Society (1792), FRS (1811), MRIA (1811), Dr Wade died at his home on Dorset Street, Dublin, on 25 July 1825.

John Templeton, ALS (1766–1825), known as the father of Irish natural history, was to become one of the more interesting contributors to botanical illustration in the second half of the 18th century. The unpublished manuscript of Templeton's illustrated *Flora Hibernica*,[12] together with his *Journal* dating between 1806 and 1825, survive and are in the Ulster Museum, Belfast. Contributors to *Flora Hibernica* included Ireland's first amateur female botanist, Ellen Hutchins (qv), and Scotsman James Townsend Mackay (1775–1862), who became Curator of the Botanic Garden, TCD, in 1806.[13]

Most of the specimens are executed in both watercolour and pencil. Templeton's portrait of *Orobanche rubra* (*Orobanche alba*) (see Figure 44, page 48) is painted in delicate tones of pink, brown and yellow. As is the case for the majority of specimens illustrated, Templeton provides the location and informs us that *Orobanche rubra* was:

> *Found on the ledges of the Basaltic Rocks of the Cave hill its angularly branching roots spreading on the Rock, not parasitic on any plant, the sun faded Flowers strongly scented August – 24 1805 being a Warm clear day.*

Judging by the contents of his *Journal*, it would appear that after 1815, the author's health was on the decline, as notes of excursions and of plants newly discovered cease to appear.

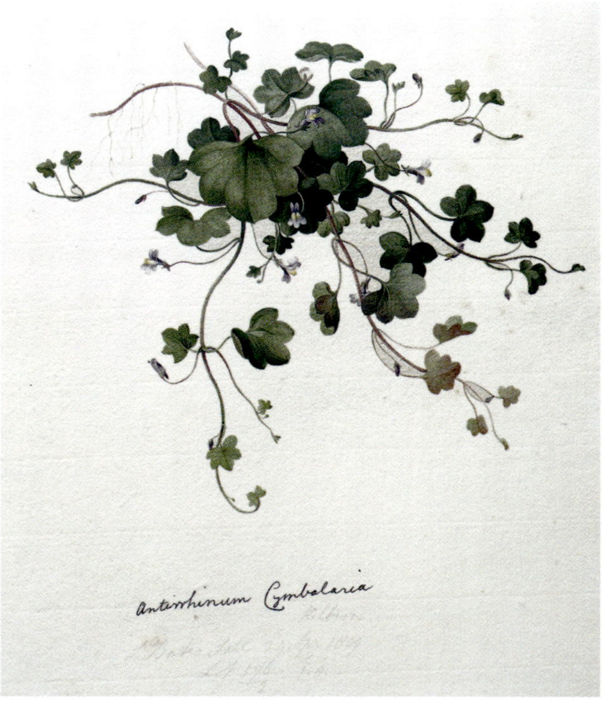

Fig. 37. *Antirrhinum cymbalaria* (*Cymbalaria muralis*)
Watercolour and pencil drawing by William Kilburn, inscribed
'*Antirrhinum cymbalaria Kilburn...*'
[Private collection. Reproduced by kind permission]

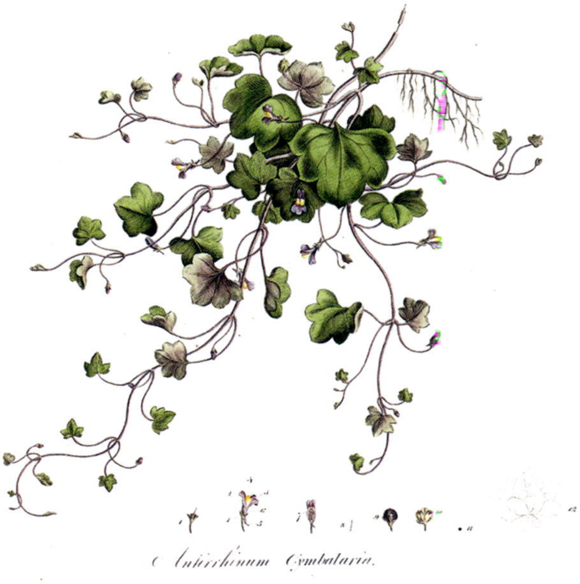

Fig. 38. *Antirrhinum cymbalaria* (*Cymbalaria muralis*)
Copperplate engraving by William Kilburn
[Courtesy, National Library of Ireland]

Drawings of Irish plants illustrated in both pencil and pen, together with one dry specimen, the Irish moss, *Sagina maritima*, recorded as being found 'at Ballycastle shore and the shores of Belfast Lough', all form part of Templeton's *Catalogue of the Native Plants of Ireland* (1793–1811) preserved in the RIA.[14] These plant portraits combine accuracy with a fine feeling for design, and confirm Templeton as being a precise and clear recorder of botanical detail.

The practical application of scientific studies was, by the mid-18th century, being actively encouraged by societies such as the DS. Templeton became part of this movement and by the age of 20 was devoting much of his time to the study of botany, carrying out research on the cultivation and improvement of plants.[15]

The Templeton family were prosperous Belfast wholesale merchants. John Templeton was born on

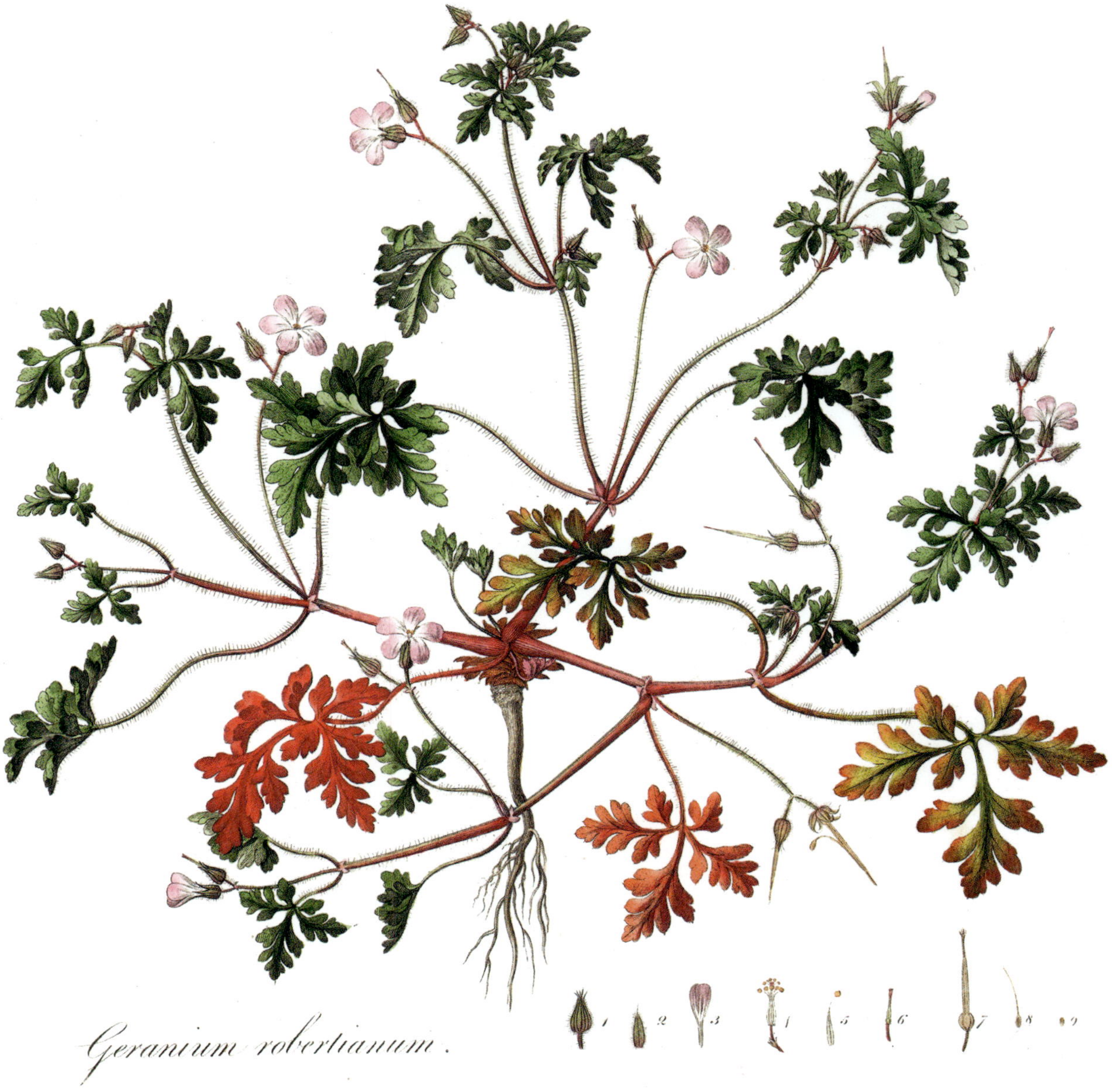


Fig. 39. *Geranium robertianum*, herb Robert
Copperplate engraving, hand-coloured from an original watercolour drawing for *Flora Londinensis* by William Kilburn
[Courtesy, National Library of Ireland]

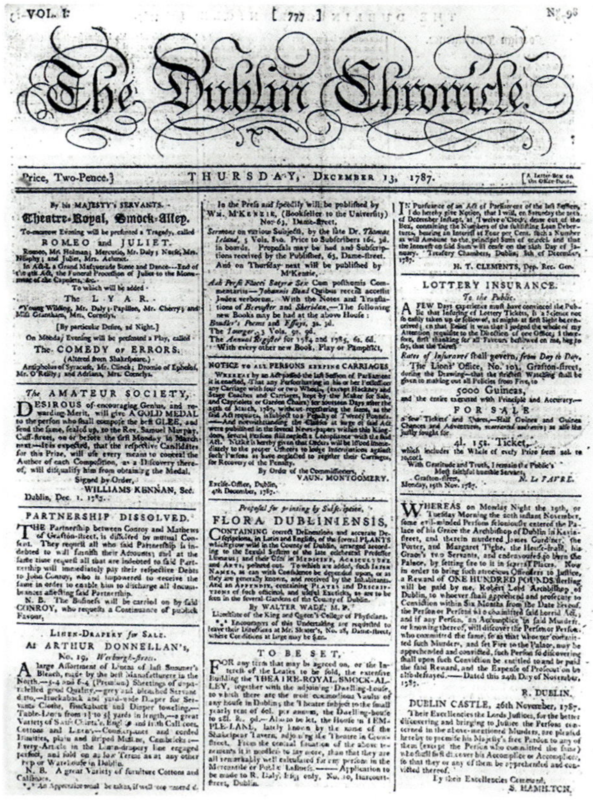

VOL. I. [ 777 ] No. 98

# The Dublin Chronicle.

Price, Two-Pence.] THURSDAY, DECEMBER 13, 1787. [A Letter-Box on the Office-Door.]

By his MAJESTY's SERVANTS.
Theatre-Royal, Smock-Alley.
To-morrow Evening will be presented a Tragedy, called
ROMEO and JULIET.
Romeo, Mr. Holman; Mercutio, Mr. Daly; Nurse, Mrs. [illegible]; and Juliet, Mrs. [illegible].
In Act I. a Grand Masquerade Scene and Dance---End of the 4th Act, the Funeral Procession of Juliet to the Monument of the Capulets, &c.
To which will be added
The LYAR.
Young Wilding, Mr. Daly; Papillon, Mr. Cherry; and Miss Grantham, Mrs. Cornelys.
[By particular Desire, 2d Night.]
On Monday Evening will be presented a Play, called
The COMEDY of ERRORS.
(Altered from Shakespeare.)
Antipholus of Syracuse, Mr. Clinch; Dromio of Ephesus, Mr. O'Reilly; and Adriana, Mrs. Cornelys.

The AMATEUR SOCIETY,
DESIROUS of encouraging Genius, and rewarding Merit, will give A GOLD MEDAL to the person who shall compose the best GLEE, and send the same, sealed up, to the Rev. Samuel Murphy, Cuff-street, on or before the first Monday in March next.—It is expected, that the respective Candidates for this Prize, will use every means to conceal the Author of each Composition, as a Discovery thereof, will disqualify him from obtaining the Medal.
Signed by Order,
WILLIAMS KENNAN, Sec.
Dublin, Dec. 1. 1787.

PARTNERSHIP DISSOLVED.
THE Partnership between Conroy and Mathews of Grafton-street, is dissolved by mutual Consent. They request all who said Partnership is indebted to will furnish their Accounts; and at the same time request all that are indebted to said Partnership will immediately pay their respective Debts to John Conroy, who is impowered to receive the same in order to enable him to discharge all Incumbrances affecting said Partnership.
N. B. The Business will be carried on by said CONROY, who requests a Continuance of publick Favour.

LINEN-DRAPERY for SALE.
At ARTHUR DONNELLAN's,
No. 19, Werburgh-street.
A large Assortment of Linens of last Summer's Bleach, made by the best Manufacturers in the North.—5-4 and 6-4 (Premium) Sheetings of unparalelled good Quality,—grey and bleached Servant ditto,—Huckaback and yard-wide Diaper for Servants Cloths, Huckaback and Diaper toweling,—Table-Linen from 1½ to 5½ yards in length,—a great Variety of [illegible], English and Irish Callicoes, Cottons and Linens,—Counterpanes and corded Dimities, plain and striped Muslins, Cambricks:—Every Article in the Linen-drapery line engaged perfect, and sold on as low Terms as at any other Shop or Warehouse in Dublin.
N. B. A great Variety of furniture Cottons and Callicoes.
*** An Apprentice would be taken, if well recommended.

In the Press and speedily will be published by WM. M'KENZIE, (Bookseller to the University) No. 63, Dame-street.
Sermons on various Subjects, by the late Dr. Thomas Leland, 3 Vols. 8vo. Price to Subscribers 16s. 3d. in boards. Proposals may be had and Subscriptions received by the Publisher, 63, Dame-street.
And on Thursday next will be published by M'Kenzie,
Auli Persii Flacci Satyrae Sex Cum posthumis Commentariis—Johannis Bond Quibus recens accessit Index verborum. With the Notes and Translations of Brewster and Sheridan.—The following new Books may be had at the above House:
Bowdler's Poems and Essays, 3s. 3d.
The Lounger, 3 Vols. 9s. 9d.
The Annual Register for 1784 and 1785, 6s. 6d.
With every other new Book, Play or Pamphlet,

NOTICE TO ALL PERSONS KEEPING CARRIAGES.
WHEREAS by an Act passed the last Session of Parliament it is enacted, That any Person having in his or her Possession any Carriage with four or two Wheels, (except Hackney and Stage Coaches and Carriages, kept by the Maker for Sale, and Caprioles or Garden Chairs) for fourteen Days after the 25th of March, 1787, without registering the same, as the said Act requires, is subject to a Penalty of Twenty Pounds.—And notwithstanding the Clauses at large of said Act were published in the several News-papers within this Kingdom, several Persons still neglect a Compliance with the said Act. Notice is hereby given that Orders will be issued immediately to the proper Officers to lodge Informations against such Persons as have neglected to register their Carriages, for Recovery of the Penalty.
By Order of the Commissioners,
VAUN. MONTGOMERY.
Excise-Office, Dublin, 4th December, 1787.

Proposal for printing by Subscription,
FLORA DUBLINIENSIS,
CONTAINING correct Delineations and accurate Descriptions, in Latin and English, of the several PLANTS which grow wild in the County of Dublin, arranged according to the Sexual System of the late celebrated Professor Linnaeus; and their Uses in MEDICINE, AGRICULTURE and ARTS, pointed out. To which are added, such IRISH NAMES, as can with Confidence be depended upon, or as they are generally known, and received by the Inhabitants. And an APPENDIX, containing PLATES and DESCRIPTIONS of such officinal, and useful Exoticks, as are to be seen in the several Gardens of the County of Dublin.
By WALTER WADE, M. D.
Licentiate of the King and Queen's College of Physicians.
*** Encouragers of this Undertaking are requested to leave their Directions at Mr. Shater's, No. 28, Dame-street, where Conditions at large may be seen.

TO BE SET,
FOR any term that may be agreed on, or the Interest of the Leases to be sold, the extensive Building the THEATRE-ROYAL, SMOCK-ALLEY, together with the adjoining Dwelling-house, to which there are the most commodious Vaults of any house in Dublin; the Theatre subject to the small yearly rent of 60l. per annum, the Dwelling-house to 28l. 8s. 9d.—Also to be let, the House in TEMPLE-LANE, lately known by the name of the Shakespear Tavern, adjoining the Theatre in Crow-street. From the central situation of the above tenements it is needless to say more, than that they are all remarkably well calculated for any person in the Mercantile or Public Business.——Application to be made to R. Daly, Esq; only, No. 10, Harcourt-street, Dublin.

IN Pursuance of an Act of Parliament of the last Session, I do hereby give Notice, that I will, on Saturday the 29th of December Instant, at Twelve o'Clock, draw out of the Box, containing the Numbers of the subsisting Loan Debentures, bearing an Interest at Four per Cent. such a Number as will Amount to the principal Sum of [illegible] and that the Interest on said Sum will cease on the 25th Day of January. Treasury Chambers, Dublin, 8th of December, 1787.
H. T. CLEMENTS, Dep. Rec. Gen.

LOTTERY INSURANCE.
To the Public.
A FEW Days experience must have convinced the Public that Insuring of Lottery Tickets, is a Science not so easily taken up or followed, as might at first Sight be conceived; in that Belief it was that I judged the whole of my Attention requisite to the Direction of one Office; I therefore, first thanking for all Favours bestowed on me, beg to say, that the Lowest
Rates of Insurance shall govern, from Day to Day,
The Lions' Office, No. 101, Grafton-street, during the Drawing—that the strictest Watching shall be given to making out all Policies from Five, to
5000 Guineas,
and the entire executed with Principle and Accuracy.—
FOR SALE
a few Tickets and Shares,—Half Guinea and Guinea Chances and Adventures, warranted undrawn; as also the justly sought for
4l. 15s. Ticket,
which includes the Whole of every Prize from 20l. to 10,000l.
With Gratitude and Truth, I remain the Public's
Most faithful humble Servant,
Grafton-street, Monday, 19th Nov. 1787. N. Le FAVRE.

WHEREAS on Monday Night the 19th, or Tuesday Morning the 20th instant November, some evil-minded Persons feloniously entered the Palace of his Grace the Archbishop of Dublin in Kevin-street, and therein murdered James Gardiner, the Porter, and Margaret Tighe, the House-maid, his Grace's two Servants, and endeavoured to burn the Palace, by setting fire to it in several Places. Now in order to bring such atrocious Offenders to Justice, a Reward of ONE HUNDRED POUNDS sterling will be paid by me, Robert Lord Archbishop of Dublin, to whoever shall apprehend and prosecute to Conviction within Six Months from the Date hereof, the Person or Persons who committed said horrid Act; and if any Person, an Accomplice in said Murder, or knowing thereof, will discover the Person or Persons who committed the same, so as that whoever committed such Murders, and set Fire to the Palace, may be apprehended and convicted, such Person so discovering shall upon such Conviction be entitled to and be paid the said Reward, and the Expense of Prosecution be also defrayed.——Dated this 24th Day of November, 1787.
R. DUBLIN.

DUBLIN CASTLE, 26th November, 1787.
Their Excellencies the Lords Justices, for the better discovering and bringing to Justice the Persons concerned in the above-mentioned Murders, are pleased hereby to promise his Majesty's free Pardon to any of them (except the Person who committed the same) who shall first discover his Accomplice or Accomplices, so that they or any of them be apprehended and convicted thereof.
By their Excellencies Command,
S. HAMILTON.

Fig. 40. Advertisement in the *Dublin Chronicle* for Dr Walter Wade's *Flora Dubliniensis*
[Courtesy, National Library of Ireland]

Bridge Street, Belfast, in 1766, the son of James Templeton and Mary Eleanor Legg, daughter of Benjamin Legg of Belfast and Malone. When he was a child, his health was delicate and he spent a good deal of his time reading; in particular, books devoted to natural history. Templeton received his early education from the educational innovator, author and pioneer, David Manson (1726–1792), whose approach to education was to have a profound effect

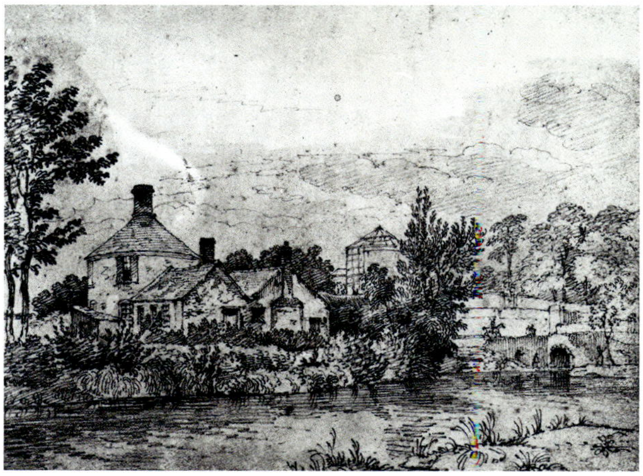

Fig. 41. View of the Royal (now National) Botanic Gardens, Glasnevin, Dublin, from the east bank of the River Tolka
[Courtesy of the Irish Architectural Archive]

on the boy. Manson's educational methods were based on encouraging success rather than punishing failure. A philanthropist by nature, Manson encouraged his pupil's study of local natural history.

In the early 17th century, the family settled on a small estate, 'Cranmore' (previously known as 'Orange Grove'), Malone, located on what was then the outskirts of Belfast. There, c.1786, John Templeton laid out a garden according to a suggestion contained in Rousseau's novel *La Nouvelle Héloise*. This was an experimental garden and he set about successfully cultivating foreign trees, flowers and shrubs grown from seed sent to him by fellow enthusiastic botanists. Today, sadly the only reminder of this historic garden is the avenue of ancient trees leading to the house, which is almost a ruin.[16]

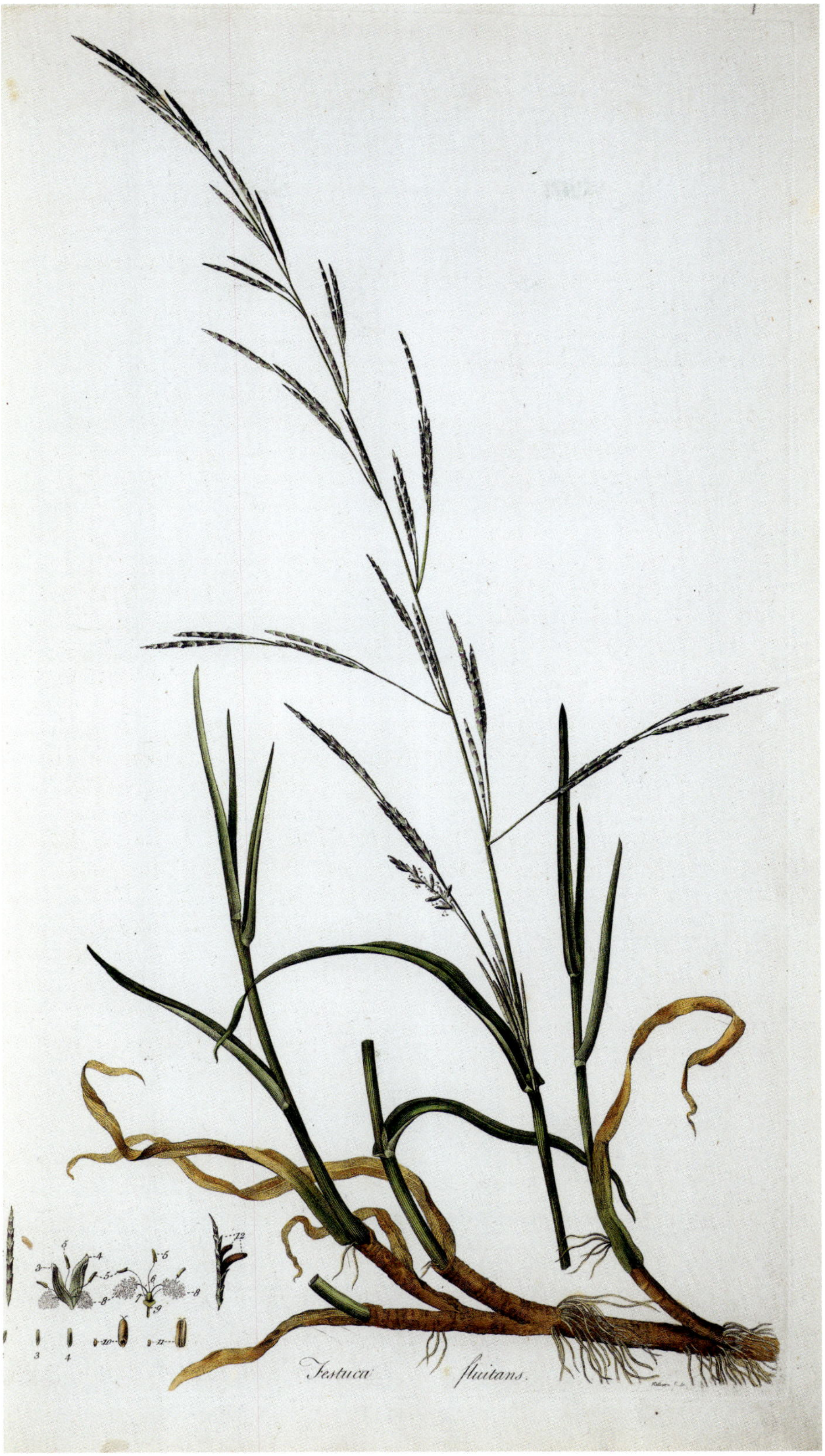


Fig. 42. *Festuca fluitans* (*Glyceria fruitans*)
Copperplate engraving, hand-coloured from an original watercolour drawing for *Flora Londinensis* by William Kilburn
[Courtesy, National Library of Ireland]

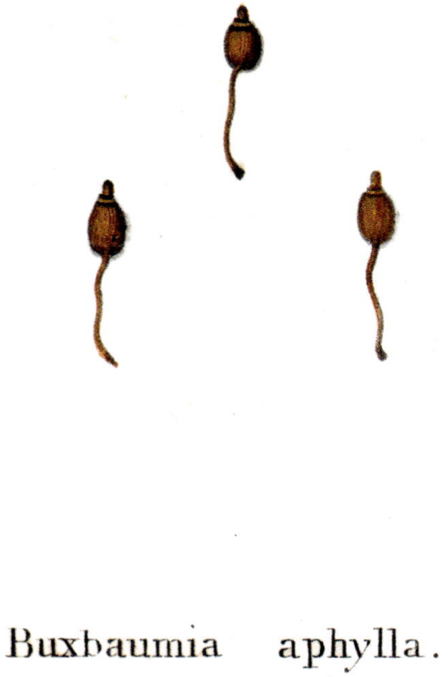


Fig. 43. *Buxbaumia aphylla,* bug-on-a-stick/hump-backed elf/ elf-cap moss
Engraving by unknown artist
[Courtesy, National Library of Ireland]

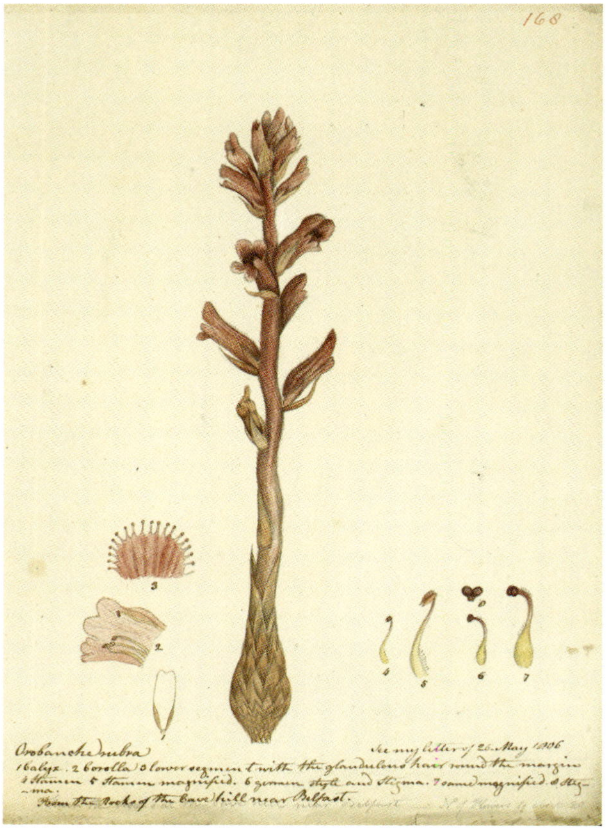


Fig. 44. *Orobanche rubra* (*Orobanche alba*), thyme broomrape
Watercolour and pencil by John Templeton
Inscription (in brown ink): *...From the Rocks of the Cave hill near Belfast.*
[Ulster Museum]

On his first visit to London in 1794, Templeton met Thomas Martyn (1735–1825), Professor of Botany at Cambridge University and one of the earliest exponents of Linnaean classification. Templeton later contributed information on cultivation for Martyn's edition of Miller's *Gardeners and Florists Dictionary.*[17] It was on his second visit to London that Templeton encountered such well-known figures in the botanical field as William Curtis, James Sowerby, Dawson Turner (qv) and Sir Joseph Banks, President of the Royal Society.

On his return to Ireland, Templeton set about collecting material for a complete natural history of Ireland, while at the same time contributing to such works as

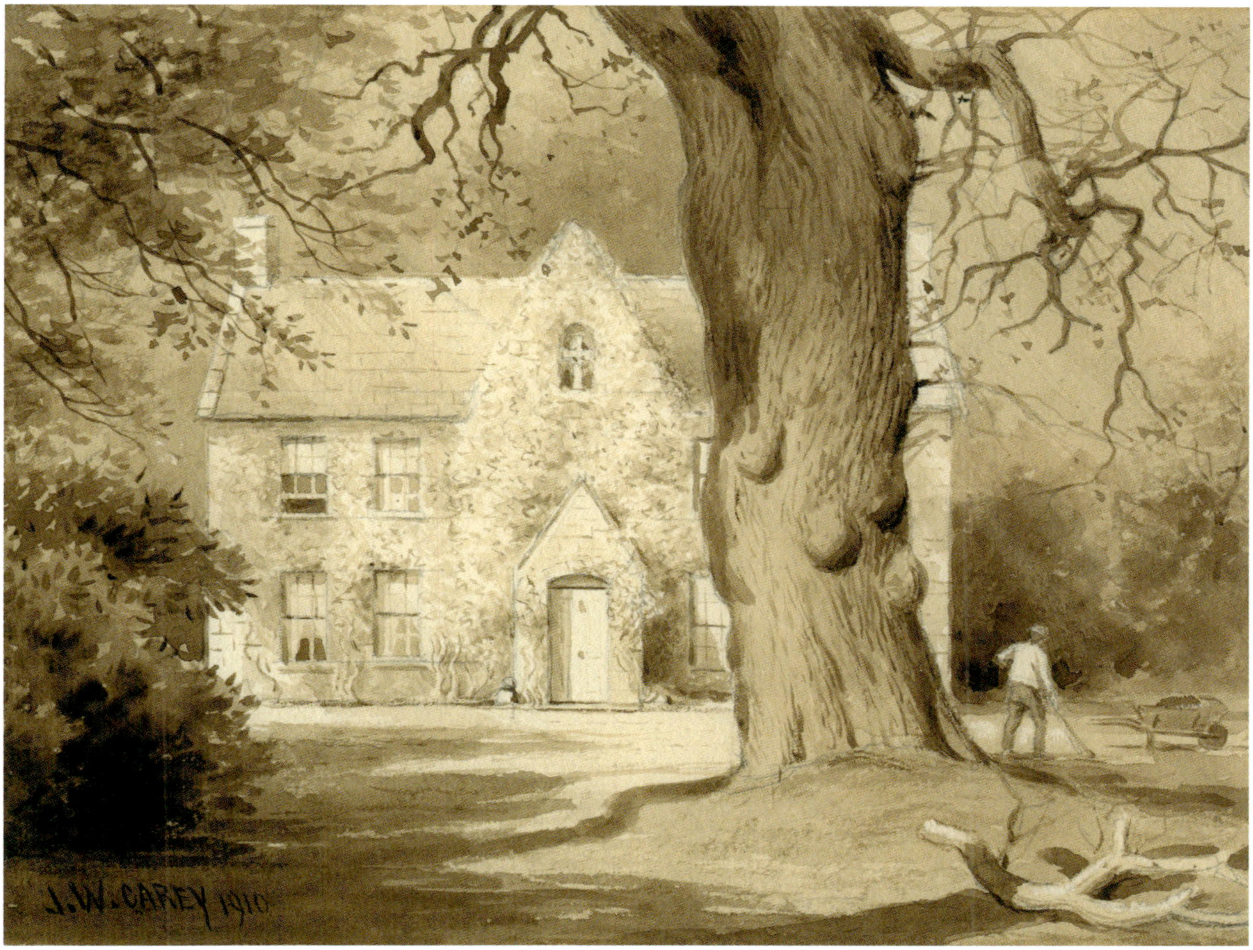


Fig. 45. 'Cranmore' (formerly 'Orange Grove'), Belfast, home of the father of Irish natural history, John Templeton, a founder member of Belfast Natural History Society
Sepia and pencil on paper (signed) by Joseph William Carey (1859–1937), 1910
[Ulster Museum]

J. Sowerby and J.E. Smith's *English Botany*. In 1802, he sent a rare hybrid rose that he had discovered in Holywood, Co. Down, to the Royal Irish Academy and was awarded a premium of five guineas. This was *Rosa* x *hibernica* (the Irish rose), *Rosa canina* x *pimpinellifolia* (*R.* x *hibernica*) Templeton-rose-Rosaceae, which will always be associated with this leading naturalist and botanist. Devoted to collecting lichens, mosses and

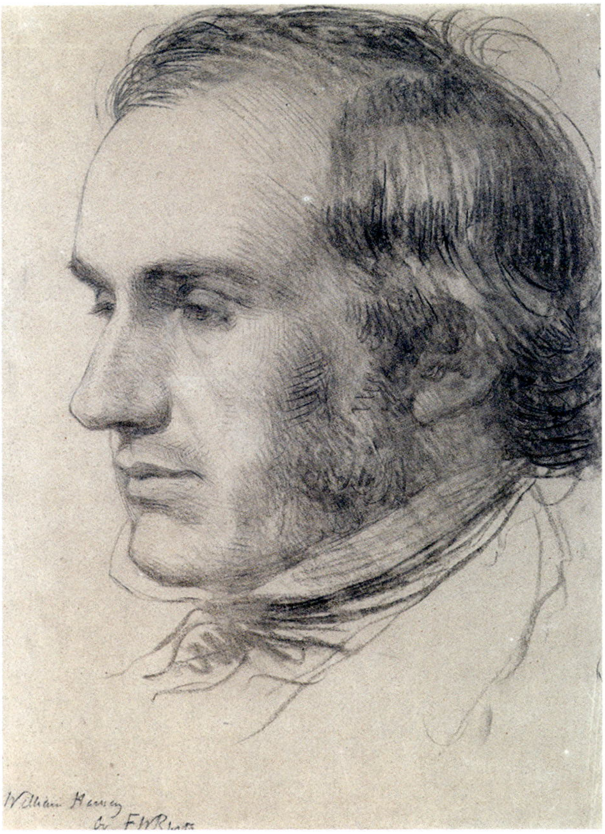

Fig. 46. William Henry Harvey (1811–1866)
Black chalk (signed F.W. Burton) by Sir Frederic William Burton
[Photo © National Gallery of Ireland]

liverworts, and frequently dissatisfied with many of the published drawings, Templeton made careful pencil studies, shading them with ink or watercolour.

A strong advocate of a botanic garden for the City of Belfast, an ALS (1794), vice-president of the Belfast Literary Society (1803), Templeton became a founder member of the Belfast Natural History Society in 1821.[18] His collections formed the basis of the Society's museum, which opened in 1831. A kind and generous man who gave freely of his time to others, Templeton donated material to the DS, which consisted largely of seed for the BG Glasnevin, Dublin, and birds for the Society's museum.[19]

Unlike Templeton, botanist, systematist and phycologist William Henry Harvey, MD, FRS, FLS (1811–1866) became a keen traveller, spending part of his early life in South Africa, where he made a significant contribution towards the study of plants.

Harvey was the 11th and youngest child of Quaker parents, Joseph Massey Harvey and Rebecca (née Mark). Born at Summerville House, Limerick, on 5 February 1811, he attended Newtown School, Waterford. At the age of 13, the young boy was sent to another Quaker school, Ballitore, Co. Kildare. The headmaster, James White, a well-known local botanist, encouraged the boy to collect shells, lichens, mosses, butterflies and algae, Harvey remarking:

> *I am very fond of botany ... I have not had much opportunity of learning anything because I have only to show a plant to James White, who tells me about it which I forget the next minute.*

Harvey's main interest was cryptogams, which included algae and mosses, and this was given added encouragement when the family visited their holiday home at Miltown Malbay, Co. Clare, each year.

Harvey left Ballitore in 1827, 'neither fit to be a doctor nor a lawyer' and joined the family business. In his spare time, he continued to study botany. In 1831, he discovered, in Killarney, a species of moss, later to be called *Hookeria laete-virens*, which led to a meeting with Sir William Jackson Hooker, LLD, DCL, FRS, FLS (1785–1865) then Regius Professor of Medicine, Glasgow, but later to become director of the Royal Botanic Gardens, Kew. Hooker came to Ireland to meet him, and a friendship developed, with Hooker encouraging the young botanist by lending him various species of algae to be identified.[20]

Harvey's mother died in 1831 and his father in 1834. Largely through the influence of Thomas Spring-Rice (1790–1866), 1st Baron Monteagle and MP for Limerick, Harvey's brother Joseph was appointed Colonial Treasurer in the Cape Colony, a British colony established in 1806 and known today as South Africa. Harvey accompanied Joseph and his family, and they arrived at the Cape on 17 September 1835. Shortly afterwards, Joseph became ill and died two weeks after embarking on a return voyage to Europe. In his place, his brother, William was nominated as Colonial Treasurer and returned to the Cape Colony in 1836, where he was to spend the next seven years.

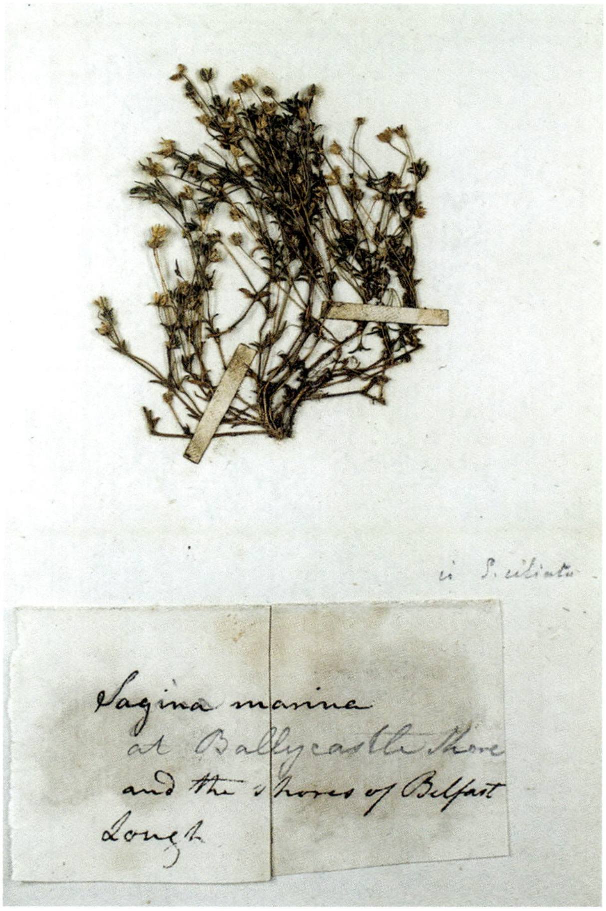


Fig. 47. Photograph of dry specimen, *Sagina maritima*, Irish moss recorded as being found 'at Ballycastle shore and the shores of Belfast Lough'
[By permission of the Royal Irish Academy. © RIA]

During this period, and with only two return trips to Ireland taking place, Harvey worked with zeal and enthusiasm. Plant collecting took place in the early mornings, he fulfilled his duties as Treasurer during the day, and in the evenings arranged his collections.

Harvey's botanical interests were of prime importance to him. In March 1857, he wrote:

*I have indeed taken so many excursions lately that I almost fear I shall earn the soubriquet of*

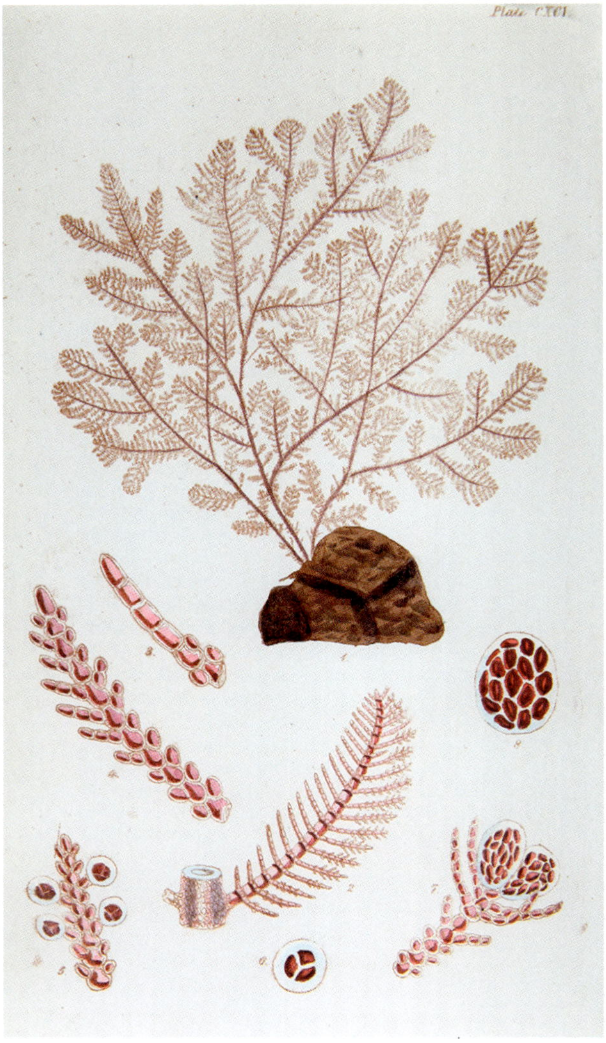

Fig. 48. *Ptilota sericea* (*Plumaria plumosa*), soft feather weed
Lithograph (coloured) by William Henry Harvey
[Courtesy, National Botanic Gardens, Glasnevin, Dublin]

*Her Majesty's pleasurer - general instead of the more dignified one of treasurer.*

He embarked on one of his many works, for which he is now well known, *Flora Capensis: Being a Systematic Description of the Plants of the Cape Colony, Caffraria, & Port Natal.* Harvey had been approached by Sir William Jackson Hooker to assist in a series of colonial floras which he had already initiated with such work as *The Genera of South African Plants* (1838) (see below). Together with German botanist and pharmacist, Dr Otto Wilhelm Sonder (1812–1881) of Hamburg, Harvey contributed the major part of the first three volumes (*Flora Capensis*), which appeared in 1859, 1862 and 1865 respectively.[21] At the same time, between 1859 and 1863, he succeeded in providing two volumes of his *Thesaurus Capensis, or illustrations of the South African flora*, each containing one hundred lithographed sketches of new or interesting plants drawn by himself and based on specimens in the Herbarium, TCD.

Harvey scorned the assistance of professional botanical artists and, as in his previous publications, executed his own line drawings, depicting with skill and accuracy details of floral anatomy and foliage. In each case, he carried out the lithographic process on stone himself, a practice he continued throughout his life.[22]

While in South Africa, Harvey collected a personal herbarium of native plants which, together with the plants he had collected in Europe, comprised around ten thousand sheets. During this period, there was no published guide to aid identification of plants in South Africa. In 1838, this hard-working botanist published *The Genera of South African Plants* (Cape Town), in which he reconstructed and revised the older genera definitions according to his own interpretations.

During his second tour of duty at the Cape, Harvey became ill. He resigned his position in 1841 and returned to Limerick. Three years later, he was appointed Keeper of the Herbarium, TCD, where his main concern was the care of the collections of dried and labelled plants, sorting, identifying and cataloguing the thousands of specimens sent to him from overseas collectors. While working in the Herbarium, he devoted his time mainly to the study of seaweeds. In 1841, he published his *Manual of the British Algae*,[23] which was followed in 1846 by the first part of *Phycologia Britannica*, completed in 1851.[24] This work contained 360 coloured figures, all drawn on stone by the author.

In 1848, Harvey was elected Professor of Botany, RDS, and in 1856, following the retirement of Professor George James Allman, he succeeded in being elected to the Chair of Botany, TCD.[25]

In the field of plant collecting, Harvey's ability and energy as a plant collector were formidable.[26] His collection trip, which he undertook in 1853, took him around the world to Malta, Gibraltar, Egypt, Sri Lanka, Tasmania, Fiji, Tonga and Valparaíso. However, the majority of his time was spent in

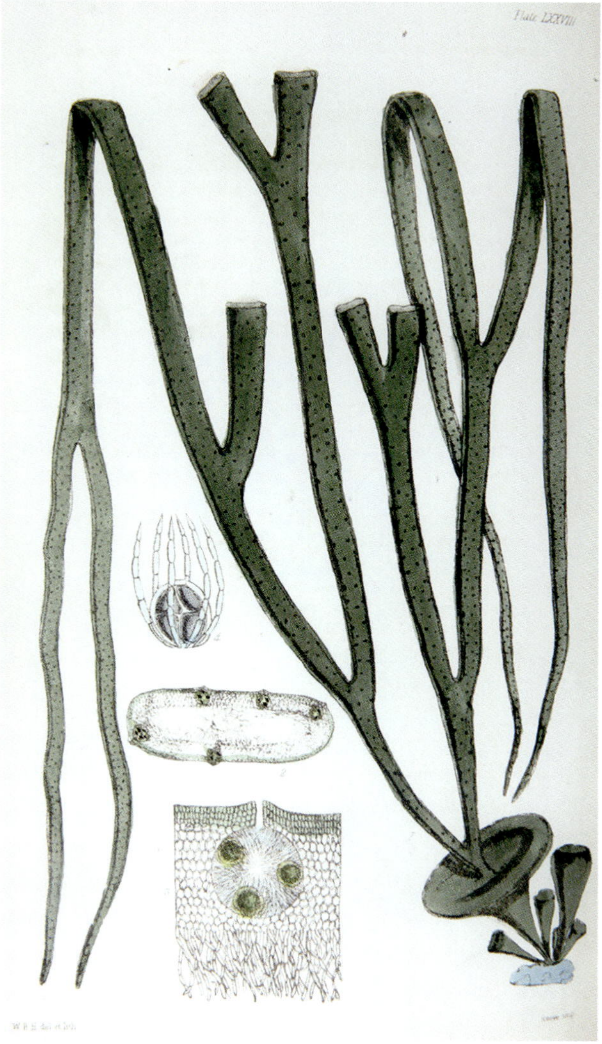

Fig. 49. *Himanthalia lorea* (*Himanthalia elongata*), button weed
Lithograph (coloured) by William Henry Harvey
[Courtesy, National Botanic Gardens, Glasnevin, Dublin]

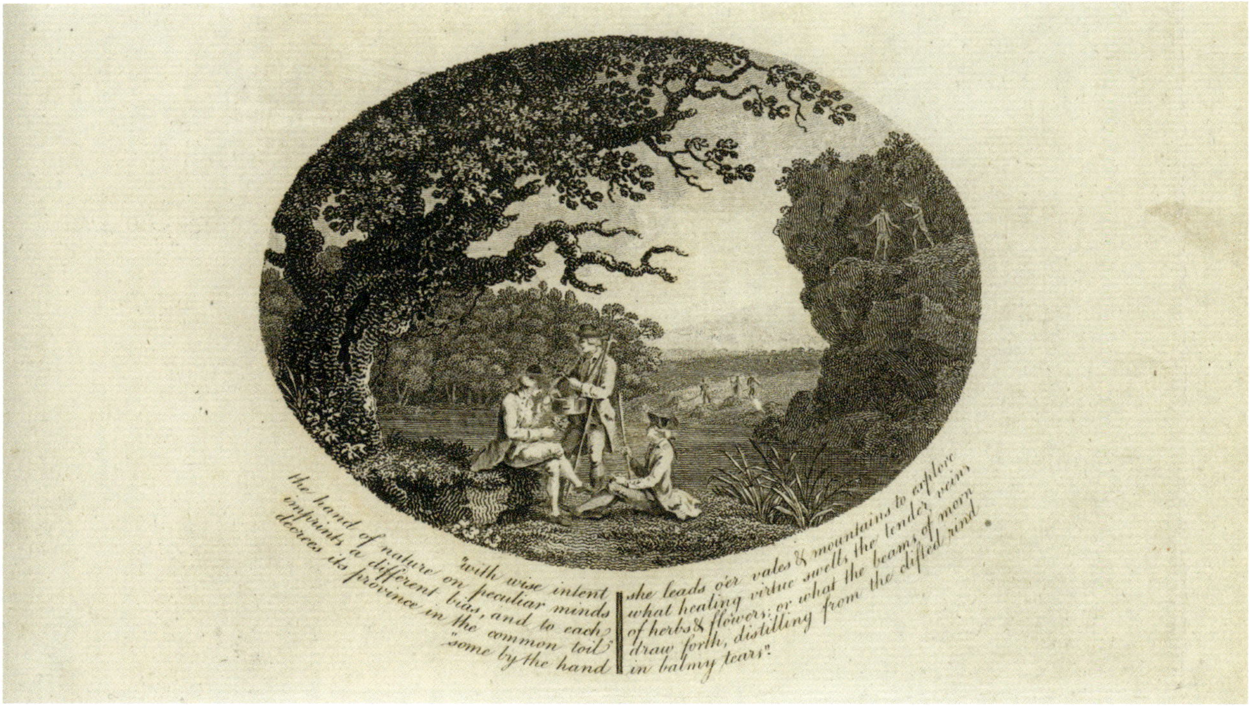


Fig. 50. Engraved design on title-page, *Flora Londinensis* vol.1 (1775), 1777 [–81] by William Curtis
[© Royal Botanic Gardens, Kew]

Australia, where it is believed he collected at least twenty thousand specimens.

In 1857, Harvey was elected FLS and a year later, FRS. In April 1861, he married Elizabeth Lecky Phelps, daughter of James Phelps of Limerick, a childhood friend. His health, which had never been very strong, continued to deteriorate and during the winter of 1865 he became ill. It was felt that a spell in a mild climate might help, so the Harveys went to stay with Sir William's recently bereaved widow, Lady Hooker, at Torquay on the south-west coast of England.

William Henry Harvey died on 15 May 1866 at Torquay. His contribution to the flora of South Africa had been outstanding. *Flora Capensis* had brought together, and summarised, descriptions of plants scattered throughout numerous publications and had provided keys for the identification of species. In the words of distinguished botanist and Chair of Botany, TCD, the late Dr David Webb (1912–1994), 'It was the vision of continuity with his successors that sustained him through hours of tedium'.[27] This Limerick-born botanist is commemorated by a South African genus *Harveya* and the species, *Albizia harveyi.*

# Chapter 4
# Early Amateur Botanists and Floras

*The power of the amateur tradition must never be under estimated*[1]

Knowledge of the flora and vegetation of Ireland, together with many European countries, is the result of early fieldwork by both amateur and professional botanists. Amateur floras are important because they allow the amateur botanist to identify plants – the first step towards developing a deeper appreciation of them – and to make contributions towards the knowledge of their species distribution.

For centuries, botanical drawing and flower painting had been at the core of female accomplishments and accepted as a 'polite' subject for keen, energetic young girls of a higher social class. During the 18th century, the drawing of flowers resulted in vast numbers of drawing-books being published for 'the use and amusement of gentlemen and ladies delighting in that art'. Towards the middle of that century, when drawing in watercolour became a necessary accomplishment for every fashionable young lady, drawing-books became more instructive. Numerous instruction 'manuals' were on offer. One of the earliest, *The Lady's Drawing Book* (1755), encouraged the 'fair sex...to engage...in a profitable Improvement of their Leisure Hours' and demonstrated how to proceed from a rough sketch to a finished drawing of both flowers and stems of plants. Interestingly, it did not reveal the roots of plants or separate out the reproductive part of the flower for special attention.

Several manuals, such as the plates found in *A New Treatise on Flower Painting, or Every Lady Her Own Drawing Master* (1797) fulfilled the author's (J. White) promise to illustrate the flowers:

> *in three different states: first the outline: second, the first tints put on, in order to shew in what manner to begin to colour or paint a flower, with proper references to the tints; thirdly, the flowers finished, with proper directions how to proceed to each state.*

Eighteenth-century young ladies were also encouraged to occupy themselves by colouring plates in natural history books which, in time, became a fashionable pastime.

Throughout the 18th and 19th centuries, women became more and more drawn to the world of botany, which became increasingly a feminine area, marked as being especially suitable for women and girls. Botany became a part of their education and recreation – observing, drawing, collecting, classifying and naming plants. This resulted in a significant number of enterprising, keen, amateur women botanists excelling in this area both as amateur botanists and botanical illustrators.[2]

# Mary Delany (née Granville, formerly Mrs Pendarves, 1700–1788)

Mary Delany was one of the most gifted women of her age, particularly in the applied arts. A talented fabric designer, creator of shell grottoes,[3] a competent needlewoman, musician and artist in both oil and watercolour, she also found the time to study mineralogy, astronomy and botany. A lively correspondent, her letters have left a rich social commentary on the age. In a letter to her sister, Mrs Dewes, dated 3 November 1759, she wrote:

> *Last Wednesday Mrs H. Hamilton and her daughter breakfasted here. After breakfast I went to my painting and settled Mrs Hamilton with watercolours and pencils; she is assisting me in colouring Sheldrake's herbal.*[4]

At the age of 72, Mary Delany embarked on her famous *Hortus siccus* (paper collages of flowers) and continued until she was 85. This unique collection (970) is now housed in the BM and, according to her biographer and descendant, Ruth Hayden,[5] the collages are botanically correct. They were assembled as follows:

> *Having a piece of Chinese paper on the table of bright scarlet, a geranium caught her eye of a similar colour, and taking her scissors she amused herself with cutting out each flower, by her eye, in the paper which resembled its hue; she laid the paper petals on a black ground, and was so pleased with the effect that she proceeded to cut out the calyx, stalks and leaves in shades of green and pasted them down–*[6]

Her collages attained such a high standard that the eminent botanist Sir Joseph Banks (1743-1820) 'used to say that he would venture to describe botanically any plant from Mrs Delany's imitation without the least fear of committing an error'.[7]

Born in Coulston, Wiltshire, on 14 May 1700, Mary Delany was the eldest daughter of Colonel Bernard Granville and a niece of Lord Granville, a noted patron of many branches of the arts. She spent her early life in London and c.1713 moved with her family to Buckland Manor in the Cotswolds, Gloucestershire. Both for political and financial reasons, she was forced into an arranged marriage with Alexander Pendarves, MP for Launceston, Cornwall, in 1717. She lived at Penryn, Falmouth, Cornwall and then in London until her husband's death. Between 1731 and 1733, she visited Ireland and became a friend of Dean Jonathan Swift. Later, in 1743, she married Swift's friend Dr Patrick Delany, Dean of Down and tutor at TCD.

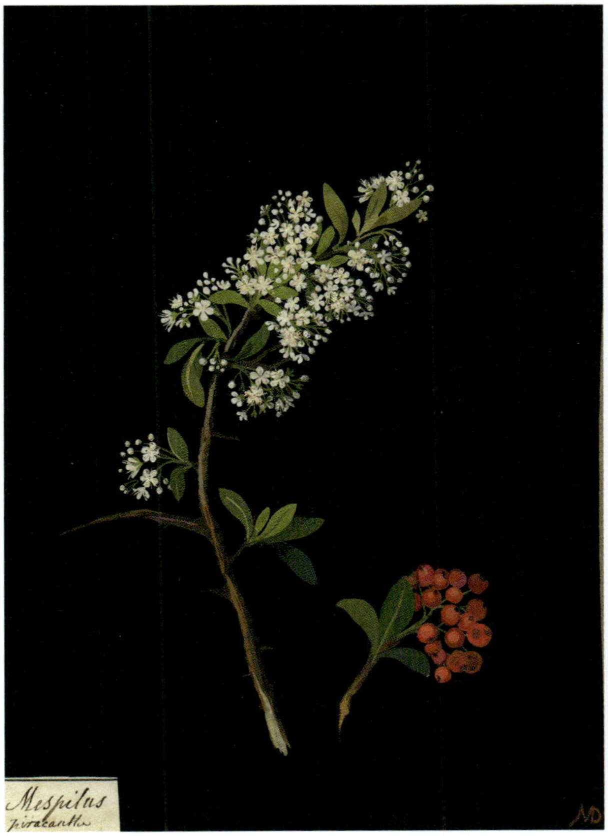


Fig. 51. *Mespilus pyracantha* (*Pyracantha coccinea*)
A paper flower collage by Mary Delany
[© The Trustees of the British Museum]

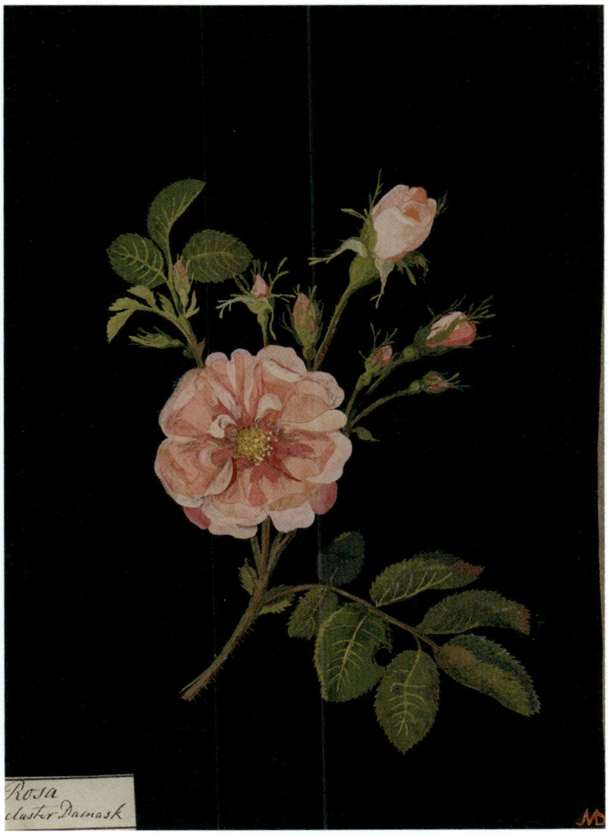


Fig. 52. *Rosa cluster Damask*
A paper flower collage by Mary Delany
[© The Trustees of the British Museum]

It was in Ireland that her career as an artist began to develop, and encouraged by her husband, she took lessons copying family portraits, constantly drawing wherever she and her husband travelled. They made many visits to England, largely to visit her sister Anne Dewes at Wellesbourn, Warwickshire, her brother Bernard Granville at Calwich Abbey, Staffordshire, and her friend the Duchess of Portland at Bulstrode, Buckinghamshire. After her husband's death in 1768, she settled in London, moving to Windsor in 1785.

Mary Delany forged, through her work in whatever media she chose – mosaic, painting, poetry, music – a strong relationship with nature and art. Her famous *Hortus siccus* is a lasting reminder of her talents.

# Frances (Fanny) Anne Edgeworth (née Beaufort, 1769–1864)

Frances (Fanny) Anne Beaufort was born at 'Flower Hill', Navan, Co. Meath, two years after the well-known novelist Maria Edgeworth (1767–1849), later to become her stepdaughter. She came from a talented family, and, like her father, the Reverend Daniel Augustus Beaufort, LLD (1739–1821), possessed outstanding gifts of scholarship combined with an enquiring mind.

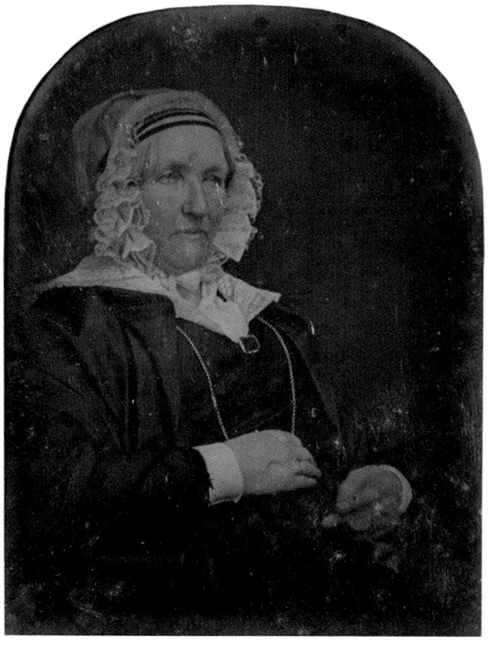

Fig. 53. Frances (Fanny) Anne Edgeworth (1769–1864)
Daguerreotype by Michael Pakenham Edgeworth (1812–1881)
[Photo © National Gallery of Ireland]

The Beaufort family had originated in France. Daniel Cornelis de Beaufort (1700–1788), the seventh child of Count François de Beaufort of Wessel, became a Huguenot refugee as a result of persecution, proceeding withdrawal of all civil rights from Protestants in France. He fled to London and became a Calvinist minister. After Lord Harrington's appointment as Viceroy of Ireland in 1746, Daniel Cornelis de Beaufort accompanied him as one of his chaplains. On arrival in Ireland, de Beaufort was given responsibility for the benefice of Navan, together with pastoral responsibility for the substantial Huguenot colony then residing in Dublin.

In London, Daniel Cornelis de Beaufort had married another French refugee from La Rochelle, Esther Gougheon. Their only child, Daniel Augustus Beaufort, was born in 1739. He also entered the church and was ordained in 1763, succeeding his father as Rector of Navan from 1765 to 1818. Described by Maria Edgeworth as 'a man of taste and literate.... possessing peculiarly the power of serving friends in society', Daniel Augustus Beaufort not only served as a rector, but was also a farmer, pioneering new methods of cereal and potato growing. He played a prominent role in the foundation of Sunday schools and helped to bring about the formation of the RIA, Dublin. A designer of houses and demesnes, a genealogist, Daniel Augustus Beaufort was knowledgeable about the identification of trees and plants. His remarks relating to towns and villages in Ireland that he visited while working on his well-known map of Ireland (1792) still arouse interest and comment.[8]

His daughter, Frances Anne, was born in 1769.[9] Frances, together with her two brothers and two sisters, grew up amidst an exceptionally talented family in a home filled with pictures. She attended the French Huguenot school run by a Mrs Terson in Portarlington to learn writing, drawing, French and dancing. From a young age, she loved drawing and c.1790 began taking lessons from Francis Robert West (c.1749–1809), son of Robert West (d.1770). Francis Robert had succeeded his father in 1777 as Master of the DS's School of Figure Drawing and was a highly respected and gifted teacher.

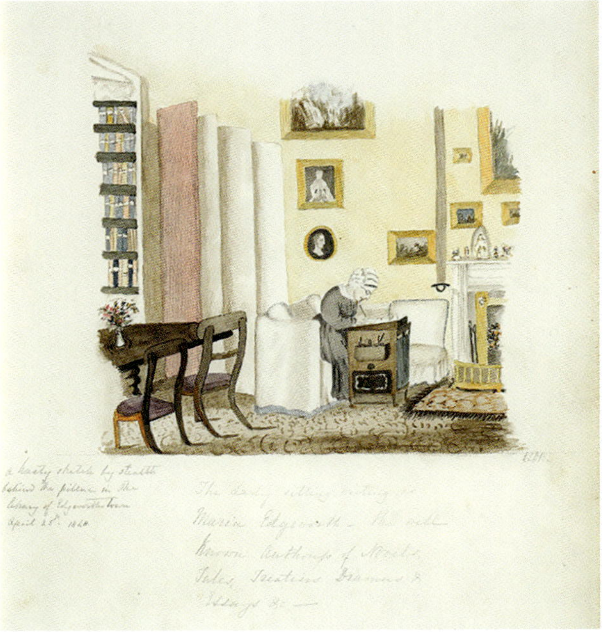

Fig. 54. Maria Edgeworth writing in the library, Edgeworthstown, County Longford dated 25 April 1848
Watercolour and pencil attributed to Louisa Catherine Beaufort (1781–1863)
[Courtesy, National Library of Ireland]

It was her talent for drawing that brought Frances into contact with the Edgeworth family. She had already illustrated, in 1792, her father's map of Ireland with an attractive and charming title vignette. Apart from drawing lessons received from West, she also received instruction from a Mr Raymond Deshouileres ('artist in crayons') on a visit to London with her parents in 1789.

The Beauforts were close friends of the Ruxtons, who lived at Blackcastle, beside the River Boyne, close to Navan. Margaret Ruxton was Richard Lovell Edgeworth's sister and she and her daughter Sophy were particular friends of Frances Beaufort. The Ruxtons obtained Maria Edgeworth's permission to ask Frances to execute some of the illustrations for Maria's lavish new edition of her book *The Parent's Assistant.* This edition, which was planned for 1800, would carry illustrations, as the publisher, Joseph Johnson, felt it would attract a wider public.[10]

The drawings were ready by March 1797. Richard Lovell Edgeworth discussed them with Frances when he was visiting her father. He also invited Frances and her mother to come and meet the family at Edgeworthstown. The visit went well and after an 'unexpected conversation of Mr. Edgeworth', Frances became, on 31 May 1798, the fourth wife of Richard

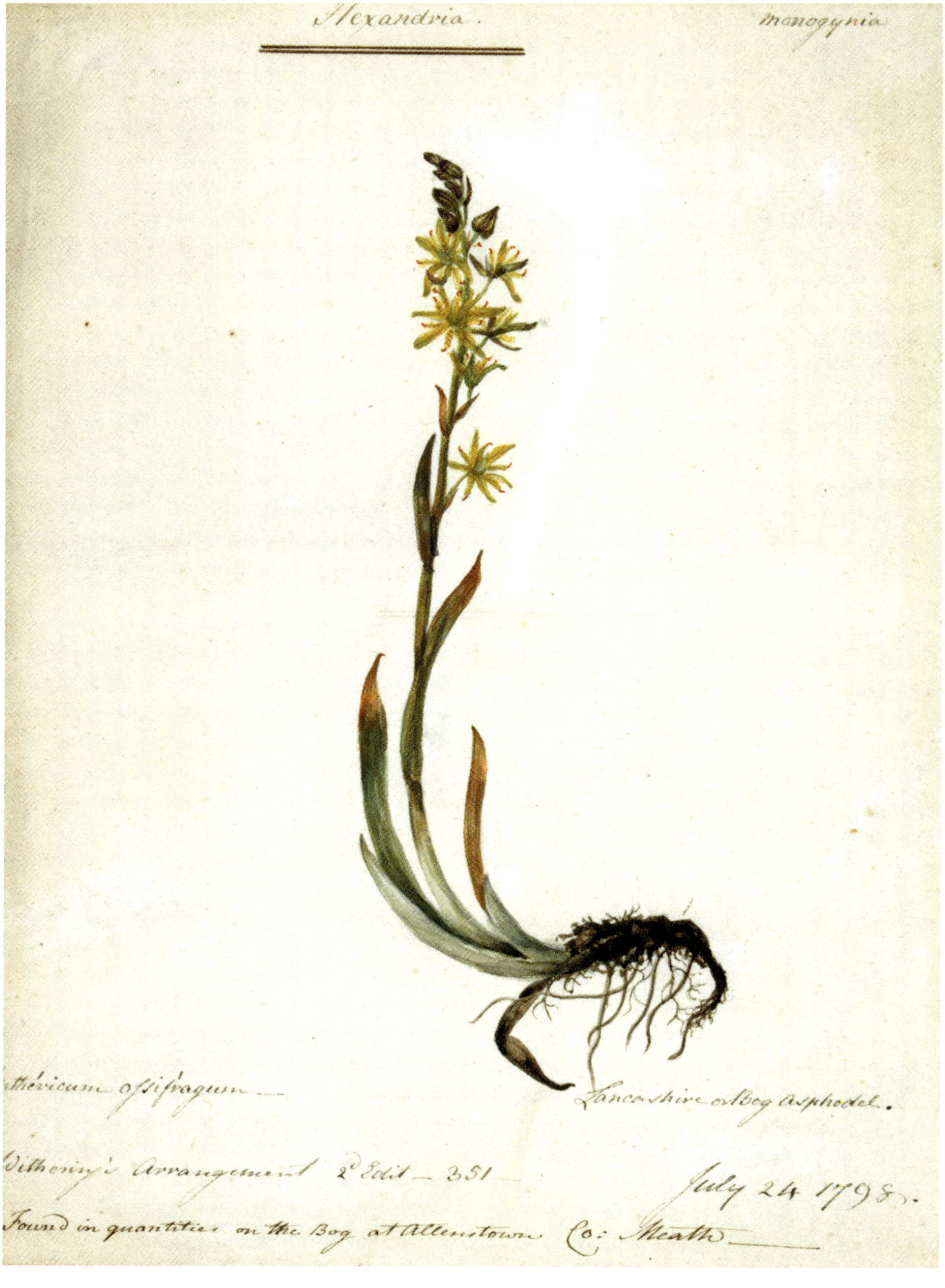


Fig. 55. *Narthecium ossifragum,* bog asphodel
Body colour by Frances (Fanny) Anne Edgeworth
Inscription: (brown ink) 'Found in quantities on the bog at Allenstown Co. Meath'
[Sir Francis Beaufort papers, 1710–1953 (bulk 178-1890). B1B 1D/UD1D: b1552512. The Huntington Library, San Marino, California. Reproduced by kind permission]

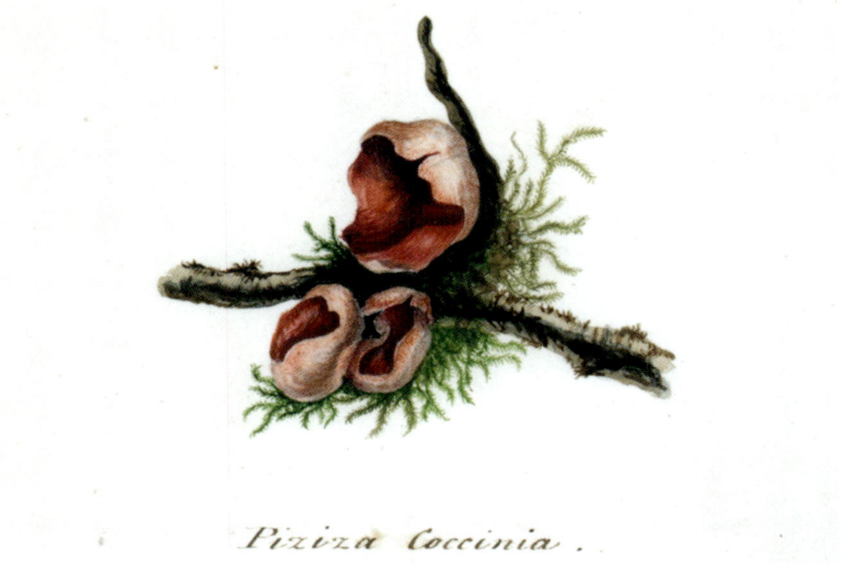


Fig. 56. *Sarcorypha coccinea*, scarlet elf cup, scarlet elf cap or the scarlet cup
By Frances (Fanny) Anne Edgeworth
[Sir Francis Beaufort papers, 1710–1953 (bulk 1780-1890). B1B 1D/UD1D: b1552512. The Huntington Library, San Marino, California. Reproduced by kind permission]

Lovell Edgeworth and stepmother to his 12 children, many of whom were already grown up. Her wry sense of humour, coupled with her genius for supplying sympathy and understanding, made Frances an effective and much-loved mother. Despite a hesitant start, she and Maria became excellent friends, Maria describing Frances as 'her beloved friend and mother'.[11] Richard Lovell Edgeworth died on 13 June 1817. Frances survived him by almost 50 years, dying at Edgeworthstown on 10 February 1865.

The Huntington Library, California, possesses a collection of botanical work by Frances Edgeworth dating from 1798–1807. These include drawings of both Irish and English plants, two examples of which are illustrated here (Figures 55 and 56, opposite and above). Both are adequately descriptive, and one is struck by the beautifully controlled tonality, coupled with a sensitive disposition that may be observed in both drawings. In each case, there is little, if any, scientific basis for their representation. Both compositions appear to be seemingly random, yet there is a regular disposition of leaf and stem across the sheet to be seen in Figure 55, with the artist emphasising not only the structure but also the graceful movement of the plant defined by leaves and stems, as they stretch and turn. The elegant outlines are carefully in-filled with various gradations of body colour.

# The Hon. Katharine Plunket (1820–1932)

'Wild Flowers, Painted from Nature' (1886–1894) contains 1,200 flower portraits and is one of the treasures of the Garden Library, National Botanic Gardens, Glasnevin, Dublin.[12]

The authors, the Hon. Katharine Plunket (1820–1932) and the Hon. Frederica Louise Edith Plunket (1838–1886) were the daughters of the Right Reverend Thomas Plunket, Bishop of Tuam, Killala and Achonry, who succeeded his father as second Baron Plunket (1845). Their mother, Louisa Jane Foster (1804–1893) was the second daughter of Rebecca M'Clure and John Foster, Baron Oriel (1740–1828), last speaker of the Irish Parliament, a vice-president of the RDS and a founder of the RBG, Glasnevin, Dublin.

Katharine, the eldest of five daughters was born on 22 November 1820 in Kilsaran, Co. Louth, where her father was curate of the parish. On her death (14 October 1932) at her home, Ballymascanlon House, Co. Louth, at the age of 111, just one month short of her 112th birthday, the *Irish Times* published an editorial appreciation of her life, the editor recalling that she had lived through the reigns of five British monarchs and:

> *in all probability, she saw both the beginning and the centenary of Catholic Emancipation... saw or could have seen the first railway, the first ocean-going steam-boat and the first aeroplane.*[13]

Katharine, together with her sister Frederica, travelled throughout Ireland, constantly collecting and recording in such counties as Cork, Down, Meath, Wicklow, Waterford and Kerry. Unlike many of their contemporaries, the sisters also travelled in Europe collecting in Austria, the Black Forest, Italy and more extensively in the Pyrenees and Switzerland. Frederica was a keen pioneering mountaineer[14] and wrote about her experiences in relation to climbing in the Alps in the 1870s.[15] It is interesting to note that in 1879, Lady Rathdonnell recorded in her diary that Frederica Plunket was acknowledged as the first woman to scale the summit of the Matterhorn.[16]

In May 1903, Katharine wrote to Professor Thomas Johnson, professor of botany at the Royal College of Science: 'I shall be pleased to present [my illustrations] to a collection in my own country rather than to any Botanical Society in England.'[17] Professor Johnson accepted the gift and in 1903 the museum received an album from her sister and herself of a fine leather-bound volume of botanical watercolours.

The Plunket album is typical of a 19th-century album of high quality. It provides a range of plant portraits, botanically correct. The character of the species is well

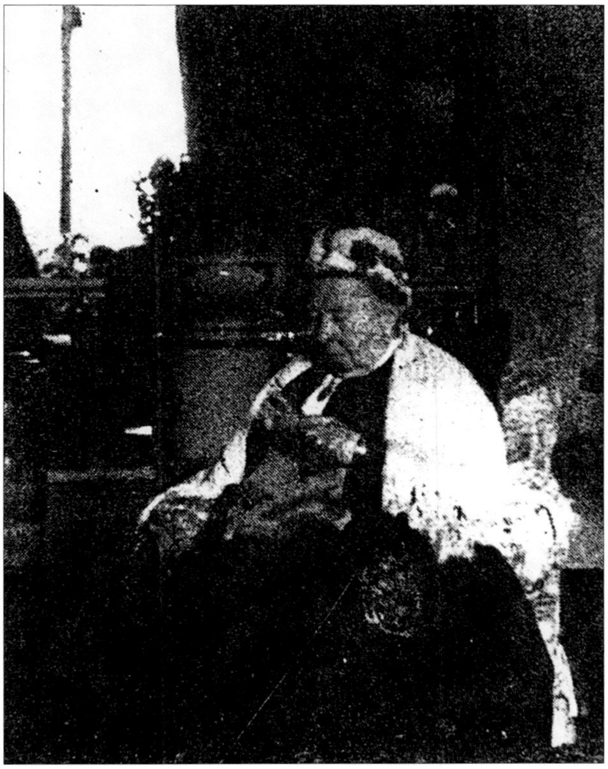

Fig. 57. The Hon. Katharine Plunket (1820–1932) photographed on her 107th birthday, 22 November 1926. From *The Tempest Annual*, 66th issue, 1927
[Courtesy, National Botanic Gardens, Glasnevin, Dublin]

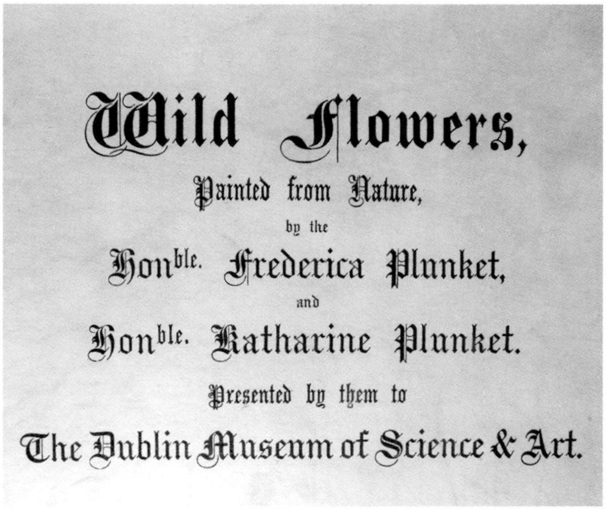

Wild Flowers,
Painted from Nature,
by the
Honble. Frederica Plunket,
and
Honble. Katharine Plunket.
Presented by them to
The Dublin Museum of Science & Art.

Fig. 58. Title page from the Plunket album, 'Wild Flowers, Painted from Nature'. The Hon. Katharine Plunket and the Hon. Frederica Plunket. The album contains 1,200 plant portraits ranging from 1886 to 1894
[Courtesy, National Botanic Gardens, Glasnevin, Dublin]

conveyed and, above all, recognisable.[18] The covers and spine are embellished with gold tooling. On the front cover, the central decorative design of entwined shamrocks, roses and honeysuckle encircles the title, 'Wild Flowers, Painted from Nature'. The mahogany case, provided to house the book, is lined with dark-green velvet. All pages are card-paper, gilt edged with eight illustrations mounted per page. Beneath each is the botanical name of the plant. The order of species follows that of George Bentham's *Handbook of the British Flora.*[19] There are no grasses, rushes or sedges included, no anatomical details and no sections. Dates for the plant portraits range from 1886 to 1894 and are drawn from France, Italy, Germany, Spain, Switzerland and Britain. In the case of Ireland, some localities are provided. 'The album is a superb achievement, incorporating a record of observations of nature over a period of time.'[20]

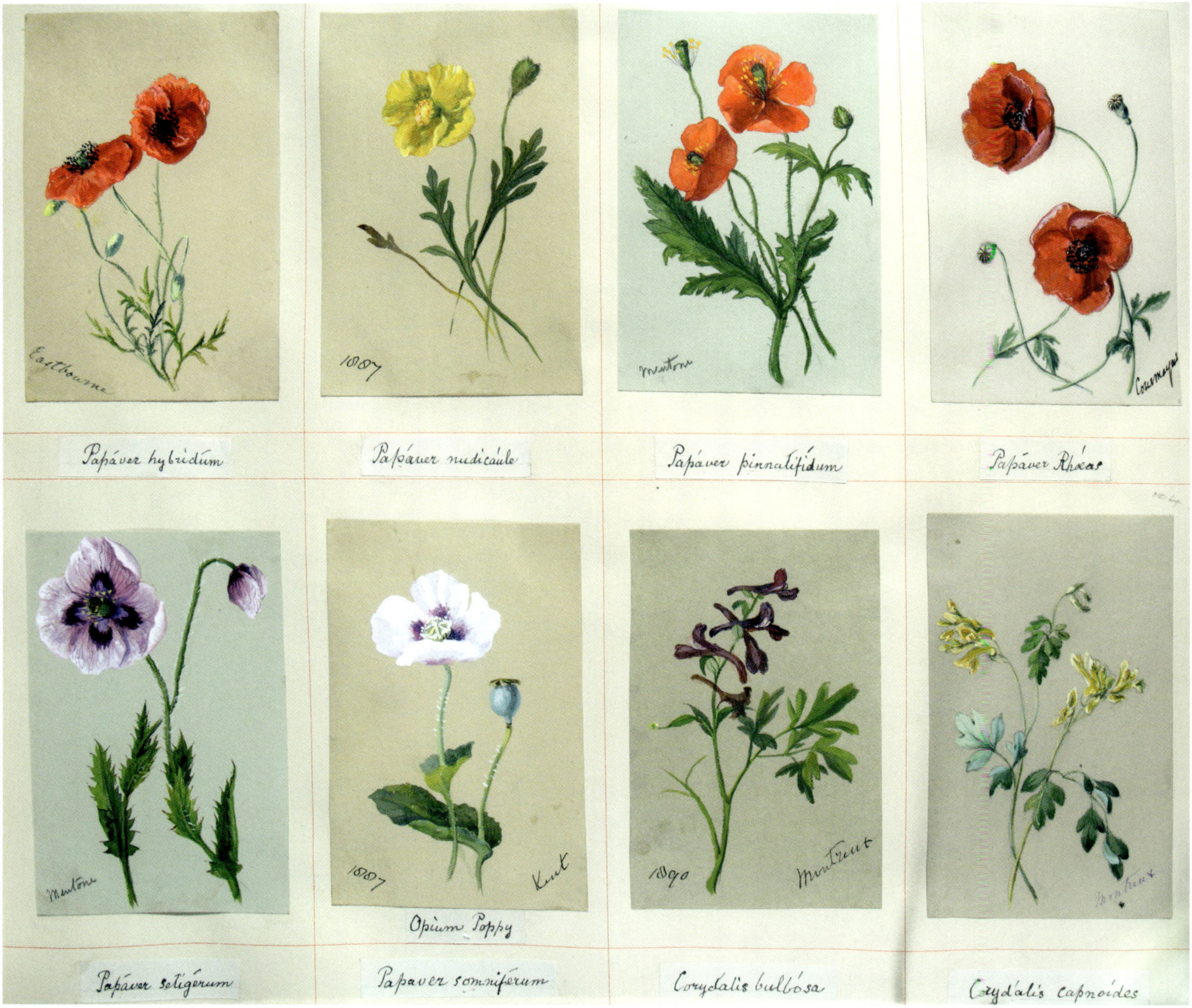


Fig. 59. A page from the Plunket album, 'Wild Flowers, Painted from Nature', showing *Papaver hybridum*, *P. nudicaule*, *P. pinnatifidum*, *P. rhoeas*, *P. setigerum* (*P. somniferum* ssp. *setigerum*), *P. somniferum*, *Corydalis bulbosa* (*C. solida*) & *C. capnoides*
Gouache on tinted card-paper by the Hon. Katharine Plunket and the Hon. Frederica Plunket
[Courtesy, National Botanic Gardens, Glasnevin, Dublin]

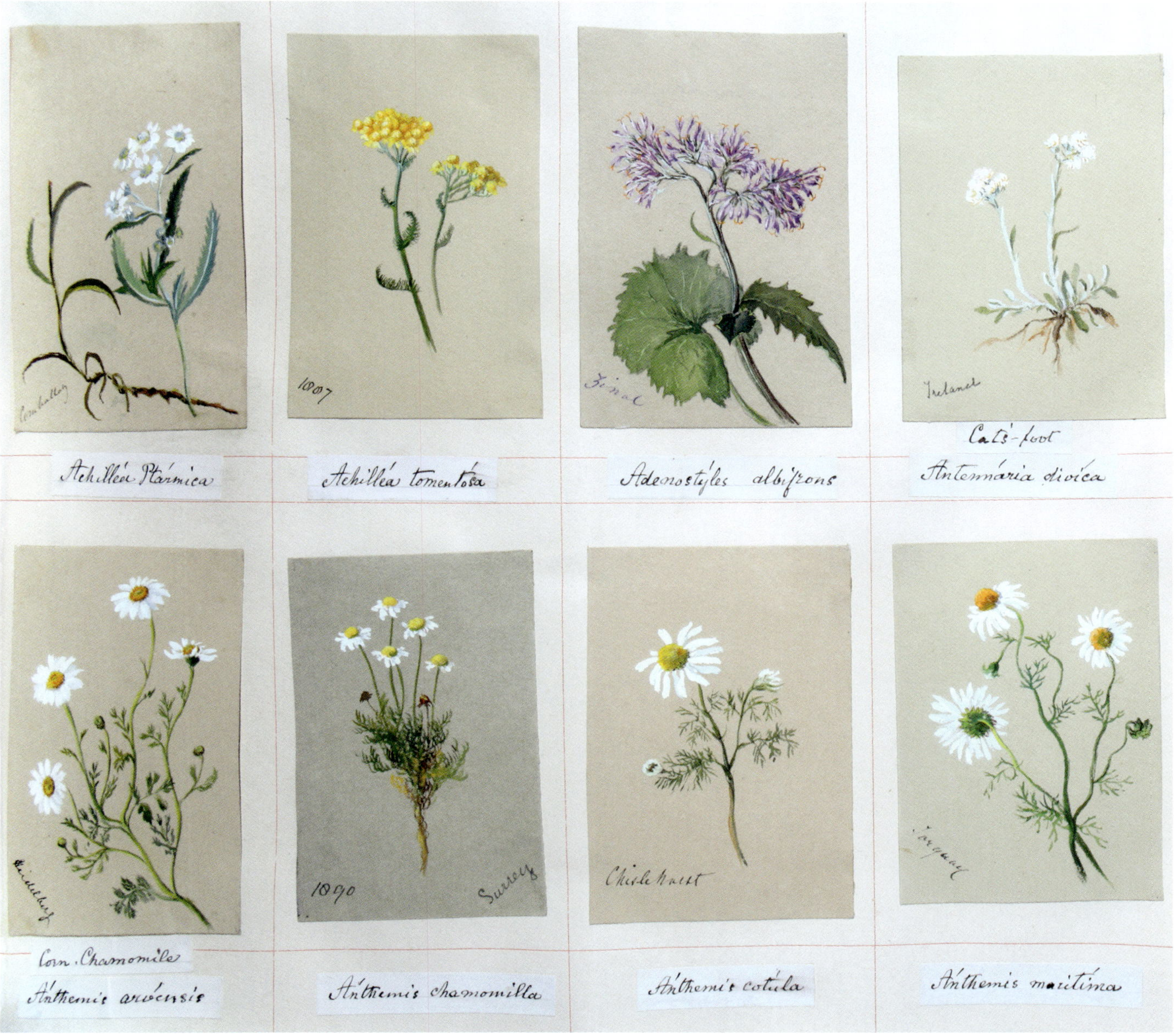


Fig. 60. A page from the Plunket album, 'Wild Flowers, Painted from Nature', showing *Achillea ptarmica*, *A. tomentosa* (*Achillea holosericea*), *Adenostyles albifrons (A. alliariae)*, *Antennaria dioica* (cat's foot), *Anthemis arvensis* (common chamomile), *A. chamomilla* (*Cota segetalis*), *A. cotula* & A. *maritima*
Gouache on tinted card-paper by the Hon. Katharine Plunket and the Hon. Frederica Plunket
[Courtesy, National Botanic Gardens, Glasnevin, Dublin]

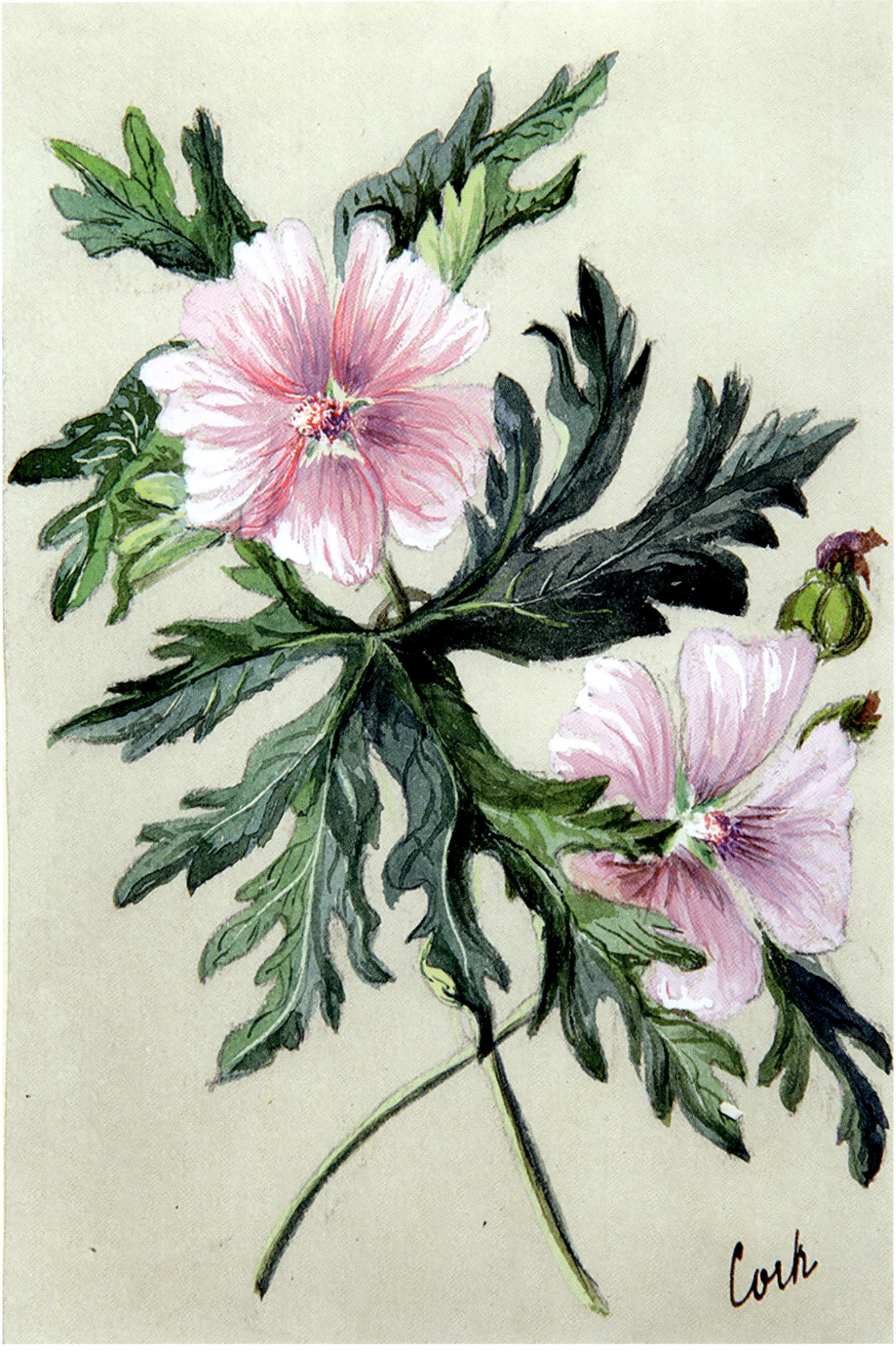


Fig. 61. Marshmallow or marsh mallow (detail from 'Wild Flowers, Painted from Nature')
Gouache on tinted card-paper by the Hon. Katharine Plunket and the Hon. Frederica Plunket
Inscription: *Cork*
[Courtesy, National Botanic Gardens, Glasnevin, Dublin]

# Mary Anne Battersby (c.1783–1841)

A keen naturalist, ornithologist and botanist, Miss Mary Anne Battersby (fl.1801–1841), in a letter from 21 North Cumberland Street, Dublin (dated 26 January 1837) to members of the RDS, stated that she wished to present:

*three books of her Drawings... one book of her Flowers to show the interest she takes in their beautiful Botanic Garden, and the amusement it affords her.*[21]

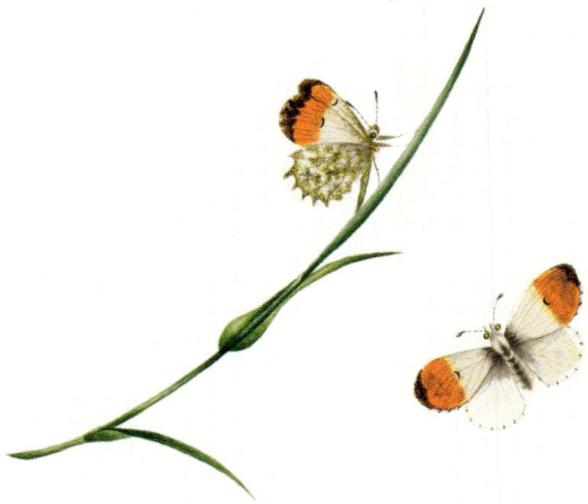

Fig. 62. Two male butterflies, *Anthocharis cardamines*, orange-tip
Body colour by Mary Anne Battersby
[Courtesy, National Library of Ireland]

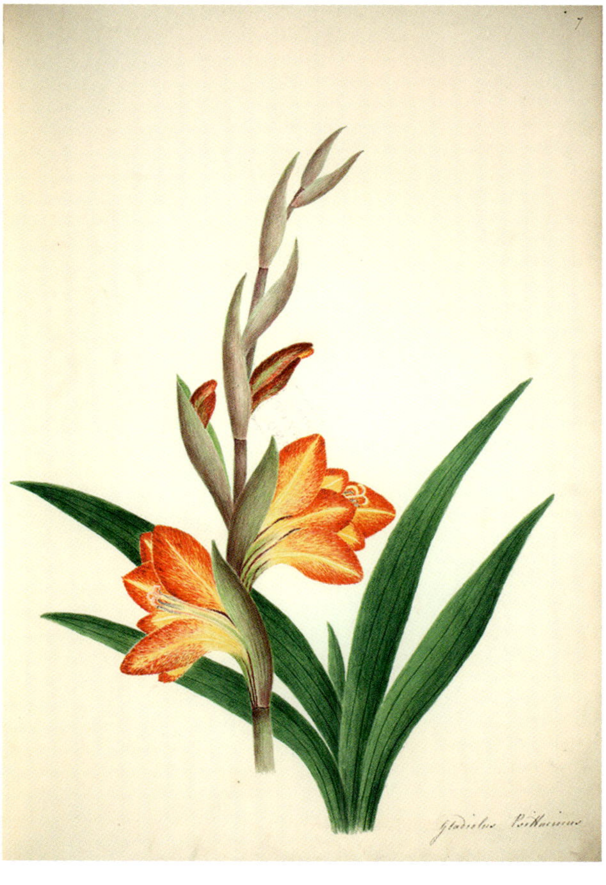

Fig. 63. *Gladiolus psittacinus*
Body colour on paper by Mary Anne Battersby
[Courtesy, National Library of Ireland]

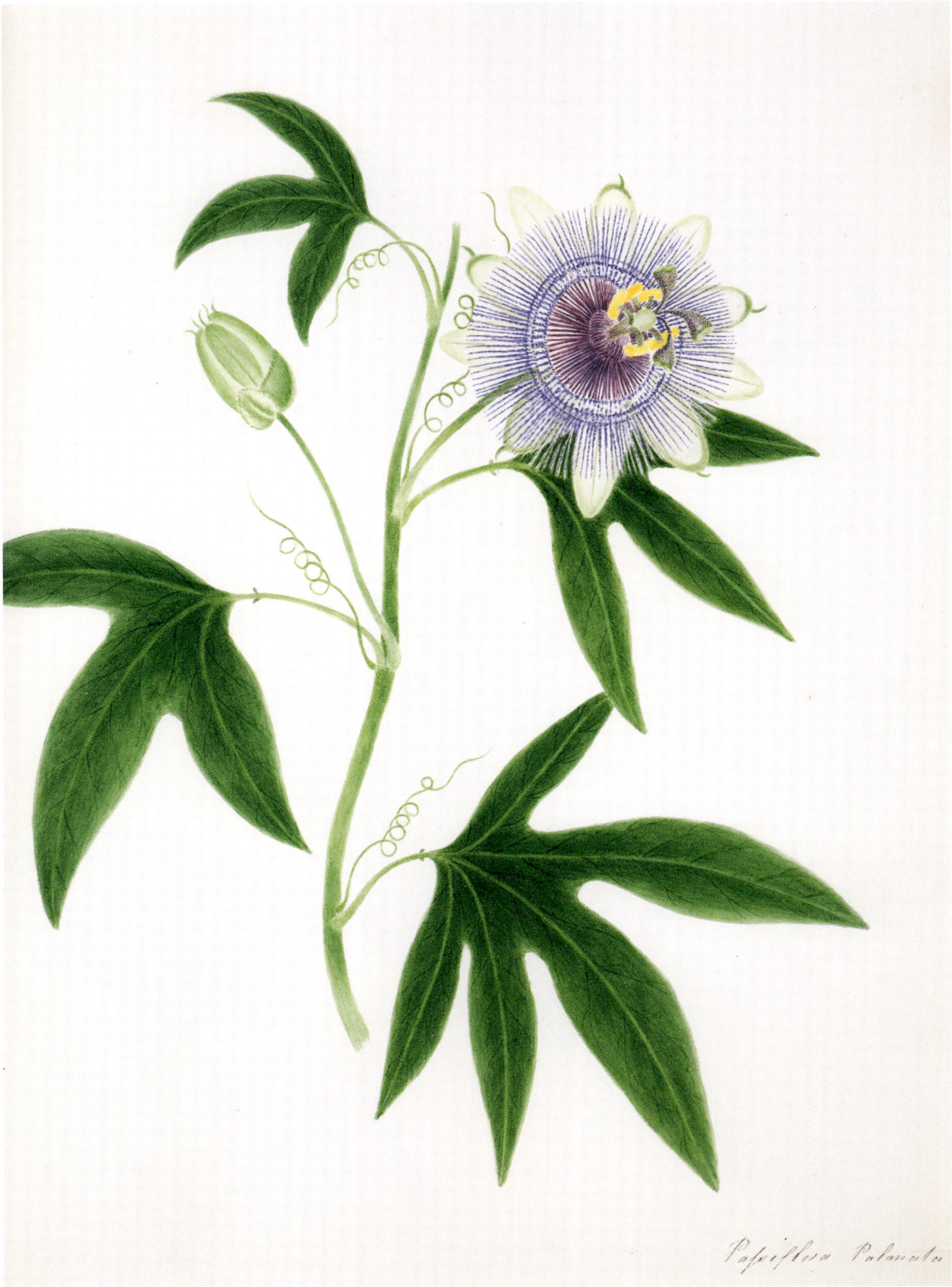


Fig. 64. *Passiflora palmata*
Body colour by Mary Anne Battersby
[Courtesy, National Library of Ireland]

The four signed albums of Mary Battersby's work, now in the NLI, together with one small sketchbook comprising studies of flowers, butterflies, insects and feathers (attributed to her) were presented by the artist to the RDS in 1820 and 1836. A further two volumes are in the Ulster Museum.

The majority of the drawings found in the NLI albums are devoted to the study of both native and exotic birds: (1) 'Drawings from a collection of birds'; (2) 'Native birds which were all shot in the County Meath'; and (3) 'Drawings taken from a collection of stuffed birds in the Dublin Museum'.

The fourth NLI Battersby album comprises 'Flowers drawn from Nature'. In this, the artist successfully combines a range of insects and butterflies with each botanical specimen. In the example illustrated here (Figure 62), the formula adopted shows two adult male butterflies (orange-tip, *Anthocharis cardamines*) together with a plant, all placed on the one page, with careful attention being paid to design. Battersby is following in the tradition of pioneers of entomological and lepidoptera painting such as Moses Harris (1731-c.1785)[22] and John Abbot (1751–c.1840).[23]

A fine feeling for detail combined with a brilliance of colour is evident throughout this artist's work. Each plant portrait is set against a plain ground. Battersby is at her best when depicting large flowering plants, such as her series relating to the passion flower, as illustrated here (Figure 64). Executed in body colour, her drawings are delicate, neat and attractive, and in the view of Dr Eimear O'Connor, 'are not simply decorative paintings for pleasure'.[24] Battersby was an artist 'interested in documenting science in general and the Linnean system of categorization in particular'.[25]

Mary Anne Battersby was a member of a branch of the Battersby family who may have lived in Bobsville House, built around 1765 near Crossakiel, Co. Meath. The family had been established in Ireland since the early 18th century. One of a large family consisting of six brothers and one sister, Mary was the unmarried daughter of Robert Battersby (1721–1785) and his wife Marianne, co-heiress of Haynes Wade, Lislin, Co. Cavan, whom he had married in 1763.[26]

# Diana Conyngham Ellis (née Monsell, 1813–1851)

Diana Monsell, born in 1813, was the eldest daughter of four children of the Archdeacon of Derry and Precentor of Christ Church Cathedral, Dublin, Thomas Bewlay Monsell (d.1846) and Jane Rae (d.1852). Her brother was the clergyman and well-known hymn-writer, John Samuel Bewley Monsell (1811–1875), Vicar of Egham, Surrey.[27] She married her first cousin, Conyngham Ellis, a barrister on 29 December 1842 at Dunloe Church, Co. Kerry. Later, her husband abandoned the legal profession to become Vicar of Cranbourne, Windsor, Berkshire.

Diana Conyngham Ellis's mounted album of 68 flower and foliage watercolour drawings in the NGI is a typical example of a 19th-century illustrated amateur flora.[28] The flowers are painstakingly depicted in watercolour, with good observation of botanical detail, and include plants found in hedgerows and fields – primroses, bluebells and violets – all of which were obviously studied directly from nature.

Diana's married life was short-lived. She died on 4 May 1851. Although the whereabouts of her art training is unknown, Co. Clare-born Sir Frederic William Burton, RHA, RWS, RSA (1816–1900), watercolourist and Director, National Gallery, London, thought highly of her work:

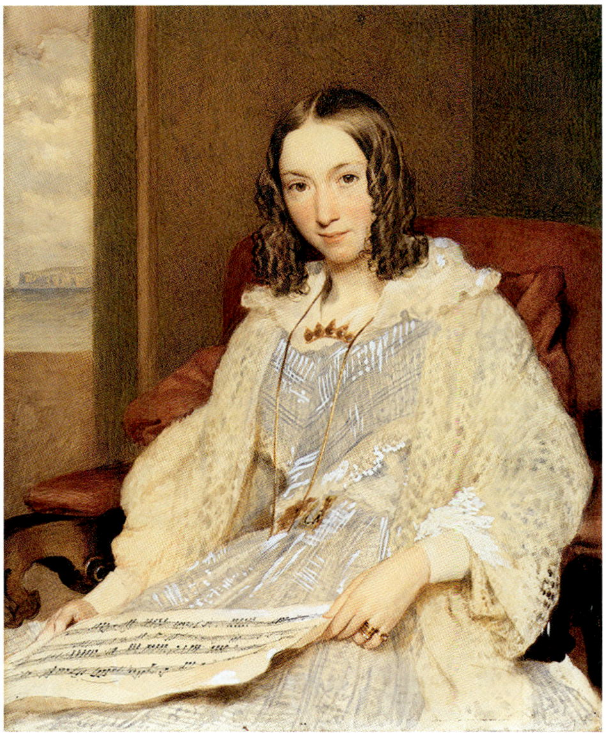

Fig. 65. Diana Conyngham Ellis
Watercolour with white highlights on paper by Sir Frederic William Burton, 1846
[Photo © National Gallery of Ireland]

*I have not for a long time seen anything that gave me so much pleasure to dwell on...they make my own work appear so rude and false that I am more than ever alive to my defects.*

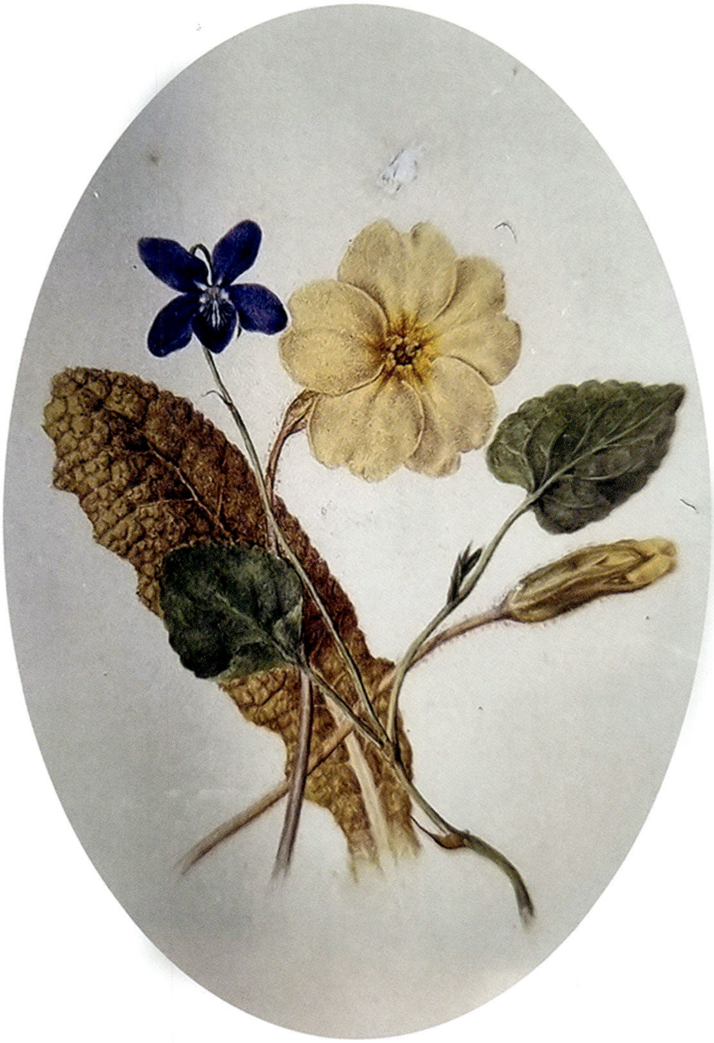

Fig. 66. A page from an album with 68 flower groups (all pre-1885)
Watercolour on paper by Diana Conyngham Ellis
[Photo © National Gallery of Ireland]

## Catherine (1815–1892) and Barbara Gage (1817–1859)

Two sisters who appear to have spent the majority of their lives depicting the plant, bird and fish life of Rathlin Island, off the coast of Co. Antrim, in the 19th century were Catherine and Barbara Gage. The family's association with this island had begun in 1746, when the Reverend John Gage of Aghadowey leased the island from the Earl of Antrim; Rathlin Island remained in the possession of the Gage family until 1925.

The family were resident on the island, living in Rathlin Manor House. Once established, they set about improving the efficiency of agriculture, the harbour and introducing horses and highland cattle from Scotland. Robert, the son of the Reverend John Gage, married Barbara, daughter of the Reverend John Richardson of Somerset, near Coleraine. Their youngest son became the Reverend Robert Gage who, in turn, married Catherine Boyd from Ballycastle, Co. Antrim, in 1812. Catherine became interested in the island and its way of life and wrote an illustrated history of Rathlin, which was published in 1851.[29] She was also an artist and produced at least one known album of flower paintings.[30]

Robert and Catherine's two daughters, Catherine and Barbara, both became artists, Catherine developing into a fine ornithological painter. Three bound albums of the sisters' work[31] depict the native wild flowers of the island, together with a cross-section of garden flowers, marine and bird life.

Each plant portrait is executed on white paper and pasted down onto pale green paper. The drawings are mounted one per page and all are carefully executed in body colour, a mixture of watercolour and opaque lead white, which gives a thicker consistency than pure, clear, transparent watercolour and is therefore easier to manipulate. On each drawing the title is inscribed in pencil with, in many instances, a note of the location. The majority are signed with the initials 'B.G.', with no signature being written out in full. Several of the botanical drawings include an example of Lepidoptera attached to the flower head. These drawings, comprising in total 316, are a remarkable and unique record of plant, bird and fish life to be found on and around Rathlin Island, Co. Antrim, in the mid-19th century.

In 1870, Catherine Gage published a list of the Rathlin flora,[32] which, according to naturalist, Robert Lloyd Praeger (1865–1953) was 'more or less incomplete'.[33] In 1850, she had prepared a list of plants for the Botanical Society of Edinburgh, which included dicotyledons (204). An abstract was published in the *Annals and Magazine of Natural History* for the same year (1850).

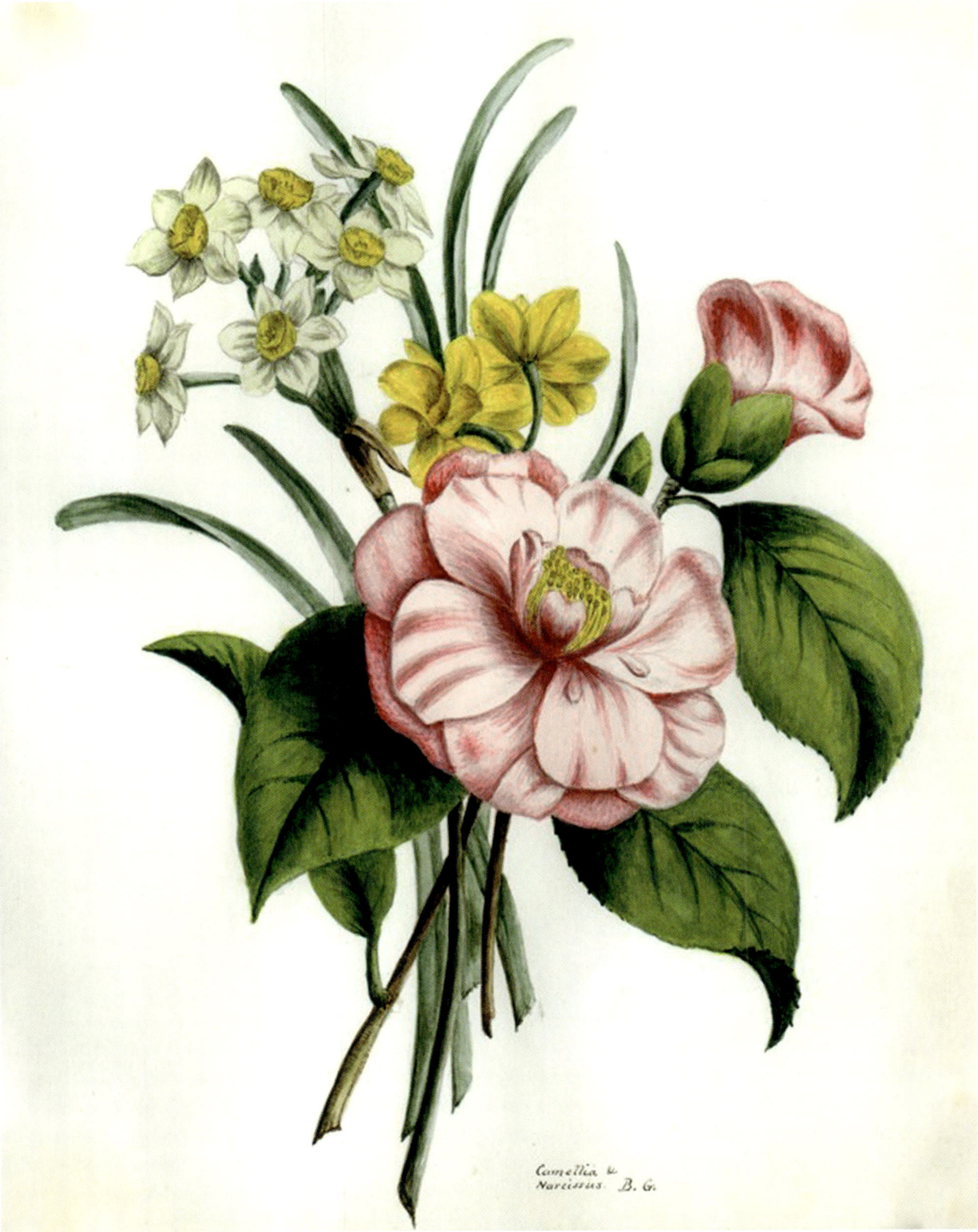


Fig. 67. Narcissi, camellia and jonquils
Body colour on paper by Catherine and Barbara Gage
Inscribed 'B.G.'
[The Linen Hall Library, Belfast]

# Susanna Grubb (1820–1911)

Susanna Grubb was a 19th-century amateur artist and botanist who contributed plant records relating to the valley of the River Suir (Clonmel area, South Tipperary) and elsewhere in Ireland. She was born on 4 April 1820 in Clonmel. Her father, Joseph Grubb (1768–1844), a greengrocer, and her mother Lydia (née Jacob) (d.1844) were both Quakers and had a large family, Susanna being the youngest of four brothers and two sisters.

From a young age, Susanna was an active and keen botanist, supplying plant records to such publications as David Moore (Curator, [Royal] Botanic Gardens Glasnevin) with Alexander Goodman More's (Natural History Museum, Dublin) *Contributions Towards a Cybele Hibernica* (1866).[34] Plant locations included her hometown of Clonmel and as far afield as Ballitore, Carrick-on-Suir and Tramore.

On 3 June 1988, two volumes of flower paintings (totalling 95 watercolours) were presented to the Head of the Herbarium, Glasnevin, Dr Maura Scannell. Volume 1 (24 portraits) was entitled 'Wild Flowers', the flyleaf inscribed, 'Susanna Grubb'; the second volume (71 portraits) read: 'Wild Flowers of Ireland. Susanna Grubb/J. Ernest Grubb, Carrick-on Suir, 1911/ Geraldine S. Cadbury/painted by Susanna Grubb of Clonmel, Ireland/Great aunt of Geraldine S. Cadbury' (flyleaf).[35] The majority of the portraits date from 1838–1848, with the exception of the fern, *Ophioglossum vulgatum* (1886), and are drawn from counties Waterford, Dublin, Kildare, Kerry, Mayo and Tipperary (south).

Susanna Grubb was an acute observer, interested in illustrating the elemental structure and precise form of the plant, each portrait conveying accurate and true colour, with the exception of leaf colouring, which is shown throughout in a uniform green, indicating a somewhat limited palette. In many cases, the artist provides the year, habitat notes and locations (for instance, *Polypodium vulgare*, found near the 'walls and banks frequent near Clonmel. 1840'). For reference, she probably used, as her guide, Mackay's *Flora Hibernica* (1836), together with J. Sowerby and J.E. Smith's well-known *English Botany* and later Bentham's *Handbook of the British Flora* (1858).

During her life, Susanna Grubb recorded plants in districts minimally worked in Ireland in the mid-19th century: 'By her work she made a contribution to knowledge of species distribution in Ireland'.[36]

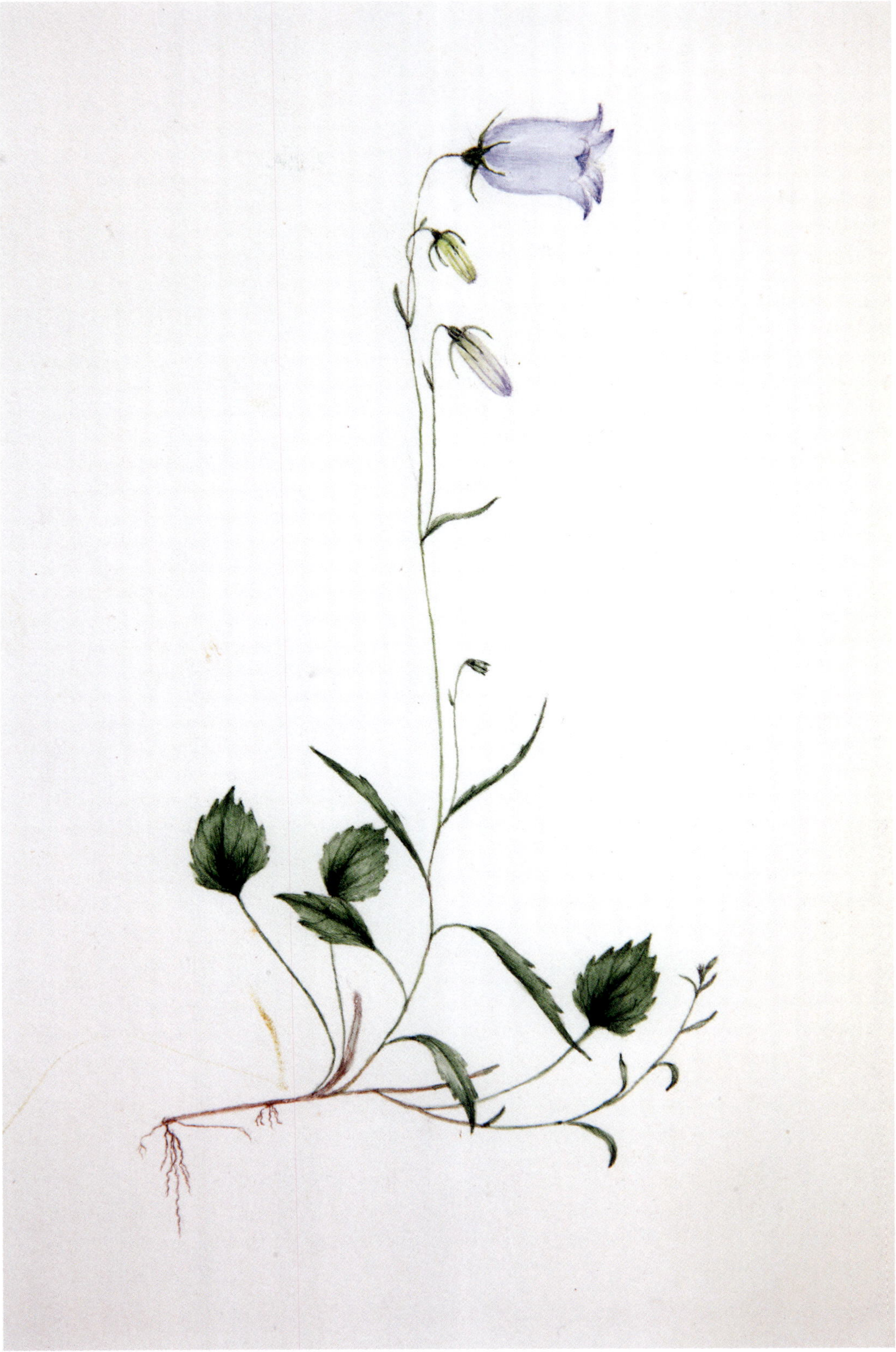

Fig. 68. *Campanula rotundifolia*, round-leaved bell-flower
Gouache by Susanna Grubb
[Courtesy, National Botanic Gardens, Glasnevin, Dublin]

# Chapter 5
# 'A Designer of Distinction' – William Kilburn

## (b.1 November 1745, Capel Street, Dublin, d.3 December 1818, Wallington, Surrey)

In the late 1970s, the V&A, London, received a handsome bound volume, with the title on the spine reading: 'Kilburn's Designs'. The volume contained 223 of Dublin-born William Kilburn's working designs for textile printing and revealed the excellence of his work – designs so fine that 'no printer could or would execute them: and no other Draper, but he for whom they were done, would have dared to engage them.'[1]

The Kilburn (or Kelburne) family originated from Rothesay on the Isle of Bute, Scotland, being descended from an Archibald Kelburne (d. before 1637), who was Burgess of Rothesay.[2] The reasons concerning why the family settled in Dublin are none too clear, but by the early 18th century, a direct descendent, William Kilburn's father Samuel (d.15 January 1770),[3] was enjoying life in Dublin, having been made a Freeman of the City in 1737. He married Sarah Johnston (c.1720–1800), a niece of General Johnston of Tyrone, around 1744. They had three children: William (1745–1818), Mary (1750–1770), who died unmarried at the age of 20, and Sarah Susannah b.1760, who was later to marry John Francillon (1744–1816) of London, 'jeweler to the King'. Samuel Kilburn, described as an architect 'of some eminence',[4] was compelled to seek an additional means of livelihood in order to support his growing family and became involved in property. He also received the patent appointment and the somewhat illustrious title of 'King's Carpenter' from King George III.[5]

From an early age, William Kilburn's health was delicate, and this may have encouraged his parents to send him into the country. In response to job advertisements from Jonathan Sissons (placed in the *Universal Advertiser* on 24 January and 7 February 1758), a firm of linen printers based around eight miles upriver (Liffey) at Bleach Green, Lucan, Co. Dublin,[6] William probably began his apprenticeship there during the same year.

However, it is likely that the Sissons firm had been established at Lucan prior to 1757, when Jonathan

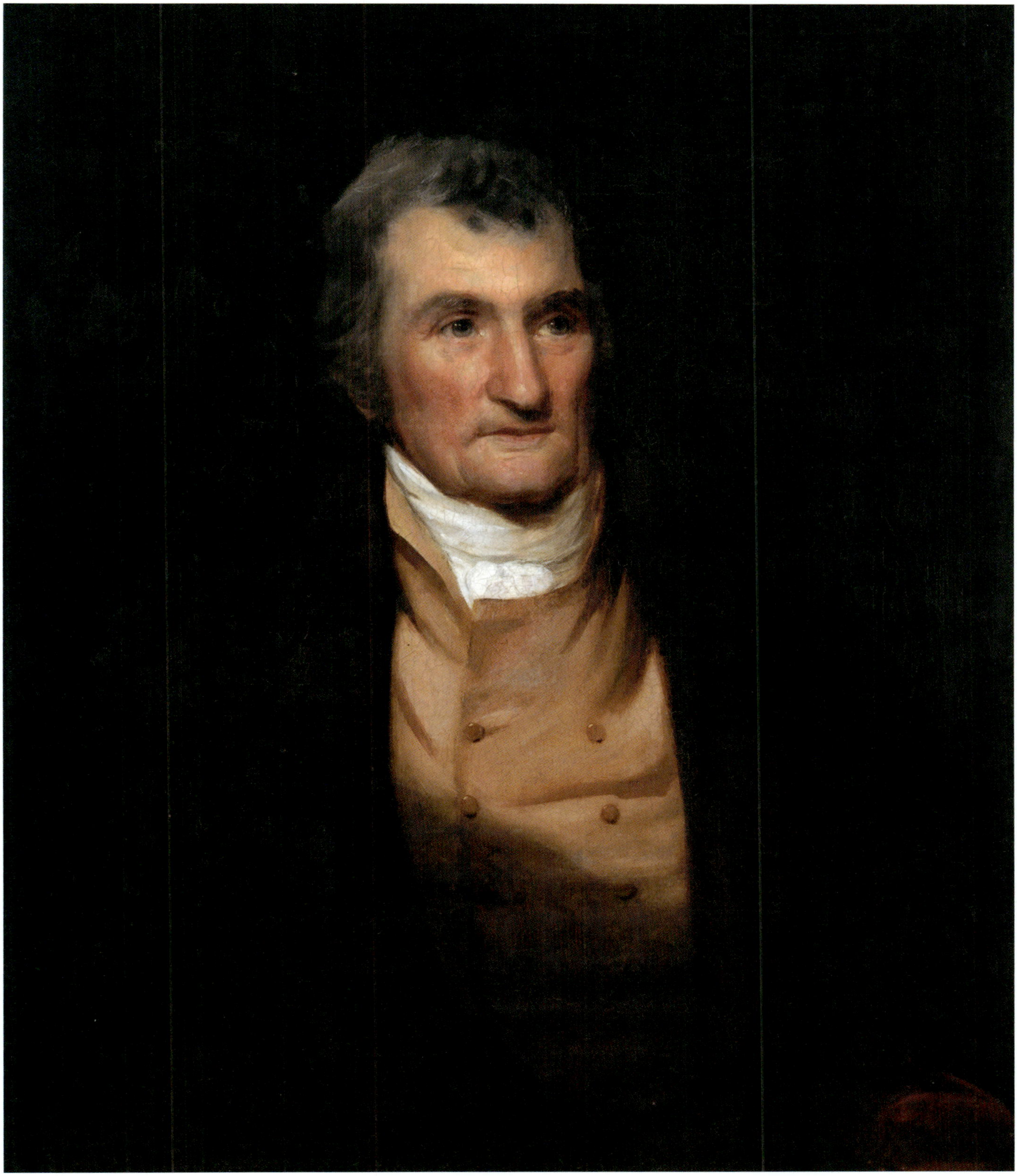

Fig. 69. William Kilburn (1745–1818)
[Private collection. Reproduced by kind permission]

Sissons sought parliamentary aid to enable him to extend and improve his business. He was successful and received £500 'to reimburse him for the Expenses he has been at in repeated Trials, in order to bring the Manufacture of printing Linen to a further Perfection'.[7] Based on the outskirts of Dublin, the firm also had a town depot at Turner's College Green, in the city centre, and would appear to have been one of the largest businesses in the country specialising in wood-block printing.[8]

The young apprentice made good progress, particularly in the areas of drawing and engraving. In his spare time, he devised patterns for 'paper-stainers' (wallpaper makers) and 'acquired an amazing readiness with his pencil. So that if a new pattern caught his eye, he would take out his pocket-book and have it ready for his master at his return'.[9] These innovative new designs generated sufficient funds to enable young William to buy a pony on which to ride from Lucan to Capel Street in the centre of Dublin, in order to visit his family on Sundays.

William's father, who had speculated in property, was forced to leave Ireland 'embarrassed in his circumstances' and moved with his family to London in the hope of 'retrieving their fortunes'. The family settled into a small house with a garden and greenhouse in Page's Walk, Bermondsey. William became a pupil of Dublin flower painter Edward Hodgson (1719–1794), who was also a drawing master with a studio in Oxenden Street, in the Haymarket area. Hodgson exhibited largely flower pieces – from 1763 to 1783 annually at the Free Society of Artists, and during the 1780s at the Royal Academy. He encouraged his Dublin pupil to exhibit work, mainly flower paintings (watercolour) at the Free Society and the Society of Artists throughout the 1770s; and Kilburn always acknowledged his teaching. In order to supplement his income, the young student sold drawings and engravings of flowers for the print shops and possibly through his interest in the world of gardeners and nurserymen, he is known to have executed a number of trade cards, one of which has survived in the BM (see Figure 72).[10]

The Kilburn family home in Bermondsey lay close to the gardens of distinguished botanist and entomologist, William Curtis, FLS (1746–1799; qv), who, in 1771, had taken an acre of land close to Grange Road, Bermondsey, where he cultivated a vast collection of native species.[11] It was during this period that Curtis began to plan his ambitious *Flora Londinensis* (or plates and descriptions of such plants as grow wild in the environs of London),[12] and invited his neighbour and friend William Kilburn to supply a substantial number of plant portraits (around 28) to Volume 1, published in May 1775.[13]

Kilburn faded out of Curtis's life around two years later; the exact date is not known, possibly sometime between 27 March 1777 and 21 December 1778. Eminent botanist and naturalist, Sir Thomas Frankland (1750–1831), who wrote regularly to Curtis with criticisms and comments in relation to Kilburn's contributions, remarked somewhat wryly:

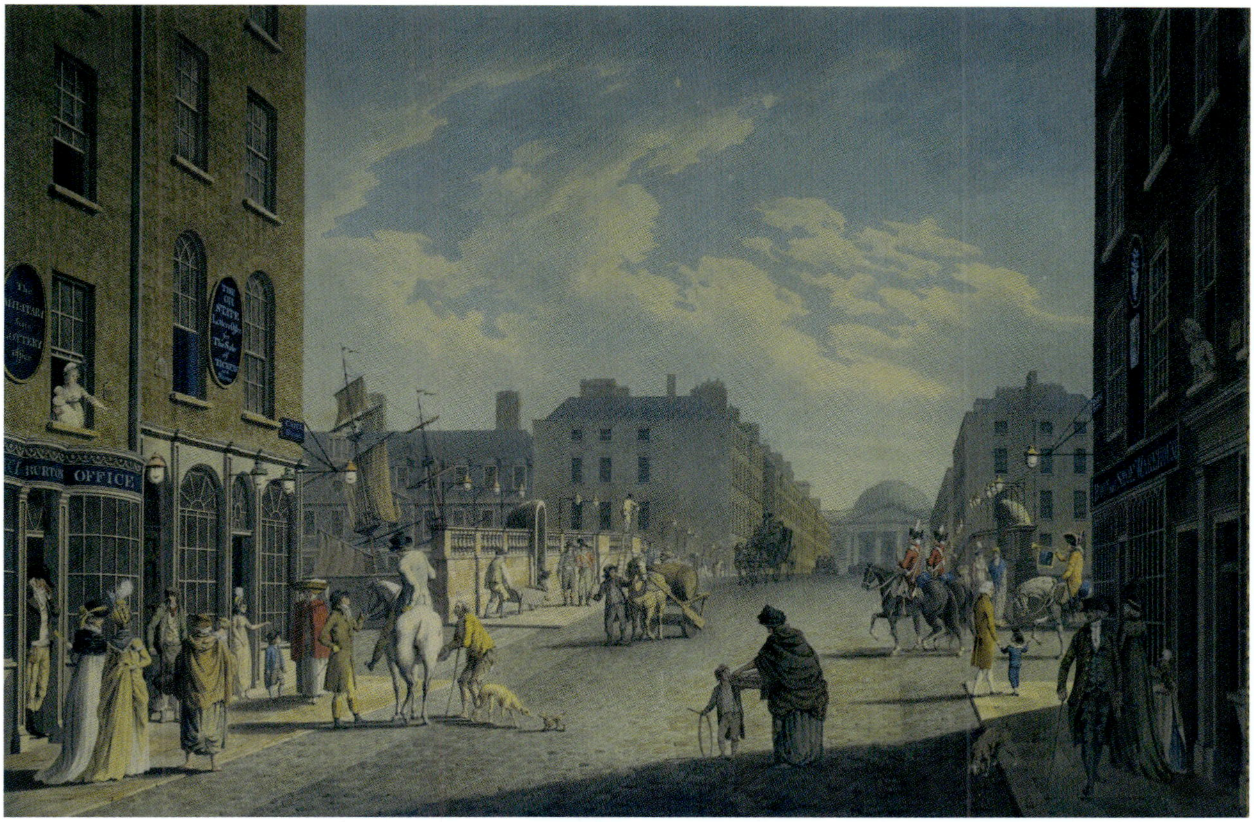


Fig. 70. View of Capel Street, Dublin with the Royal Exchange in the distance
[© Victoria and Albert Museum, London]

'There is an uncommon taste in his [Kilburn's] drawing & I often regret he has deserted you.'[14]

Kilburn had accepted a proposal from a James Newton – a contract issued on the understanding that he would have a share in the profits without having to inject capital. James Newton had been employed as a calico printer on the banks of the River Wandle at Wandsworth and resigned that position in November 1778. A year later, a lease on the calico printing works at Wallington, Surrey, about 15 miles from London, was taken out. The lessees were James Newton, James Morison and William Kilburn, calico printers and partners.

The premises included a colour house and cutting shop, a printing shop, a pencilling shop with folding loft above, and a warehouse, 'on the opposite side of

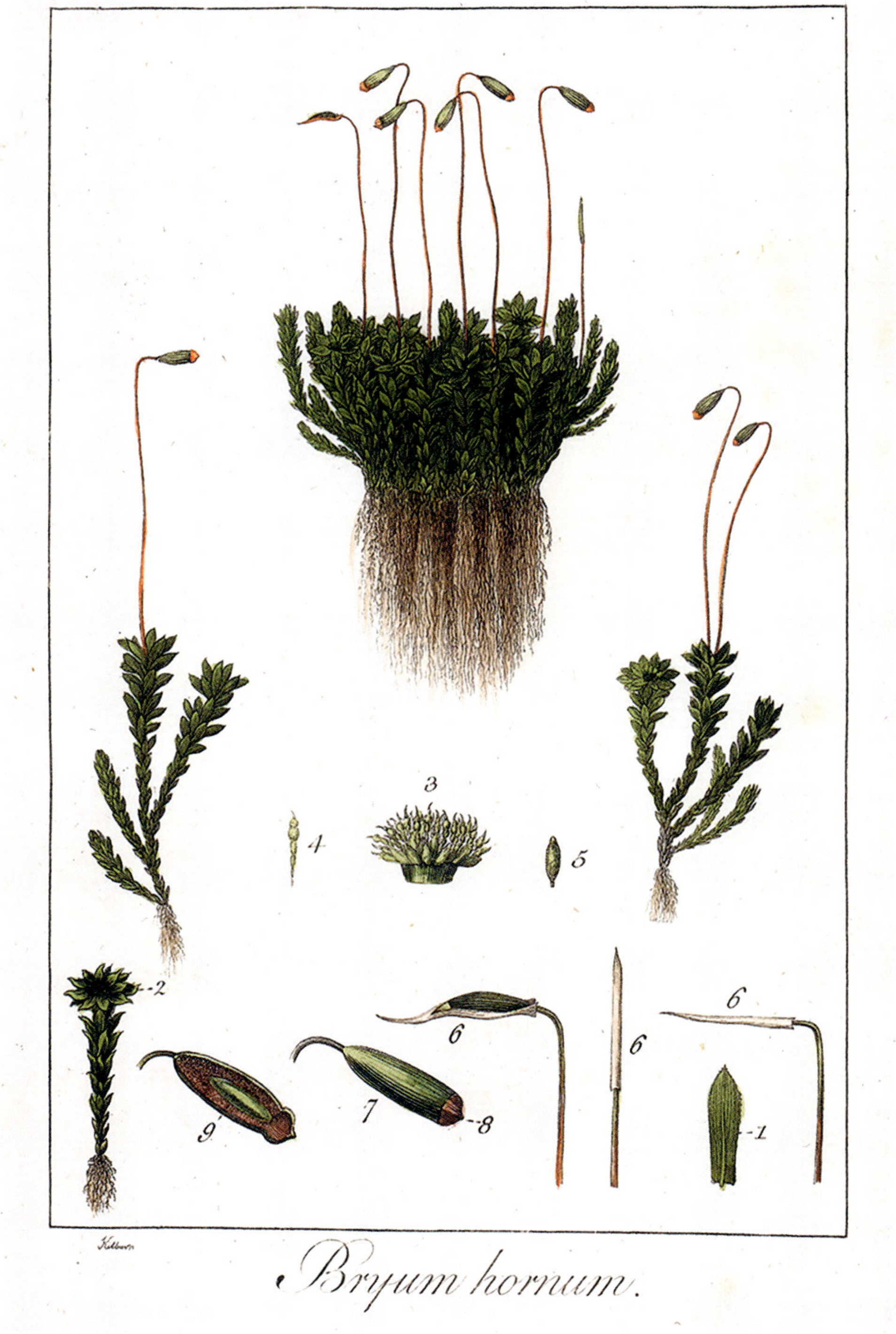


Fig. 71. *Bryum hornum*, swan's-neck thyme-moss
Original copperplate engraving (hand-coloured) by William Kilburn, inscribed '*kilburn*'. Published in *Flora Londinensis*, vol. 1, fasc. no. 8, no. 71 (after December 1775)
[Courtesy, National Library of Ireland]

the River'.[15] An account dating from 1789 describes the site of the factory and Kilburn's house:

> *...a small triangular area of waste land called Brewer's Green. On the middle of the west side is a pleasant little white house belonging to Mr. Kilburn, a noted callico-printer. His manufactory lies about a hundred paces southwest from the house.*[16]

Later, in 1791, Kilburn purchased a lease on a logwood mill near Wallington Bridge. He demolished the mill and built a replacement designed for the making of cotton. The factory flourished and within seven years this young Irishman was in a position to purchase the entire concern, becoming 'the most eminent calico printer in England'.[17]

Kilburn's success was founded on a combination of circumstances – a sound network of both business and family contacts; Freedom of the City of London Admission Papers granted to him on 8 October 1776, which permitted him to play a meaningful role in the business of the City; his partnership with James Newton in calico printing; and his second marriage,[18] on 10 May 1785,[19] to Elizabeth Brown (1765–1848). His new wife was the daughter of Thomas Brown, a director of the East India Company, a draper and importer of Indian muslins and cashmere shawls and involved in Brown, Rogers & Co., linen-drapers, Cheapside, London. Following his daughter's marriage, Thomas Brown was to be responsible for looking after his son-in-law's production of fabrics and promoting them.

Kilburn was fortunate in his ability to develop design motifs that appealed, in particular, to his female customers who, during this period, were developing a keen interest in collecting natural history specimens.[20] It should also be mentioned that he had the satisfaction of knowing that several of his plant portraits for *Flora Londinensis* were being used by a number of leading printing firms as copperplate designs for furnishing chintzes. These had been adapted with the minimum of stylisation or simplification.

As mentioned at the beginning of this chapter, the V&A possesses a bound album containing 223 outstanding designs in watercolour by this gifted manufacturer and designer (see Figures 93 and 125).[21] Designs include naturalistic flowers in a floral lattice, many of the flowers being found in both Britain and Ireland (see Figure 214); floral motifs accessorised with leaves, shells, ribbons or architectural elements (see Figure 215); seaweeds and other marine organisms (see Figure 79).[22] The latter are depicted both in naturalistic and more stylised forms and further demonstrate this artist's skill as a botanical illustrator, which had already been noted in his contributions to Curtis's *Flora Londinensis*. The artist's unique reputation for novelty, his search for something that 'shall strike the Trade as something new, and not seen before',[23] was developed and explored when he introduced into his designs the decorative potential of seaweeds and other marine organisms. This talented designer was to become particularly well-known and admired for his seaweed prints throughout the 1790s.[24]

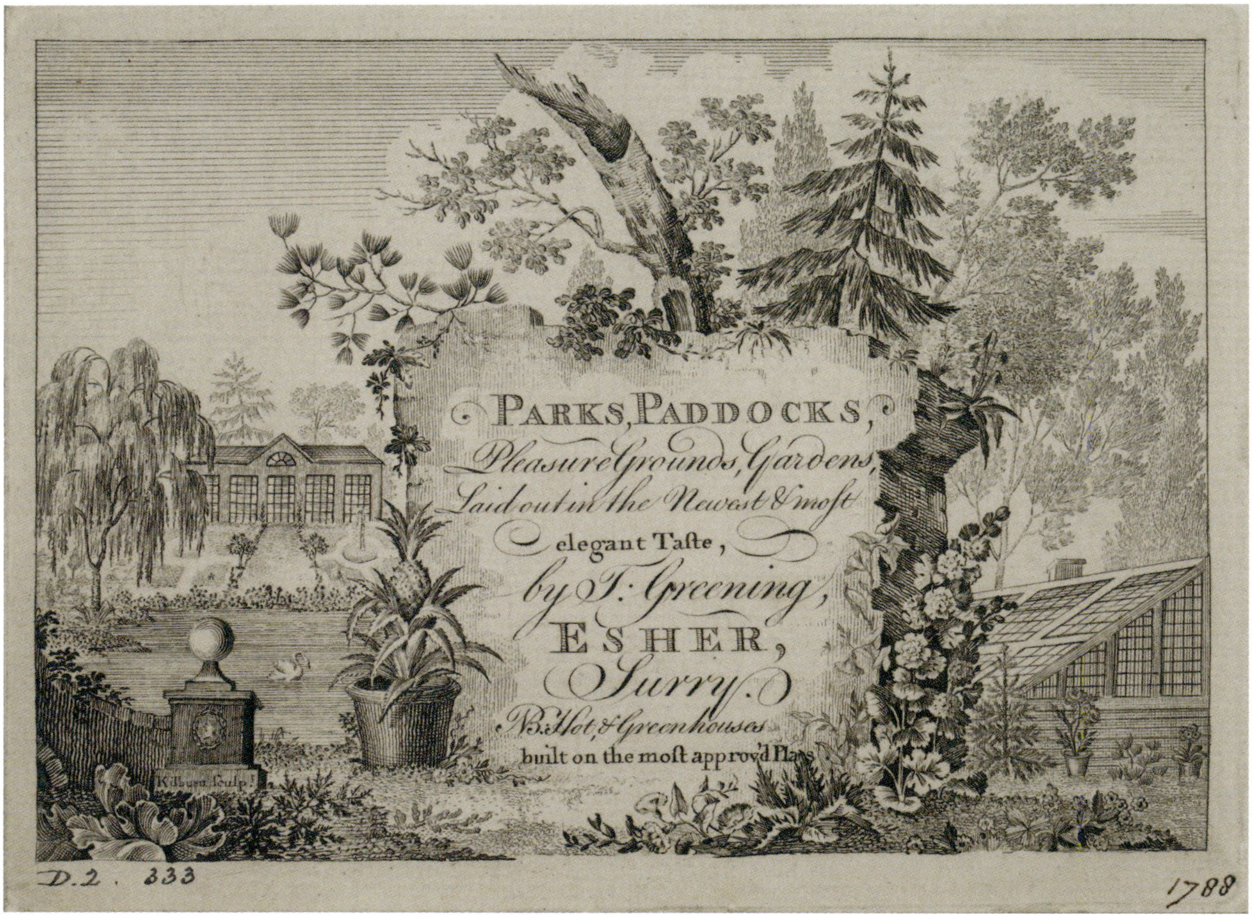


Fig. 72. Trade card of Thomas Greening, Gardener, Esher, Surrey
Etching with engraved lettering by William Kilburn, c.1777–88. Prominent in the foreground (left) is the pineapple *(Ananas comosa)* which, during the 18th century, was considered to be a precious commodity and status symbol.
[© The Trustees of the British Museum]

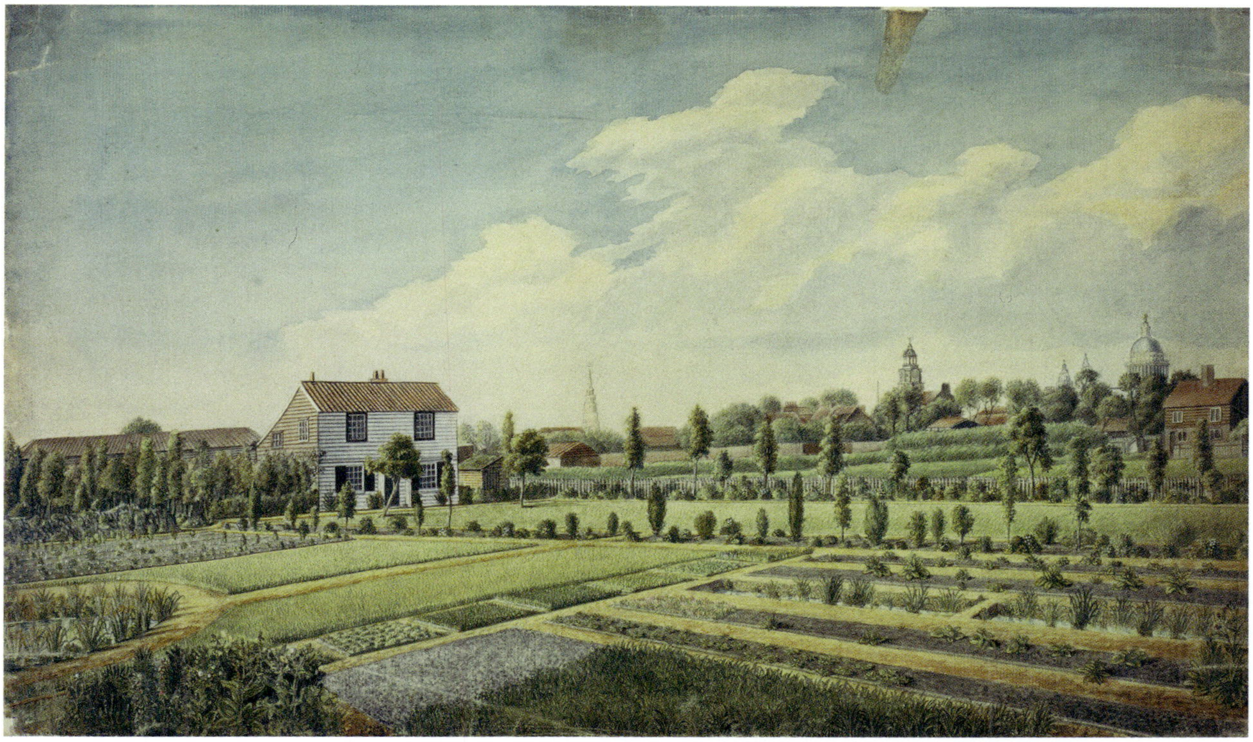

Fig. 73. *William Curtis's Botanic Gardens, Lambeth Marsh*
Watercolour by James Sowerby, ALS, FLS, c.1787
[Photo © Christie's Images / Bridgeman Images]

During the latter part of the 18th and early 19th centuries, seaweeds were being collected, studied and classified by naturalists, particularly women.[25] This fashionable subject area was being provided with an added impetus by such publications as *Coloured Figures of Marine Plants, Found on the Southern Coast of England* (1795), one of the earliest works to be published on algae. Kilburn, with his love of naturalistic plant forms, appealed to young ladies 'conversant in Natural History' and to royalty and the Court. His muslin chintzes proved to be highly fashionable and were much admired, in particular:

> *his pieces of muslin chintzes sold for a guinea per yard, and he had the honour of presenting one of them, the sea-weed pattern designed by himself, to her Majesty Queen Charlotte.*[26]

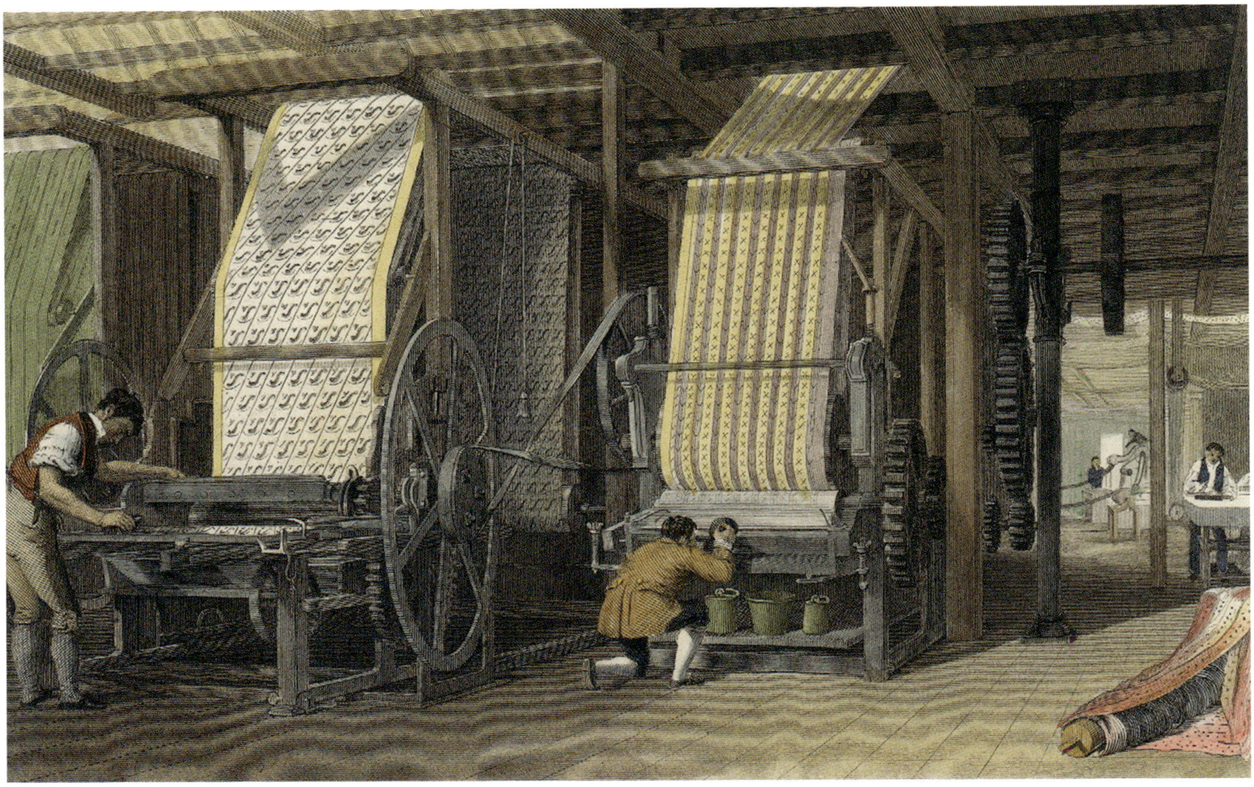

Fig. 74. Calico-printing machines powered by belt and shafting through cog wheels from a central energy source (either steam or water) [World History Archive / Alamy Stock Photo]

Highly regarded in the trade, Kilburn was looked upon as a fair employer, awarding annual premiums for the best designs and providing the 'highest wages to his workmen, some of whom came from the continent'.[27] As a 'Master Printer'[28] and 'Pattern-drawer', his designs were attracting the attention of the Lancashire calico printers. Competition between London and Lancashire for the cotton textile market had always been strong. Original designs produced at Wallington for 6*s* 9*d* per yard were now being copied by wealthy calico-printing firms such as that founded by Robert Peel and William Yates, Bury, Lancashire,[29] and arrived in London in less than 10 days priced at only 4*s* 6*d* per yard. In most cases, these patterns were copied 'upon coarser Cloth and in bad Colours'.[30] Due to stiff competition,

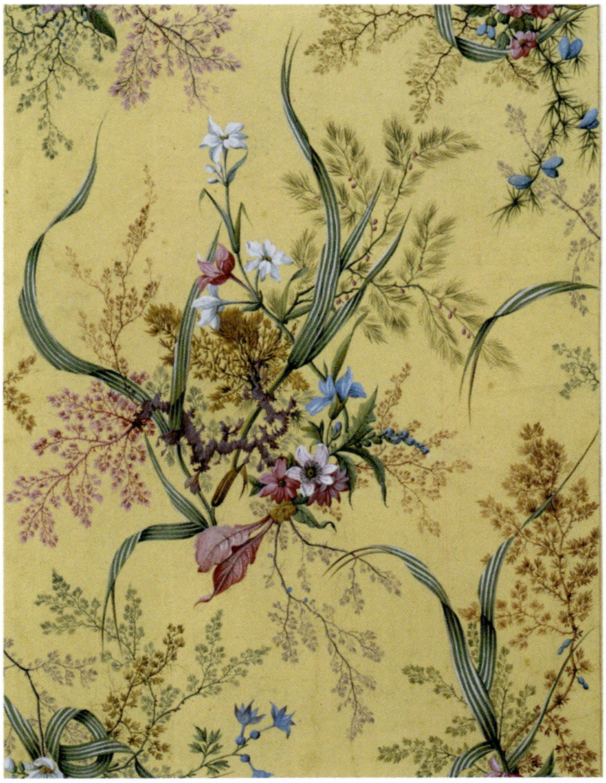

Fig. 75. Design for a furnishing chintz; leaves of a spider plant and flowers
Watercolour by William Kilburn, c.1788–1792
[© Victoria and Albert Museum, London]

Kilburn now began to find himself in severe financial difficulties. Determined to prevent the illegal copying of patterns, he set about seeking copyright protection for calico printers. A petition dated 15 March 1787, led by distinguished Irish politician Edmund Burke (1729–1797), and supported by many London firms including Kilburn, resulted in the passing of an Act in May 1787.[31] This provided for a restriction on copying for only two months from the date of publication of the design. The Act may have served as a somewhat weak deterrent and it is interesting to note that it was necessary to renew it two years later, without too much opposition.

Despite this Irish designer's struggles to protect his friends and his trade, the rise of increasing competition from Lancashire and other northern counties could not be halted. In April 1802, William Kilburn was declared bankrupt, and his calico-printing factory ceased production.[32]

Various factors had led to this sorry state of affairs: the invention of calico-printing machines powered by either steam or water allowed for printing a number of colours in one printing operation, while adding considerably to daily output; the need for water and the high cost of labour in and around London; the challenges brought about by French designers; and finally, the onset of the Industrial Revolution. All of these factors combined to make it a difficult and volatile time in which calico printers had to operate.

On 13 April 1802, an advertisement appeared in the *Manchester Mercury* declaring Wallington Mill, Surrey for sale, as follows:

> *valuable Plant, Implements and Utensils in Trade and complete fittings up of the Cotton Mills and Printing Grounds at Wallington, late of the property of Mr. Wm. Kilburn, Calico Printer and Cotton Spinner were being offered for sale.*

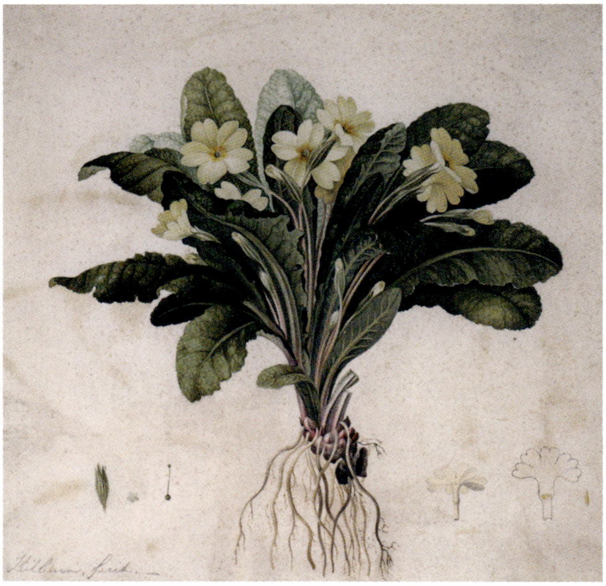

Fig. 76. *Primula vulgaris* (the common primrose)
Watercolour by William Kilburn
[Trustees of the Natural History Museum, London]

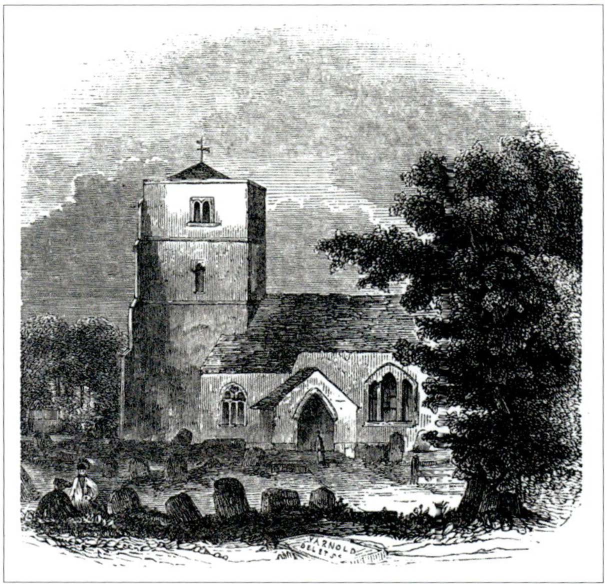

Fig. 77. St Mary's Church, Beddington
[© The Print Collector / Alamy Stock Photo]

Also included were:

> *several thousand Blocks for Calico-printing, amongst which are some of the most curious of sea weed chintzes, and others that have been in constant work.*[33]

And the following year, on 2 February 1803, the *Morning Post* advertised for sale building materials associated with the printing offices, workshops and stables.

Despite the termination of William Kilburn's printing works, there is evidence to prove that he did not cease working either at his cotton mill or his printing works. Later references prove that he continued to be associated with his business. His name appears in Holden's directories from 1802 until 1811, with his premises described as the 'very extensive calico and printing grounds of Mr. W. Kilburn at Wallington'.[34]

Towards the end of his life, and in an attempt to improve his declining health, Kilburn paid a visit to Brighton. This proved to be unsuccessful, and he returned to Wallington, where he died on 3 December 1818. He was buried on 9 December in the graveyard of St Mary's Church, Beddington, Surrey.

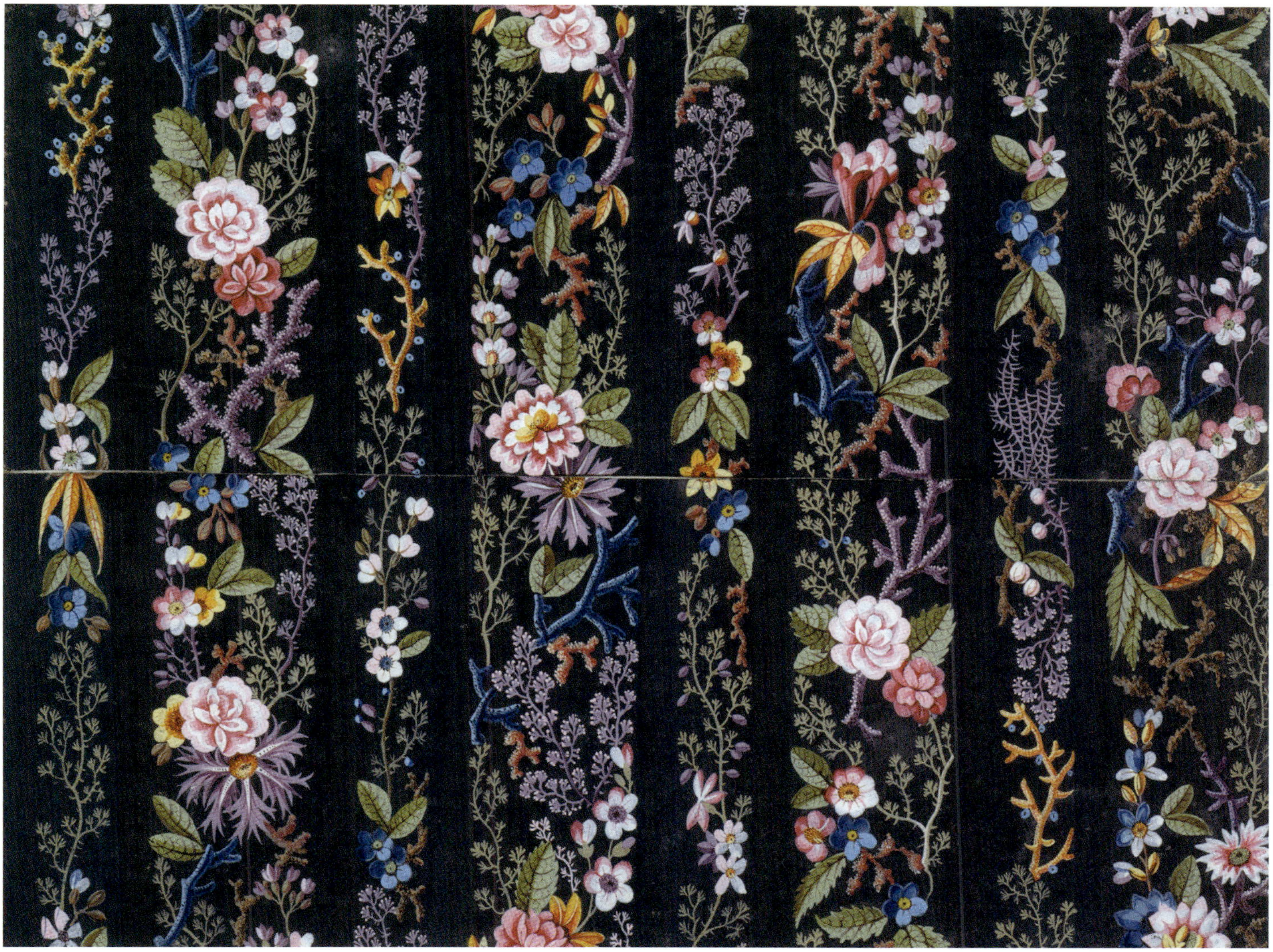

Fig. 78. Design for a printed textile
Watercolour by William Kilburn, c.1791
[© Victoria and Albert Museum, London]

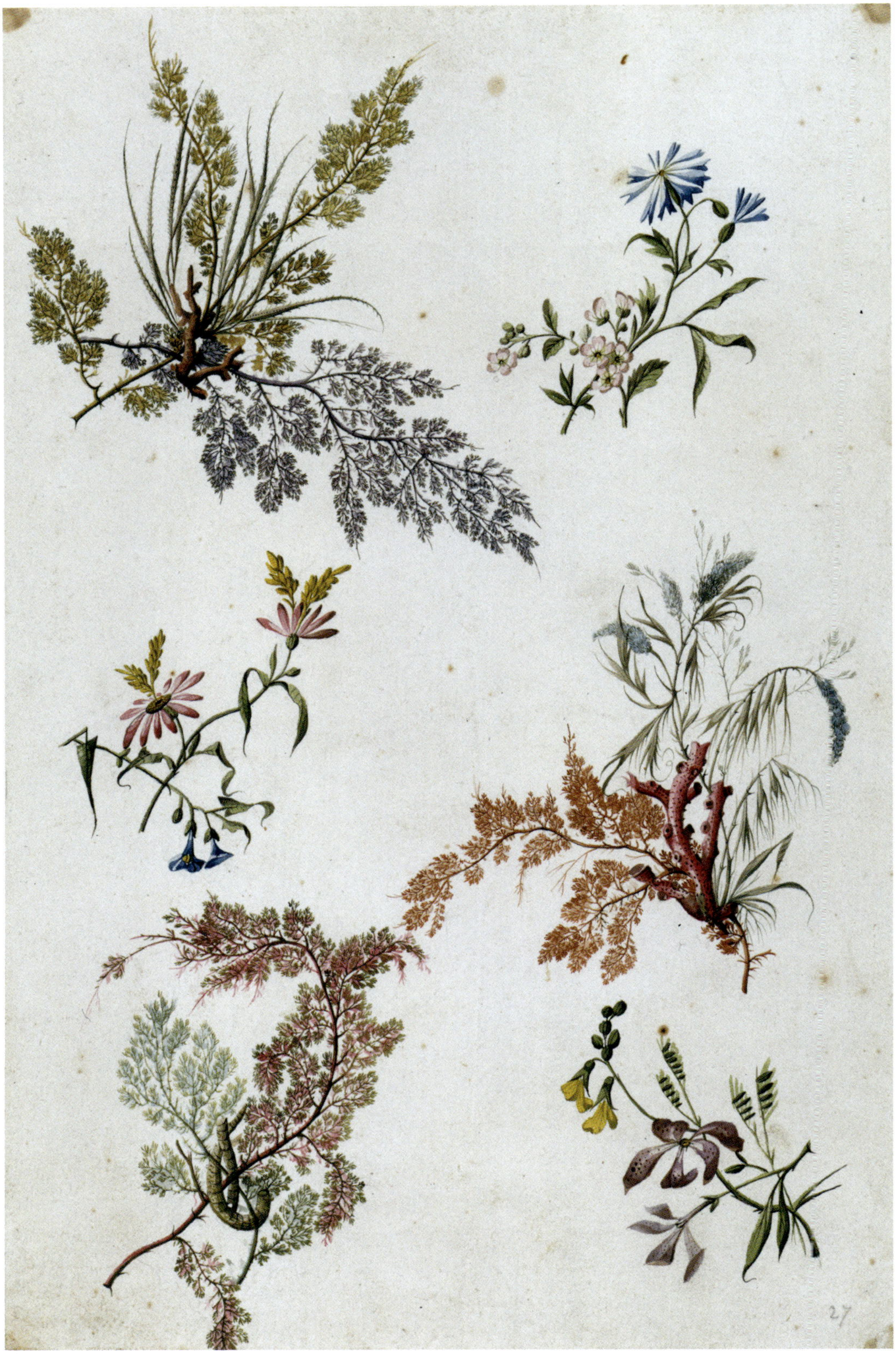

Fig. 79. Design for a printed cotton
Watercolour by William Kilburn, made c.1788–1792
[© Victoria and Albert Museum, London]

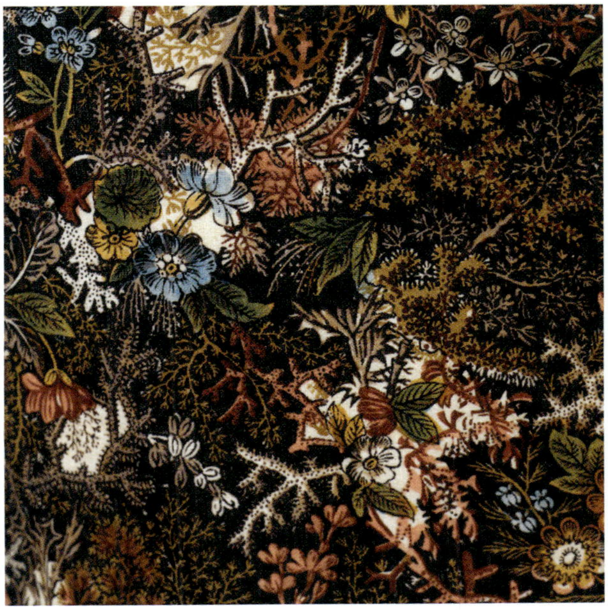

Fig. 80. William Kilburn's seaweed pattern was used for the fabric of this dress (right), priced at one guinea per yard, c.1790 [Reproduced courtesy of the Rhode Island School of Design Museum, Providence, RI]

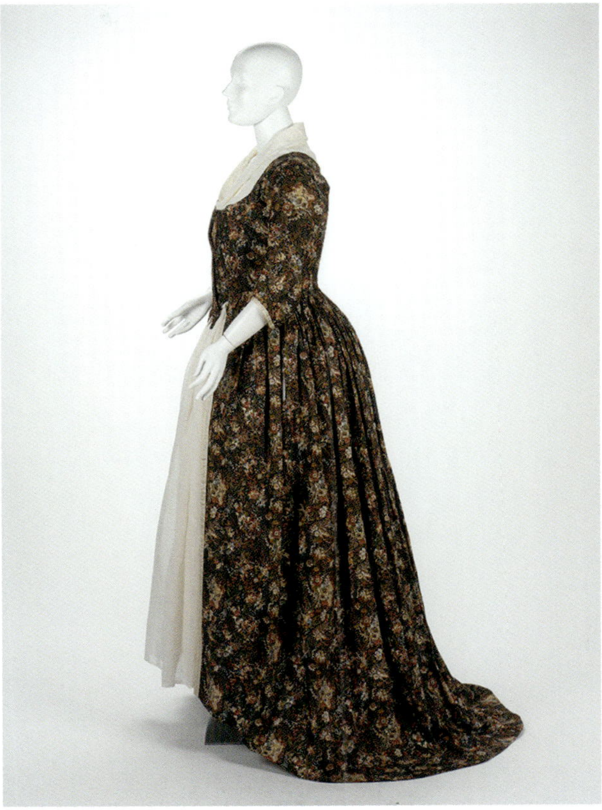

Fig. 81. Dress, c.1790
Cotton plain weave, block printed, by William Kilburn
[Reproduced courtesy of the Rhode Island School of Design Museum, Providence, RI]

During his ownership of the printing works at Wallington, Kilburn had brought into the business as a partner, a man named Clarkson. Following Kilburn's death, Clarkson's son, Thomas took over his share. Unfortunately, the business did not last long and in November 1819 the following notice appeared:

> *by order of Messrs. Kilburn and Clarkson, bleachers, retiring from business. Valuable Plant and Utensils in Trade will be offered for sale at an auction to be held on the factory premises on 25 November 1819.*[35]

A man of integrity, William Kilburn was a remarkable and gifted Irish artist/designer/illustrator who strove hard to render 'the nearest approaches to nature',[36] articulating aspects of 18th-century culture, fashion and design. Furthermore, his originality triumphed over the technical limitations imposed upon him by the age in which he lived.

# Chapter 6
# Contributions from Ireland to *Curtis's Botanical Magazine*

*The Botanical magazine, or, Flower garden displayed,* founded by William Curtis (qv), is the longest-running botanical magazine in the world, being published down to the present day. Renowned for featuring the work of over 200 years of botanical illustration, its aim is to illustrate and describe:

> *the most Ornamental Foreign plants, cultivated in the Open Ground, the Green-House and Stove with illustrations always drawn from the living plant, and coloured as near to nature, as the imperfection of colouring will admit.*

The first part, containing three plates (hand-coloured copperplate engravings), was published on 1 February 1787, the first botanical portrait being executed by James Sowerby, *Iris persica* (see Figure 84, p. 92).[1]

*The Botanical Magazine* has retained a consistently high standard throughout its history. The plant portraits, initially hand-coloured copperplate engravings, were intended to complement the text; the latter described the plant's properties, history, growth characteristics and provided common names for the species. Unlike William Curtis's *Flora Londinensis* (qv), this was his most successful literary venture and the encouragement it received was 'great beyond the author's warmest expectations'.[2] Known in

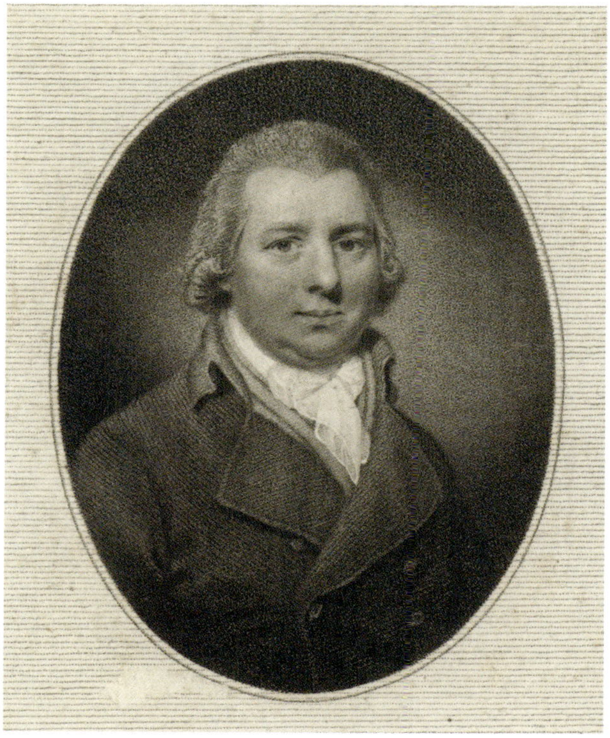

Fig. 82. Botanist, entomologist and author, William Curtis, FLS (11 January 1746–7 July 1799) [© Royal Botanic Gardens, Kew]

the trade as *Curtis's Bot. Mag.* (*Botanical Magazine*), it continues to be published today by the RBG Kew, London, and aims to serve all those interested in horticulture, botanical illustration or ecology.

The first contribution from Ireland was *Leptospermum laevigatum* (the Australian coast tea-tree) found in the coastal regions of Tasmania and south-eastern Australia and published in 1810 (see Figure 85). Although raised in Ireland since 1790, the specimen grown at Glasnevin was the first to flower, in May 1810.[3] Despatched by Dr Walter Wade (qv), Professor of Botany, [Royal] Dublin Society to Dr John Sims, MD, FRS, FLOS (1749–1831) who, following William Curtis's death in 1799, succeeded him as editor,[4] the plant portrait appeared in July 1810 with the minimum of detail, drawn by English botanical artist Sydenham Teast Edwards.[5] A skilled draughtsman and engraver of natural history subjects, Edwards had already drawn many of the figures for the plates in the sixth fascicle of Curtis's *Flora Londinensis* (qv) and was to execute many hundreds of drawings for this new publishing venture.

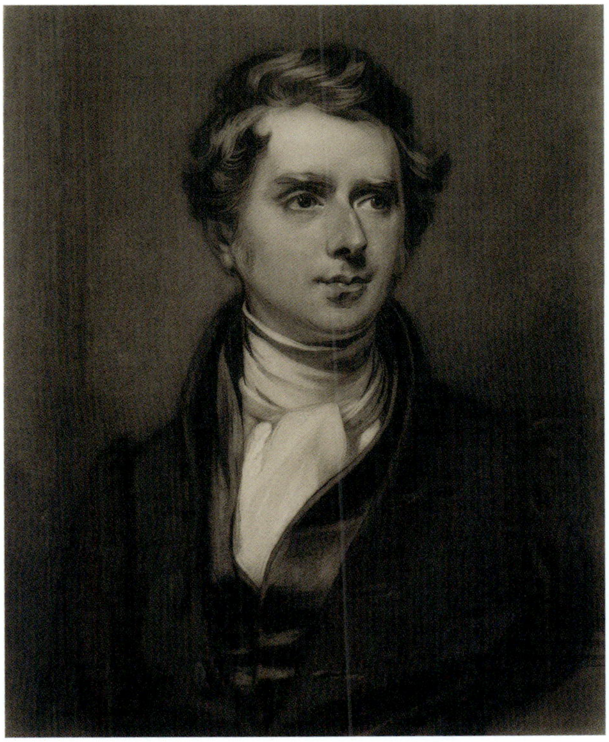

Fig. 83. Dr John Sims (1749–1831)
[© National Portrait Gallery, London]

Under the guidance of Sims, the magazine became more scientific, and the publication became known as *Curtis's Botanical Magazine.* Twenty-six years elapsed before the next Irish link to this distinguished publication was established. In 1829, the Belfast Botanic Gardens opened as the private Royal Belfast Botanic Gardens, covering an area of just over 14 acres.[6] One of its earliest curators was naturalist, John Campbell (d.1836), who resigned after a short period but not before submitting the first plate to be sent from the gardens, *Rodriguezia planifolia* (*Gomesa planifolia;* see Figure 87).[7] Published in July 1836, it was probably drawn by Sim's successor, editor, Sir William Jackson Hooker.

Between 1836 and 1844, no fewer than 12 plates associated with Glasnevin appeared and were largely based on plants and seeds collected by Scottish plant collector John Tweedie (1775–1862),[8] with original

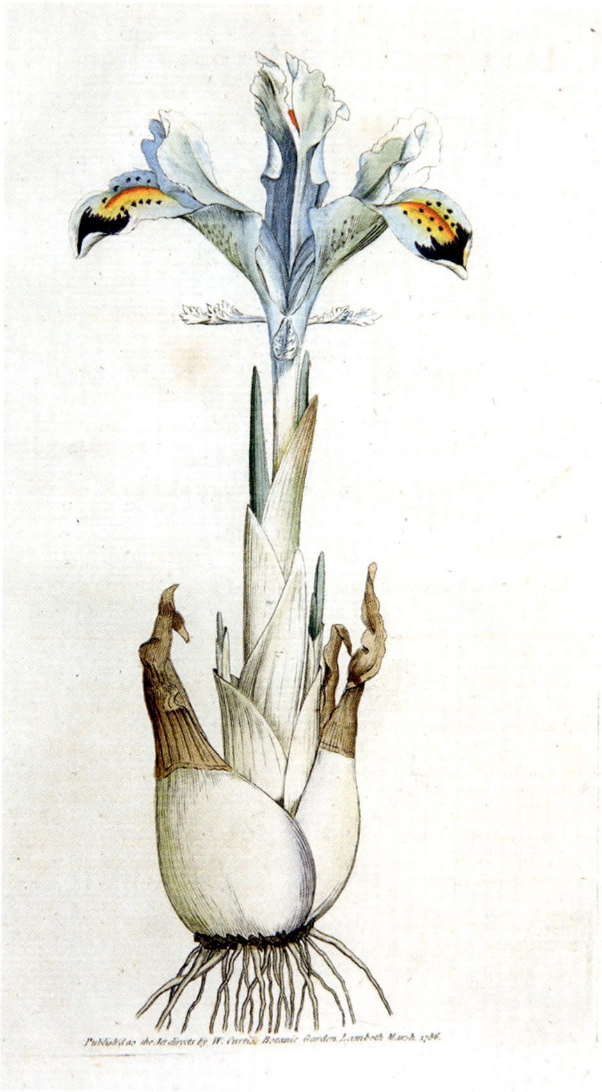

Fig. 84. *Iris persica*, Persian iris
Hand-coloured copperplate engraving by James Sowerby.
The first plate to appear in *The Botanical magazine, or, Flower garden displayed*, vol. 1, no. 1.
[Courtesy, National Botanic Gardens, Glasnevin, Dublin]

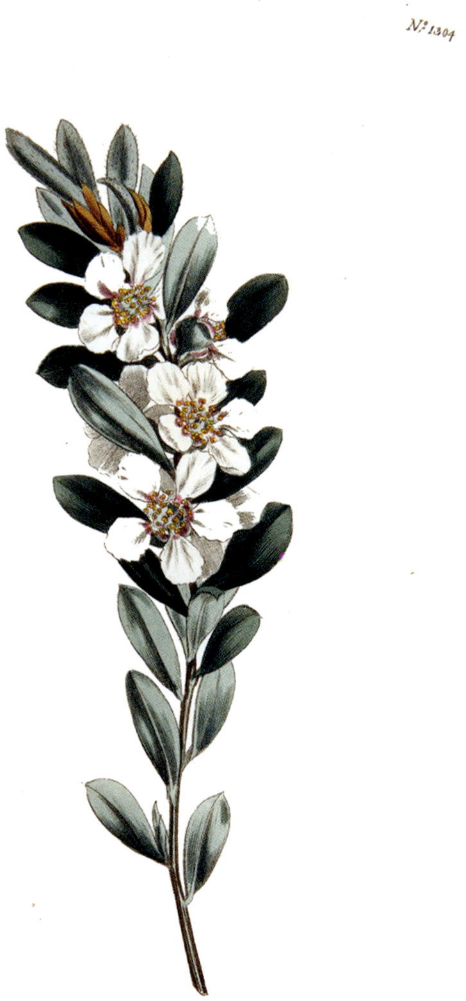


Fig. 85. *Leptospermum laevigatum* (Australian coast tea-tree)
Original watercolour by Sydenham Teast Edwards FLS, hand-coloured copperplate engraving by F. Sansom, Jr (fl.c.1797–1819), reproduced in *Curtis's Botanical Magazine*, vol. 32, tab. 1304
[Courtesy, National Botanic Gardens, Glasnevin, Dublin]

drawings by Ninian Niven (c.1799–1879), Curator, Glasnevin (1834–1838). Following his appointment at Glasnevin, Niven had begun to restock the gardens, which had reached a low ebb.

Nevin's five years as curator saved the gardens from total degradation. He succeeded in re-establishing Glasnevin as a major centre for botanical and horticultural communities within these islands.[9, 10] Niven was succeeded by Scotsman, David Moore (*olim* Muir), ALS, FLS (1808–1879), appointed Curator, 1838,[11] and he remained in charge until his death. Under Moore's leadership, the Gardens passed from the control of the RDS to the State and became known as the Royal (later National) Botanic Gardens, Glasnevin.

David Moore built on Niven's work and succeeded in transforming the gardens into one of the most outstanding in the world. His international reputation was growing, particularly his remarkable achievements in relation to orchids, which he raised from seed to flowering stage. This was the first time any botanic garden in the world had achieved this goal. In 1873, Sir Joseph Dalton Hooker (1817–1911), who had succeeded his father both as editor of *Curtis's Botanical Magazine* and Director, RBG, Kew, London (1865–1885), dedicated the publication in that year to David Moore.[12]

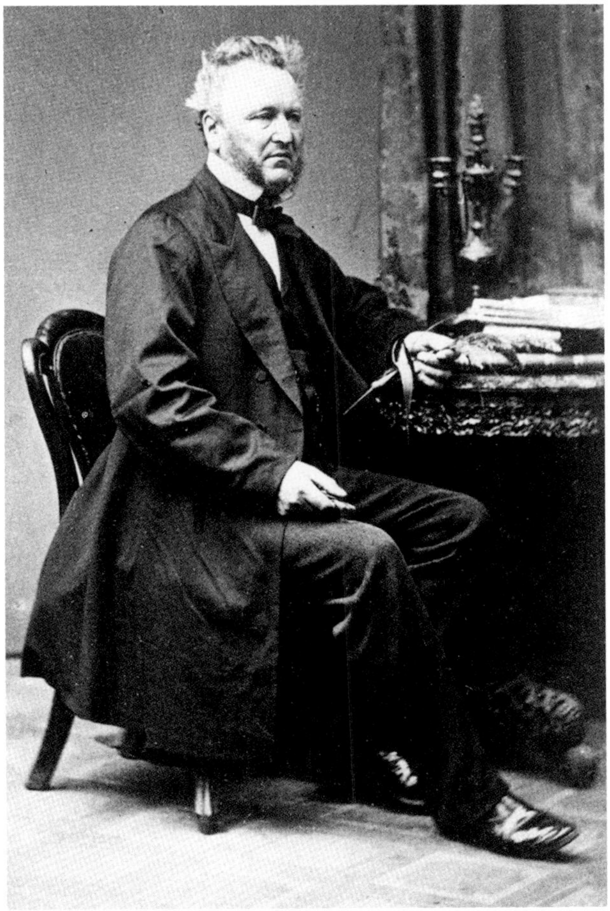

Fig. 86. Dr David Moore (Muir), ALS, FRS (1808–1879)
[Courtesy, National Botanic Gardens, Glasnevin, Dublin]

Sir Frederick William Moore, ALS, FLS, VMH, VMM (1857–1949)[13] succeeded his father at Glasnevin and established an outstanding collection of orchids that resulted in a steady stream of orchid plates being sent from Glasnevin to the editors. Sir Frederick, like his father, also had the distinction of having two volumes dedicated to him (1909, 1938).[14]

Contributors of botanical drawings for published plates connected to Ireland included the curator, Trinity

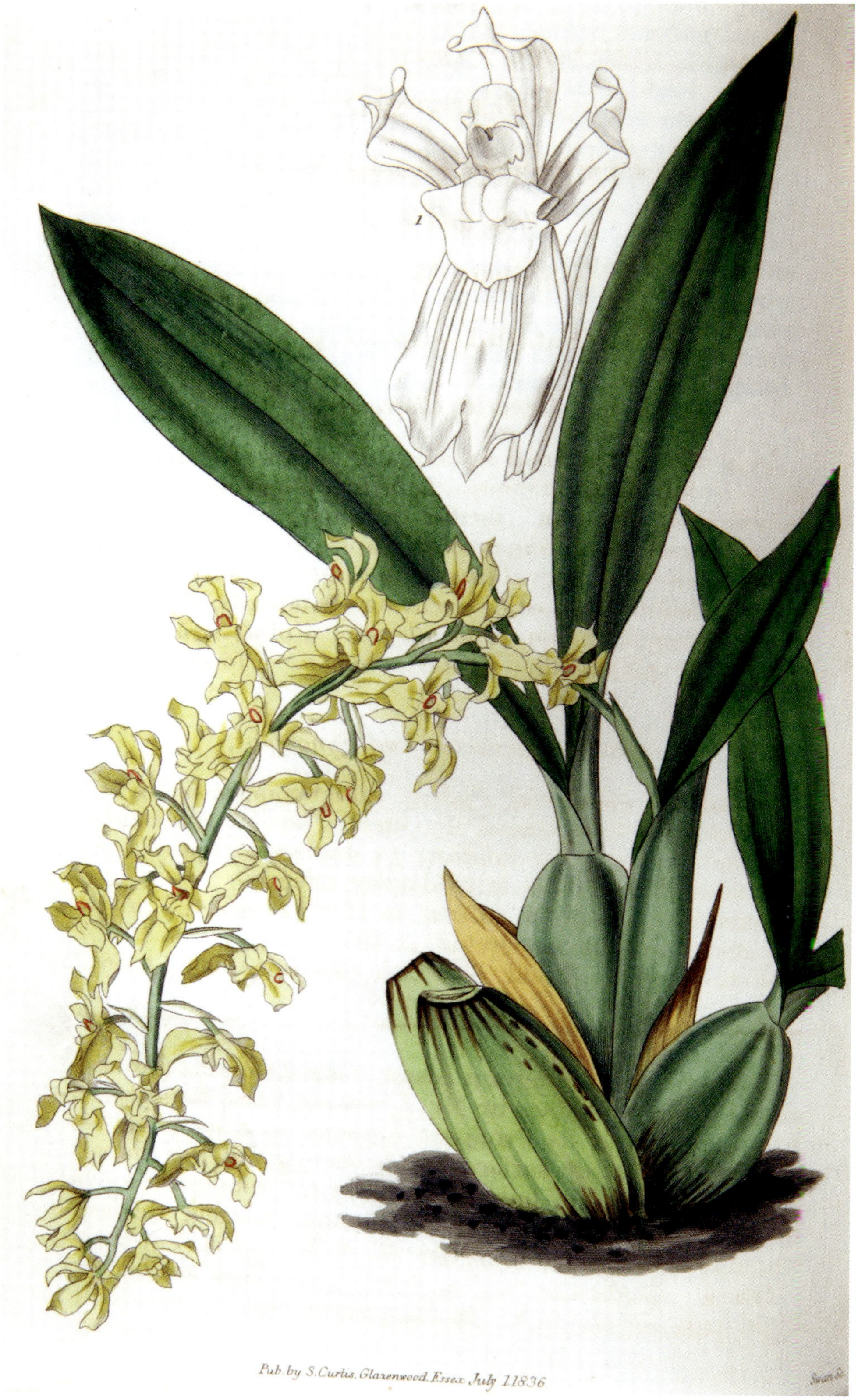


Fig. 87. *Rodriguezia planifolia* (*Gomesa planifolia*)
Attributed to Sir William Jackson Hooker (1785–1865). Hand-coloured copperplate engraving reproduced in *Curtis's Botanical Magazine*, vol. 10, tab. 3504. This orchid was the first of a short run of plates (10) to be sent from Belfast, published July 1836; the last a Mexican orchid, *Coelia macrostachya* (tab. 4712) published May 1853.
[Courtesy, National Botanic Gardens, Glasnevin, Dublin]

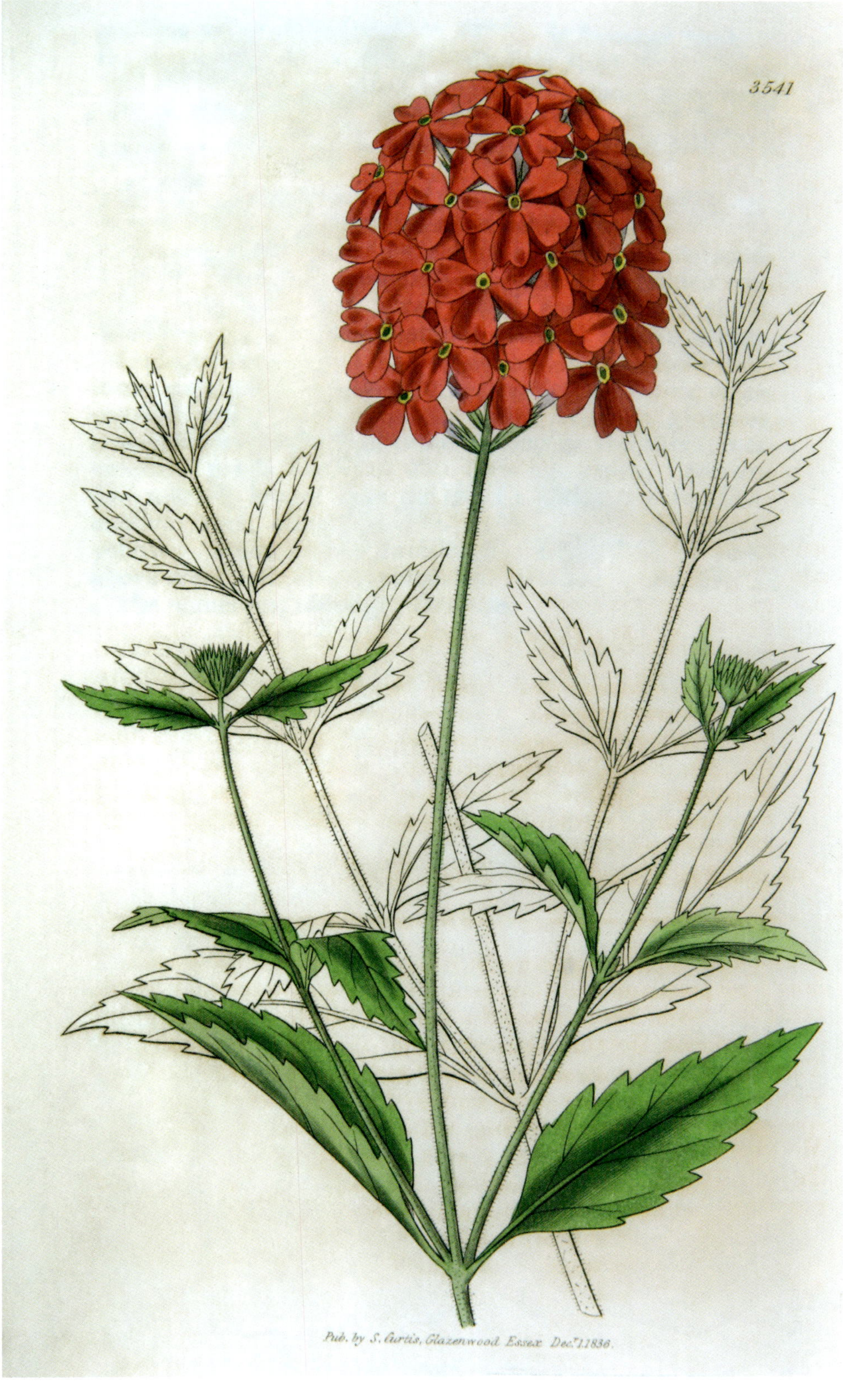


Fig. 88. *Verbena tweediana* (*Verbena megapotamica*)
Original drawing by Ninian Niven (c.1799–1879), hand-coloured copperplate engraving, inscription: (printed) 'Published by S. Curtis. Glazenwood Essex Dec. 1 1836', reproduced in *Curtis's Botanical Magazine*, vol. 10, tab. 3541.
[Courtesy, National Botanic Gardens, Glasnevin, Dublin]

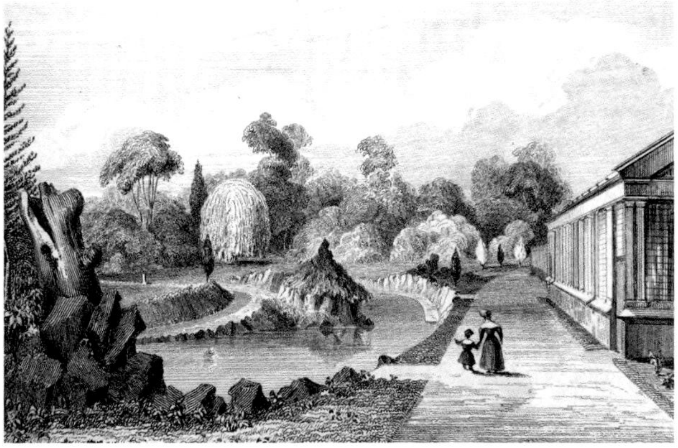

Fig. 89. *'View from the front of Hothouses'*
Engraving by John Kirkwood (d.1853) from Ninian Niven's *The Visitor's Companion to the Botanic Garden, Glasnevin* (Dublin, 1838)
[Courtesy, National Botanic Gardens, Glasnevin, Dublin]

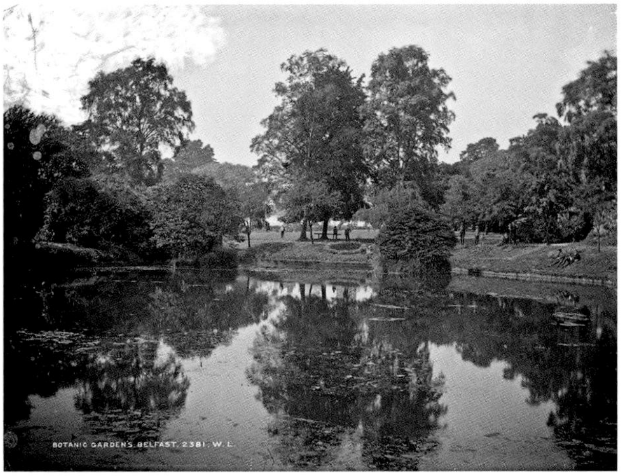


Fig. 90. Botanic Gardens, Belfast, Co. Antrim
[Courtesy, National Library of Ireland]

College Garden, Dublin (1879–1905) Frederick William Thomas Burbidge (1847–1905) (see pp. 97–101):

> *Our plate [Iris kolpakowskiana] was made from specimens and a coloured sketch sent by Mr. F.W. Burbidge, with whom it flowered under glass in the botanic garden at Trinity College, in the middle of January this present year.*[15]

The consistent quality of the superb hand-coloured plates prepared for *Curtis's Botanical Magazine* made it one of the most widely cited works of its kind in the horticultural world.[16] However, the technical processes were labour-intensive and after February 1948, due to rising costs, finance finally forced the move to photo-lithography.

In 1984, *Curtis's Botanical Magazine* underwent a change of title and became known as *Kew Magazine.* After ten years, it reverted to its original title. Firm Irish links had already been well established. Between 1810 and 2022, a significant number of plates were illustrated in the pages of this distinguished horticultural magazine, and all were connected in some way with Ireland.

# Frederick William Thomas Burbidge, MA, VMH (1847–1905)

During the period June 1827 to September 1904, Trinity College Botanic Garden, Lansdowne Road, Ballsbridge, Dublin, contributed over 30 plants to *Curtis's Botanical Magazine.* Among the College contributions was the blue-flowered *Iris kolpakowskiana*, which appeared in 1880,[17] drawn by the newly appointed curator of the garden, Frederick William Thomas Burbidge.

Burbidge, botanist and artist, was born at Wymeswold, Leicestershire, his father being a fruit grower and farmer. From an early age, his son showed considerable talent as a draughtsman. Burbidge served his apprenticeship in the gardens of the RHS at Chiswick and while there enrolled for an art course. From Chiswick, he moved to Kew, where he was employed as a student in the Herbarium, his plant portraits becoming known for their considerable accuracy. After completing his studies (1870), Burbidge remained on the staff at Kew both as a writer and an artist for the *Garden* journal. During this period, he produced four books, two of which are considered to be major contributions to the world of horticultural literature: *The Narcissus: Its History and Culture*,[18] which he both illustrated and wrote, and *Cultivated Plants, Their Propagation and Improvement*,[19] which Sir Joseph Hooker firmly believed 'should be in every gardener's library'.

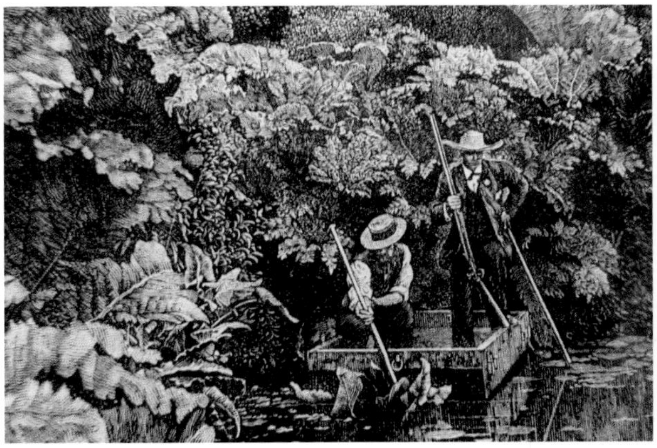

Fig. 91. Frederick William Burbidge punting on the pond, Trinity College Botanic Garden, Lansdowne Road, Ballsbridge, Dublin, steel engraving
[Courtesy, National Botanic Gardens, Glasnevin, Dublin]

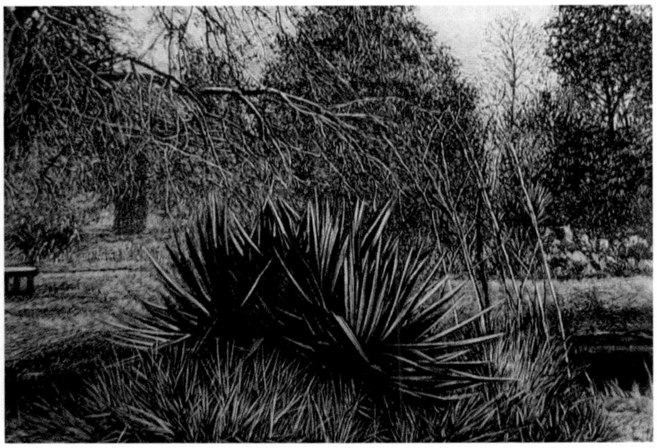

Fig. 92. Winter 1892, Trinity College Botanic Garden, Lansdowne Road, Ballsbridge, Dublin, steel engraving
[Courtesy, National Botanic Gardens, Glasnevin, Dublin]

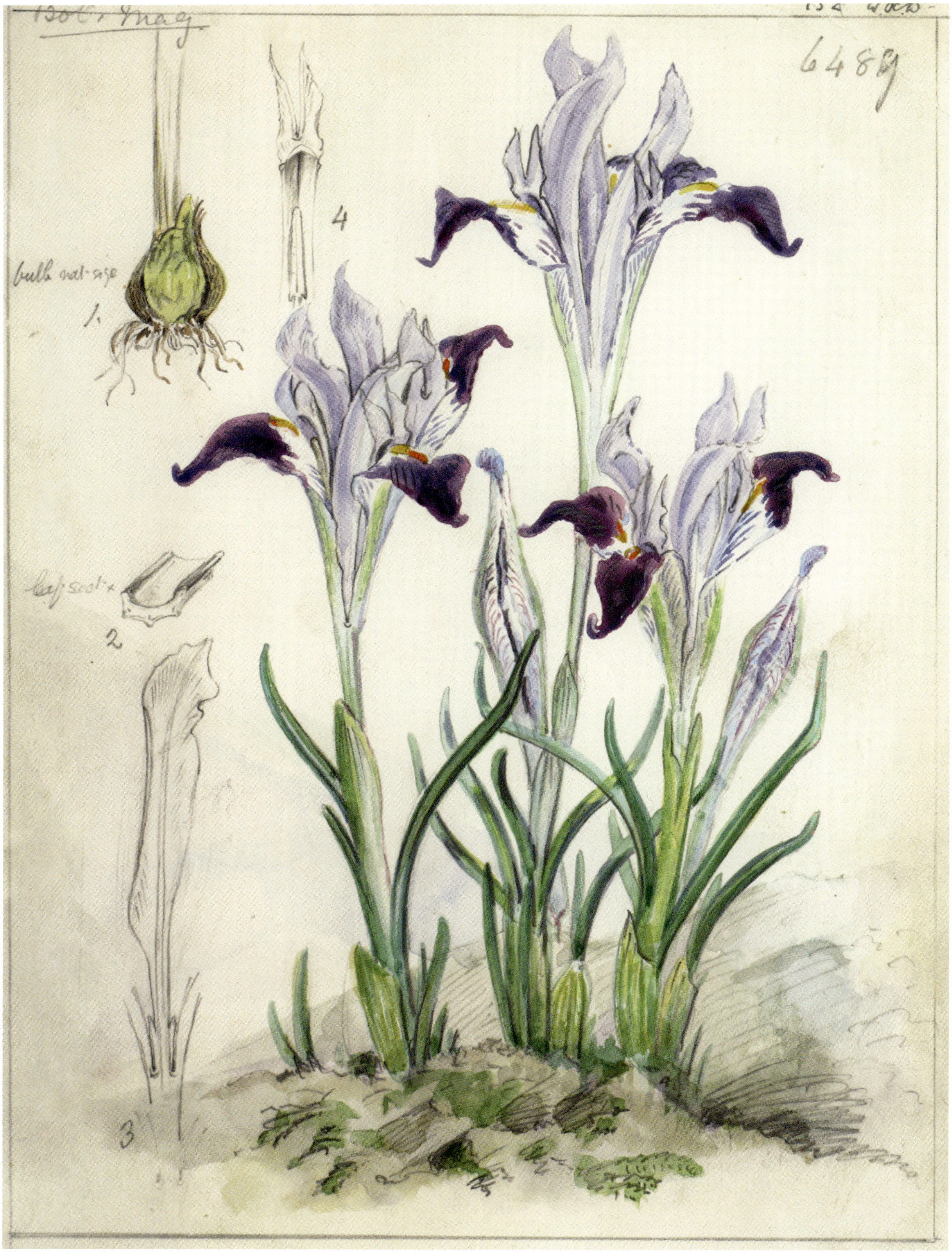


Fig. 93. *Iris kolpakowskiana*
Watercolour and pencil by Frederick William Thomas Burbidge.
Original drawing for *Curtis's Botanical Magazine*, vol. 36, 3rd series, tab. 6489
[© Royal Botanic Gardens, Kew]

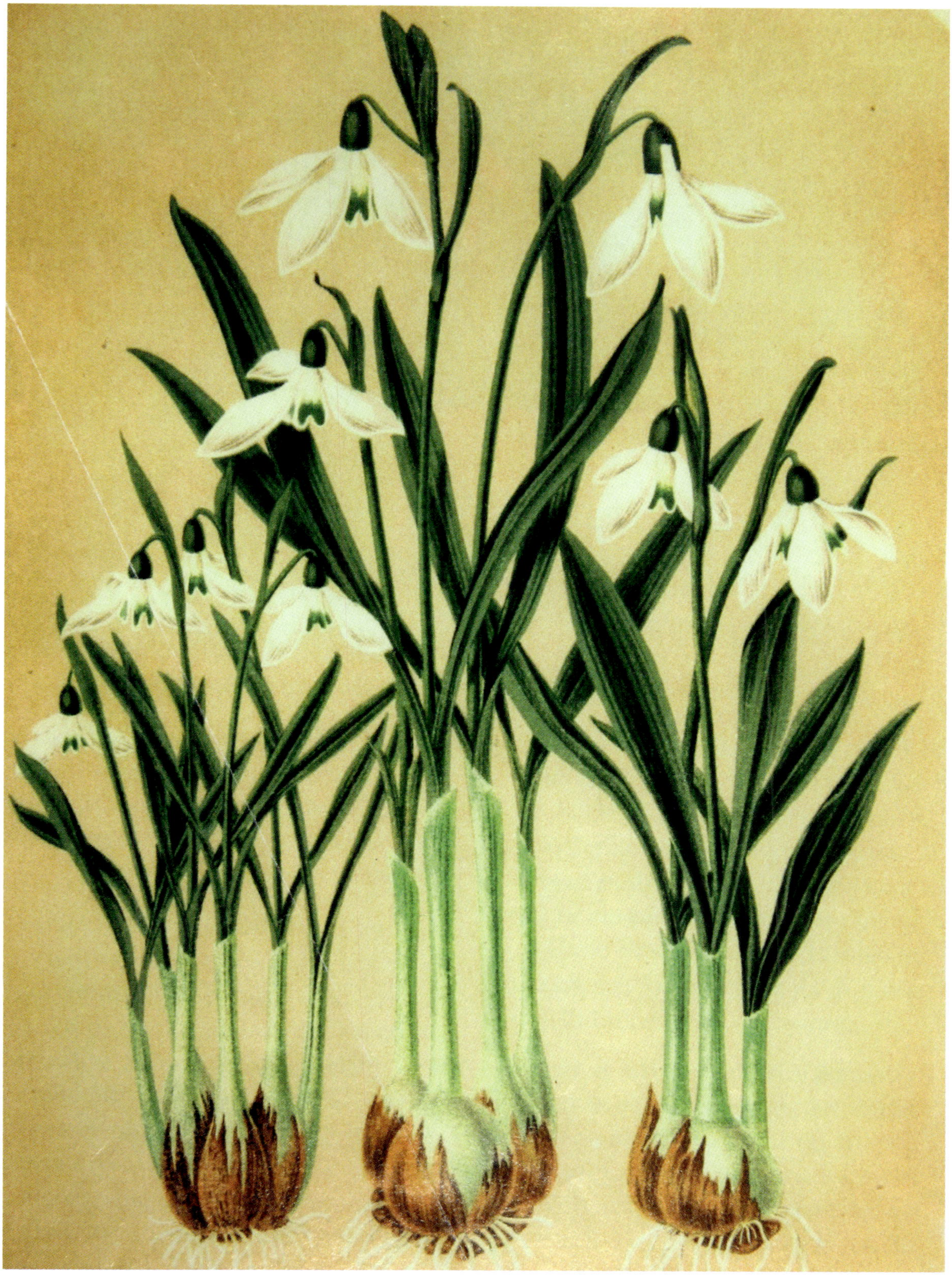

Fig. 94. *Galanthus* 'Straffan'
Watercolour by Frederick William Burbidge, a noted galanthophile responsible for writing and illustrating several monographs in the 1880s
[Private collection. Reproduced by kind permission]

In 1877, Burbidge was sent by the well-known London nursery firm, James Veitch & Sons to Borneo. After an absence of two years, during which he also visited Johore, Brunei and the islands of the Sulu Archipelago, he returned to England bringing back almost one thousand specimens of plants, including orchids, pitcher plants and rare ferns. Several orchids and ferns were named in his honour, for example, *Burbidgea nitida* (orchid) described by Sir Joseph Dalton Hooker as 'This very beautiful, plant... an entirely new genus...' (*Curtis's Botanical Magazine*, 1879, tab. 6403) and *Polypodium burbidgei* (fern). In 1880, as a result of his travels in Borneo, Burbidge published *The Gardens of the Sun: or a Naturalist's Journal.*[20]

Following his appointment (1880–1905) as Curator of the College Botanic Garden, Burbidge became renowned for his enthusiasm in encouraging both students and members of staff to bring him seeds and bulbs from their travels. He was considered to be a leading authority on daffodils and narcissi, building up one of the world's major collections of bulbous plants in the College Botanic Garden. Awarded an honorary MA by Trinity College Dublin, and appointed Keeper of College Park, 1894, Burbidge was among the first to receive the Victoria Medal of Honour awarded by the RHS (1897).

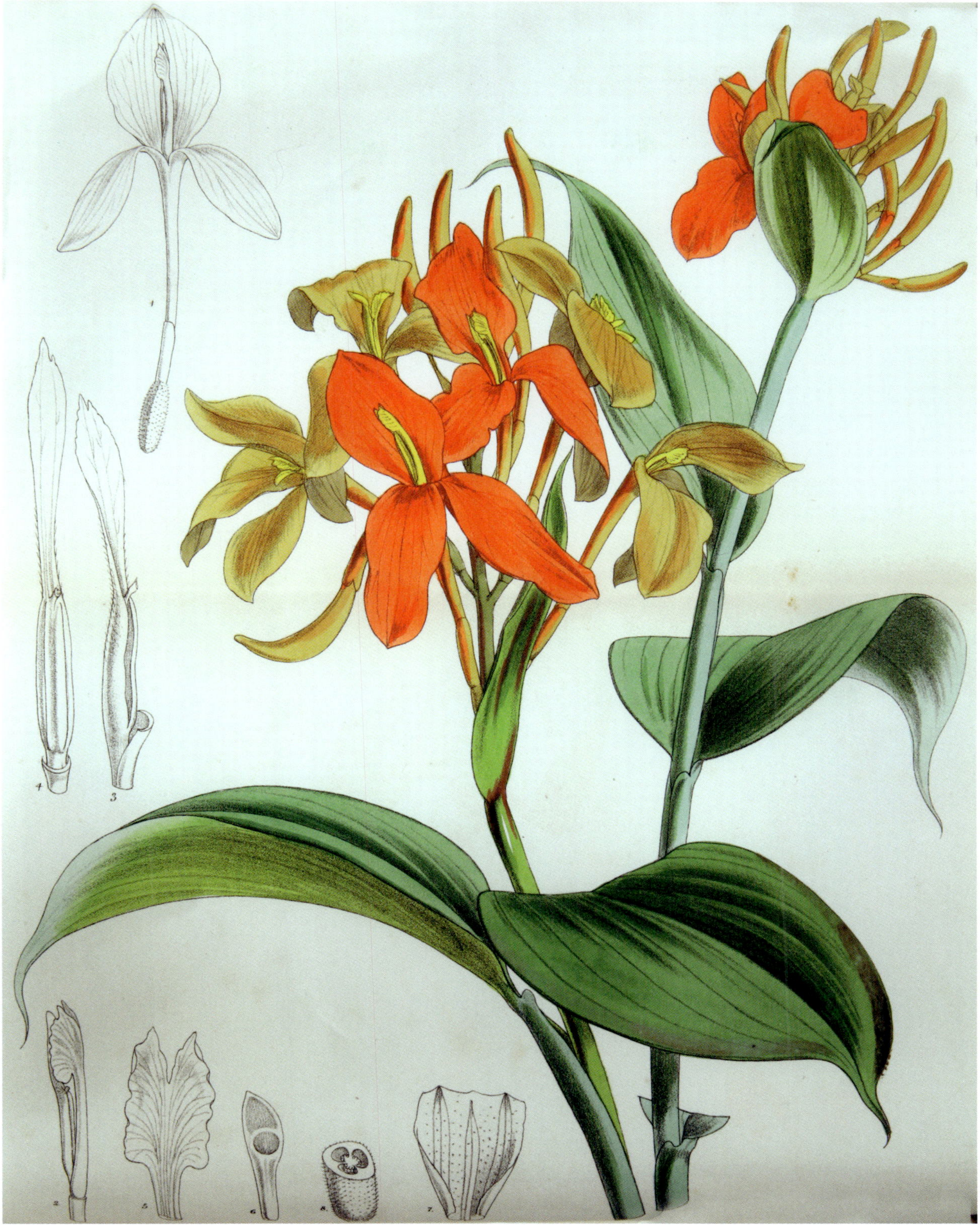

Fig. 95. *Burbidgea nitida*
Lithograph (coloured) by J.N. Fitch (John Nugent Fitch, FLS, 1840–1927), reproduced in *Curtis's Botanical Magazine*, vol. 35, tab. 6403. Sir Joseph Dalton Hooker, editor, *Curtis's Botanical Magazine* described this orchid as *'a very beautiful plant...an entirely new genus...Mr. F.W. Burbidge who discovered it when travelling in Borneo, for Messrs. Veitch, informs me that it grows in shady forests of the Murut district in N.W. Borneo, between the Lawas and Trusan rivers, at an altitude of 1,000 to 1,500 feet...'* It was named in honour of Frederick William Thomas Burbidge, MA, VMH (1847–1905).
[Courtesy, National Botanic Gardens, Glasnevin, Dublin]

# William Edward Trevithick
# (1899–1958)

William Edward Trevithick was described by his friend John Hutchinson, FRS, FL (1884–1972)[21] as 'a cheerful and jolly companion with a strong sense of humour....applying his great talents wholeheartedly and unselfishly to whatever he undertook'.[22] A ledger in the NBG, Dublin, records the fact Trevithick began as a 'pupil gardener' at Glasnevin on 4 April 1918, serving his apprenticeship under the director, Sir Frederick W. Moore (qv).

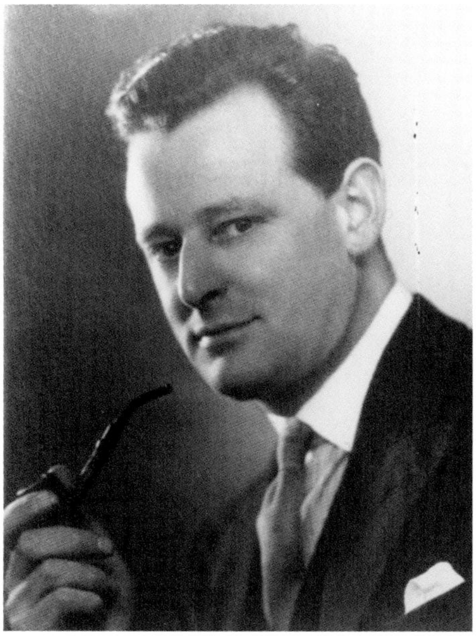

Fig. 96. William Edward Trevithick (1899–1958)
[© Royal Botanic Gardens, Kew]

His father, William Edward Roberts Trevithick (1858–1929),[23] born Helston, Cornwall, served as gardener to the Earl and Countess of Fitzwilliam at Wentworth Woodhouse, Yorkshire, before becoming head gardener on the Headfort estate near Kells, Co. Meath, between 1912 and 1921. His son was born at Headfort on 30 April 1899. The young boy left school at 13 to work with his father in these great gardens, remaining there for three years. He then spent a short period on the Duke of Rutland's estate, Belvoir Castle, Grantham, and it was noted that he was 'clever at drawing, both freehand and plans and in colour work'. In 1918, Trevithick went to Glasnevin. He was a keen photographer and in the year he left Glasnevin (1920), his photographs were published in *Irish Gardening*. Trevithick worked at the RBG Kew, London, and was promoted to sub-foreman in 1922. A year later, he was transferred to the Herbarium as a temporary technical assistant.

While at Kew, Trevithick was recognised for his skills as a botanical artist. In 1924, he began contributing to *Curtis's Botanical Magazine* (1924–1942).[24] Many of the specimens he illustrated were drawn from either the Marquis of Headfort's estate or Glasnevin and included *Encyclia mooreana*, a native of Costa Rica which was first sent to Kew in 1889 by Frederick W. Moore, Curator, RBG Glasnevin, Dublin. In 1927, the

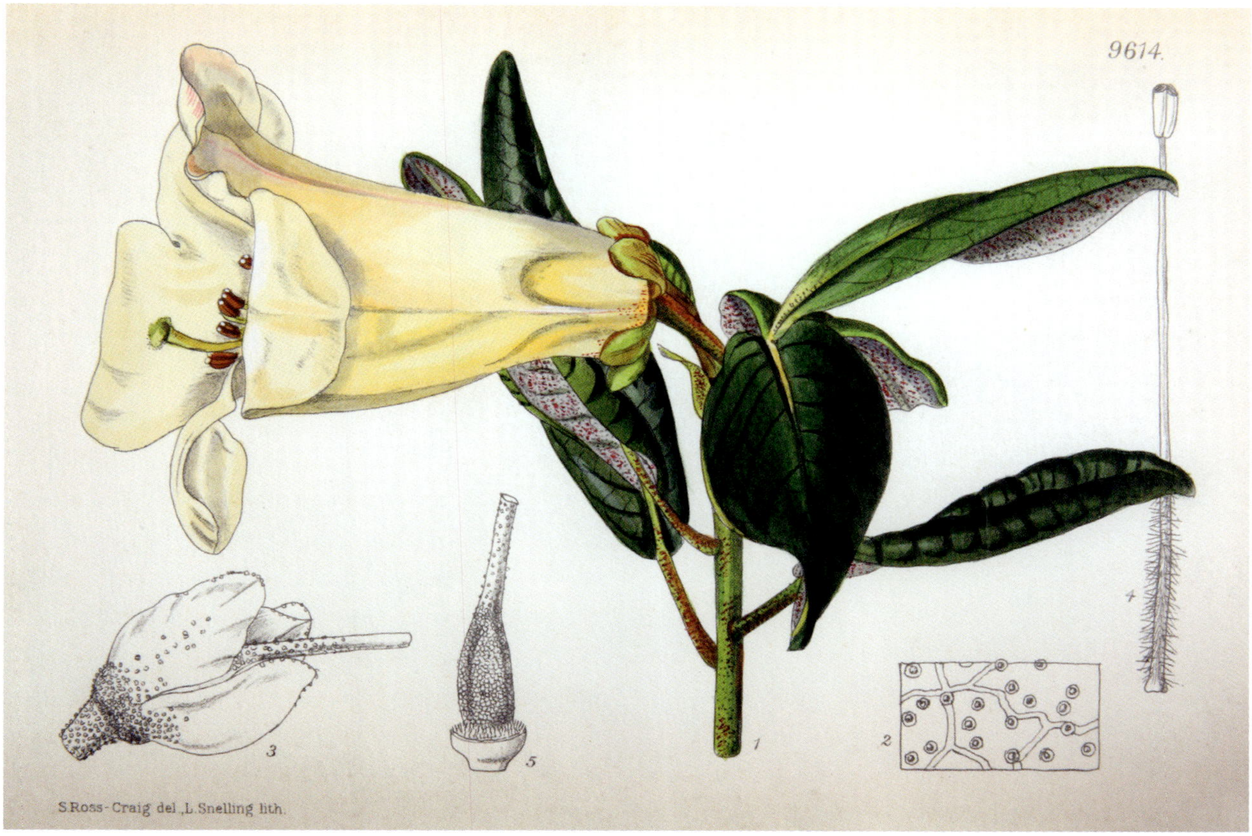


Fig. 97. *Rhododendron headfortianum* (*Rhododendron taggianum* Headfortianum Group)
Original watercolour by William Edward Trevithick, coloured lithograph reproduced in *Curtis's Botanical Magazine*, vol. 163, tab. 9614. *R. headfortianum* was described as a plant raised by Lord Headfort from seeds collected by botanist, plant hunter/collector and author, Frank Kingdon-Ward (1885–1958), November 1924 in the Tsangpo gorge, Southeast Tibet.
[Courtesy, National Botanic Gardens, Glasnevin, Dublin]

plant portrait, drawn by Trevithick and lithographed by Lilian Snelling (1879–1972)[25] appeared in the periodical named after Sir Frederick Moore.

In the winter of 1912–1913, Lord Headfort, with the assistance of Sir Frederick Moore, had begun assembling and planting his collections – *Rhododendron* species, shrubs and trees, particularly conifers. This extensive planting would result in one of the most outstanding arboreta in these islands. As Trevithick was the son of Lord Headfort's head gardener, it comes as no surprise to see a number of plates based on the collections grown at Headfort and executed by this artist appearing in the pages of *Curtis's Botanical*

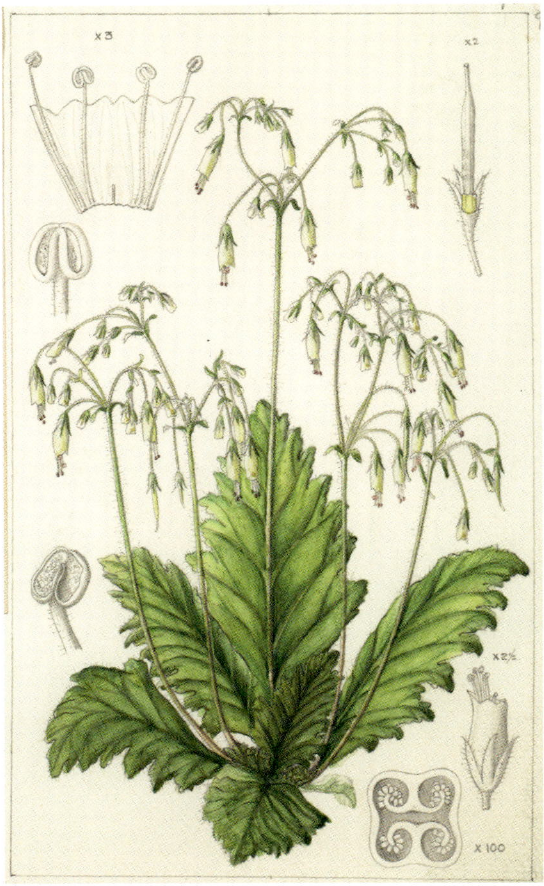


Fig. 98. *Tremacron forrestii* (*Oreocharis craibii*)
Original watercolour and pencil by William Edward Trevithick, lithograph by Matilda Smith (1854–1926) reproduced in *Curtis's Botanical Magazine*, vol. 154, tab. 9224
[© Royal Botanic Gardens, Kew]

*Magazine*, for example *Rhododendron headfortianum* (*Rhododendron taggianum*, Headfortianum Group) (see Figure 97), *Cupressus lusitanica* (table 9434) and *Tremacron forrestii* (*Oreocharis craibii*) (see Figure 98). Many of Trevithick's plant portraits were drawn and lithographed in conjunction with such well-known English botanical artists as Lilian Snelling, and artists and photographers such as Gerald Atkinson (1893–1971) and Robert Moyes Adam (1885–1967).

Besides being a contributor to John Hutchinson's *Families of Flowering Plants* (1926), Trevithick also submitted plates for the *Flora of West Tropical Africa* (1927–29).[26]

This artist's plant portraits, largely executed in body colour and/or watercolour with pencil notations, are simple, straightforward and descriptive, displaying his ability to place plants upon the page with skill and accuracy. The original drawing, *Brunnera macrophylla*, perennial forget-me-not (*Curtis's Botanical Magazine*, May 1924; see Figure 99)[27] emphasises not only the structure but the graceful movement defined by leaves and stems, as they stretch and turn, their elegant outlines being carefully infilled with various gradations of green.

Trevithick left Kew to study full time at the Chelsea School of Art and supported himself by freelance work. When he qualified, he joined his brother, a commercial artist, and spent three years working with him. Later, he established his own commercial art advertising business while living in Barnes, Surrey.

Today, the Hibernian link is kept alive with contributions by distinguished botanical artists such as: Dr Wendy F. Walsh, Deborah Lambkin, Susan M. Sex and Lynn Stringer.

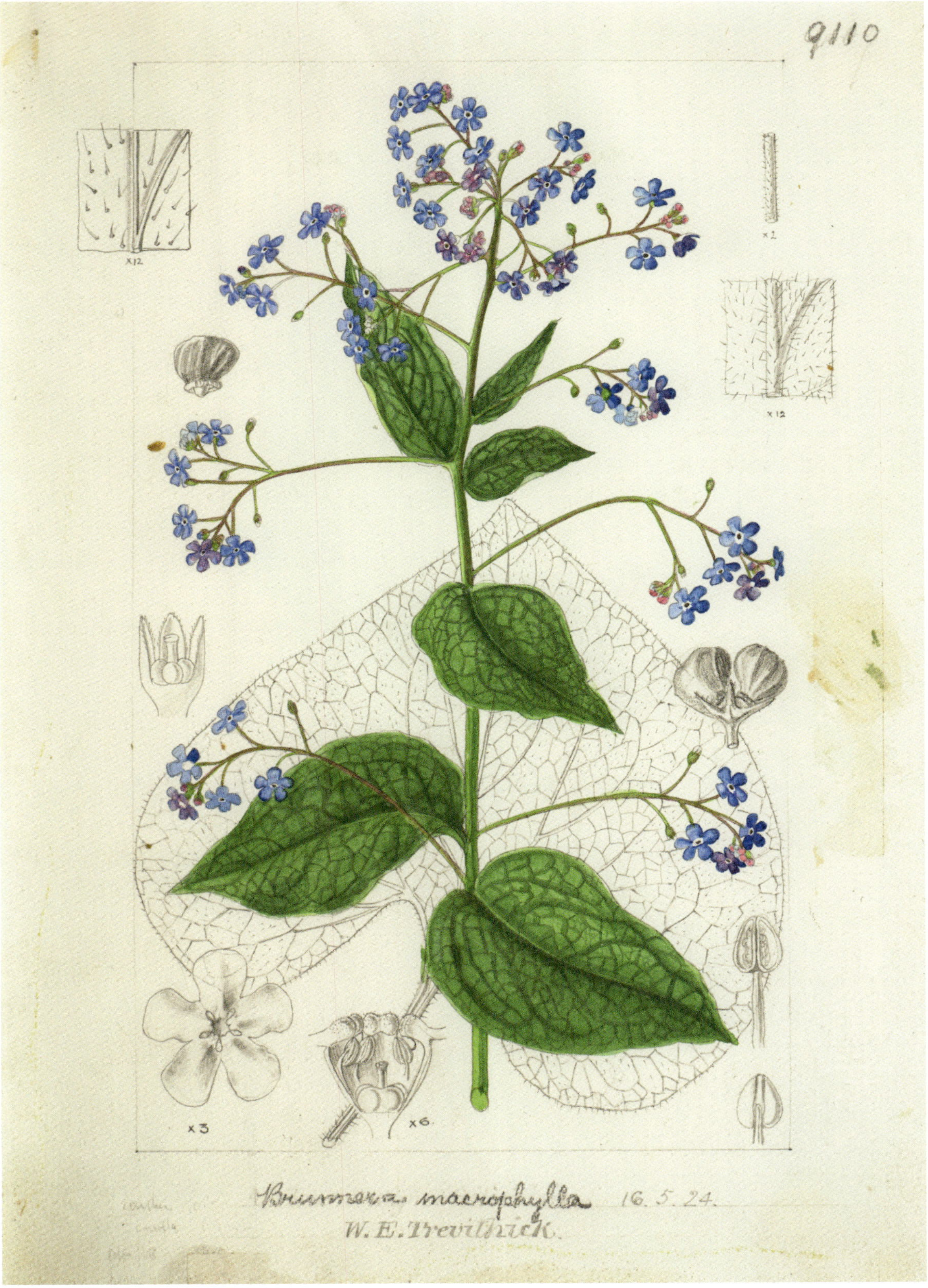


Fig. 99. *Brunnera macrophylla*, perennial forget-me-not
Original watercolour by William Edward Trevithick, lithograph reproduced in *Curtis's Botanical Magazine*, tab. 9110
[© Royal Botanic Gardens, Kew]

# Dr Wendy Felicité Walsh (née Storey), Doctor in Litteris (1915–2014)

> *Botanical art is a very, very demanding discipline, because you have to get everything right, and at the same time produce a good picture. And you have to be able to paint in watercolours.*

Wendy Walsh, born on 9 April 1915, in Cumbria, 'retired' with her husband John to north Co. Dublin and lived and worked in Ireland for over 40 years. During recent decades, she devoted her life to producing outstanding examples of botanical art. Self-taught, she combined good eyesight with formidable powers of concentration and an enviable steadiness of hand, all essential in a discipline where each brush stroke had to be perfect first time. In Dr Walsh's view, rigorous discipline and self-training are essential:

> *You must know exactly what you are doing. I trained myself by doing exercises, painting squares, and learning exactly what my colours did, so that now I can look at a flower, or a stem, or a leaf and know exactly what colours would be needed to recapture it.*[28]

Her work has included designing postage stamps, first in 1978 for the Gilbert Islands (now Kiribati), which she visited in the 1970s. This was followed by a Dublin fauna and flora series from 1979 to 1986 first-day covers for the Department of Post and Telegraphs and Unicover Corporation, Wyoming, USA). She worked closely with Dr E. Charles Nelson, formerly taxonomist at the NBG Glasnevin, Dublin. Published works included two volumes of *An Irish Florilegium: Wild and Garden Flowers of Ireland* in 1983 and 1987,[29] followed, in 1984, by *An Irish Flower Garden Replanted,*[30] a collection of botanical portraits employing watercolours and Chinese inks. Other collaborations included:[31] *The Burren: Companion to the Wildflowers of an Irish Limestone Wilderness* (1991), *Trees of Ireland: Native and Naturalized* (1993), and *The Flowers of Mayo* (1995).

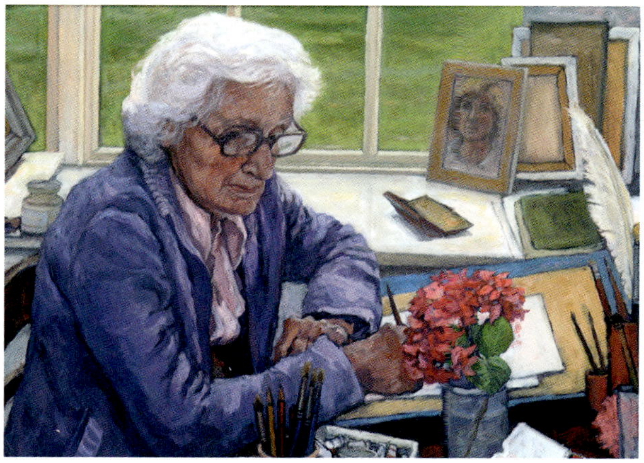

Fig. 100. Dr Wendy Felicité Walsh in her studio
Oil on canvas by Lesley Fennell
[Private collection. Reproduced by kind permission]

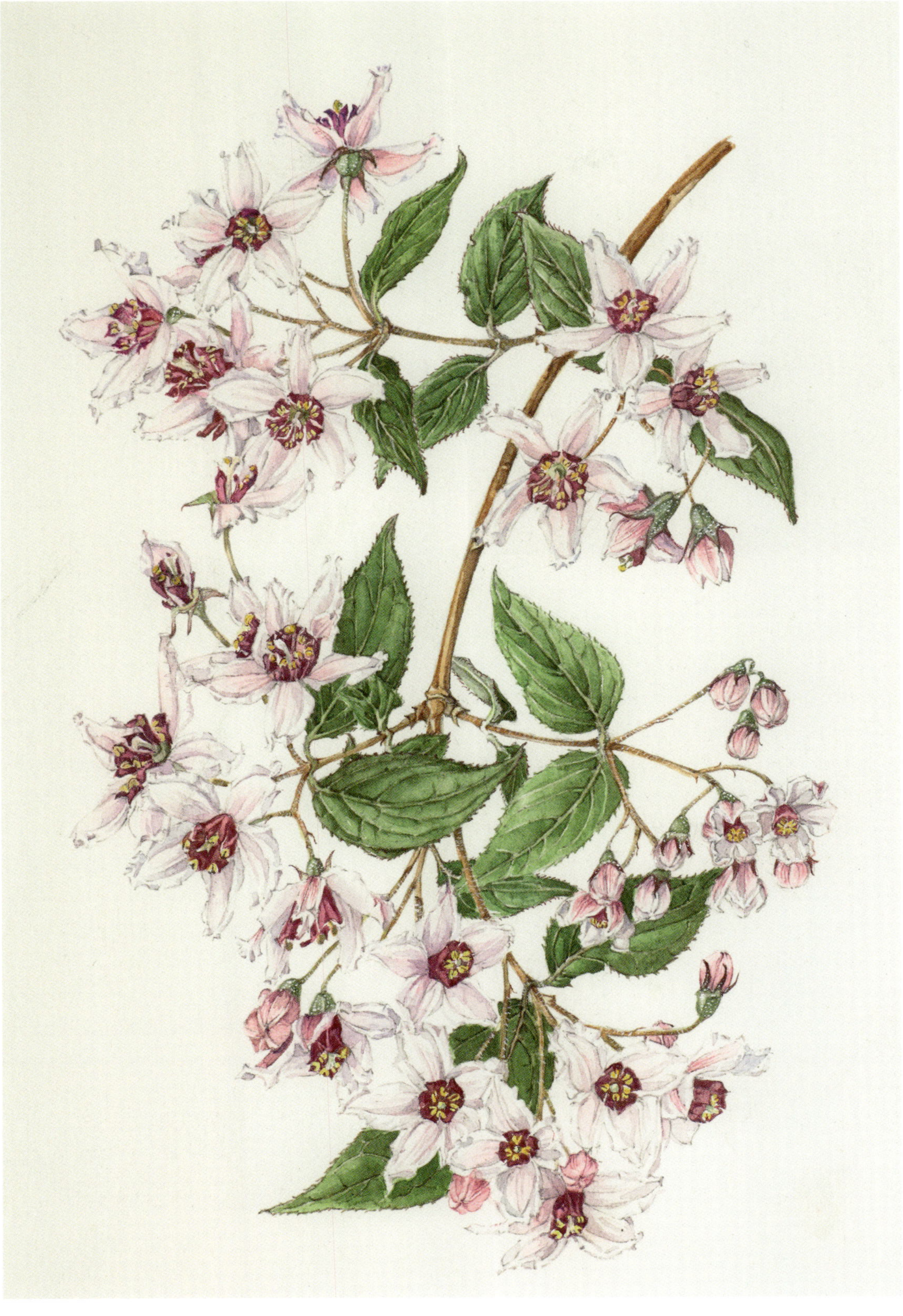

Fig. 101. *Deutzia purpurascens* 'Alpine Magician'
Watercolour by Wendy F. Walsh
Original drawing for *The Kew Magazine* (incorporating *Curtis's Botanical Magazine*), vol. 10, part 4, plate 234
[© Estate of Wendy Walsh. Royal Botanic Gardens, Kew]

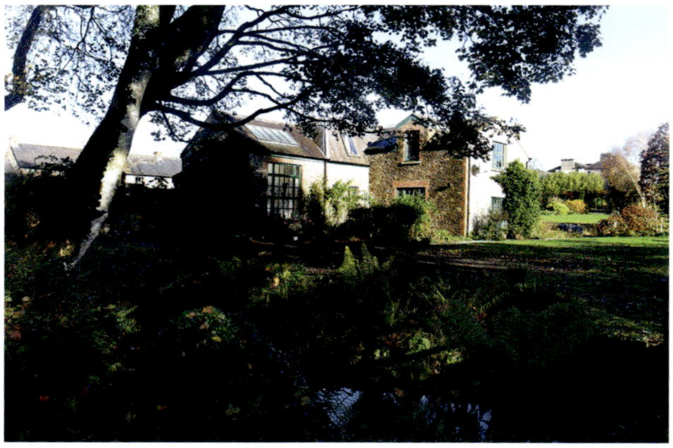

Fig. 102. View of the studio, Burtown House, Co. Kildare, home of the late Wendy Walsh
[Private collection. Reproduced by kind permission]

Throughout her range of publications, which also included four illustrations for a history of the NBG Glasnevin, Dublin, Dr Walsh contributed a number of plates to *The Kew Magazine* (*Curtis's Botanical Magazine)*, beginning in 1989 with *Rhododendron burtii* Ericaceae (Plate No: 130) and continued until 1995 with *Cotoneaster bradyi* (Plate No: 280).[32] *Deutzia purpurascens*, 'Alpine Magician' (Figure 101) was published in 1993, a seedling raised at Glasnevin.

> *The cultivar was, and remains a compliment paid to Reginald Farrer by the great Irish gardener, Lady Phyllis Moore, whose husband, Sir Frederick Moore, was director of the Royal (now National) Botanic Gardens, Glasnevin.*[33]

Dr Walsh's artistic capabilities have augmented materially the current literature relating to plants. Her portraits, whether executed in watercolour or Chinese inks, combine botanical accuracy with exactness of colour and detail. An outstanding botanical artist and illustrator, she has been the recipient of many honours and international awards. In 1997, she received an honorary degree from the University of Dublin, and the following year was made an Honorary Life Member of the RDS and an Honorary Member of the Irish Garden Plant Society. A recipient of a number of gold and silver gilt medals from the RHS, she was awarded their Medal of Honour in 1996. She was also awarded the Alpine Garden Society Gold Medal Award twice, in 1991 and 1993. Her work has been exhibited worldwide, including the US (Hunt Institute for Botanical Documentation, Pittsburgh), South Africa, Melbourne, London and many times in Ireland, including the Water Colour Society of Ireland from 1979 to 1999. A botanical artist who succeeded in 'gain[ing] international recognition for the beauty of Irish Flora, which had never been shown before,'[34] Dr Walsh died on 3 March 2014.

# Susan Mary Sex (née Byrne, b.1947, Dublin)

A recipient of the RHS's gold medal for three consecutive years (2000–2002) and a silver gilt medal in 2004 for her portraits of Irish orchids, Susan Sex is internationally recognised as a major exponent of this most mysterious and diverse form of art. Her frequently exotic interpretations stand at the forefront of botanical illustration, both in this country and throughout the world.

Born in Dublin, the artist was involved at an early stage in the make-believe world of magic – making displays, special effects and props. Educated at Maryfield College, Drumcondra, Dublin, Sex did not continue with full-time academic training but, despite a young and growing family, managed to find the time to paint for pleasure.

> *I began to notice the wild plants that appeared in the ditches and roadsides,' she says, 'My husband bought me a copy of Wild Flowers of Britain and Ireland, illustrated by Marjorie Blamey, and I was hooked.*

She spent much of her time in the nearby NBG Glasnevin, Dublin, and attended a weekend course in botanical painting under the tutelage of Dr Wendy Walsh. This she found to be both practical and inspiring: 'In fact,' she says, 'I have modelled my teaching on Walsh's ever since as I found it so helpful.'

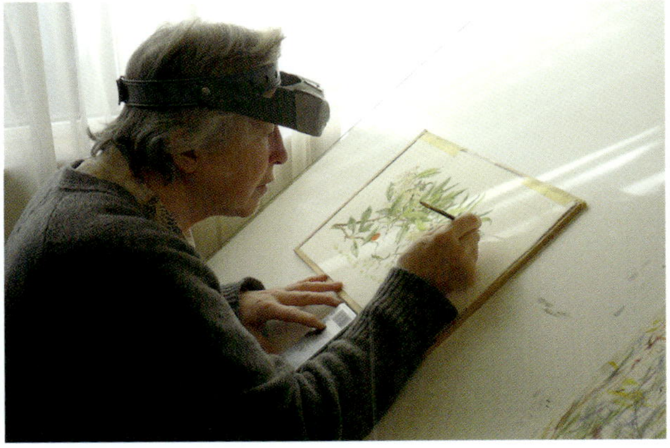

Fig. 103. Botanical artist, Susan Mary Sex
[Private collection. Reproduced by kind permission]

She was introduced to horticulturist and orchid keeper at the NBG, Brendan Sayers, who quickly spotted her talent and started to point out tropical orchids from the collections that included five native Irish species. She became fascinated by the latter and thus began her involvement with Ireland's native orchids. In December 2016, her portrait of *Platystele ovatilabia,* a creeping miniature orchid, the second of two *Platystele* species, appeared in *Curtis's Botanical Magazine*.[35] For the next six growing seasons, the artist devoted her time to depicting all species of the known native orchid genera, around 30 in all. The portraits, accompanied by Brendan Sayers's text, were exhibited in groups of eight at the RHS January shows in London and duly honoured.

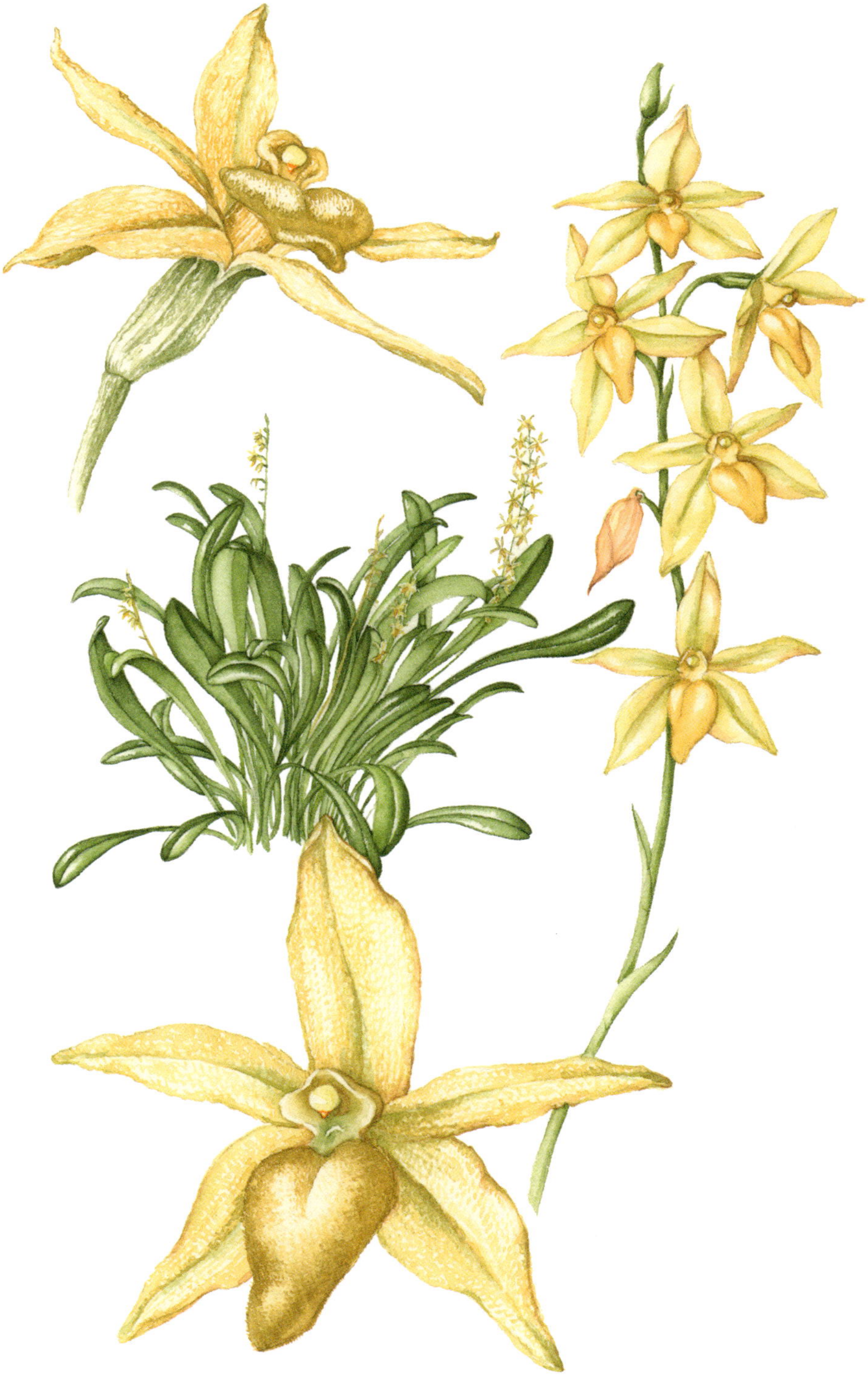

Fig. 104. *Platystele ovatilabia*
Original watercolour by Susan Sex, reproduced in *Curtis's Botanical Magazine*, vol. 33, part 4, plate 849
[© Susan Sex. Royal Botanic Gardens, Kew]

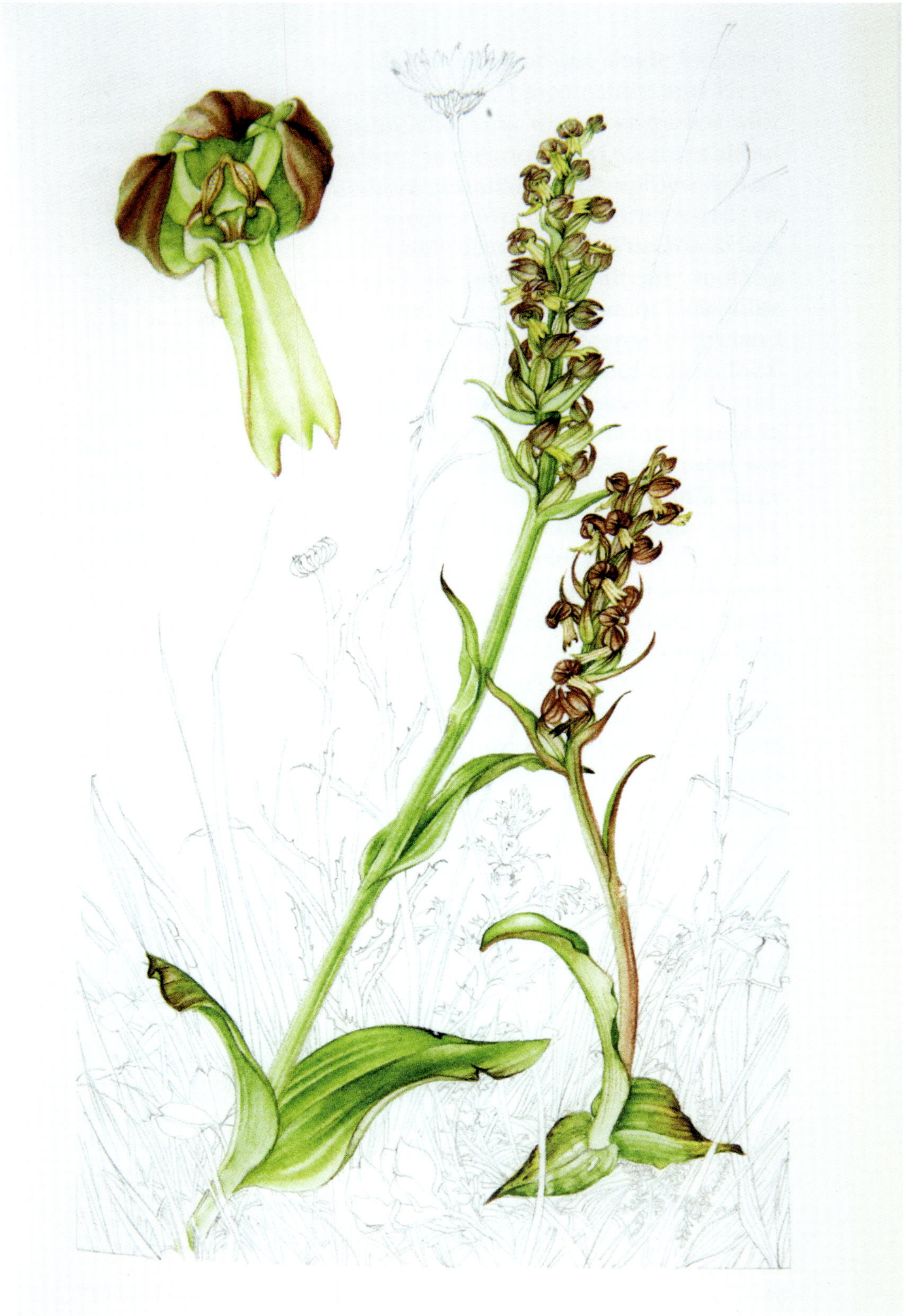

Fig. 105. *Dactylorhiza viridis*
Original watercolour by Susan Sex, reproduced in *Curtis's Botanical Magazine*, vol. 32, part 1, plate 802

The first complete record of Ireland's wild orchids, published as the eponymously titled *Ireland's Wild Orchids* (2004), followed by a smaller, pocket-sized book, *Ireland's Wild Orchids: A Field Guide* (2008), with Sayers responsible for the text and Sex executing the orchid portraits.

In 2014, she was commissioned by RHS Gold Medallist, Billy Alexander, Kells Bay House and Gardens, located on the ring of Kerry, to paint their specialities; southern-hemisphere tree ferns and ground ferns from Australia, New Zealand, South Africa and Chile. 'I commence with a light pencil drawing, no shading or feathered lines, and always, striving for accuracy,' says Sex.

*Then, a first wet-on-wet wash, freely applied, showing light and shaded areas with graduated colour, with any patterns or variations hinted at from the beginning. A second, mostly wet-on-dry, wash follows, with more intense colour, carefully retaining any highlights. When all is dry, small detail, shadows, perhaps a glaze of extra colour are added, and any corrections are made.*

A recipient of the Jill Smythies Award, presented by the Linnean Society, London, Susan Sex also teaches, conducting art courses at the Burren College of Art in Co. Clare each year.

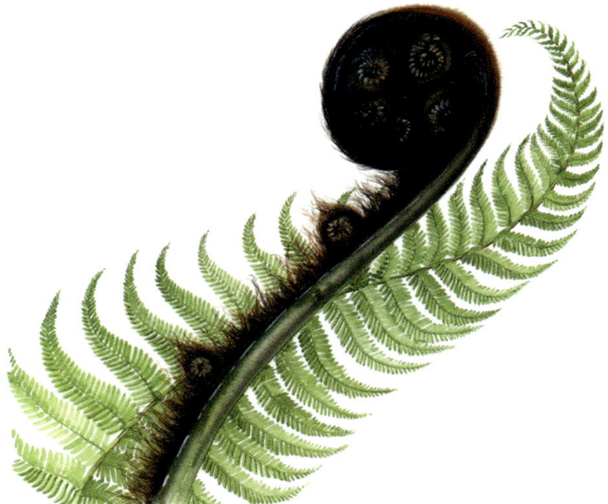

Fig. 106. *Cyanthea medullaris*, black tree fern
Watercolour by Susan Sex
[© Susan Sex. Private collection. Reproduced by kind permission]

# Deborah Lambkin (b.1970, Dublin)

'I sit down and look at it for ages before I do anything ... I look at all the colours and do a few colour tests,'[36] so explains Deborah Lambkin. Her career began not in botanical illustration but rather in the field of visual communications at NCAD. Always interested in plants and gardening, she chose botanical painting as the subject for her final year thesis. Amongst the botanical artists she studied was Dr Wendy Walsh (qv), whom she maintains to have been a consistent source of inspiration and encouragement throughout her career. After her degree, she decided to travel, recording local plants in Central America, India and Europe. In 1994, she joined a Dublin advertising agency, becoming a director. She never abandoned botanical illustration and in her free time completed a number of commissions, including a series on Irish endangered species (1996) for which, in 1997, she was awarded a silver medal. Other commissions included *Chaenomeles* x *superba* 'Rowallane', executed for the National Trust, Northern Ireland (1996) and *Arbutus unedo* (strawberry tree), commissioned by the National Botanic Gardens for a poster commemorating their bicentenary, in 1995.

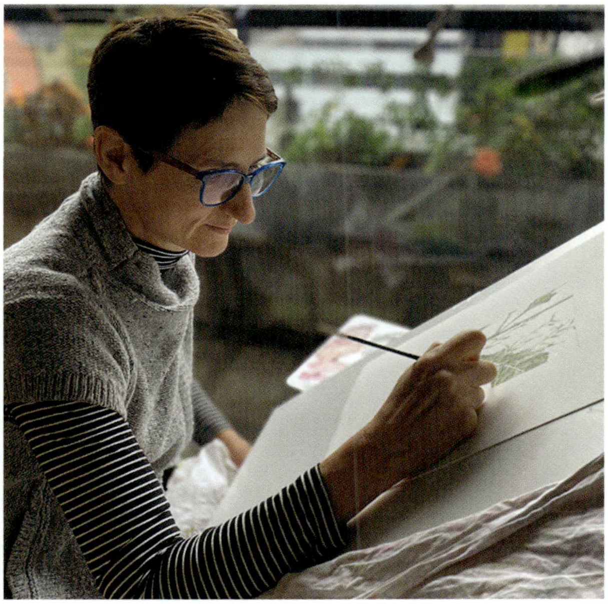

Fig. 107. Botanical artist, Deborah Lambkin at work in her studio, 2019
[Private collection. Reproduced by kind permission]

In 1998, Lambkin decided to concentrate full time on botanical illustration and abandoned her job in advertising. She began working on a series of studies of *Vireya*, a tropical group of rhododendrons[37] that form part of the collections in the restored curvilinear range at the NBG Glasnevin.[38] Her botanical portraits were the first illustrations of the *Vireya* collection, grown at Glasnevin, to be recorded. This led to an exhibition, in May 1998,[39] with 20 of her works being purchased by the NBG Glasnevin, Dublin. This Irish artist has received the Grenfell Silver Medal twice, presented by the RHS (1997, 1998), and in 1999 was awarded its Gold Medal for her plant portrait, *Nerine bowdenii.* Deborah Lambkin has exhibited at the Society of Botanical Art, Westminster Hall,

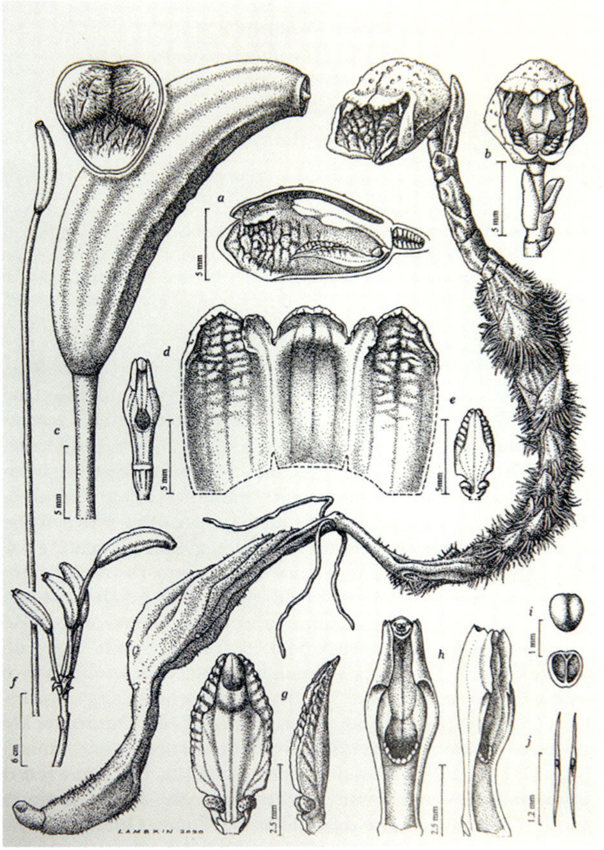

Fig. 108. *Gastrodia agnicellus*
Original watercolour by Deborah Lambkin, reproduced in *Curtis's Botanical Magazine*, vol. 37, no. 3, pp. 385–395. '*A new holomycotrophic orchid from southeast Madagascar...flowering beneath leaf humus*' (Johan Hermans, p. 385).
[© Deborah Lambkin. Courtesy, National Botanic Gardens, Glasnevin, Dublin]

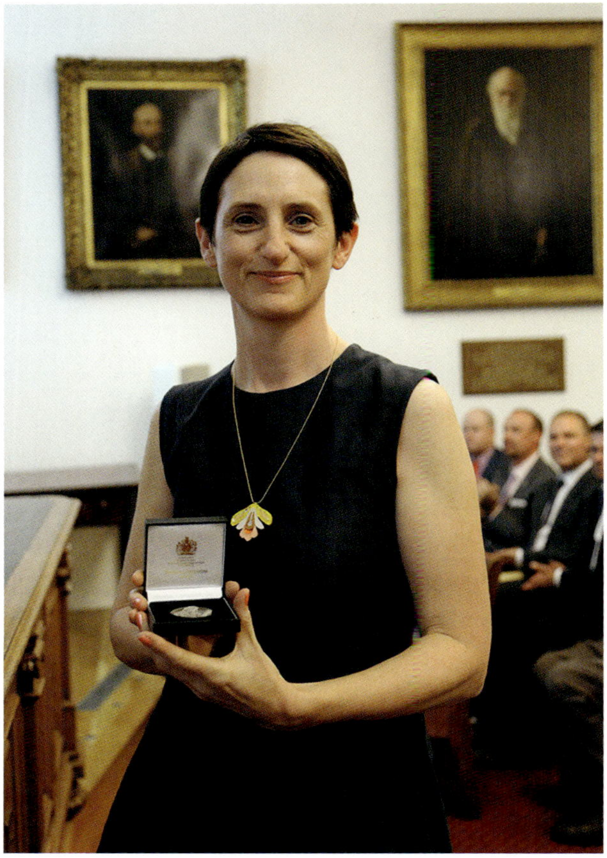

Fig. 109. Deborah Lambkin accepting the Jill Smythies Medal awarded by The Linnean Society, London, May, 2019. The Jill Smythies Medal was established in 1986 by the late Mr B.E. Smythies, FLS in honour of his wife, Florence Mary Smythies ('*Jill*').
[Courtesy, The Linnean Society, Burlington House, London]

London (1994–1996) and in 2005 became the official Orchid Artist for the RHS Orchid Committee. She continues a tradition that began in 1897 when Nellie Roberts, VMM (1879–1959) was appointed as the first Orchid Artist. The orchid portraits are used by the committee for reference when new awards are being made. Composition and style of the orchid portraits is dictated by the committee and always includes colour together with details of form and pattern found on the inflorescence.

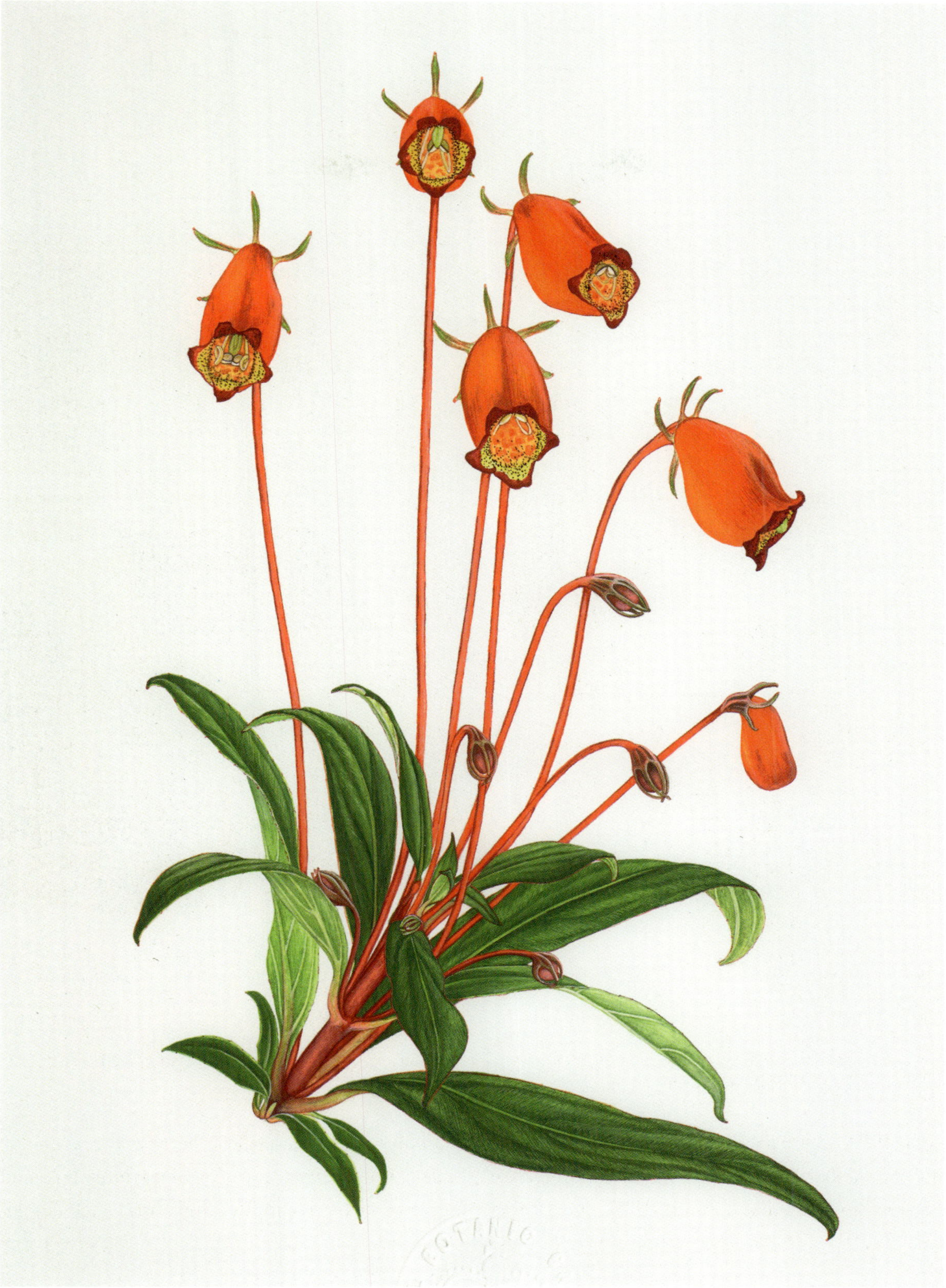

Fig. 110. *Seemannia sylvatica*
Watercolour by Deborah Lambkin, original drawing for *Curtis's Botanical Magazine*, vol. 12, no. 4, plate 278
[© Deborah Lambkin. Royal Botanic Gardens, Kew]

The Linnean Society[40] presented its distinguished Jill Smythies Medal to this gifted artist in 2019. The medal is awarded annually to a botanical illustrator for excellence in publishing botanical illustrations that contribute to plant identification. In 2020, she received the Margaret Flockton Award (presented annually by the Royal Botanic Garden, Sydney) 'for excellence in scientific botanical illustration for her illustration of the new orchid species, *Gastrodia agnicellus*. The latter, a strange, tiny new orchid from Madagascar was painted by Lambkin and appeared in *Curtis's Botanical Magazine* (September 2020).[41]

Lambkin's portraits can take anything from a week upwards to complete, the artist working largely in watercolour and pencil. In the past, she has used gouache:

> *A completely different medium from watercolour. I feel I'm only learning to paint in watercolour now. But one of the things that keeps you interested is that you are learning as you are doing it…I am not a botanist but I've learnt an awful lot about plants as I paint them. Even two different specimens of the same plant can be quite different. There is always more scope for learning.*[42]

# Lynn Stringer

In an interview with Jane Powers,[43] the artist Lynn Stringer spoke about her introduction to botanical art. Having completed a three-year course in fine art at the College of Marketing and Design, Mountjoy Square, Dublin, in the late 1990s, Lynn Stringer attended a series of three week-long summer workshops under the guidance of botanical artist, Susan Sex (qv) between 2005 and 2007:

> *I had come across Susan's book on orchids and was intrigued. Someone told me that she ran courses as part of the Burren College of Art and so in the summer of 2005 a friend and I decided to enrol on one of them....and it was as if a door opened into another world. I fell in love with it, instantly.*

This was followed by a year-long artist's residency at the Vermont Studio Center, the international artists and writers' residency programme in the United States.

Lynn Stringer lives in east Co. Wicklow, her studio located in a low-ceilinged, single-storey stone-built wing of a Victorian farmhouse, where she has lived all her life surrounded by a garden filled with fine specimen trees, shrubs and flowers. A founder member of ISBA, established in 2014, Stringer teaches botanical art, insisting anyone can learn to be proficient:

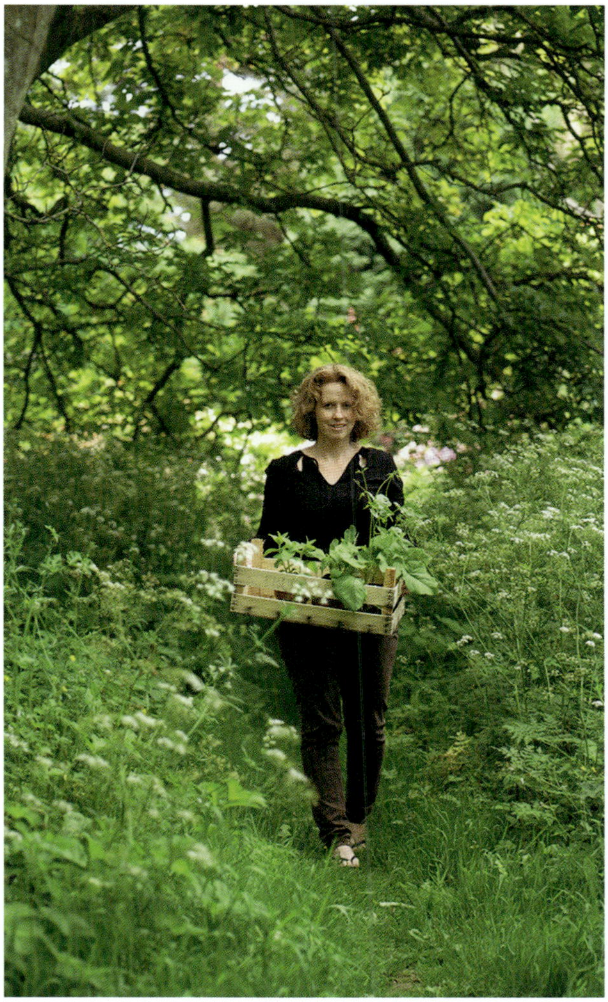

Fig. 111. Botanical artist, Lynn Stringer in her garden, Co. Wicklow
[Photograph: Courtesy of Richard Johnston]

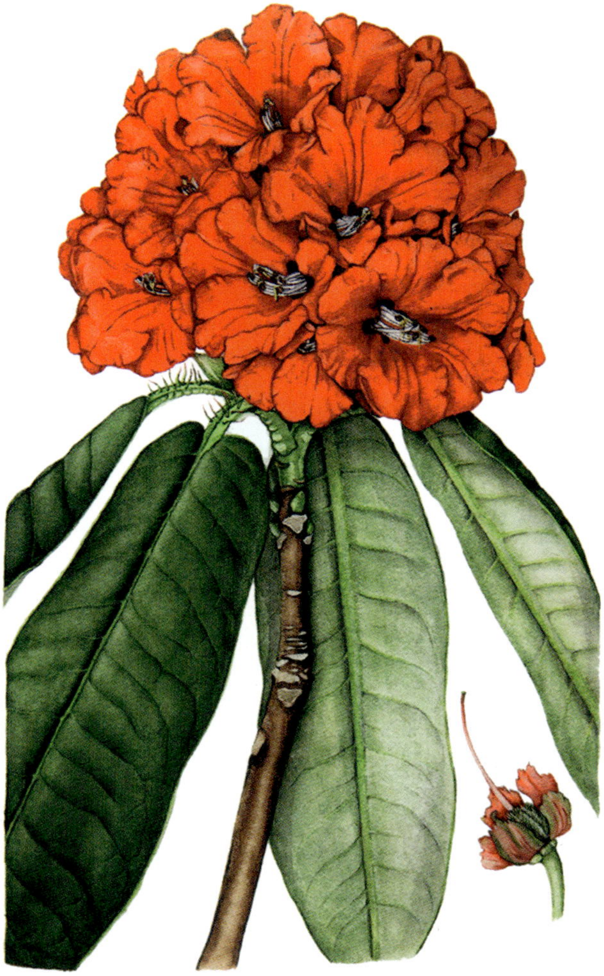

Fig. 112. *Rhododendron barbatum*
Watercolour by Lynn Stringer, reproduced in *Curtis's Botanical Magazine*, vol. 37, no. 2
[© Lynn Stringer. Courtesy, National Botanic Gardens, Glasnevin, Dublin]

*It's about being observant and accurate – even the smallest botanical details need to be correct, whether that's counting the number of petals on a flower, or the way in which the leaves are arranged along a stem...*[44]

The artist has also embarked on a series of plant portraits relating to the NBG Kilmacurragh, Kilbride, Co. Wicklow. Since 2009 and working closely with Seamus O'Brien, Head Gardener, Kilmacurragh, this artist has completed a number of portraits based on plants and shrubs grown in these historic gardens, for example, *Rhododendron grande, Rhododendron* 'Thomas Acton', *Rhododendron falconeri, Rhododendron arboreum and Rhododendron barbatum*. The series, inspired by the gardens at Kilmacurragh, formed the basis for an exhibition held at the NBG, Glasnevin, Dublin in August 2014. The year before, a selection of Stringer's portraits (six), all based on plants and shrubs raised at Kilmacurragh, were awarded a Silver Medal for excellence at the RHS London Botanical Art Exhibition.

As part of the Kilmacurragh series, Stringer was invited to illustrate Seamus O'Brien's text for *Curtis's Botanical Magazine – Aextoxicon punctatum*,[45] a poisonous, evergreen tree. This portrait appeared in June 2012 (part 2). A male specimen, it first flowered in the autumn of 2010 at Kilmacurragh and was described by O'Brien as:

*...native to the sub-Antarctic forests of Chile and Argentina... At Kilmacurragh, its fruits ripen and the end of September and persist on the tree until blossoms open in mid-November. The flowers are scented, though not pleasantly*

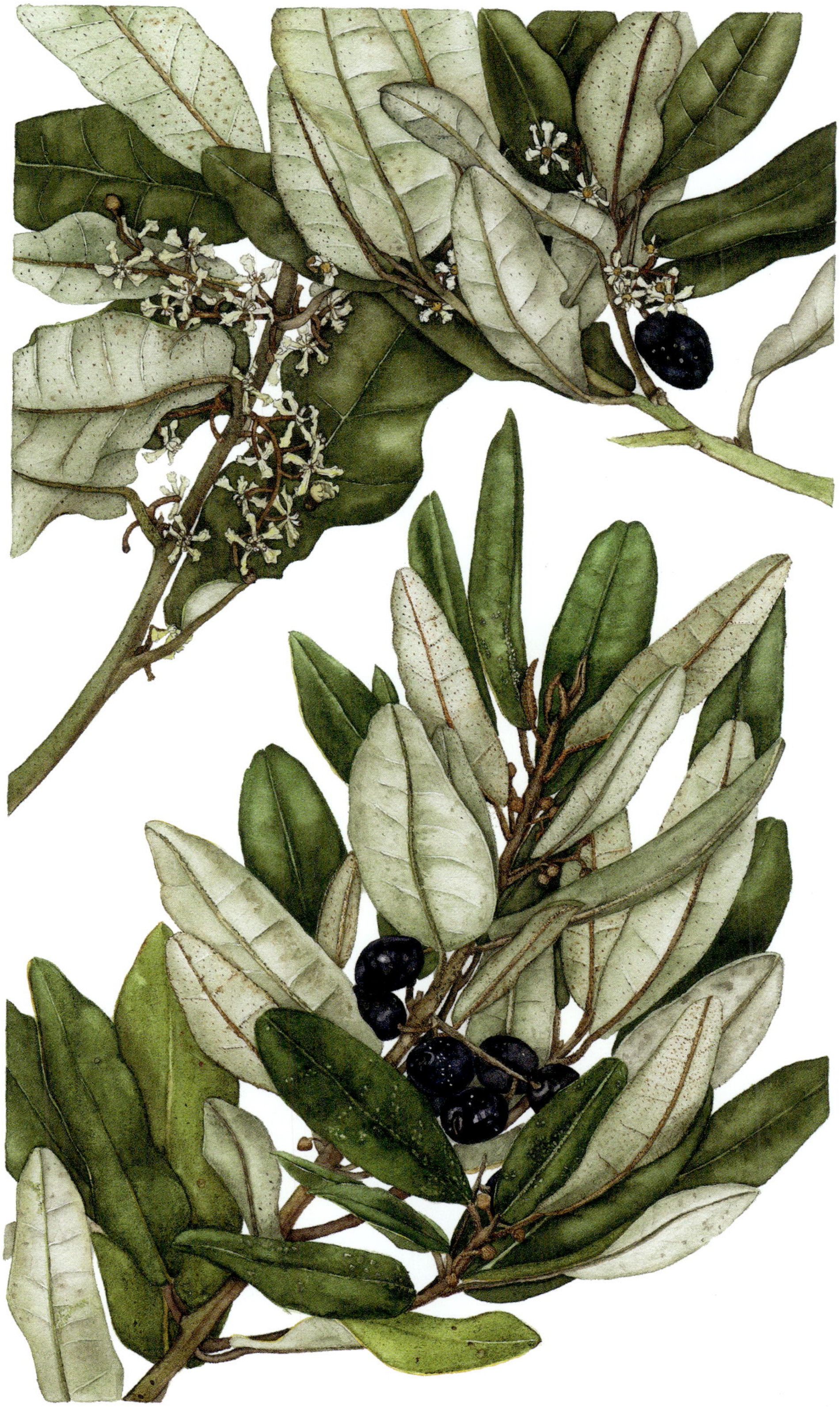

Fig. 113. *Aextoxicon punctatum*
Original watercolour by Lynn Stringer, reproduced in *Curtis's Botanical Magazine*, June 2012, vol. 29, no. 2, tab. 945. '*The olivillo is a poisonous dioecious evergreen tree native to the sub-Antarctic forests of Chile and Argentina. At Kilmacurragh, its fruits ripen at the end of September and persist on the tree until blossoms open in mid-November. The flowers are scented, though not pleasantly so and the waxy, creamy-yellow dentate, claw-like petals when viewed beneath a hand lens are both unusual and attractive. In its native Chile, it is said to be a valuable timber tree and the source of a high-quality timber used in furniture making and interior carpentry.*' (Seamus O'Brien, Head Gardener, National Botanic Gardens, Kilmacurragh, Co. Wicklow, pp. 182–190, 191)
[© Lynn Stringer. Royal Botanic Gardens, Kew]

*so and the waxy, creamy-yellow dentate, claw-like petals when viewed beneath a hand lens are both unusual and attractive. In its native Chile, it is said to be a valuable timber tree and the source of a high-quality timber used in furniture making and interior carpentry.*[46]

A substantial contributor to *Curtis's Botanical Magazine*, Stringer has completed around seven portraits,[47] working both in watercolour and pencil and depicting her portraits life-size. Awarded a Silver Gilt Medal at Bloom Botanical Art, Dublin (2017) and a Gold Medal (2022), she is a founding member of ISBA, a member of the American Society of Botanical Artists and a member of the Water Colour Society of Ireland.

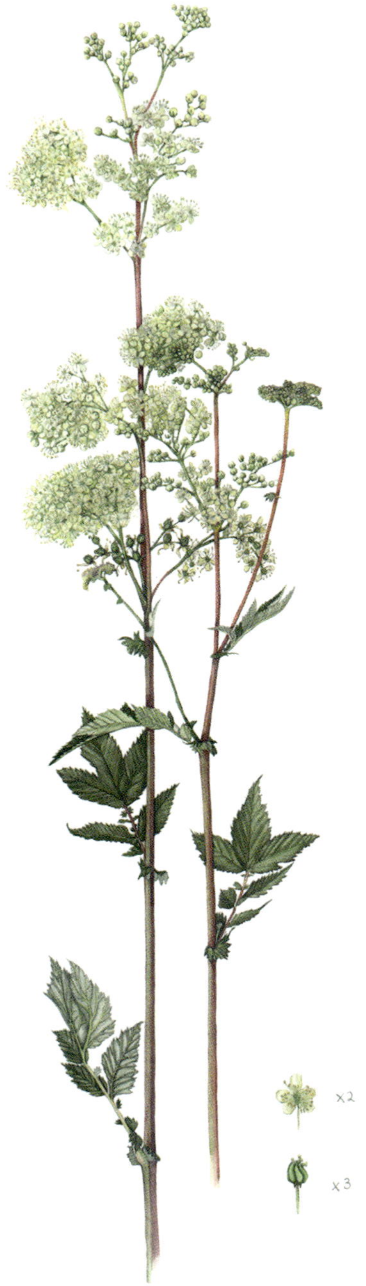


Fig. 114. *Filipendula ulmaria*, meadowsweet or mead wort
Watercolour by Lynn Stringer
[© Lynn Stringer. Private collection. Reproduced by kind permission]

# Chapter 7
# 'A Recorder of Life' – George Victor Du Noyer, MRIA

### (b.1817, Blackrock, Dublin; d.3 January 1869, Co. Antrim)

George Victor Du Noyer made a substantial contribution to botanical illustration and publication during the 19th century. A 'recorder of life', he more than fulfilled that role, becoming a field geologist, palaeontologist, archaeologist, zoological artist and antiquarian.[1]

Du Noyer was born in Blackrock on the outskirts of Dublin in 1817 into a family of Huguenot descent, the first son of Louis Victor Du Noyer (1782–1868), music teacher and Margaret Du Bédat (1794–1876). He was educated in the strict surroundings of the Reverend Jones's seminary 'in Great Denmark Street', and the family moved from Blackrock when the young boy was around 10 years old, to the city. There, his mother ran a school for young ladies from their home in Charlemont Street, while his father taught French. A bright pupil, Du Noyer excelled, needless to say, in French, writing and drawing. His drawing teacher was artist and antiquarian George Petrie, PRHA, LLD (1790–1866), who had trained at the RDS School of Landscape and Ornament.[2] He began to give the young boy lessons at the family's home in Charlemont Street, not only instructing his young pupil in the gentle art of watercolour technique, but also instilling in him an interest in antiquities and archaeology. This was later to reflect itself in Du Noyer's love of recording ancient churches, abbeys and castles, and capturing the Irish landscape, together with vivid scenes of everyday life in Ireland.

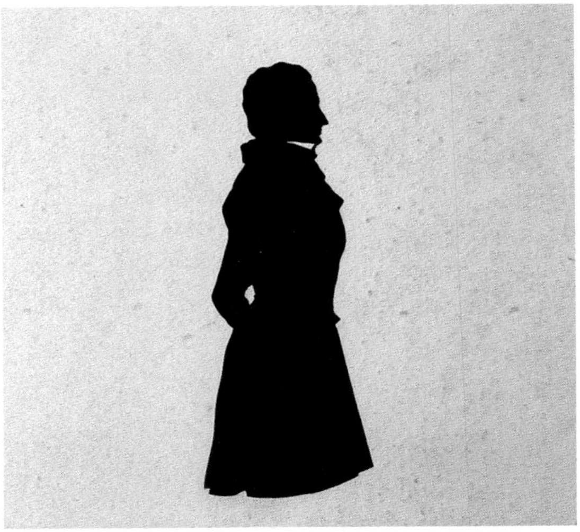

Fig. 115. Silhouette of George Victor Du Noyer
[© Royal Society of Antiquaries of Ireland]

During this period, Petrie was establishing himself as a topographical artist whose easy, graceful style in both

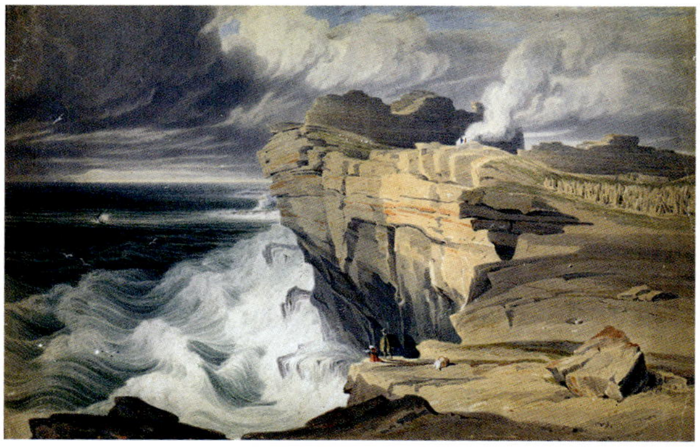

Fig. 116. Dun Aengus fort, Inishmore, Aran Islands
Watercolour by George Petrie, c.1850s
[Photo © National Gallery of Ireland]

watercolour and pencil adapted itself well to the world of book publishing. Later, he was to be appointed head of the Topographical Department (Antiquities division) of the OS of Ireland in 1833 (–1843), which he ran from his home, 21 Great Charles' Street, Dublin.[3] It appears that it was largely due to Petrie's influence that Du Noyer was later invited to join the OSI, aged 18, on 6 April 1835.

As early as 1814, plans for an Irish OS were discussed in the House of Commons and a recommendation made that a survey and valuation of Ireland should be carried out that would include the fields of 'botany, zoology, geology archaeology' and 'productive economy'. In 1824, the Spring Rice Committee recommended to the House of Commons that a survey of Ireland, at a scale of six inches to the mile, would be required to provide a definitive indication of acreages and rateable value for the purpose of establishing local taxes in Ireland.

The Irish OS, under Major Thomas Colby (1784–1852),[4] began work on 22 June 1824 and had completed the world's first large-scale mapping of an entire country by 1846. The work was conducted by specially trained Royal Engineers and Artillery Officers, with men drawn from the ranks of the Royal Sappers and Miners. From the early 1830s, it was agreed the Survey should also include civilians – distinguished Irish scholars, artists and antiquarians such as George Petrie, William Wakeman (1822–1900),[5] John O'Donovan (1806–1861)[6] and 'a labourer in the fields of art and science', George Victor Du Noyer. The botanist attached to the OSI was David Moore (qv), later to be appointed Curator, Royal Dublin Society's Botanic Gardens, Glasnevin (1838). Subjects covered in the natural history area of the Survey included marine algae, fungi (mushrooms, toadstools and others), flowering plants such as studies of the rose family (*Rosaceae*); also brambles, blackberries (*Rubus*), wild dog roses (*Rosa*) and apples (*Malus*).

Du Noyer's association with the Survey (orthography section) began on 6 April 1835 as a civilian assistant, where his drawing skills quickly began to attract the attention of his employers. This is reflected in his salary which, in 1835, was increased from 2*s* 6*d* a day in May of that year to 4*s* per day by September.[7] By the end of that year, Du Noyer was no longer employed in the orthography section but had left to join the geological and trigonometric division branch of the Survey,[8] led by Captain Joseph Ellison Portlock (1794–1864),[9] the aim of the team being to record the geology in the

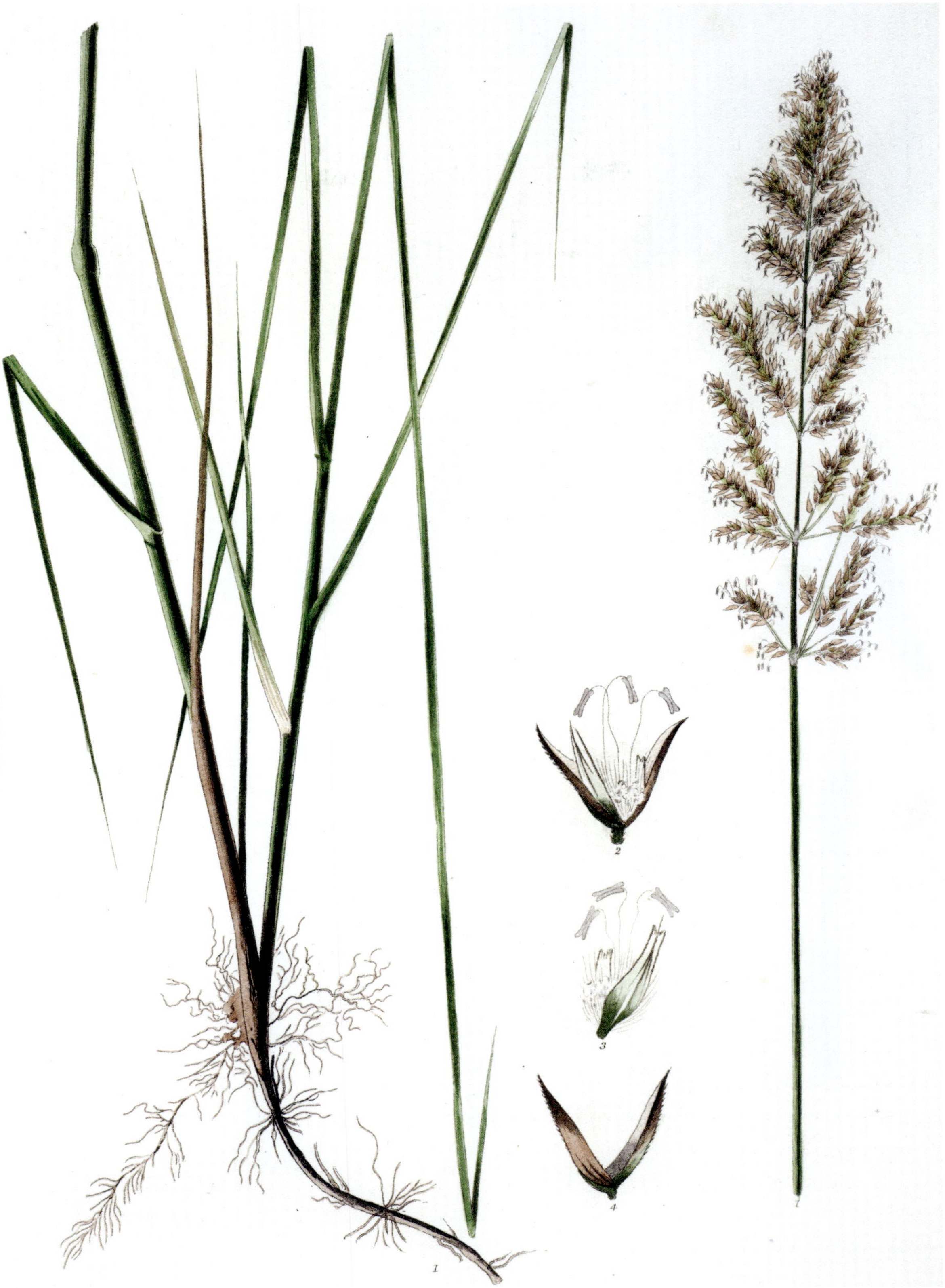

Fig. 117. *Calamagrostis lapponica*, narrow small-reed
Original watercolour by George Victor Du Noyer. Engraving from *The Templemore Memoir* (Appendix, 2nd ed., Dublin, 1837), plate 4
[Courtesy, National Library of Ireland]

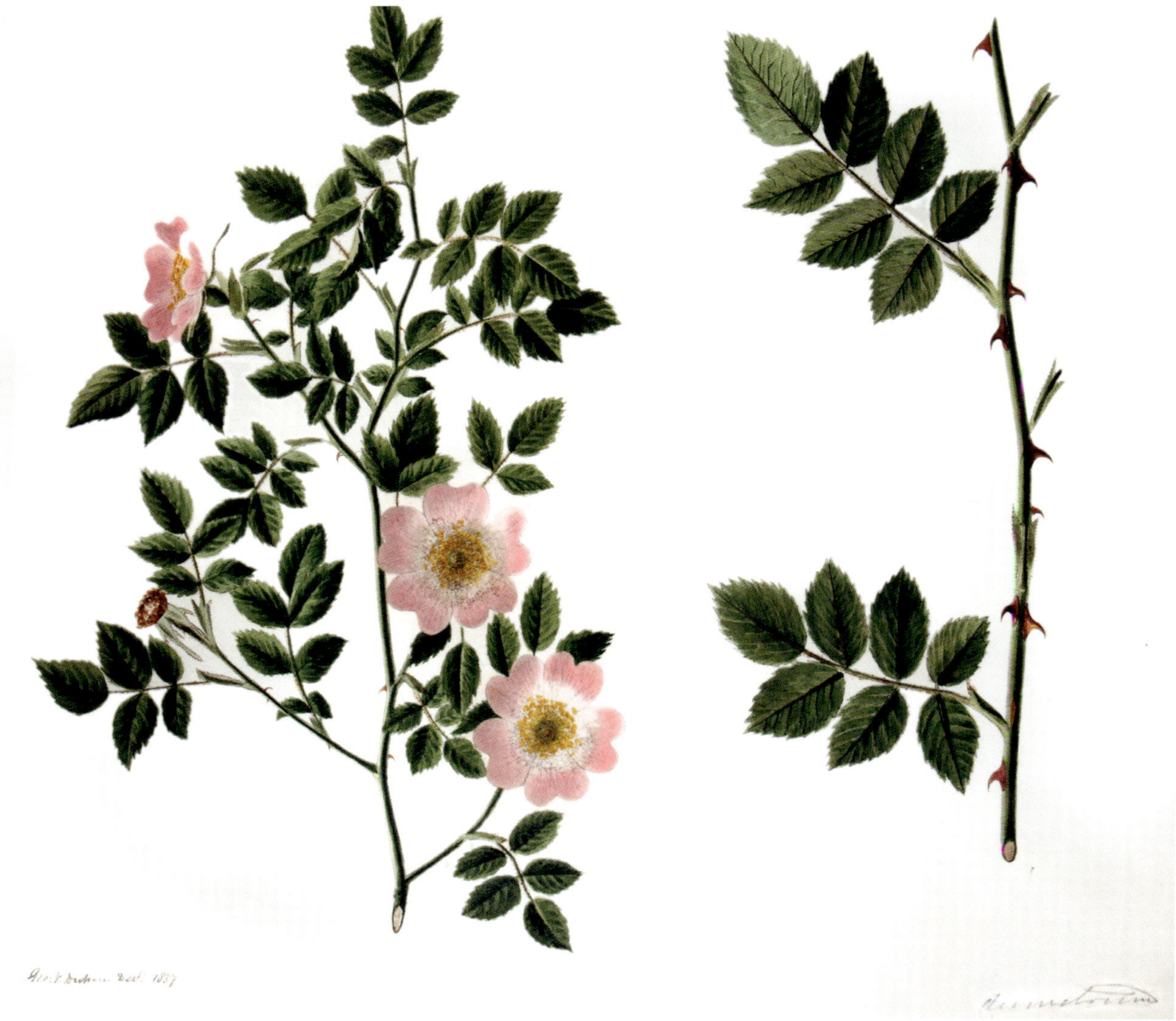

Fig. 118. *Rosa* x *dumetorum*
Watercolour by George Victor Du Noyer, inscribed (lower left) '*Geo. V. Du Noyer 1837*', (lower right) '*dumetorum*'
[Courtesy, National Botanic Gardens, Glasnevin, Dublin]

field. Du Noyer was to remain with them until the end of his working period with the Survey.

It would appear that, throughout Du Noyer's term attached to this particular division, Portlock thought highly of the young man's artistic skills and employed him to execute a wide range of subject matter, both in the office and in the field.[10] Evidence is to be found in progress reports submitted by Portlock, which indicate the tasks Du Noyer was engaged in: 'examining, classifying, arranging, drawing and setting up objects of natural history'.[11] The previous month, November 1837, the young artist was busy executing:

> *drawings of three specimens of fish, three of trilobites, three of zoophytes, two varieties of apples, arranging specimens of recent and fossil crustacea, and also arranging and labelling rocks.*[12]

It is evident from correspondence at Kew that when it came to botany, Du Noyer was following a clear course of direction laid down by botanist David Moore (qv), rather than conducting a random survey. This first comes to light in a letter by Moore to Sir William Jackson Hooker, Professor of Botany, University of Glasgow, dated 18 October 1837, in which Moore would appear to have encouraged Du Noyer to concentrate on various species of *Rubus* and *Rosa*, particularly the latter:

> [Rosa] *will form an interesting feature of the botanical section of the book. We have given portions of root shoots along with each species where such formed any very essential part of their character.*[13]

In earlier correspondence (letter of 9 October 1837) exchanged between the two men, Moore expressed his belief that Du Noyer had not practised as a botanical artist and that there was no qualified botanist to supervise the artist's work.[14]

Despite these difficulties, and as a member of the geological and trigonometric division of the Survey, Du Noyer worked hard six days a week and frequently in difficult weather conditions. Both he and Moore appear to have worked well together; Moore, in particular, making two outstanding discoveries – the grass, *Calamagrostis stricta* (as *Calamagrostis lapponica*) (Figure 117) and the sedge, *Carex buxbaumii* (Figure 119), which he found growing on the shores of Lough Neagh. Both were later to appear (as lithographs) in the second edition of the publication, *Templemore Memoir* (1837).

The artist's earliest known plant portraits date from 1836. All carry a high degree of technical and artistic excellence, with meticulous attention being paid to texture and detail. In his series of roses found in Western Europe, depicted in watercolour and in this particular case, collected in Co. Antrim in 1836/37, Du Noyer's ability to convey accurate colour is well displayed in his portrait of *Rosa* x *dumetorum* (Figure 118). The botanical detail is treated with great care and the subject is drawn life-size. The artist would appear to have shown a reluctance to name any of the species or localities, with the possible exception of *Orobanche alba.* Several of his studies in this section appear to be preliminary sketches for final work.[15]

In the 1830s, the Survey had considered the idea of issuing a memoir descriptive of each parish in Ireland, around 2,400 parishes in all. In the event, and largely due to financial constraints, only two publications appeared: *The Templemore Memoir...* (Dublin, 1837), devoted to the parish of Templemore, Co. Londonderry,[16] and a report on the geology of Co. Londonderry, published in 1843.[17]

The *Memoir* itself contained no botanical illustrations but in an appendix attached to the second edition (1837), entitled 'Notices', eight pages were devoted to both botanical and geological illustrations executed by Du Noyer.[18] It is obvious from the artist's work with David Moore that his knowledge and understanding of plant life deepened, as can be clearly seen from these remarkable studies, which include four examples of plant species – *Calamagrostis lapponica, Carex buxbaumii, Polysiphonia atropurpurea* (*Vertebrata fucoides*) (Figure 123) and *Vertebrata fucoides.* Originally executed in watercolour, they possess a high degree of technical skill, showing Du Noyer's awareness and appreciation of natural forms. Both form and colour are true. Strict botanical details have been adhered to, with no attempt at embellishment and, as always, a feeling for texture is meticulously conveyed. All are depicted life-size.

The process of translating Du Noyer's image from plant portrait into print format was carried out by a number of engravers: J. Duncan, J.J. Macaulay, W. Archibald and G. McCoy. The finished plates are superb, with clear, fine lines being carefully inked prior to being printed by Graisbury of Dublin. The final stage of colouring by hand was helped by Du Noyer's careful annotations for the colourist, seen, for example, in his study of *Calamagrostis lapponica* (Figure 117).

Du Noyer's contributions were extraordinarily wide-ranging and included the areas of fungi (Figure 120) and apple portraits (Figure 121). Due to their ripe condition, the latter were probably executed by the artist in the autumn of that year and are depicted with a high degree of realism and accuracy that includes blemishes and scabs. None are believed to be of Irish origin, although the folio is entitled 'Irish Apples Collected at Belfast in 1837'.

The artist's fungi series indicates a diverse range of dates, 1837–1839, and was painted after the resignation of David Moore from the Survey, following his appointment as curator of the RDS's BG Glasnevin, Dublin. There would appear to be little taxonomic purpose behind the arrangement of each individual fungi drawn on the separate sheets, the species of individual genera not being grouped together.

During this period, it is interesting to note that a new Geological Survey Office in Belfast had opened (1837) under the command of Captain Portlock (see

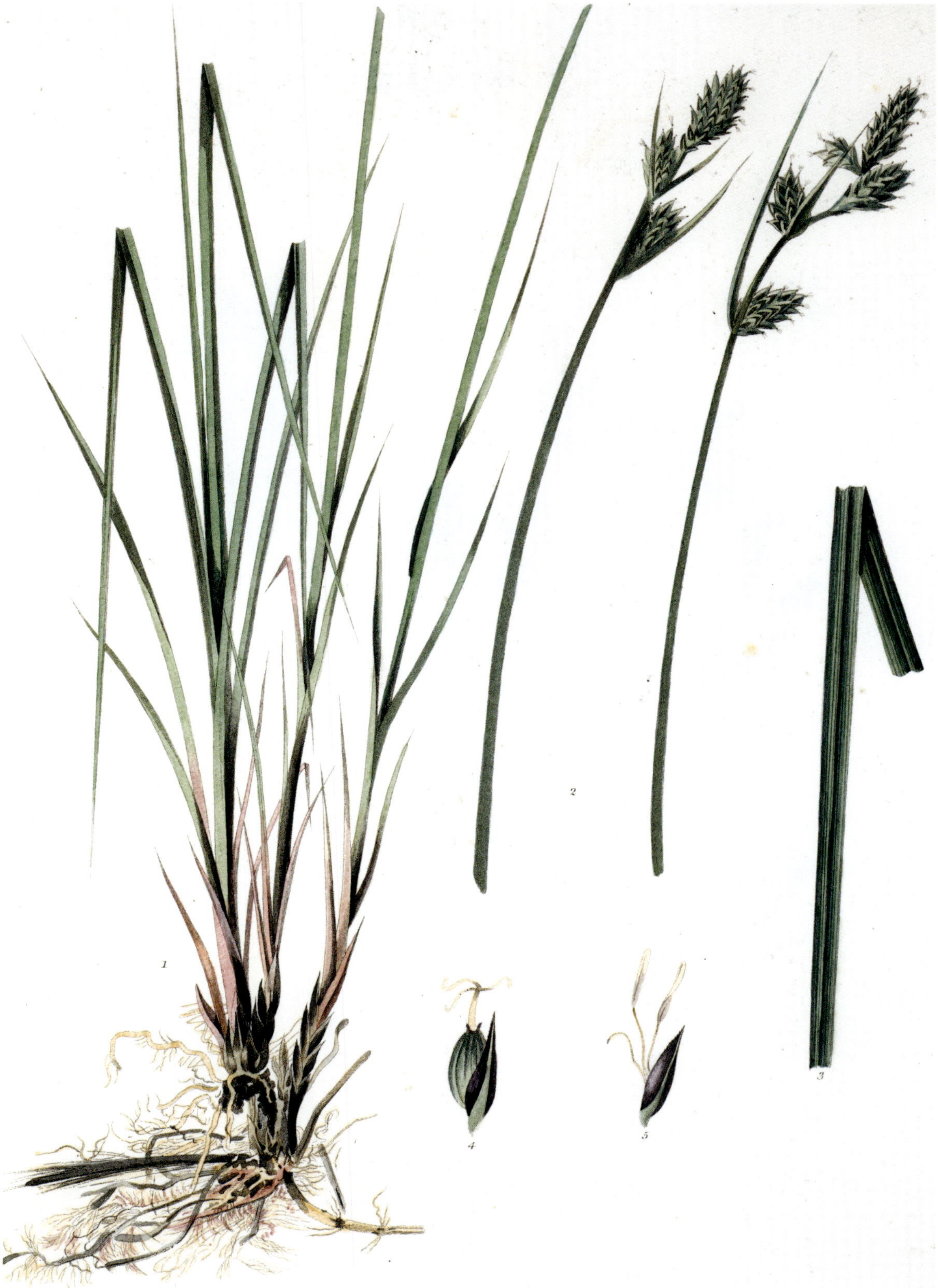


Fig. 119. *Carex buxbaumii*
Original watercolour by George Victor Du Noyer, MRIA (1817–1869), engraving by G. McCoy, from *The Templemore Memoir* (Appendix, 2nd ed., Dublin, 1837), plate 5. Found by David Moore (1808–1879) growing on the shores of Lough Neagh.
[Courtesy, National Botanic Gardens, Glasnevin, Dublin]

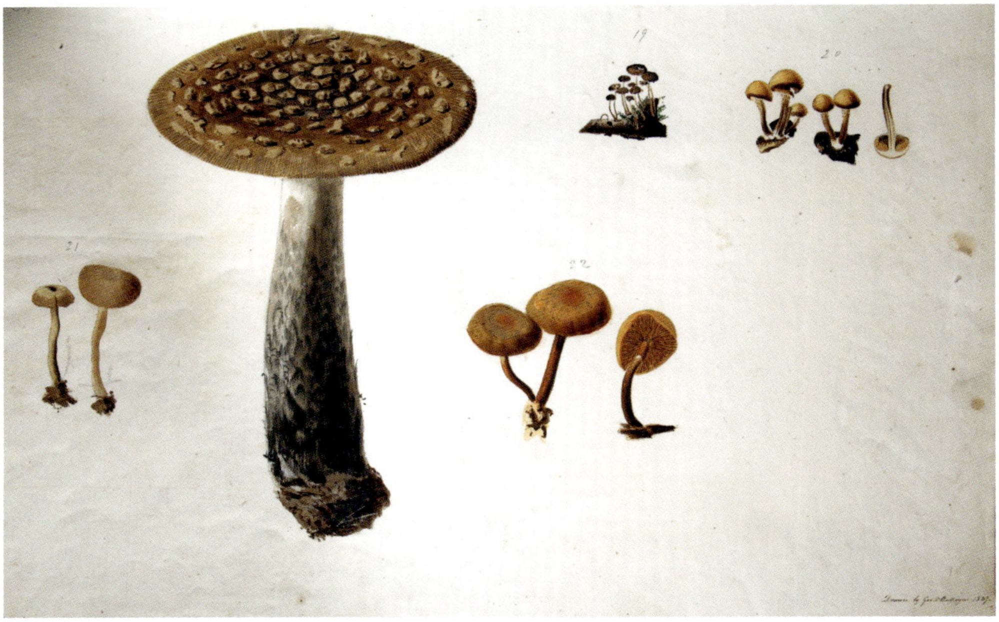

Fig. 120. Fungi
Watercolour and pencil drawing by George Victor Du Noyer, signed (bottom right) '*Drawn by Geo V Du Noyer 1837*'
[Courtesy, National Botanic Gardens, Glasnevin, Dublin]

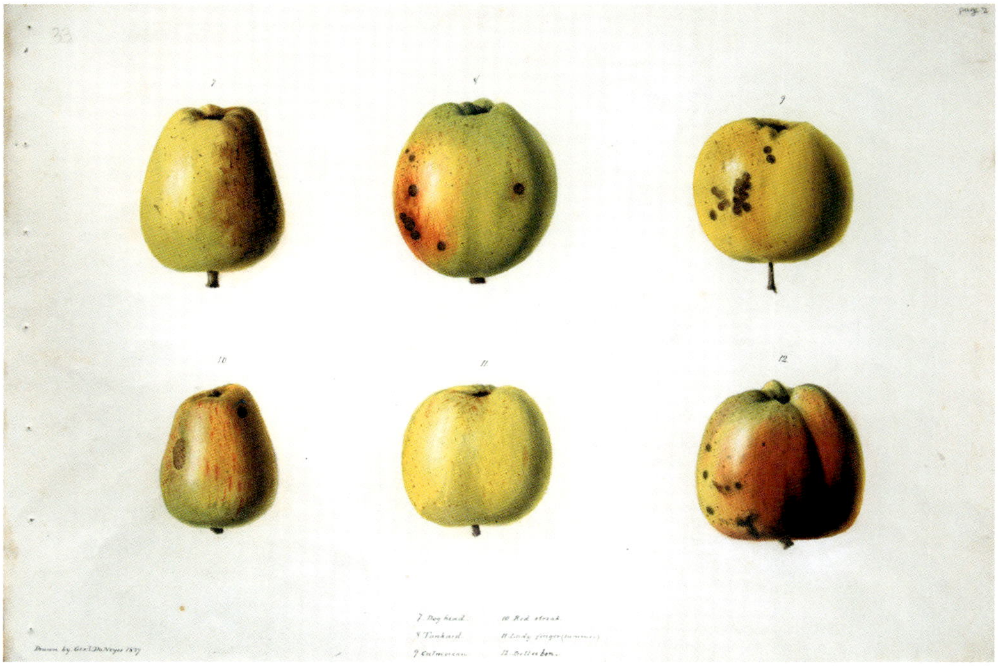

Fig. 121. A collection of apples
Watercolour by George Victor Du Noyer, inscription (in pencil): '*7. Dog head; 8. Tankard. 9. Culmorian; 10. Red Streak; 11. Lady finger (summer); 12. Bell et bon*'
[Courtesy, National Botanic Gardens, Glasnevin, Dublin]

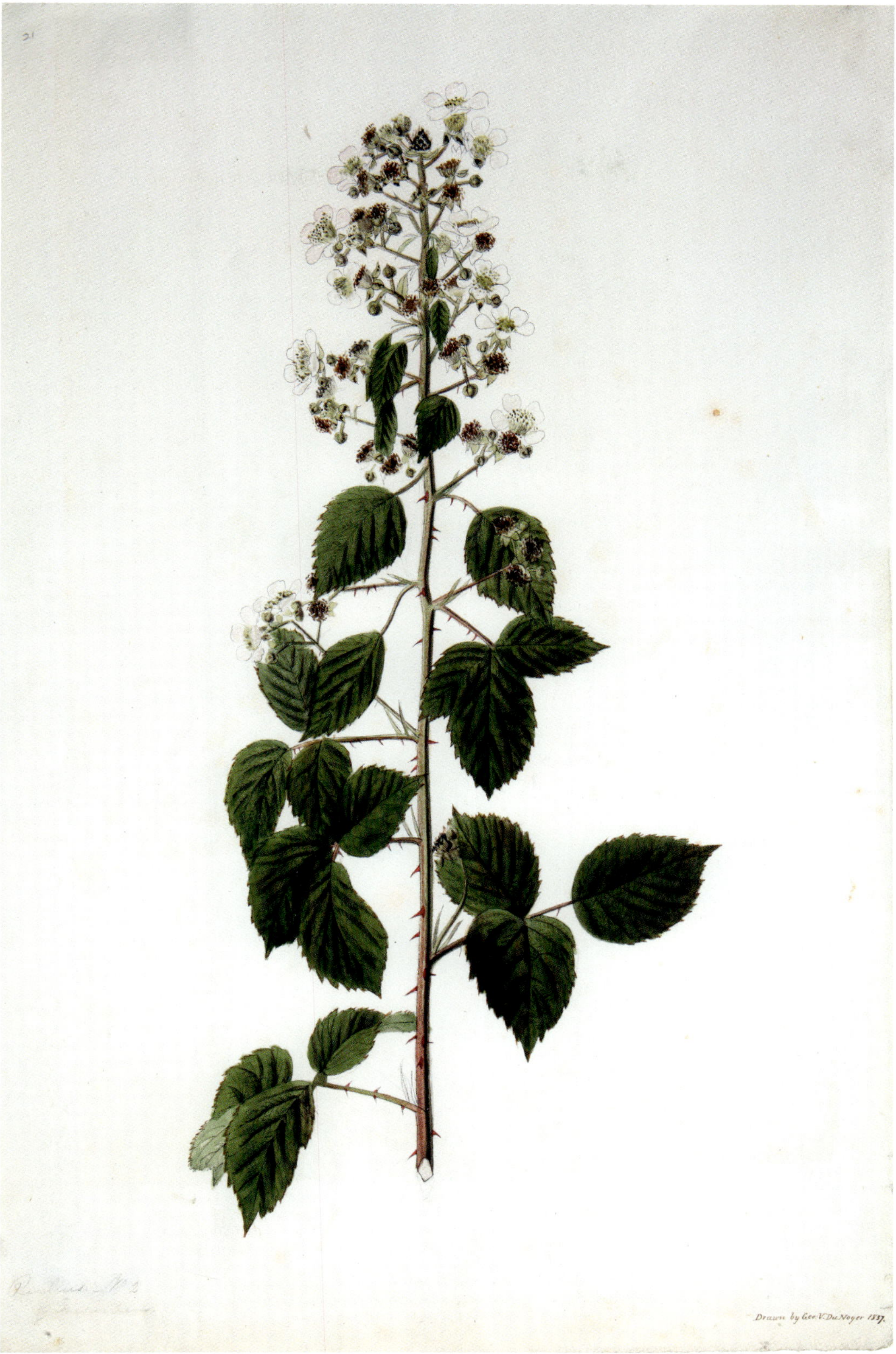

Fig. 122. *Rubus fruiticosus*
Watercolour and ink by George Victor Du Noyer, 1837, signed (bottom right, in brown ink) '*Drawn by Geo V Du Noyer 1837*', (bottom left, in pencil) '*Rubus No.2*'
[Courtesy, National Botanic Gardens, Glasnevin, Dublin]

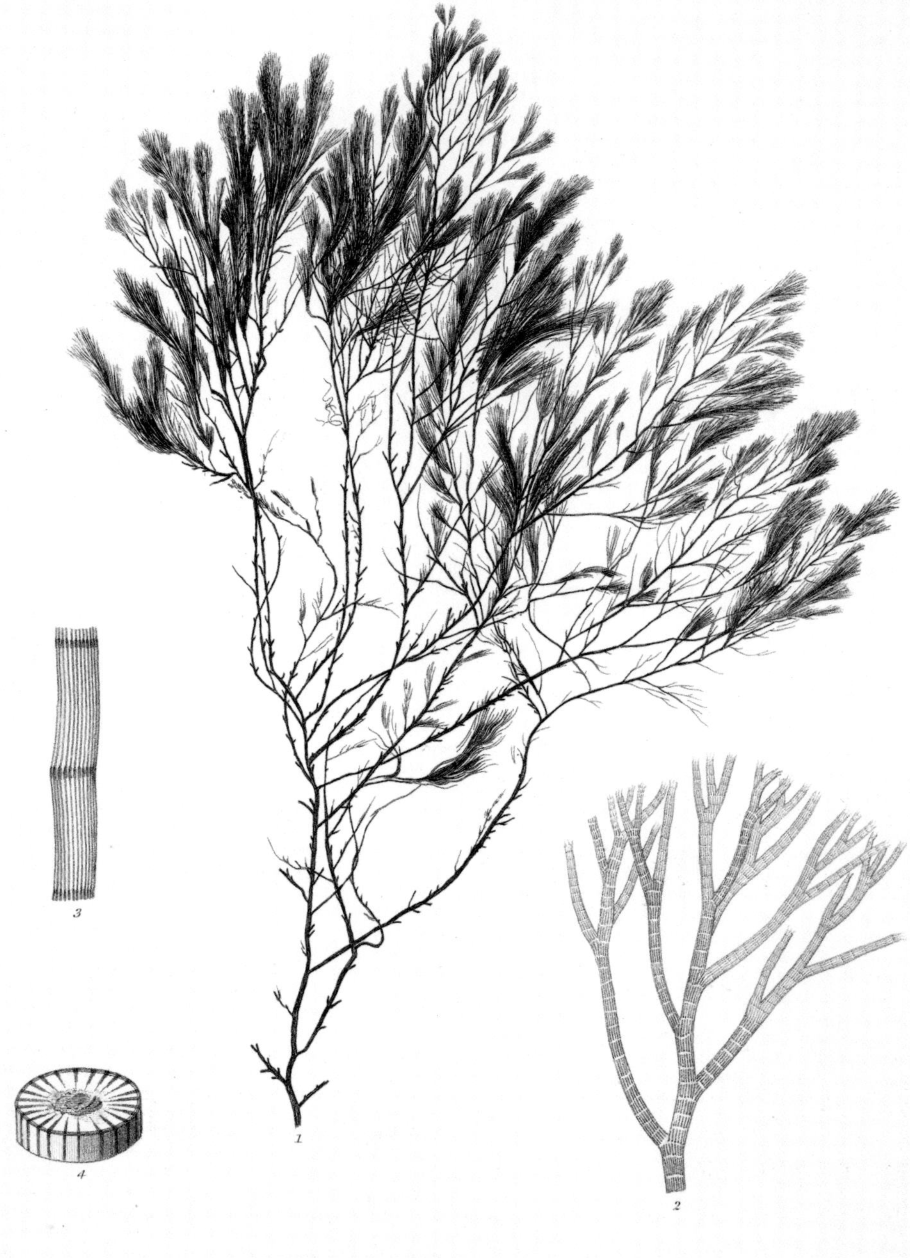


Fig. 123. *Polysiphonia atropurpurea* (*Vertebrata fucoides*)
Original watercolour by George Victor Noyer. Engraving from *The Templemore Memoir* (Appendix, 2nd ed., Dublin, 1837), plate 6
[Courtesy, National Library of Ireland]

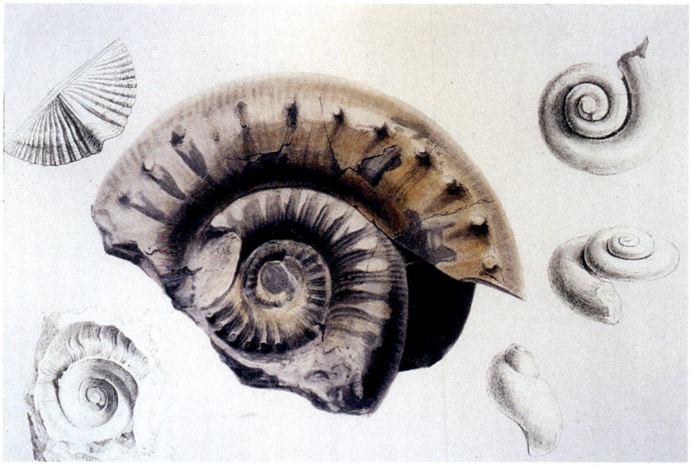

Fig. 124. Fossil
Drawing by George Victor Du Noyer. Colour lithograph from *Report on the Geology of the County of Londonderry and Parts of Tyrone and Fermanagh by Joseph Ellison Portlock* (Dublin: HMSO, 1843)
[Private collection. Reproduced by kind permission]

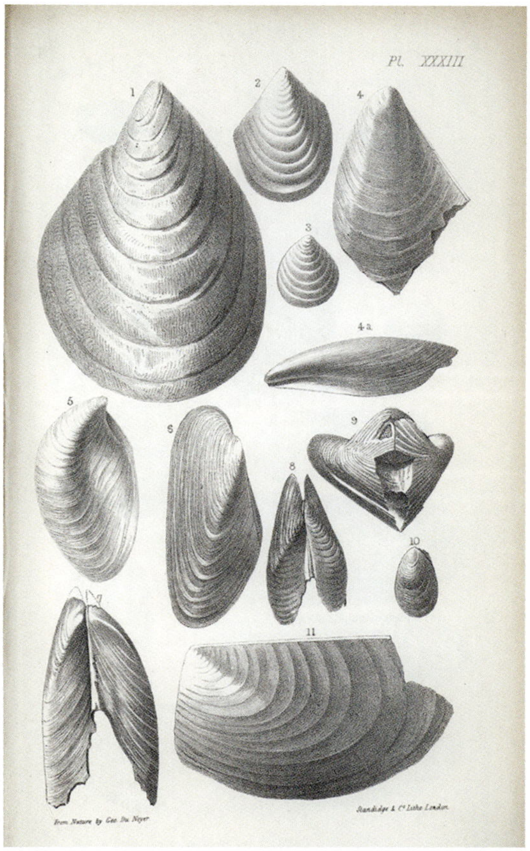


Fig. 125. A collection of shells drawn *'From Nature by Geo Du Noyer'*
Lithograph, from *Report on the Geology of the County of Londonderry and Parts of Tyrone and Fermanagh by Joseph Ellison Portlock* (Dublin: HMSO, 1843), plate 33.
[Courtesy, National Library of Ireland]

below). This included a soils laboratory, a museum, botanical and zoological departments and a statistical bureau, with a total staff of around 35. Among the eight civilian geologists employed was Du Noyer.

Du Noyer's range of subject matter was extended further when he worked on the preparation of Portlock's *Report on the Geology of the County of Londonderry and Parts of Tyrone and Fermanagh*, published in 1843 by the OSI,[19] and still recognised today as one of the classic studies in the development of Irish geology. The original 38 watercolours, all executed by Du Noyer, comprised many illustrations of fossils. For publication, the artist, with the assistance of an engraver, printer and colourist, translated his watercolours into lithographic form.

By 1840, due to rising costs, the geological division was in crisis and Du Noyer was moved to the orthography branch, working under Petrie. In July 1840, his 'employment [within the geological department] was suspended'.[20]

From September,1840, Du Noyer continued to work in the field but began to realise the divisions in which he had been employed were becoming depopulated and he would have to find an alternative.

Therefore, the artist began to raise his profile as an illustrator supplying sketches (Holy Cross Abbey and Cahir Castle) for the *Irish Penny Journal*, of which Petrie was editor.[21] Between 1841 and 1843, Du Noyer also submitted a number of topographical illustrations to such publications as Hall's *Ireland: Its Scenery and Character*[22] and *Picturesque Ireland.*[23] He also began exhibiting straightforward, topographical landscapes at the RHA (1841–1863), a total of 48 paintings. By February 1842, Du Noyer's employment with the OS had come to an end.[24]

For almost two years, Du Noyer worked as a freelance artist and illustrator but in March 1844, he was appointed drawing master attached to the newly founded St Columba's College (1843), located in Stackallan House, Navan, Co. Meath, a post he occupied until December the following year.

During this period, Du Noyer was becoming part of the community of antiquarians in Dublin, as reflected in his watercolours submitted to the RHA, for example 'Dunmore Castle on the Boyne near Navan' (1844).

He also played a leading role in the Geological Society of Ireland's activities and became a member on 20 November 1843. A year later, he was elected a member of council. Always regarded as an outstanding artist, it would appear that Du Noyer wanted to push the boundaries further and he began presenting his original research revealed in a paper relating to the geology of west Clare, which he read at the Society's Dublin meeting in 1846.

The Geological Survey of Great Britain and Ireland, based in London, was founded in May 1845. Two years later, Du Noyer joined its ranks. There he was to remain for the rest of his life. As a geologist 'on special service', his task was to record and map geological sections that were exposed as a direct result of railway construction taking place around Dublin and in counties Waterford, Cork, Kerry and Wexford. In April 1849, he was appointed assistant geologist with the Survey and as a permanent member of staff, succeeded in completing six-inch-to-the-mile geological field-sheets for 'reduction' to one inch to the mile, publishing not only maps, but drawings and watercolours of coastal scenes, rockscapes and geological features. His handsome, attractive field-sheets are preserved in the archives of the GSI and are looked upon today as an invaluable inventory of geological information. In May 1867, Du Noyer was promoted to senior geologist.

An active member of the Natural History Society of Ireland, he was elected a member of council in 1849. On 14 August 1857, he became a member of the Royal Irish Academy[25] and a life member, 1863. From c.1841, the RIA had begun purchasing archaeology drawings from this artist.[26] Du Noyer, realising the importance of his work in the field of archaeology, landscape and antiquities, presented 11 folios of

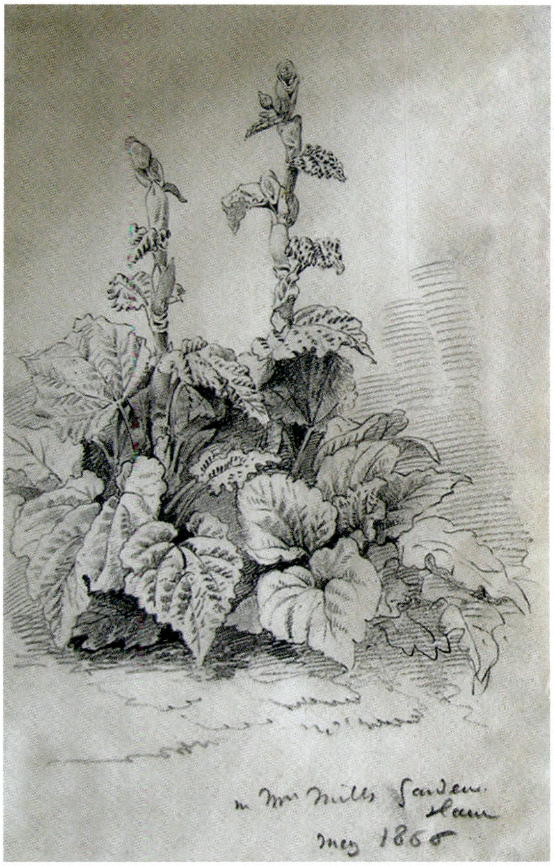

Fig. 126. *'In Mr. Mills Garden Slane, May 1866'*
Pencil drawing by George Victor Du Noyer
[© Royal Society of Antiquaries of Ireland]

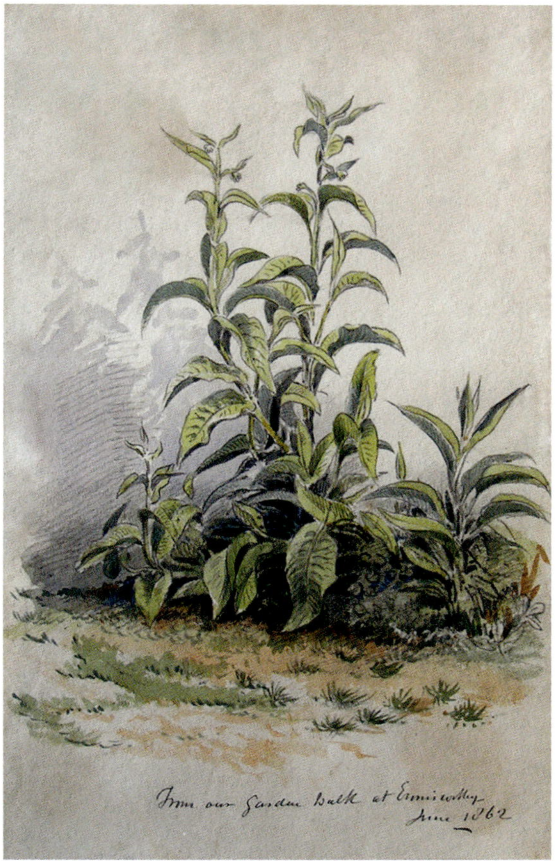

Fig. 127. *'From our Garden Walk at Enniscorthy, June 1862'*
George Victor Du Noyer
Watercolour and ink
[© Royal Society of Antiquaries of Ireland]

drawings and sketches to the RIA between the years 1859 and 1863.[27]

In January 1858, the artist married, in St Mary's Church, Donnybrook, Dublin,[28] Frances Adelaide du Bédat (1833–1914), daughter of William du Bédat, who was employed as transfer officer by the Bank of Ireland, and his wife, Mary Allee. They had five children, William Victor, Fanny, Charlotte Eugenie and twins, Henry Westropp and Joseph Du Bédat.

In 1850, Joseph Beete Jukes (1811–1869) was appointed director of the GSI in place of Thomas Oldham, who had left to take up an appointment

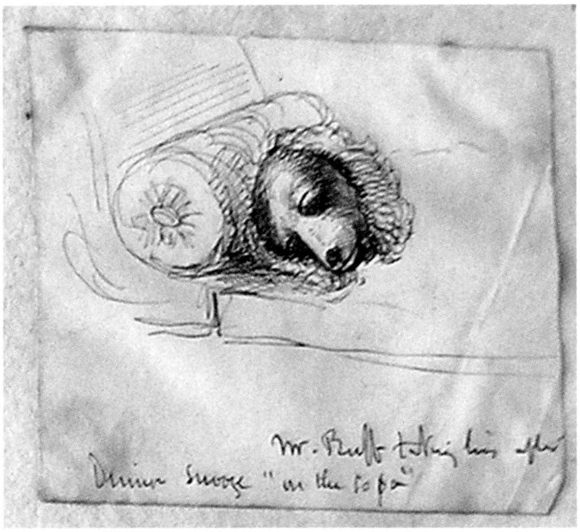


Fig. 128. *'Mr Buff taking his afternoon snooze on the sofa'*
Pencil drawing by George Victor Du Noyer
Mr Buff was a constant and faithful companion throughout Du Noyer's travels.
[© Royal Society of Antiquaries of Ireland]

with the Geological Survey of India.[29] Always acutely conscious of being an 'artist' of architecture, antiquities and archaeology, rather than a fully fledged geologist specialising in the study of rock formations, Du Noyer appeared conscious of his own limitations in this field. This fact was not lost on Jukes, who remarked at the beginning of his appointment in Ireland:

> *Our fellows here seem all good fellows, as good as on the English survey, but sometimes they do astound me not a little and then that leaves an uncomfortable feeling afterwards.*[30]

Du Noyer, despite possessing reservations about his own limitations as a geologist, was appointed by the GSI as its first Irish District Surveyor, in April 1867. As a result, he and his family moved to Carrickfergus, Co. Antrim. Always acutely aware of the historical importance of his work, the artist continued to record archaeological and geological sites, thus providing a vital record of what had been destroyed.

In late December 1868, while on survey in Co. Antrim, and based at his field-station in Antrim town, the family began to suffer from scarlet fever. George Victor Du Noyer died on 3 January 1869, aged 52. The day before, his daughter, Fanny had passed away from the same disease. They were buried together in the graveyard of All Saints' Church, Antrim town, on the same day, 4 January 1869. Following his premature death, his widow, Frances, received no financial support, despite the efforts of leading members of the Geological Survey and scientific community. As a result, the family was left in severe financial difficulties.

A superb 'recorder of life', and always describing himself somewhat modestly as 'a labourer in the field of science', Du Noyer had achieved his aim to be looked upon not only as an artist but also as a 'geologist'. As his biographer, Petra Coffey commented, Du Noyer had:

> *no formal academic or military training in the days when those were essential for advancement, his achievements were overlooked and credit sometimes went to another. His unambitious and modest attitude allowed his work to go unrecognised and only lately has the extent and breadth of his work been acknowledged.*[31]

# Chapter 8
# 'The Fair Discoverers' – Women Botanical Illustrators and Naturalists

In 19th-century Ireland, as elsewhere, the sciences, until around the 1880s tended to be male-dominated. Women's contributions to research in the fields of botanical illustration were largely ignored, the subject being looked upon as a leisure pursuit and their efforts going largely unrecorded. If fortunate enough to come from either an aristocratic or professional family, a young lady's passion for this particular branch of the natural sciences could be nurtured at home, many being fortunate enough to possess outstanding libraries and collections drawn from the natural world.[1]

While boys were encouraged to progress to university, their female counterparts were usually educated at home, often under the eagle eye of a governess, who channelled their curiosity towards the 'polite' subjects. The ideal of femininity was produced and promoted through activities such as music, painting and needlework,[2] with women's botanical interests always being underlined and governed by gendered beliefs that they should adhere to their role as wives and mothers. There was no doubt, in the realm of science, that the 19th century was decidedly male-dominated.

Almost on a consistent basis, the 'fair discoverers' found that their artistic activities equated to their emerging femininity. Unable to nurture 'unnatural' ambitions such as membership of a university, women had to conform to the strict ideals of their sex laid down by society. Acceptance by the latter was relatively straightforward if confined to 'feminine' and fashionable subjects that included botany, so long as home, family, the domestic scene (considered to be their natural habitat), marriage and motherhood remained their eventual goal.

From c.1830, botany and natural history in Ireland and abroad began to possess a more modern profile as a science and became accepted and integrated into the daily round of upper- and middle-class women. Both subjects were looked upon as 'respectable' pursuits, where knowledge, based on observation and close familiarity, were valued. Botanical activities offered a temporary escape for women from the constraints of indoor society. Outdoor excursions, frequently in mixed company, provided many with an opportunity to meet the leading botanists and scientists of the day.

In the early decades of the 19th-century Ireland witnessed a remarkable flowering and thriving of scientific culture represented mainly in TCD,[3] the RDS, the RIA[4] and the Royal Cork Institution. Female admittance to these venerable institutions

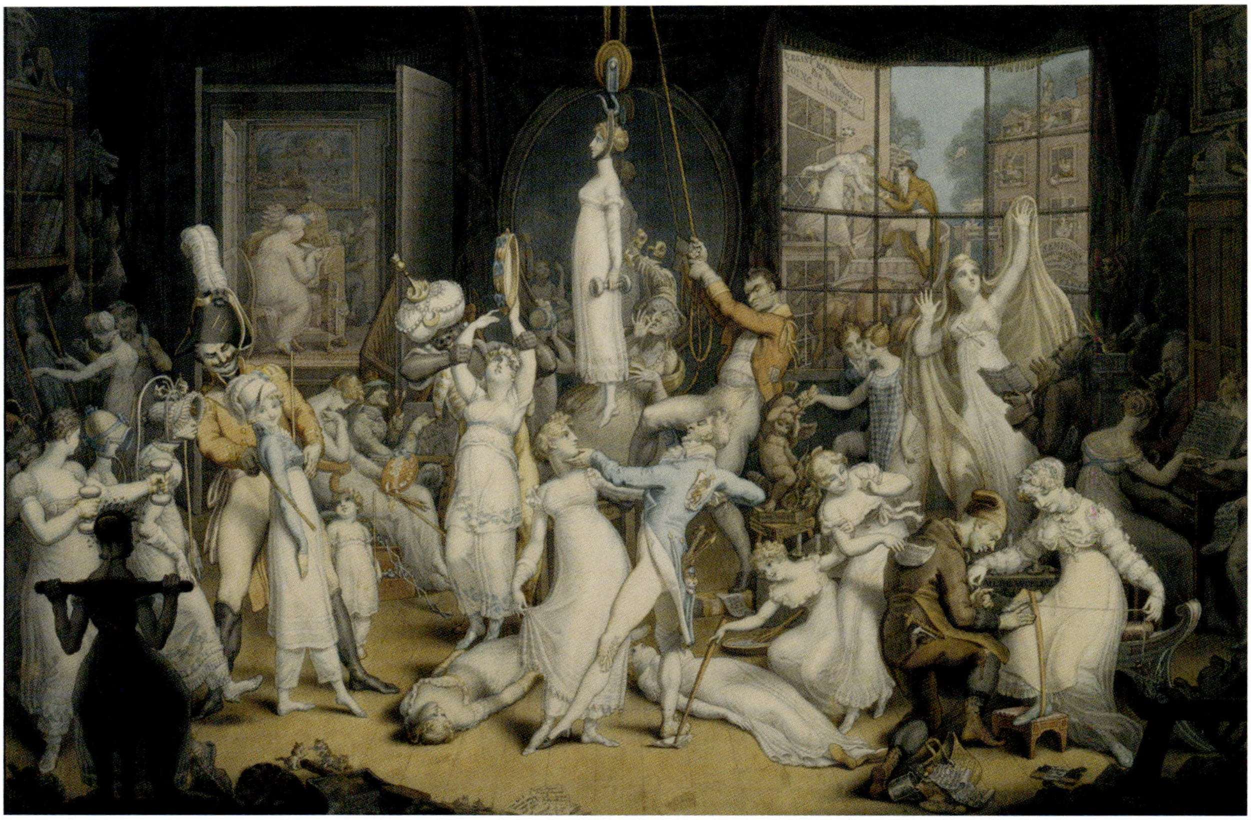

Fig. 129. *An Elegant Establishment for Young Ladies*
In this caricature, artist, Edward Francis Burney (1760–1848) implies that women's education in deportment, dress, dance and music is self-indulgent and superficial, and the only accomplishment thought necessary by society is for a career devoted to marriage and motherhood.
[© Victoria and Albert Museum, London]

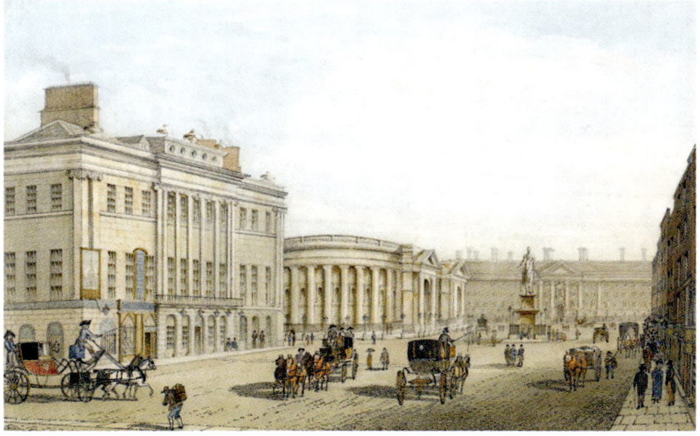

Fig. 130. *View of Trinity College and College Green, Dublin*
Ink and watercolour by Samuel Frederick Brocas, 1818
[Reproduced by kind permission of Whytes Fine Art, Dublin]

was not an easy path and in the majority of cases it was barred altogether.

The growth and interest in natural history and botany by 'the fair sex' may have been due to a number of factors. Firstly, young women were permitted to take a far greater interest in the development of these subjects in Ireland than elsewhere, but very rarely received public recognition for their work. Secondly, few were involved, and social barriers were less developed. Thirdly, natural history and botany were largely unaffected by existing precedents and were therefore relatively young disciplines, offering an opportunity for exploration and research.

This level of curiosity and interest in Ireland is reflected in the birth of new societies, together with the foundation, in the 19th century, of the three Queen's Colleges in Belfast, Cork and Galway. Again, female membership was frequently denied, with women increasingly being kept on the margins and expected to adhere to the dominant Victorian ideas relating to separate spheres, sexual difference, and gendered activities.

The spasm of institutional creation in Ireland continued well into the 1850s with the founding of the NHM. Seven years later, the NGI opened its doors. Access to these institutions was available to all, but equal opportunities for women relating, for

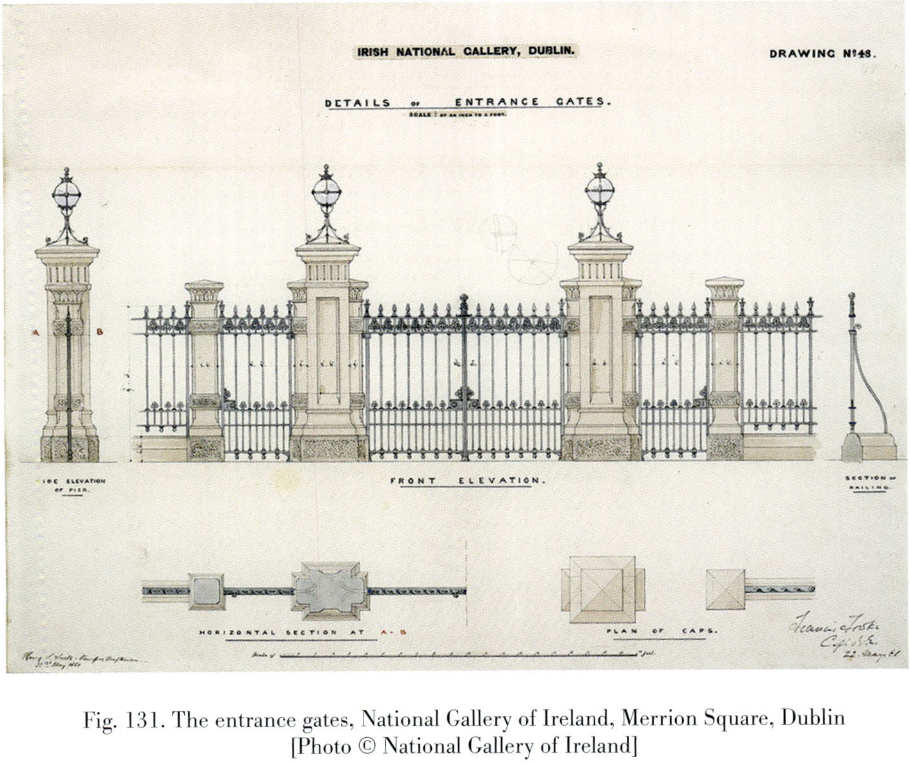


Fig. 131. The entrance gates, National Gallery of Ireland, Merrion Square, Dublin
[Photo © National Gallery of Ireland]

example, to employment remained closed. In vain, and struggling with a social structure shaped by sexual difference, they found that access to contribute on an equal footing with men was frequently denied.

Because of their gender, and confined to working on the margins of these academic and scientific institutions, women in the 18th and early 19th centuries were limited in their public contribution to the fields of botany and the natural sciences. However, with little or no public acknowledgement during their lives, their travels, studies and social activities did contribute towards helping to form a firm foundation for the development of these fields in Ireland.

One such case was the publication of the first complete descriptive work on Irish flowering plants and vascular cryptogams published in Dublin, in 1833. The author of this remarkable publication, *The Irish Flora*,[5] wished to remain anonymous but was later identified as being botanist and horticulturist, Katherine Sophia Baily (later Lady Kane) (1811–1886).[6] The author's modesty and reluctance to publish under her own name are typical of the lack of self-confidence and acknowledgement that many female amateur botanists, illustrators and naturalists experienced during this period and indeed had to endure until well into the mid-20th century.

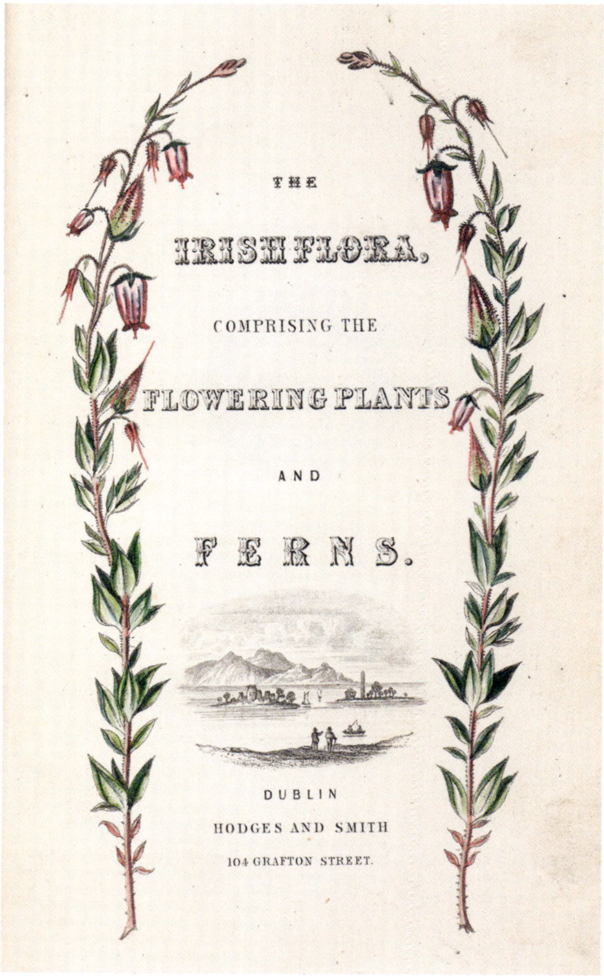


Fig. 132. Frontispiece from *The Irish Flora*, published anonymously and assisted by John White. [Courtesy, National Library of Ireland]

Despite being denied a lack of formal training, the four 19th-century women outlined below laboured with courage and spirit as pioneers in their own particular fields; and struggled to overcome the social constraints that held them back from participating fully in their chosen subject. In discussing their lives in more detail, some aspects of their work have been stressed, in order to illustrate diversity of approach rather than common ground.

# Ellen Hutchins (1785–1815)

During the early 19th century, and in a cultural genealogy of female botanists, lady algologists were a distinguished subset. Ireland's first female amateur field botanist, an energetic algologist and bryologist who 'could find almost anything',[7] was Ellen Hutchins a woman of extraordinary talents. She combined these gifts with a disarming modesty which, at first, prevented her from allowing her name to be published as the collector, discoverer and recorder of many non-flowering plants – lichens, mosses, liverworts and seaweeds – that she discovered in and around her native West Cork.

Prior to the birth of photography, and as organisms were not easy to preserve, it was essential to draw and record them efficiently and accurately. This provided Ellen Hutchins with an opportunity to contribute to plant records. The artist's attention to naturalistic detail, together with a strong sense of line, a thorough understanding of the species' structure and a high degree of accuracy, all ensured that Ellen Hutchins's work was represented and included in many of the leading publications of the day, though frequently with little or no acknowledgement by the author(s).[8] Occasionally, species were named in her honour, including mosses, liverworts, lichens and marine algae as well as certain flowering plants.

A short memoir, 'Ellen Hutchins: A Botanist',[9] written by a niece of the subject, reveals that Hutchins, born at Ballylickey House close to the shores of Bantry Bay, West Cork, was sent at an early age to school in Dublin, near Donnybrook.[10] Her father, a magistrate, had died in 1787 when she was two years old, and left behind him a wife and six children.

Throughout her short life, Ellen Hutchins frequently endured bouts of ill health; it is thought she probably suffered from tuberculosis.[11] It was therefore suggested that she would stay in the family home in Harcourt Street, Dublin, which belonged to physician, Dr Whitley Stokes (1763–1845), Professor of Medicine, TCD (1798–1811), who was himself a keen naturalist.[12] On her return to Ballylickey House, and acting on the advice of Dr Stokes, who had encouraged her to take up an outdoor pursuit in order to improve her health, Hutchins decided to explore the world of botany. A keen and avid collector, and a skilled botanical artist, she was to make a substantial contribution to the world of cryptogamic botany – lichens, algae and mosses.

Following a letter of introduction from Dr Stokes, James Townsend Mackay, Curator, BG, TCD, visited Ballylickey in July/August 1805 confirmed by the date of a plant he found north of the Priest's Leap and which he recorded on the day he left Ballylickey. Stokes found Hutchins 'amiable and accomplished'. Both began to correspond. While he assisted and advised her on how to classify the specimens she had

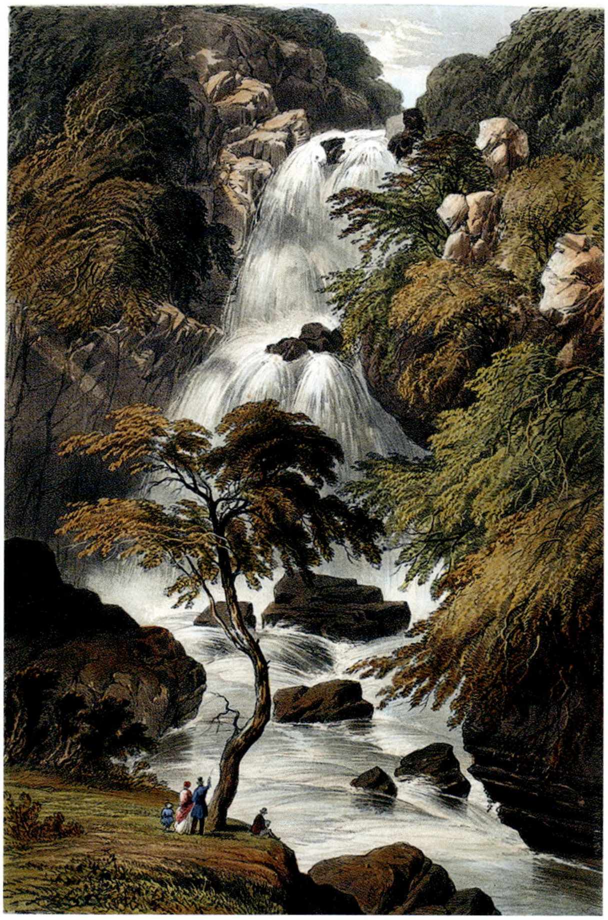

Fig. 133. Torc waterfall, Killarney, Co. Kerry
It was in areas such as Torc waterfall, Killarney that Ellen Hutchins collected her mosses
[Courtesy, National Library of Ireland]

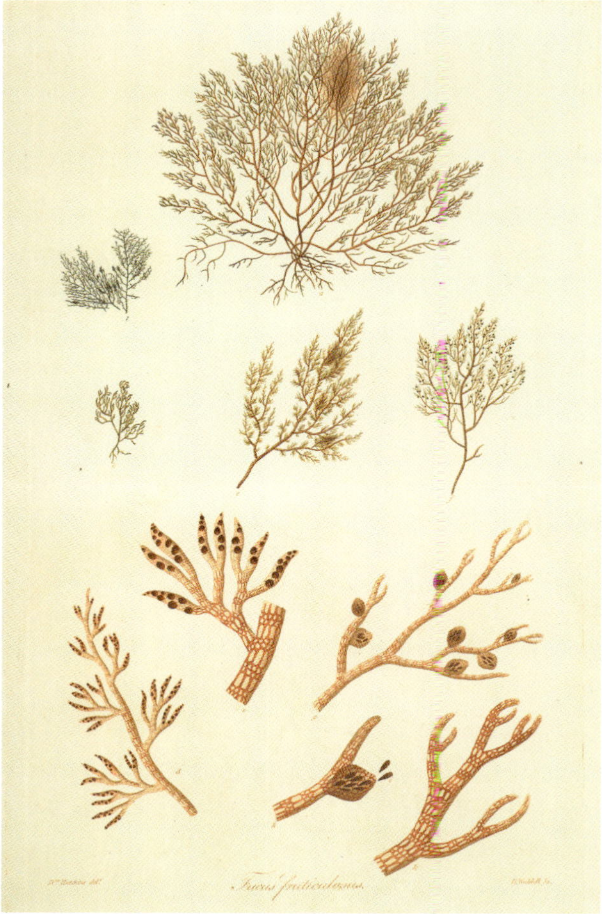


Fig. 134. *Fucus fruticulosus (Boergeseniella fruticulosa)*, from Dawson Turner's *Historia Fuci*, vol. 4, 1819
[© Royal Botanic Gardens, Kew]

collected, this young botanist also contributed to his seminal work, *Flora Hibernica*.[13]

Hutchins's contribution regarding the collection and line drawings of seaweeds was to be considerable. In 1807, she began to correspond and supply a number of rare species and drawings to botanist, Dawson Turner's (1775–1858) *Fuci*.[14, 15] Turner lived at Bank House, Yarmouth (now known as Great Yarmouth), Norfolk, and thought highly of her work. Writing to her, he praised one of her drawings and stated: 'it was one of the most beautiful plants I ever saw, either this [n.21], or [no.5 or no.7] must be called *Conferva hutchinsiae* – Choose which you please'. Describing *Cladophora hutchinsiae*, William Henry Harvey (qv), Professor of Botany, RDS,[16] wrote:

> *a very beautiful and strong growing species discovered about the year 1808 by the late Miss Hutchins of Ballylickey near Bantry whose explorations of her neighbourhood were as unremitting as they were successful and whose name is deservedly held in grateful remembrance by botanists in all parts of the world.*

*Fucus tomentosus*, now called *Codium tomentosum*,[17] (common name. velvet horn; Figure 135) is believed to be her first drawing of a plant. Ellen drew the enlarged details of the spores in July 1808 and succeeded in despatching the finished drawing in December of that year. It later appeared in Dawson Turner's *Fuci*. The portrait confirms Hutchins's ability as a botanical artist. Through the medium of watercolour, she reveals her thorough understanding of the species' structure. Dawson Turner was:

> *extremely pleased with the drawing [Fucus tomentosus], amazed at Ellen's artistic ability, and begged her to draw many more, which she did.*[18]

Responsible for producing hundreds of highly accurate watercolour drawings of fuci (see Figures 137–139), Hutchins's outstanding collection – seaweeds or marine and freshwater algae (see Figure 140), lichens, mosses and liverworts passed to Dawson Turner on her death.[19] Later, her collection was given to Turner's son-in-law, Sir William Hooker.[20]

Prior to 1805, Hutchins had travelled further afield to Belfast[21] and to the west of Ireland. Her contributions to J. Sowerby and J.E. Smith's well-known *English Botany*[22] included such mosses as *Ulota hutchinsiae* (*Orthotrichum hutchinsiae* Hutchins' pincushion; Figure 136).

> *This new Orthotrichum [Ulota] was gathered near Bantry by Miss Hutchins, a lady whose numerous discoveries in the more difficult departments of Botany justly entitle her to commemoration in the specific name.*[23]

Following the publication of Dawson Turner's *Muscologiae Hibernicae Spicilegium* (1804),[24] the first to be devoted entirely to the mosses of Ireland, *Ulota hutchinsiae* (*Orthotrichum hutchinsiae* Hutchins' pincushion) was named by James Edward Smith (*English Botany*) in her honour.

At the beginning (1805–early 1807), Hutchins shunned publicity and was reluctant to allow her work to be acknowledged. This may have been due to her essential modesty and her hesitancy in allowing her name to appear in print. Writing to her elder brother, she said:

> *I desired that my name should not be published. I have since been asked to allow it to be*

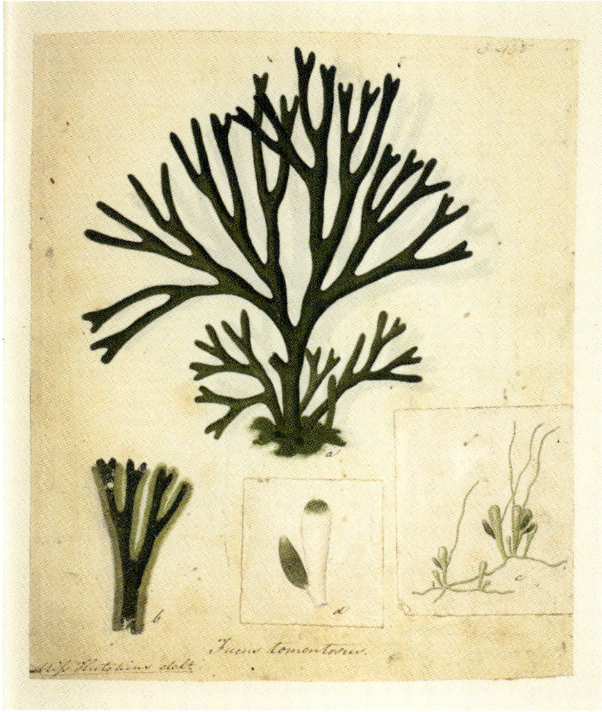

Fig. 135. *Codium tomentosum* (*Fucus tomentosus*) velvet horn
Watercolour by Ellen Hutchins
[© Royal Botanic Gardens, Kew]

> *mentioned. I am doubtful whether I ought to do so or not, I beg you to tell me what I should do.*[25]

Her many unique finds also include lichens. Three species bear witness to her work in this field and commemorate her name.[26] A keen correspondent, she communicated with her friends, many of whom were leading botanists and naturalists of the day. Writing to Sir William Jackson Hooker, LLD, DCL, FRS, FLS (1785–1865)[27] she said: 'I know not how to thank you sufficiently for the many beautiful engravings you have sent me.'[28] For a period of seven years, Dawson Turner and Ellen Hutchins frequently wrote to each other. They developed a strong friendship and discussed not only botany but also the range of books they were reading, together with news of their families; her friendship with Dawson Turner providing her 'with the only brightness or light in her life'.[29] Her last letter (an extract) to Dawson Turner dated 30 November 1814, just over two months before her death on 9 February 1815, is poignant:

> *My dear kind friend I am settled up in bed to write you a line to tell you I read your letters long after they came here with tears of gratitude & affection for such kindness. I have been many months in bed not able to turn or move myself, stupid except when roused by violent pains.... I cannot write more. I cannot read at all now or amuse my mind in any way & this is worse than pain to a mind once active & tho ever struggling with disadvantages seldom unemployed. Send me a moss anything just to look at.*
> *Yours ever affectionately E.H.*[30]

Ellen Hutchins also corresponded with James Townsend Mackay (Curator, BG, TCD). In a letter dated 1 February 1807, she mentions:

> *You will no doubt be surprised to see a parcel from me so soon again but as your pleasure in plants equals mine, I could not delay writing with the enclosed minute species of Conferva... I shall spread some specimens for you and shall*

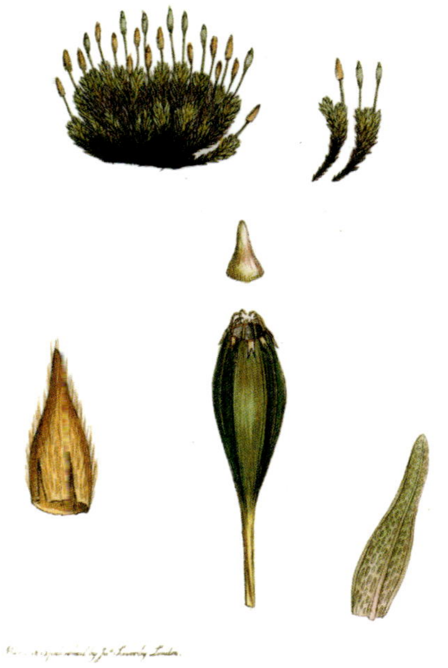

Fig. 136. *Ulota hutchinsiae* (*Orthotrichum hutchinsiae*) Hutchins' pincushion
Named in honour of Ellen Hutchins
[Private collection. Reproduced by kind permission]

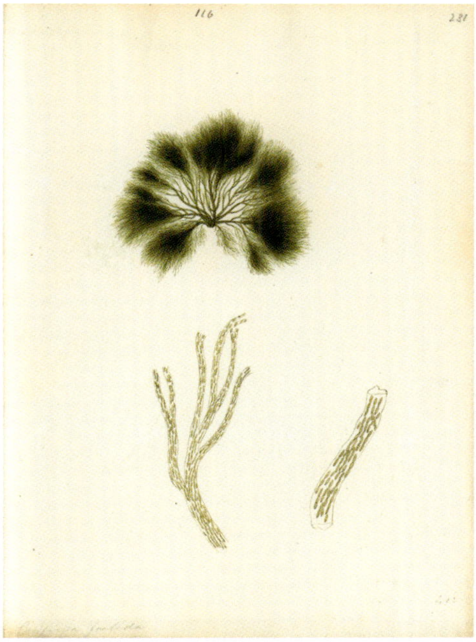

Fig. 137. *Hydurus foetidus* (*Conferva foetida*)
Watercolour by Ellen Hutchins
[© Royal Botanic Gardens, Kew]

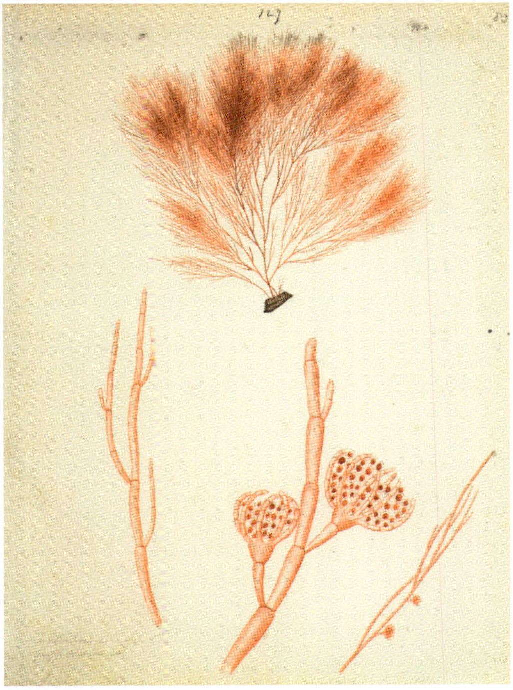

Fig. 138. *Halurus flosculosus* (*Conferva setacea*)
Watercolour by Ellen Hutchins, 1810
[© Royal Botanic Gardens, Kew]

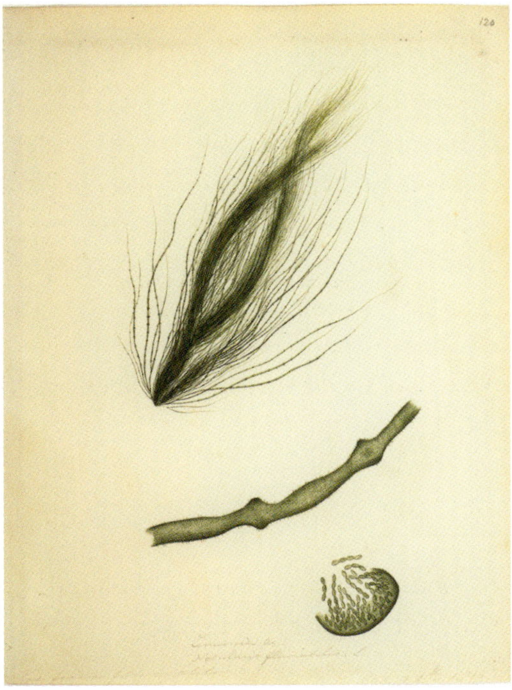

Fig. 139. *Lemanea fluviatilis* (*Conferva fluviatilis*)
Watercolour by Ellen Hutchins, March 1810
[© Royal Botanic Gardens, Kew]

*take the very first opportunity the weather will allow of to get a good number of them.*[31]

Mackay also helped her to obtain useful books and sent her several consignments of plants for her garden at Ballylickey House.[32]

From early in 1813, Ellen Hutchins's health continued to deteriorate and she was unable to continue to botanise. She and her mother made the decision to move to Bandon in order to avail of better medical care. Following the death of her mother in March 1814, Hutchins moved to the home of her elder brother, Arthur, Ardnagashel House on the shores of Bantry Bay.[33] Through the years, the estate had been carefully cultivated and planted with many rare trees and shrubs, and this was to continue with owners of the estate such as Samuel Hutchins (owner, 1839–1862) enjoying many visits to Kew Gardens and benefiting from the advice of Sir William and Lady Hooker.

At Ardnagashel House, Hutchins's letters, dated 4 August and 30 November 1814 indicate that she was very ill indeed: 'I am not able to sit up an hour and am a perfect skeleton'. At the early age of 29, just short of her 30th birthday, this 'young botanist of great promise'[34] died.

William Henry Harvey paying tribute to her (*Phycologia Britannica, or a History of British Seaweeds*, 1847), wrote:

*[Her] name is held in grateful remembrance by botanists in all parts of the world. To her, the botany of Ireland is under many obligations, particularly the crypotogamic branch, in which field until her time little explored. She was particularly fortunate in detecting new and beautiful objects, several of which remain the rarest species to the present day.*

Ellen Hutchins is a prime example of a pioneering female botanist who managed to overcome considerable problems in her short life with remarkable courage. She left behind an outstanding contribution to the field of botany and to botanical illustration.[35]

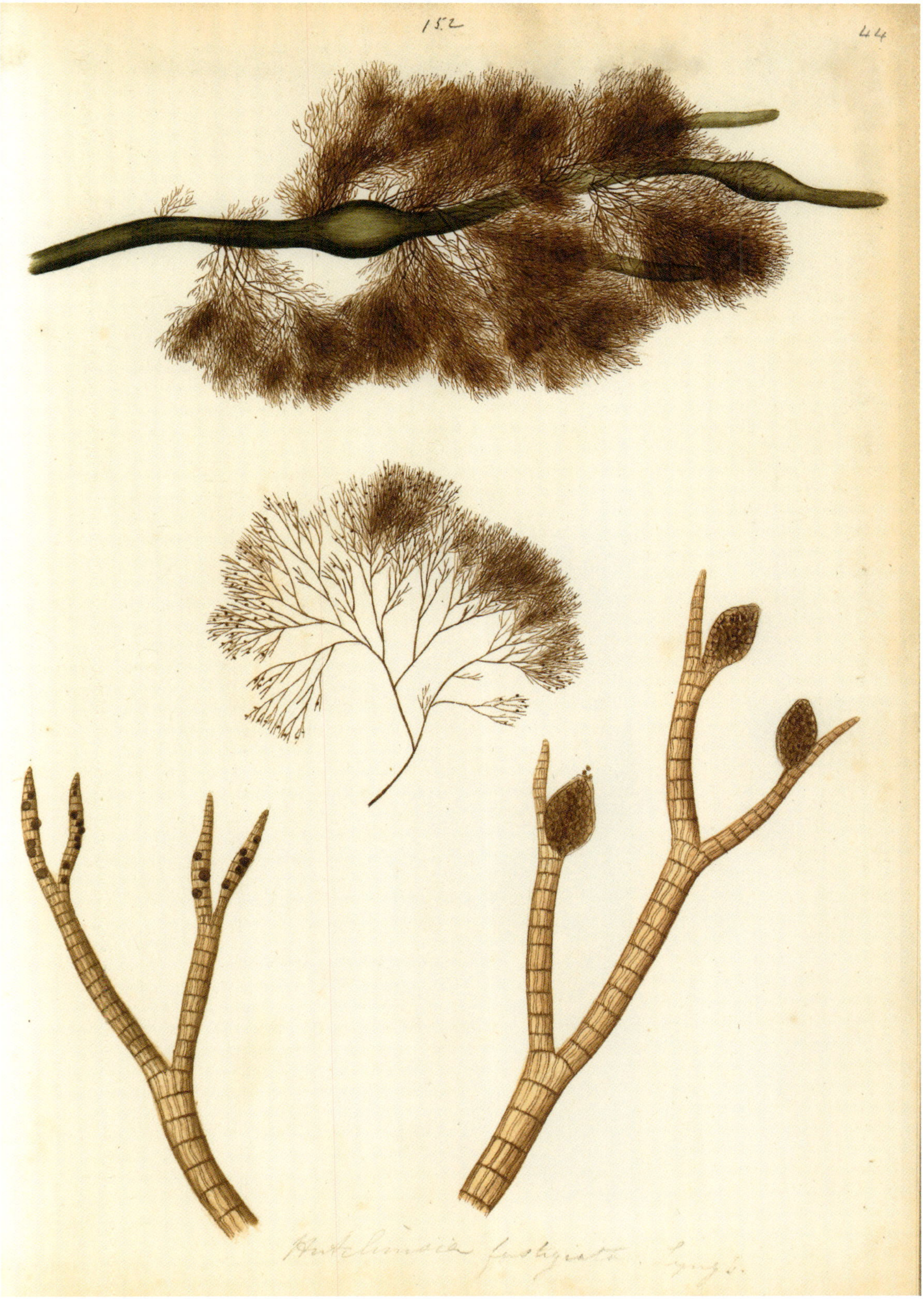


Fig. 140. *Vertebrata lanosa* (*Hutchinsia fastigiate, Ceramium fastigiatum*)
Watercolour by Ellen Hutchins
[© Royal Botanic Gardens, Kew]

# Anne Elizabeth Ball (1808–1872)

'The fair discoverer ... from whom I have, during the course of this publication, received much assistance.' William Henry Harvey (qv)[36] and Anne Elizabeth Ball grew up in an age when the rise in popularity of natural history study made it a fashionable pursuit for women. The romance of nature, plants and flowers influenced the objects to be found in a Victorian woman's cabinet. Anne Elizabeth Ball was no exception. She enjoyed excursions, gathered and studied specimens under microscopes, and read journals, books and picture books. More or less any activities connected to nature satisfied both family and cultural mandates and, in Anne Elizabeth Ball's case, an interest in the natural world was given further emphasis by her father, Bob Stawell Ball (1768–1841) and his wife, Mary (née Green).

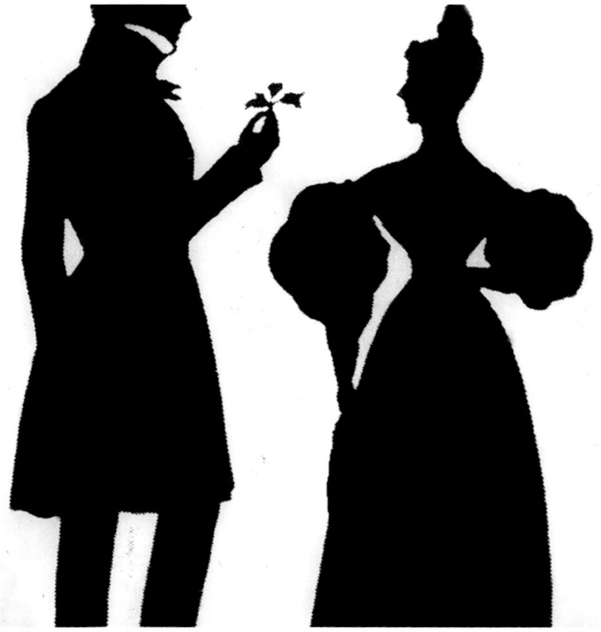

Fig. 141. Silhouette of Robert Ball (1802–1857) and his sister, Anne Elizabeth Ball (1808–1872)
[Private collection. Reproduced by kind permission]

They fostered, in their three surviving children, a love of natural history coupled with a keen curiosity. In the first half of the 19th century, it is remarkable that of the three, the two girls became naturalists, each forming collections of specimens. Anne's sister, Mary (1812–1898), studied insects and molluscs and was a keen entomologist.[37] Their brother Robert (1802–1857), while appointed assistant librarian and keeper of records at Dublin Castle, was also a keen zoologist and naturalist, devoting the majority of his spare time to natural history. He was elected Hon. Secretary of the Zoological Society of Ireland and in 1844 became curator of the university museum at TCD, a post he held until his death in 1857.[38] In that year, he was elected a Fellow of the RS.

Anne Elizabeth Ball's family had originated in Bampton, Devonshire. Her father was the youngest of nine children of Robert Ball (1729–1802). His grandfather, Robert Ball, had settled in Youghal, Co.

Cork, in 1674. Anne's father was a customs officer and lived at Cobh (Queenstown), Co. Cork from c.1799 onwards and returned to Youghal in 1815 for health reasons. The family eventually settled in Dublin on the northside at no. 28 Eccles Street.

Ball became an enthusiastic algologist, collecting and recording seaweeds, which in turn brought her into contact with distinguished botanists such as William Henry Harvey (qv). He was a long-standing friend of her brother Robert and held her work in high esteem. Harvey was to honour Anne Elizabeth Ball by naming the genus of red seaweed after her, the type species being *Ballia callitricha*. However, before conferring this distinguished honour upon his keen algologist, he sought the advice of physician Dr Nathaniel Ward (1791–1868), begging him 'to ask the great Robert Brown' (1773–1858):[39]

> *if there [were] any reasons as to why he should not dedicate it to [his] friend Miss Ball, a zealous and successful Irish algologist and who would rival Miss Hutchins had she the equal opportunities.*[40]

Anne Elizabeth Ball contributed a number of records to Harvey that were used by him in his algological section of Mackay's *Flora Hibernica* (1836) and later in his (Harvey's) *Phycologia Britannica* (1846–1851). Harvey continued to recognise and admire her collecting powers. *Cladophora balliana* (Figure 143), which he believed to be new from specimens found by Anne Elizabeth Ball on 16 May 1843, on the

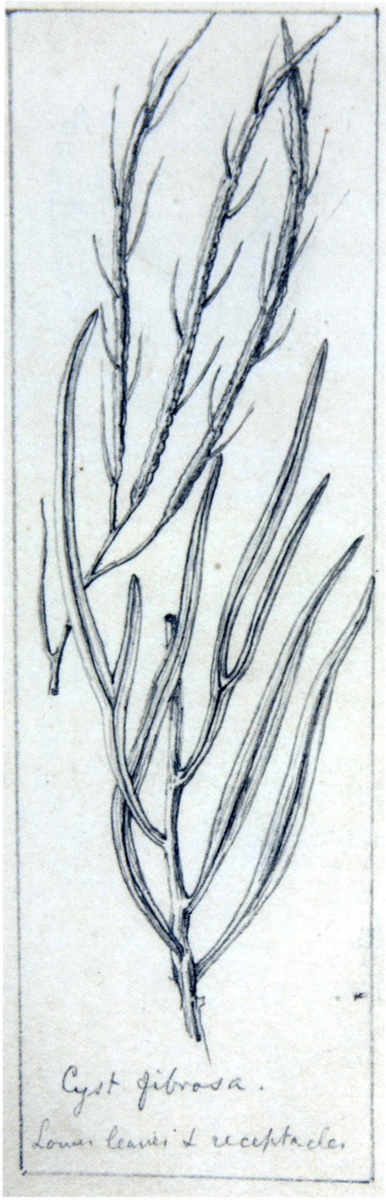


Fig. 142. *Cystoseira fibrosa* (seaweed)
Pen and ink drawing by Anne Elizabeth Ball
[Courtesy, National Botanic Gardens, Glasnevin, Dublin]

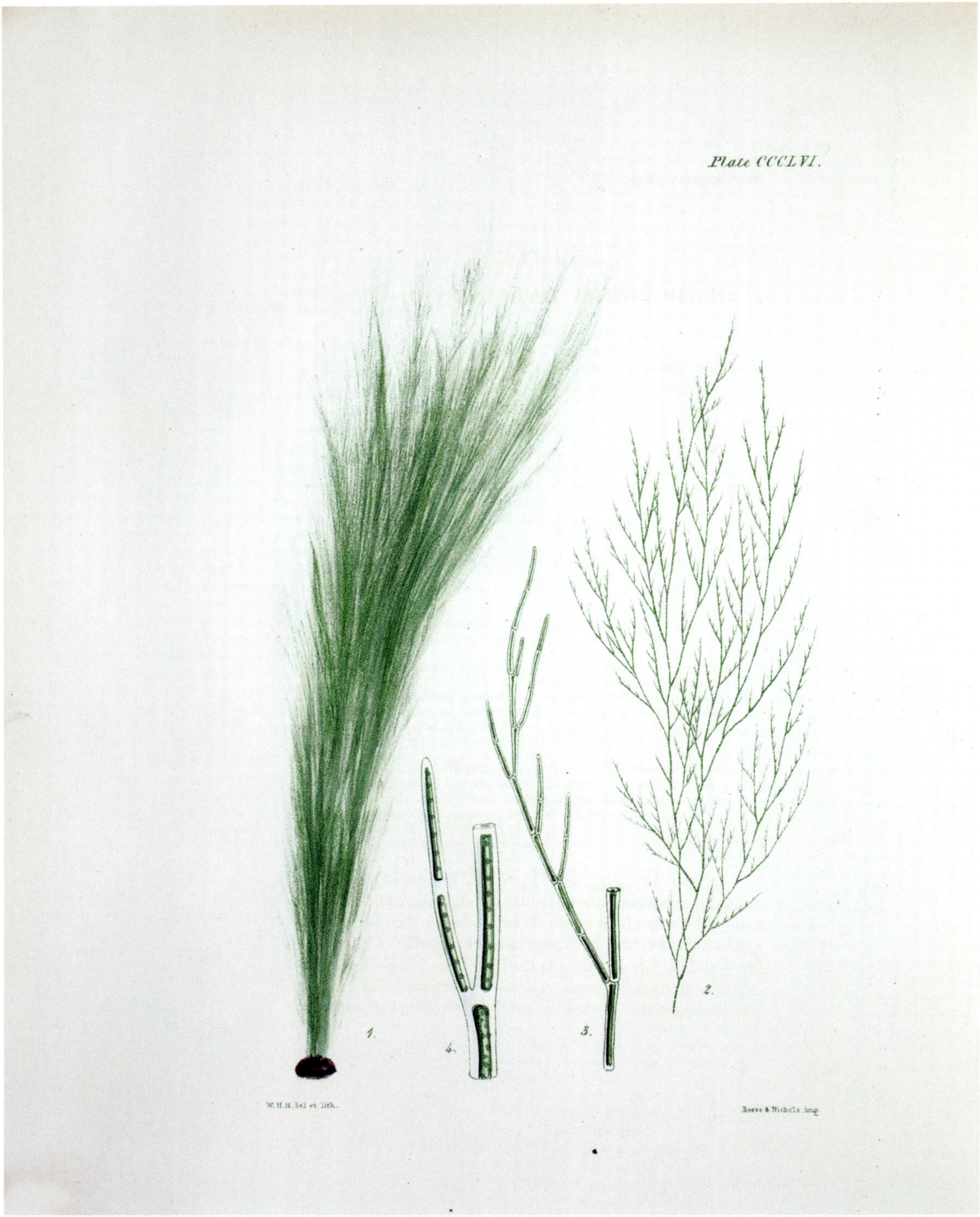


Fig. 143. *Cladophora balliana*
Drawing and lithograph by William Henry Harvey, reproduced in *Phycologia Britannica, or a History of British Sea-weeds*, vols 1–4. This particular specimen was found at Clontarf, Dublin by Miss Ball on May 16, 1843. William Harvey noted: 'I am glad... to have an opportunity of paying a grateful tribute to a fair discoverer'
[Courtesy, National Botanic Gardens, Glasnevin, Dublin]

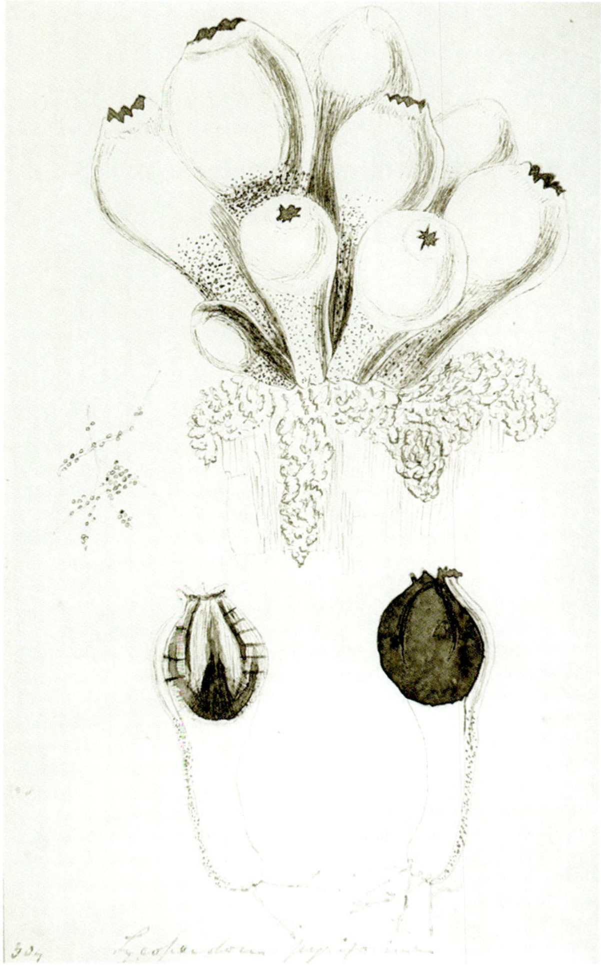

Fig. 144. *Lycoperdon pyriforme*, stump puffball
Watercolour, pen and ink on cream paper by Anne Elizabeth Ball
[Courtesy, National Botanic Gardens, Glasnevin, Dublin]

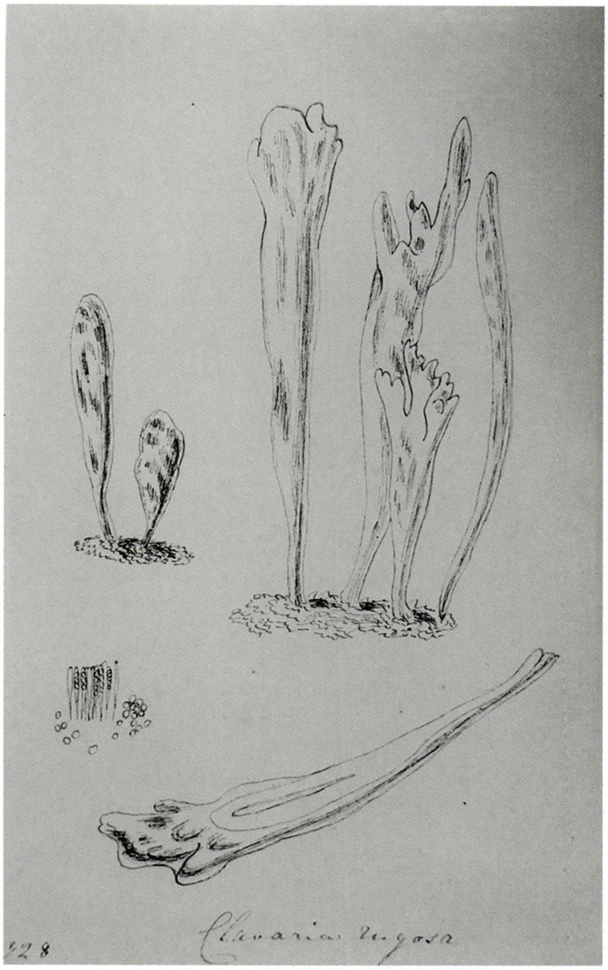


Fig. 145. *Clavaria rugosa*, wrinkled coral fungus
Pen and ink drawing by Anne Elizabeth Ball
[Courtesy, National Botanic Gardens, Glasnevin, Dublin]

seashore at Clontarf, Dublin, was named after her. He wrote:

> *I am glad, in closing the 'Phycologia' to have an opportunity of paying a grateful tribute to the fair discoverer ... from whom I have during the course of this publication, received much assistance - in supplies of specimens, etc., - and to whose acute eye the Irish Flora is indebted for the addition of many interesting specie.*[41]

Both Anne and her sister Mary donated material (algae and insects) to Trinity College museum, following their brother Robert's appointment as curator and later to Cork University's Herbarium.[42] Anne Ball's pen, ink and watercolour drawings of algae[43] are housed in two bound volumes in the Herbarium, NBG Glasnevin, Dublin. In the majority of cases, she does not record the full tonal complexities of each specimen, but confines herself to simple, elegant outlines with, in the case of a few examples, careful pen and ink notations on verso (Figures 142 and 144). With regard to her fungi drawings (see Figure 145),[44] several of the specimens are carefully infilled with a modulated wash. However, this is not applicable to her algae drawings, which are executed entirely through the medium of pen and ink.

Despite making a considerable contribution,[45] Anne Ball never published her findings. Perhaps it was felt that publication by a woman was somewhat immodest. Following her father's death, she continued to live with her sister Mary in Eccles Street, Dublin. Resourceful, and not having a garden, they built a rockery in the basement of the house, where they cultivated ferns. When their mother died in 1862, they moved to Belmont Avenue, Dublin; each sister had her own garden. Anne Elizabeth Ball died in 1872.

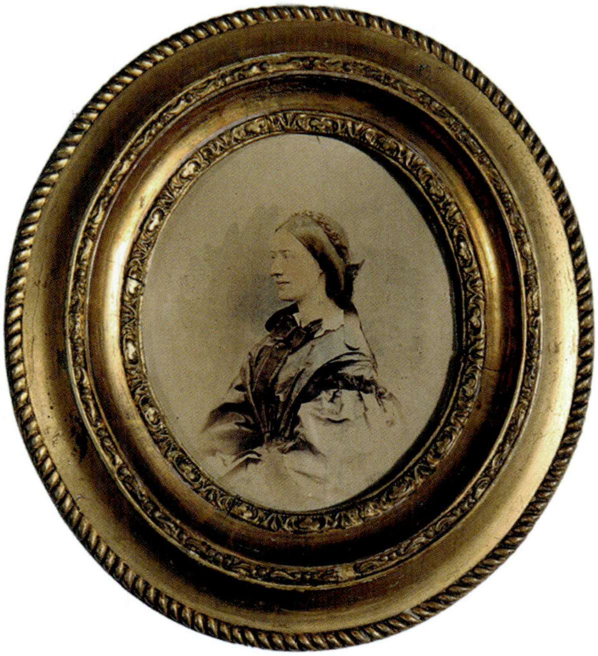

# Hon. Mrs Mary Ward (née King, 1827–1869)

Books illustrated with women's drawings and watercolours, some of them privately printed, began to appear in the 1840s. The Hon. Mrs Mary Ward, a distinguished artist, astronomer, naturalist and microscopist, was no exception. She became widely known largely due to her three books, all privately printed, relating to scientific subjects. Acknowledged as Ireland's First Lady of the Microscope, Ward was the first woman to write and publish a book on the subject: *Sketches with the Microscope* (1857),[46] which did much to popularise astronomy and microscopy in the second half of the 19th century. She did not use her full name, instead preferring to publish under the name 'The Hon. Mrs W'.

The Hon. Mrs Mary Ward was an artist, astronomer and naturalist who executed her own beautiful, detailed drawings of bird feathers, fish scales, insects and botanical material in the mid-1800s. She became the author of three books relating to scientific subjects

Fig. 146. The Hon. Mary Ward
[National Trust]

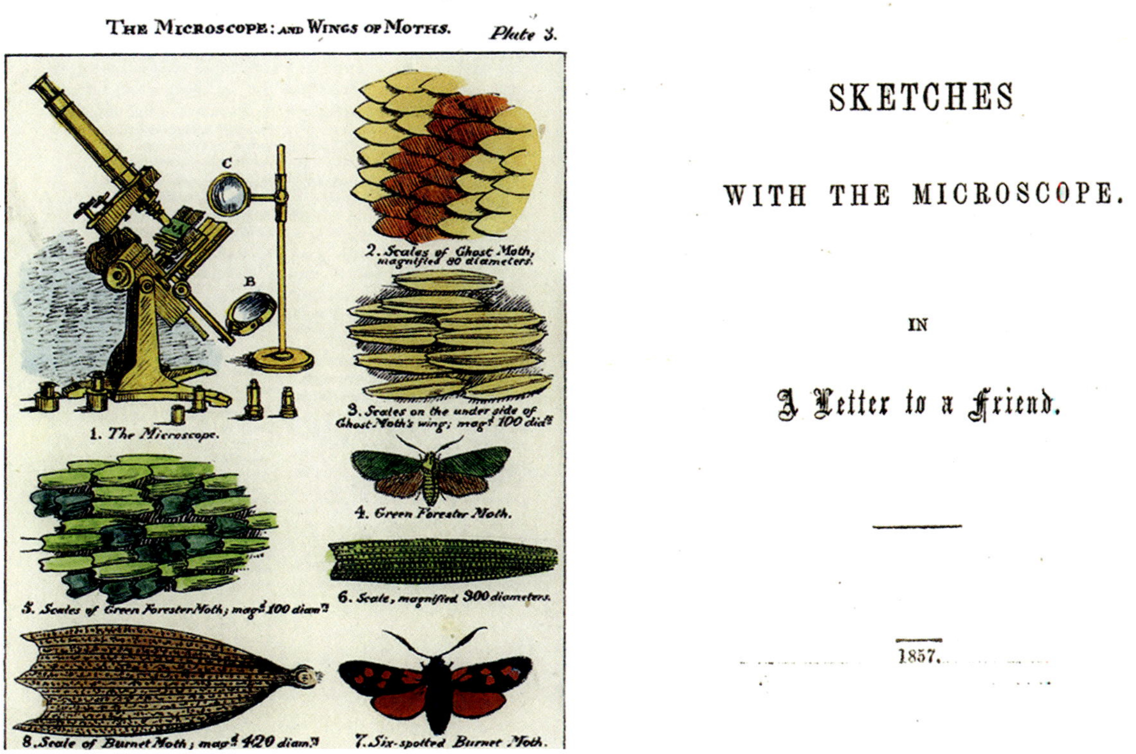


Fig. 147. Frontispiece from *Sketches with the Microscope* by the Hon. Mary Ward, 1857
[Private collection. Reproduced by kind permission]

and painted over 200 illustrations of insects, fishes, birds and landscapes for several books and articles relating to science and natural history.

Daughter of the Reverend Henry King (1799–1857) and Harriette King (née Lloyd of Gloster, King's Co. [Co. Offaly]; 1789–1847), Mary was born on 27 April 1827 at Ballylin, Ferbane, King's Co. (now Co. Offaly), located between Tullamore and Birr. Her mother was the sister of Mary Lloyd, who had married William, 2nd Earl of Rosse (1758–1841). Mary was educated privately at home and from early childhood her parents had fostered and encouraged her interest in natural history, presenting her, at the age of seven, with a copy of *Buffon's Natural History*.[47] As a young girl, she was a regular visitor to Birr Castle,[48] which was around 15 miles from her home. It was largely due to her family's connections

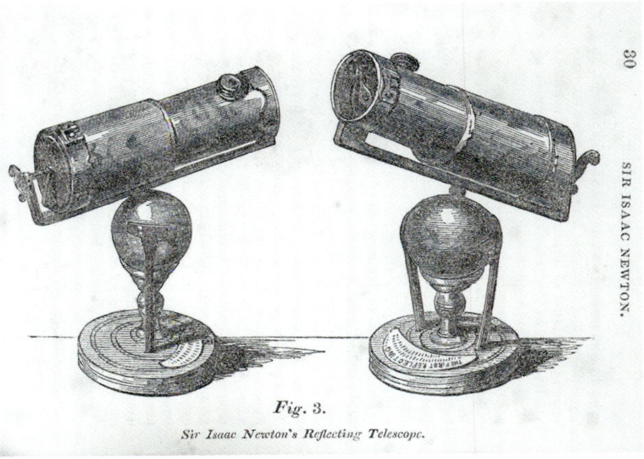


Fig. 148. Sir Isaac Newton's reflecting telescopes
Original drawing by the Hon. Mary Ward, reproduced in Sir David Brewster, *The Life of Sir Isaac Newton* (London, 1831), p. 30
[Courtesy, National Library of Ireland]

and her passionate interest in astronomy that Mary took a keen interest in observing and recording the building of the giant 'Leviathan of Parsonstown' telescope and its installation, by her cousin, the 3rd Earl of Rosse (1800–1867), in the castle grounds at Birr.

At the age of 18, Mary's parents presented her with her first Ross microscope recommended by distinguished astronomer, Sir James South (1785–1867). She taught herself the techniques required to use it and how to prepare objects for microscopic examination. Her microscope proved to be a constant source of fascination for her throughout her short life helping her to unlock many mysteries of the natural world.

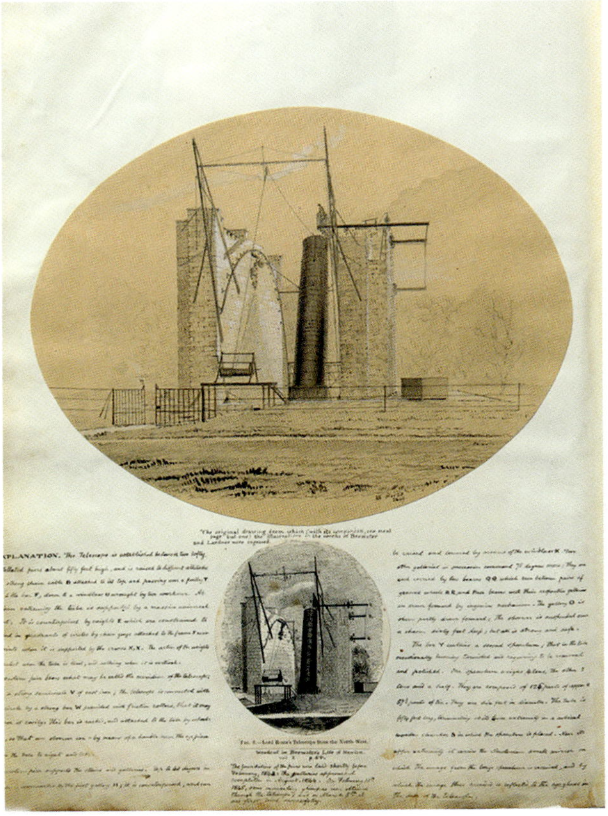

Fig. 149. The Great Telescope, Birr Castle, Co. Offaly
Pen, pencil and gouache by the Hon. Mary Ward
[National Trust]

As a young woman, Mary was fortunate to have plenty of social opportunities to meet many eminent scientists of the day. Scottish scientist, Sir David Brewster, KH, PRSE, FRS, FSA Scot., FSSA, MICE (1781–1868),[49] inventor of the kaleidoscope, was a frequent visitor to her father's house. Her drawings of the telescopes of Sir Isaac Newton and the 3rd Earl

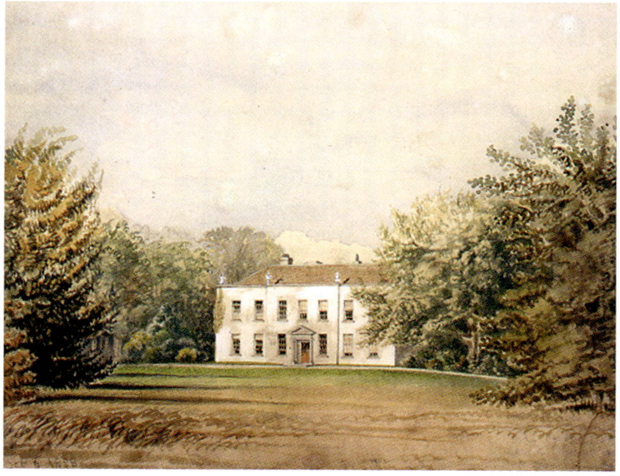

Fig. 150. Entrance front, 'Ballylin', Ferbane, Co. Offaly, home of the Hon. Mary Ward (née King)
Watercolour by the Hon. Mary Ward, signed 'M.W', 1858
[Private collection. Reproduced by kind permission]

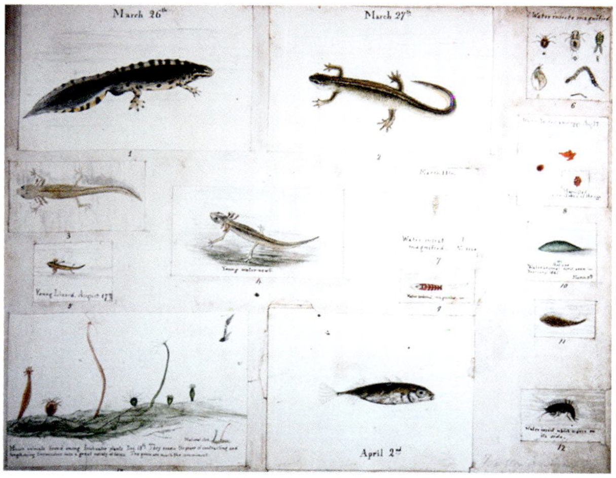


Fig. 151. A page from the Hon. Mary Ward's nature notebook, 1847
[National Trust]

of Rosse are printed in Brewster's *The Life of Sir Isaac Newton* (see Figure 148).[50] Ward also prepared microscopic specimens for Brewster. She both drew and painted them, the coloured illustrations appearing in the *Transactions of the Royal Society of Edinburgh,* 1864.[51]

Employing her microscope, which did not possess a light source or rotating eyepieces, she used a candle and a condensing lens to focus the candlelight on to a mirror, which then reflected it through a microscope. Using her microscope in this way, she executed many fine and detailed drawings of animals and plants (see Figure 151). Insects would appear to have been her favourite subject matter. An article entitled *Natterjack Toads in Ireland* had been written and published by her, later to be reprinted in full in the *Irish Times* in May 1864.[52] This led to an invitation by Sir Richard Owen, KCB, FRMS, FRS (1804–1892),[53] for her to send him a copy of her painting of the natterjack toad to form part of the collections in the British Museum (NH). Her research/writings attracted the attention of a number of men of science. In 1867, Sir Warren De La Rue (then secretary, Royal Astronomical Society) contacted her in response to an article relating to astronomy that she had published in the *Irish Times*, 21 August 1867:

> *Permit me to say that such articles do much to encourage the cultivation of science by*

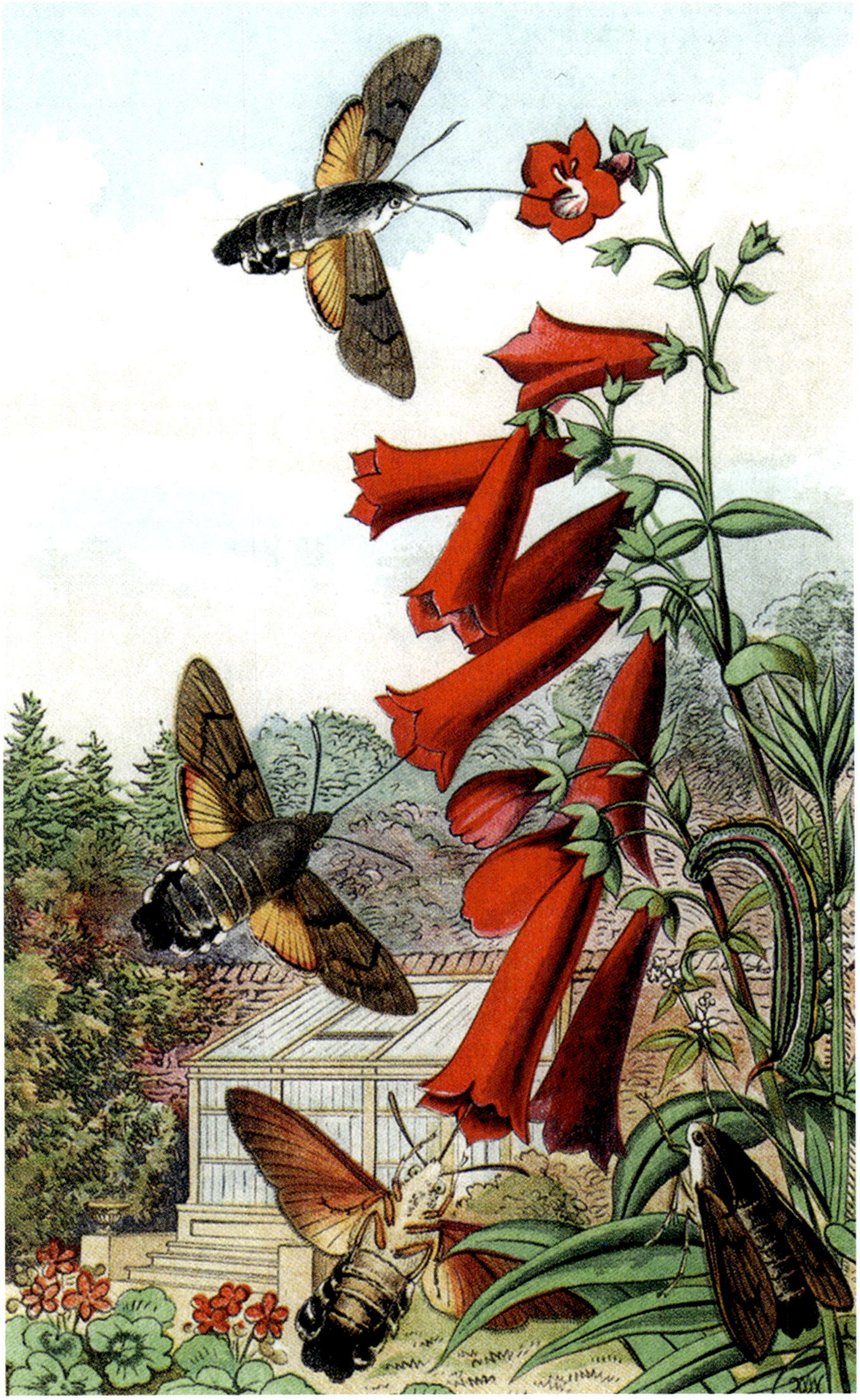

Fig. 152. A hummingbird hawk-moth drawn at 'Ballylin', Co. Offaly by the Hon. Mary Ward [National Trust]

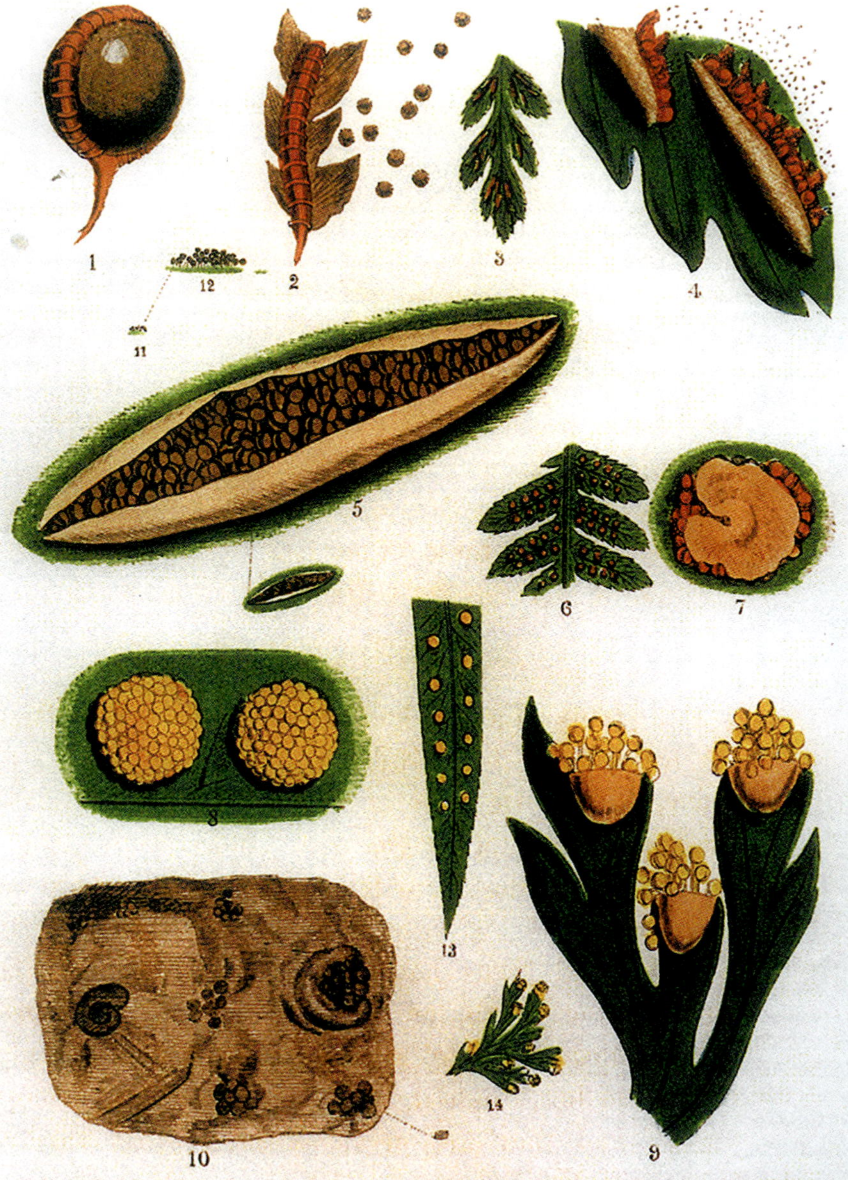


1. Seed-vessel of Fern when unripe, magnified 60 diameters. 2. Seed-vessel of Fern, at the moment when the ring straightens itself. 3. Leaflet of Black Maiden-hair Spleenwort Fern. 4. Two sori, or collections of seed-vessels, of Spleenwort Fern, magd. 12 diams. 5. Sorus of Hart's-tongue Fern, magd. 6 diams. 6. Part of a leaflet of Shield Fern. 7. Sorus, magd. 10 diams. 8. Sori of Polypody Fern, magd. 7 diams. 9. Sori and part of leaflet of Hare's-foot Fern, magd. 5 diams. 10. Thin section of Limestone, magd. 20 diams. 11. Group of twenty seed-vessels, natural size. 12. Group of twenty seed-vessels, magd. 6 diams. 13. Leaflet of Polypody. 14. Part of a leaflet of Hare's-foot Fern.

Fig. 153. Seed-vessels of ferns and section of limestone
From *A World of Wonders Revealed by the Microscope, a book for young students* (London, 1858, p. 48).
[Private collection. Reproduced by kind permission]

*amateurs - and that England (in which I of course include Ireland) has much to be proud of the work done by non-professional cultivators of science.*

*Sketches with the Microscope*,[54] published privately in 1857, began as a series of letters to her childhood friend, Emily Filgate. A year later, this small, privately printed book was published in London by Groomsbridge as *A World of Wonders as Revealed by the Microscope.* Reprinted a number of times between 1858 and 1864, it was enlarged, revised and published as *Microscope Teachings.* In the 1855 edition of the book, she wrote:

*The collector of objects for the microscope will most probably have a bias in favour of some particular branch of Natural History. Entomology was my favourite pursuit and this will account for the prominent place occupied in these pages by specimens taken from the insect world.*[55]

Ward's publications and scientific papers always included up-to-date information relating to function, structure and development. She described vision in insects, the structure of insect and fish scales, a method for observing the circulation of the blood in small vertebrates, the development of insect larvae, the dispersal of seeds.

Responsible for making her own microscopic slides that were assembled over a period of 25 years, the earliest dates from 1845; they include a wide range of subject matter:

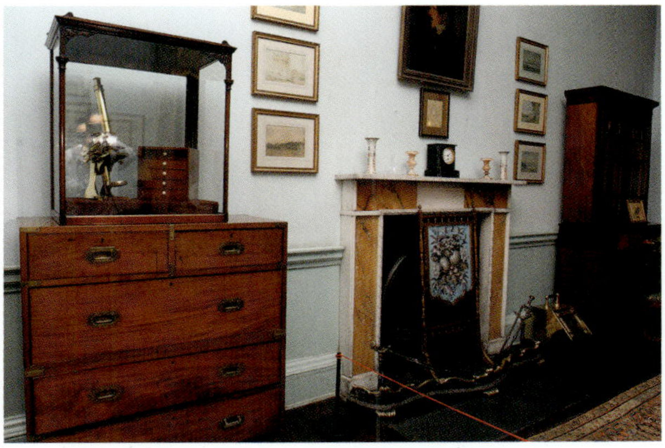

Fig. 154. The Hon. Mary Ward's bedroom, Castle Ward, Co. Down [National Trust]

*They are not merely a collection of curiosities but were used to illustrate all the features of structure and function outlined in her books....*[56]

In 1854, she married Henry William Crosbie Ward, later to become 5th Viscount Bangor (1828–1911), Castle Ward, Co. Down. The marriage resulted in eight children, six of whom reached adulthood. Despite her rapidly growing family, Ward never abandoned her research in the fields of microscopy and entomology. She retained her 'talents and energy, her scientific acquirements, her genial and affectionate disposition and her many virtues'[57] throughout her short life. This was brought to a tragic and sudden end on 31 August 1869. On a visit to Birr, she and her husband

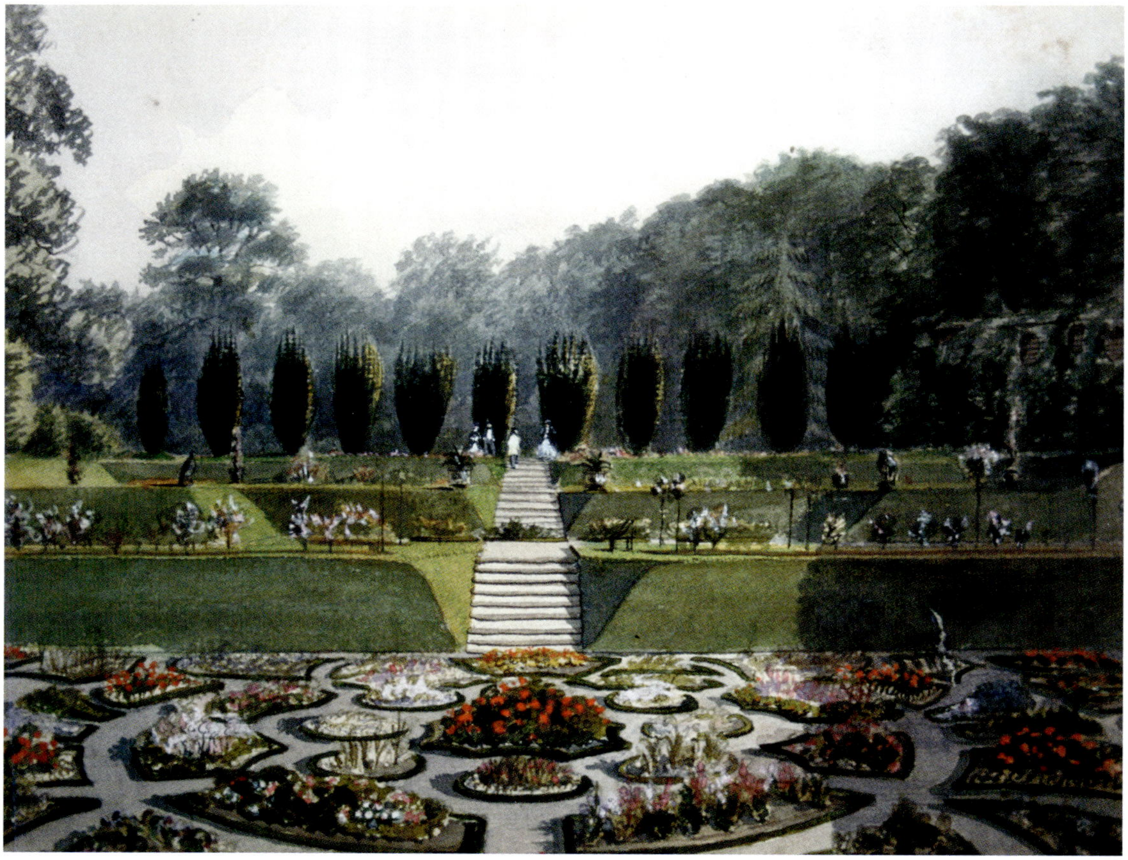

Fig. 155. View of the gardens, Castle Ward, Co. Down
Watercolour by the Hon. Mary Ward
[National Trust]

went to pay their respects at the grave of her cousin William, who had died in 1867. They were travelling along the mall, Birr, in a steam-powered road carriage invented by William, when the carriage hit a stone. Ward was thrown from the vehicle which then rolled backwards. She was instantly crushed under one of the wheels.

*It is possible only to speculate on the impact she might have made in the scientific and literary fields had she not died at such a tender age. There is no doubt that she would have eventually established a considerable reputation in the field of scientific endeavour to which she had already made significant contributions.*[58]

# Eveline Elizabeth ('Eileen') Barnes (1870–1956)

Eveline Elizabeth ('Eileen') Barnes appears to have spent the majority of her working life as a part-time craftworker/botanical and scientific illustrator in the NMI (previously known as the Museum of Science and Art), Kildare Street, Dublin. Despite her outstanding work from 1932 onwards as an illustrator, little is known about her career. Her 'life story is one of quiet achievement rather than acclaim'.[59]

Barnes was born on 3 May 1870 at 137 Great Britain Street (now Parnell Street), daughter of Edwin and Elizabeth (née McKay); her father was a grocer, wine and spirit merchant.[60] After attending Rutland School for Girls, Dublin, Barnes received her early training at the Dublin Metropolitan School of Art, Kildare Street, Dublin (1898–1899), which included not only the 'traditional' subjects such as life drawing and drawing from the antique, but also sculpture and clay modelling. Her early work with the NHM, Dublin, shows her ability and versatility in the field of model making. She executed models in wax of Mollusca (slugs and snails) that were injurious to crops, to enable farmers and gardeners to recognise the species. To construct a good model of a snail or slug required close study of anatomy and a heightened awareness of detail.

Her early association with the NMI may have begun around 1907. It was spent in the Natural History Division assembling models of natural habitats and wax models, as well as setting up exhibition cases. She also served in the Antiquities Division.

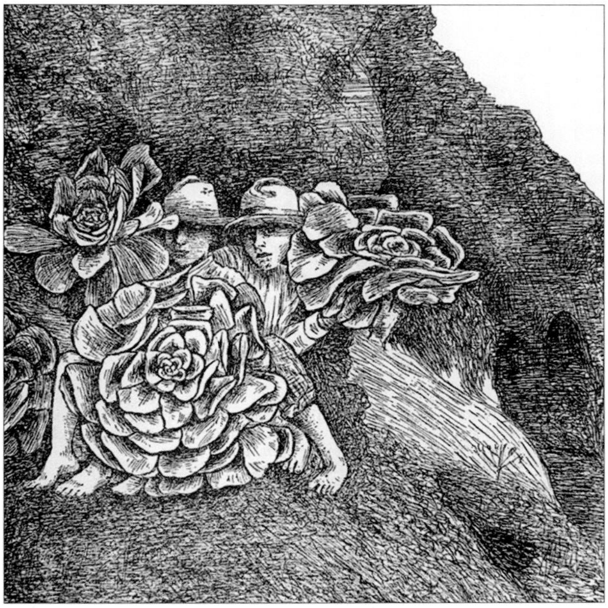

Fig. 156. The artist's interpretation of the rosette nature of *Aeonium canariense*. Pen-and-ink drawing by Eileen Barnes, reproduced in Robert Lloyd Praeger, 'An Account of the Sempervivum Group', *Journal of the Royal Horticultural Society of London*, 1932, pp. 1–265, Fig. 53. [Courtesy, National Botanic Gardens, Glasnevin, Dublin]

A skilled botanical illustrator, Barnes contributed a number of line drawings relating to spores and spore-bearing structures to established botanist,

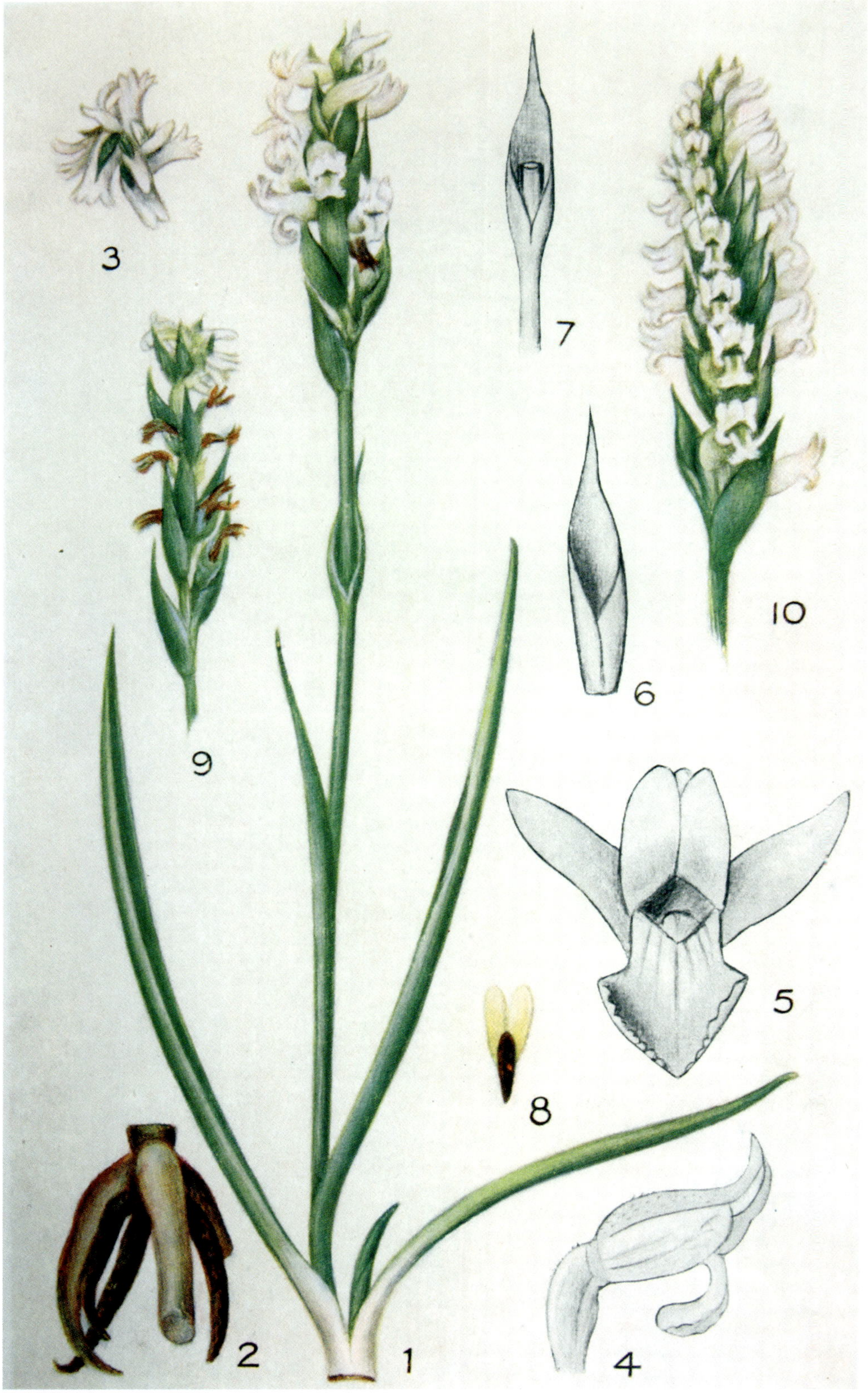


Fig. 157. *Spiranthes stricta* (*Spiranthes romanzoffiana*) Irish lady's tresses
Colour lithograph based on a watercolour drawing by Eileen Barnes, reproduced in *The Irish Naturalists' Journal*, vol. 11, January 1928–November 1929, plate 1
Until 1892, the Irish orchid, *Spiranthes romanzoffiana* was only known in Ireland from a few southern stations, all located in Co. Cork – Castletown Berehaven (North side), Bantry Bay, Dunmanway.
[Courtesy, National Botanic Gardens, Glasnevin, Dublin]

Matilda Knowles's[61] work *The Maritime and Marine Lichens of Howth* (1913). She also provided a colour portrait showing details of the structure of the rare orchid, *Spiranthes stricta* (now known as *Spiranthes romanzoffiana*; Figure 157) for Knowles's paper relating to this orchid, which appeared in the *Irish Naturalists' Journal*.[62]

She was responsible for submitting two plates to Anne Massy's report (1927) on the collection of Cephalopoda[63] in the South African Museum, which were collected during the British Antarctic expedition, 1910–1913. Her skills as a scientific illustrator were much in demand and her illustrations appeared in many publications, including several by distinguished Irish zoologist and Irish sponge specialist, Jane Stephens (1879–1959; see Figure 159):[64]

> *I recall with special gratitude the drawings of sponges and their skeletal spicules, which she made for my papers on sponges. She had to draw these minute spicules under a high-power microscope – work which demanded great accuracy and patience.*

As far as can be ascertained, she never signed her work but in the case of Jane Stephens's papers, the plate usually indicated that Barnes was responsible for the scientific illustration.[65]

It was largely through her collaboration with Robert Lloyd Praeger that Barnes is remembered today. In 1915, Praeger began a study of the genus *Sedum*.[66] *Sedums* are members of the Crassulaceae family of succulent plants and are commonly known as stonecrops (a literal name as these small fleshy-leaved plants 'crop' the exposed surface of stones). With financial support from a number of sources, including the RHS London, the monograph was to be illustrated. Praeger approached Barnes, who agreed to work with him as illustrator on this important study.

The 185 drawings were executed in black and white (pen and ink) with the morphological features of each leaf, stem and flower being depicted. Barnes drew them from living plants. The line drawings are clear, concise and well drawn, with no detail being lost. It is clear that the published portraits did not differ from the originals, with the exception of a small number that were annotated for printing purposes and indicate that they were to be reduced.

Today, Barnes's original line drawings are in the RIA manuscripts collection.[67] They are not coloured – colour is not considered to be of vital importance in a monograph as it can be conveyed in words. In 1921, 'An Account of the Genus Sedum as Found in Cultivation' was published by the RHS. For this study, Praeger was awarded the RHS Veitch Silver Medal.

Praeger's success generated a further approach by the Council of the RHS 'to prepare an illustrated account of the Semperviva', which was to be similar to his work on sedums. Once again, Barnes was to act as his collaborator. She provided 107 line drawings for this study,[68] which appeared in 1932. For the

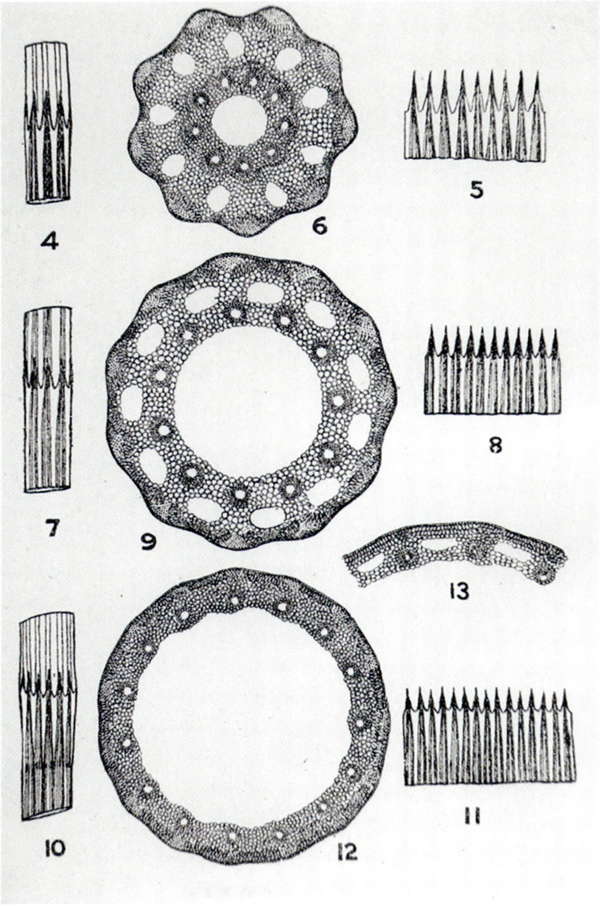


Fig. 158. *Equisetum arvense* (*E. fluviatile* and *E. litorale*, horsetails) showing characteristic stems
Original drawing by Eileen Barnes, reproduced in R.L. Praeger, *Irish Naturalists' Journal,* vol. 26, plates 6 and 7.
[Courtesy, National Botanic Gardens, Glasnevin, Dublin]

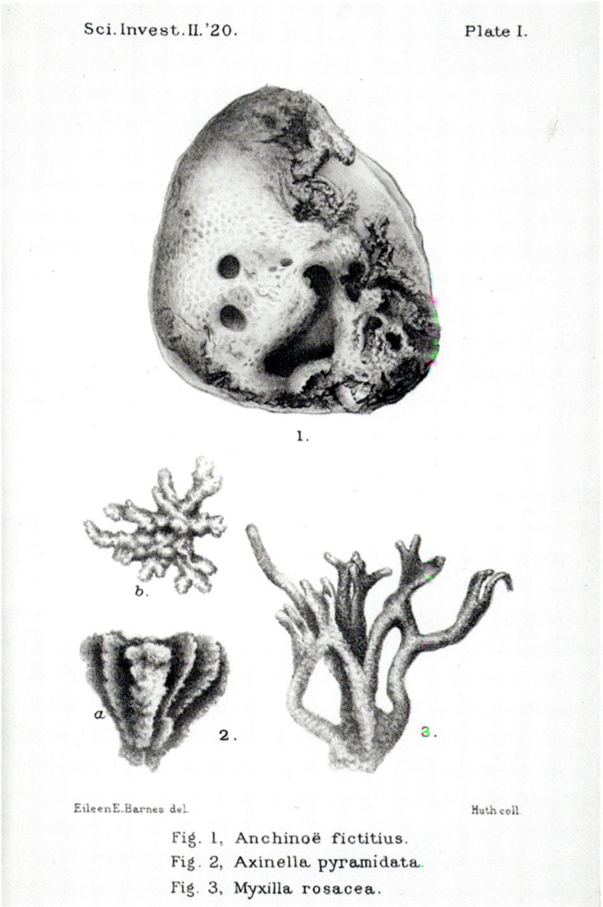


Fig. 159. A collection of sponges. 1. *Anchinoe fictitius* (Bowerbank), on oyster shell. 2. *Axinella pyramidata*, Stephens. Seen from the side (a) and from the top (b) of the sponge. 3. *Myxilla rosacea* (Lieberkuhn). Branching specimen. All natural size.
Pen and ink drawing by Eileen Barnes.
From Jane Stephens, *Sponges of the Coasts of Ireland, vol. 2, The Tetraxonida* (concluded) (Dublin: The Stationery Office, 1921).
[Courtesy, National Library of Ireland]

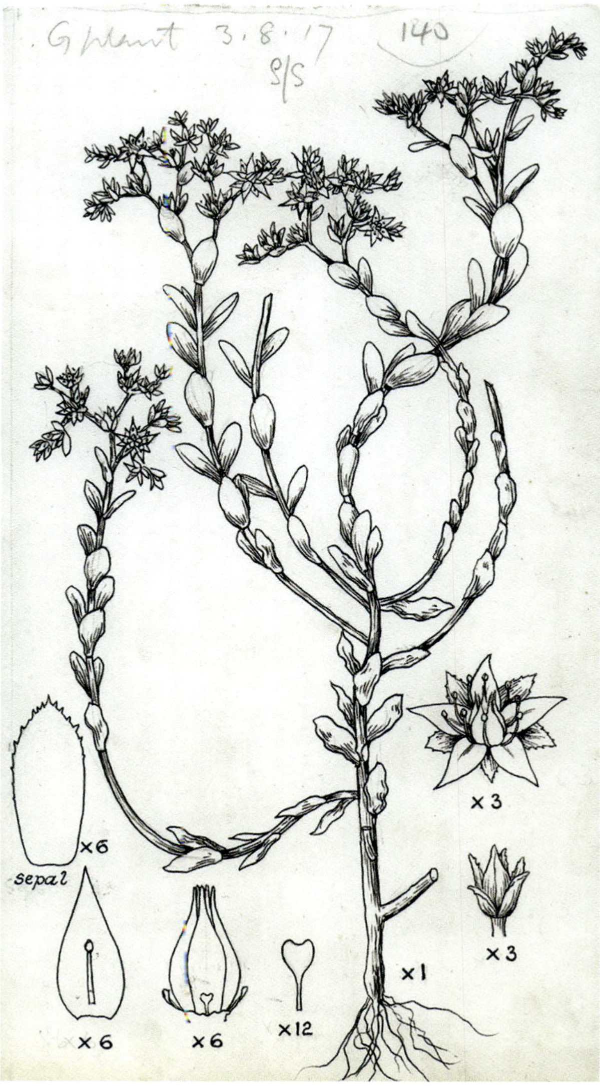


Fig. 160. *Sedum somenii,* sedum
Pen and ink on card by Eileen Barnes, 1917
Original pen and ink drawing (No. 140) executed by Eileen Barnes and reproduced in Robert Lloyd Praeger, 'Account of Genus Sedum as Found in Cultivation', *Journal of the Royal Horticultural Society*, 1921, pp. 296, 297.
[By permission of the Royal Irish Academy © RIA]

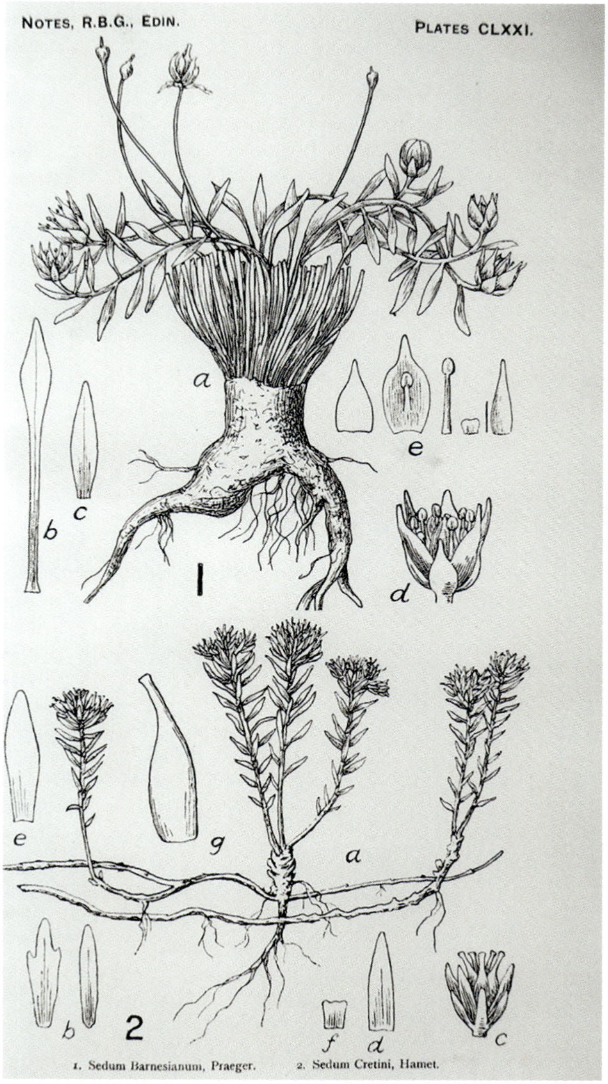


Fig. 161. *Sedum barnesianum* (*Rhodiola humilis;* plate 171)
Published line drawing based on an original drawing by Eileen Barnes
Reproduced in Robert Lloyd Praeger, 'Some Asiatic Sedums in the Edinburgh Herbarium; with supplementary notes from Kew and the British Museum', *Notes from The Royal Botanic Garden,* Edinburgh, vol. 12, 1920–1922, p. 72.
The original line drawing of this plant species from East Himalaya was executed by Barnes and is dedicated to her by Praeger.
[By permission of the Royal Irish Academy © RIA]

second time, Praeger was awarded the RHS Veitch Silver Medal. However, this time, he did acknowledge Barnes's contribution:

> *I owe special obligations to Miss Eileen Barnes of the National Museum, Dublin, the artist to whom the figures in this volume are due; her patience and skill in portraying the plants and making analyses of the flowers, etc., have resulted in drawings which add very greatly to whatever value the present account possesses.*[69]

In addition, Barnes illustrated a number of Praeger's articles (see Figure 158). In a publication relating to Asiatic sedums in the Edinburgh Herbarium, published in 1921,[70] Praeger named *Sedum barnesianum* (*Rhodiola humilis*; see Figure 161) after her, commenting that it was the artist's 'industry and skill [to which he owed] drawings of nearly two hundred species of Sedum'.

Eileen Barnes lived with her family at 2 Cabra Terrace on North Circular Road, Dublin and, from 1901 until her death, at 45 Kenilworth Square, Dublin. On 12 March 1956, following an accident, she died in Sir Patrick Dun's Hospital. Despite a record of almost 50 years' association with the National Museum, its archive holds no record of her service. It is good to learn that Eileen Barnes's life story was 'one of quiet achievement rather than acclaim'[71] and that it is recognised and publicly acknowledged today.

Often perceived as working on the margins, the women cited above succeeded in managing families, husbands and households in a social structure shaped by sexual difference. Frequently suppressing intellectual frustration and romantic daydreams, they broke through that barrier. We are fortunate that the majority of their work has survived and is recognised today.

# Chapter 9
# 'A Woman of Substance' – Lady Edith Blake

### (née Bernal Osborne; b. Clonmel, Co. Tipperary, 1846; d. Youghal, Co. Cork, 1926; Irish botanical artist, author, diplomat and polyglot)

Lady Edith Blake was born on 7 February 1846 at 'Newtown Anner', a late Georgian house belonging to her mother's family (see Figure 163). The house is located around two miles from Clonmel, Co. Tipperary, on the Tipperary side of what is known as the Golden Valley, where the broad River Suir runs between the Comeragh Mountains and Slievenamon. Edith was the eldest daughter of Catherine Isabella Osborne (1818–1880) and Ralph Bernal Osborne (1808–1882), a liberal MP.

The latter was educated at Charterhouse School and entered Trinity College Cambridge in 1829 but never settled and was removed from the university and sent into the army. There, Ralph Bernal remained, being promoted to Captain until he entered Parliament in 1841. As MP, he held a number of seats, including Waterford (1870–1874). An able, if controversial, debater in the House, he supported the liberal interests and with his engaging and witty personality was considered to be the licensed jester of Victorian high society – the 'enfant terrible'. Contemporary accounts recall his remarks, considered devastatingly witty at the time, but which today sound somewhat out of tune. When he retired from politics, many felt that his loss 'contributed to the decline of the House of Commons and the decline and fall of statesmanship'.[1]

His wife, Catherine, was the daughter of Catherine Rebecca Osborne (née Smith) and Sir Thomas Osborne (1757–1821), a prominent landowner in counties Tipperary (south) and Waterford, who served as MP for Carysfort, Co. Wicklow from 1776 to 1797. Catherine's only brother, William, died, aged eight in May 1824, which left her the sole heir to the Osborne estates. On a visit to London, she met her future husband, Ralph Bernal, at a salon hosted by Irish novelist, Lady Morgan (née Sydney Owenson; 1781–1859). The couple were married on 20 August 1844, Ralph Bernal assuming his wife's surname, Osborne, by royal licence. The marriage would not appear to have been a happy one. In 1863, Catherine published, anonymously, a thinly disguised attack on her husband entitled *False Positions*,[2] which succeeded in bringing his extramarital affairs to the public's attention.

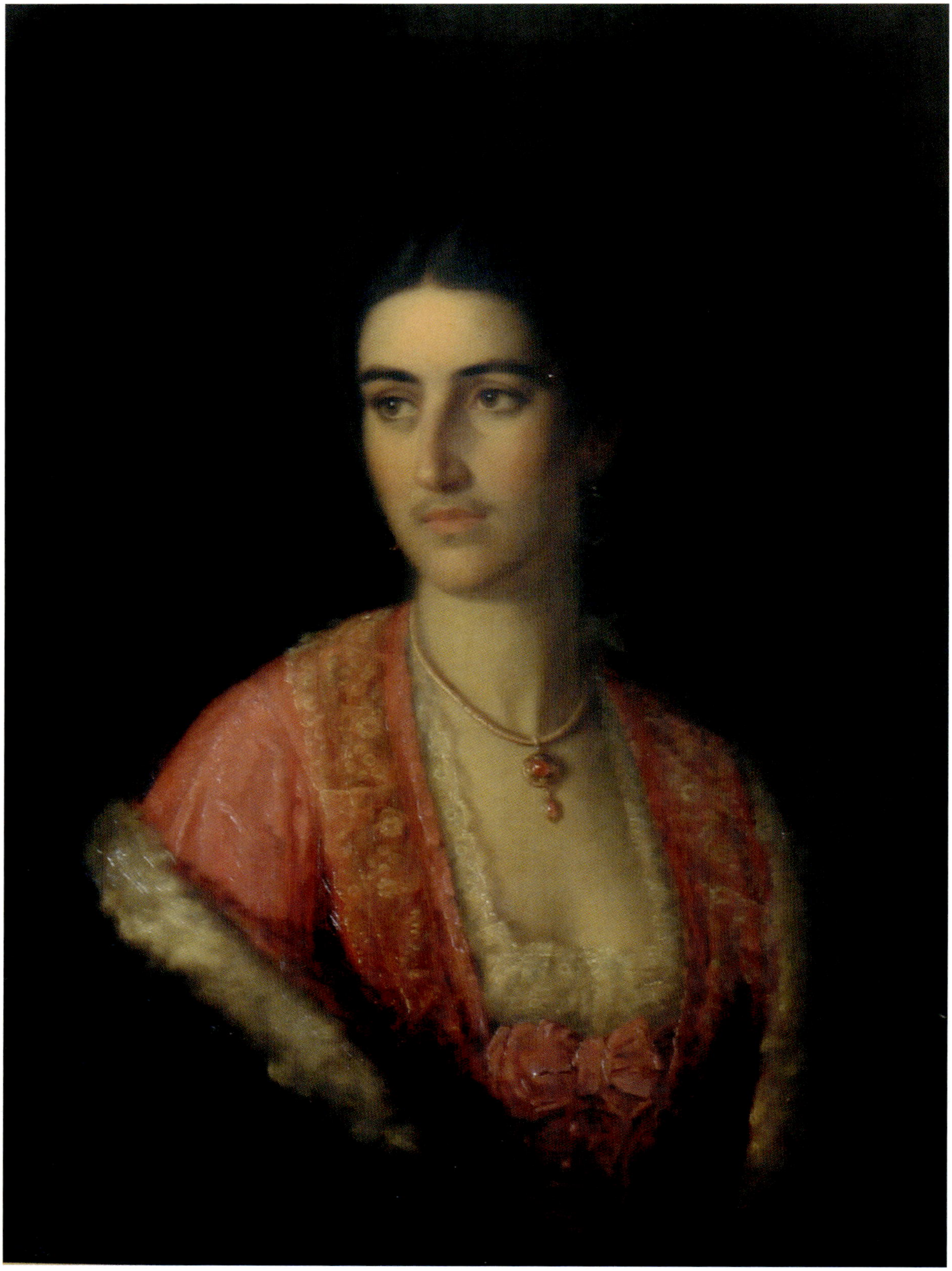

Fig. 162. Edith Osborne (later Lady Edith Blake; 1846–1926)
[Private collection. Reproduced by kind permission]

Ralph Bernal Osborne was based largely in London, and this resulted in his wife being responsible for the raising of their two daughters at 'Newtown Anner'. Edith was born in 1846 and Grace (1848–1926) two years later. Their mother, a lively and cultivated woman who played host to many of the well-known 'personalities' of the day, ensured that her daughters had ample opportunity to meet figures of distinction drawn from the world of politics, science, art, philosophy and literature – leading English watercolourist/engraver Thomas Shotter Boys, William Despard Hemphill, photographer, together with Joseph Paxton, designer and landscape gardener responsible for the design of the gardens at 'Newtown Anner' were all frequent visitors. Catherine, herself a talented artist, became an early patron and admirer of such artists as Swiss landscape painter, Alexandre Calame (1810–1864); she consistently encouraged her two daughters in their artistic activities.

It was against this background that Edith and her sister, Grace, developed wide-ranging interests. In Edith's case, these included anthropology, art, social issues and a love of natural history. She became an excellent linguist and could:

> *speak nine languages: Irish, English, Spanish, French, German, Portuguese, Italian, Russian and Chinese, which later she learned to both read and write.*[3]

Founders of the Water Colour Society of Ireland (known then as the Amateur Drawing Society)[4] paid many visits to the Osborne home and included

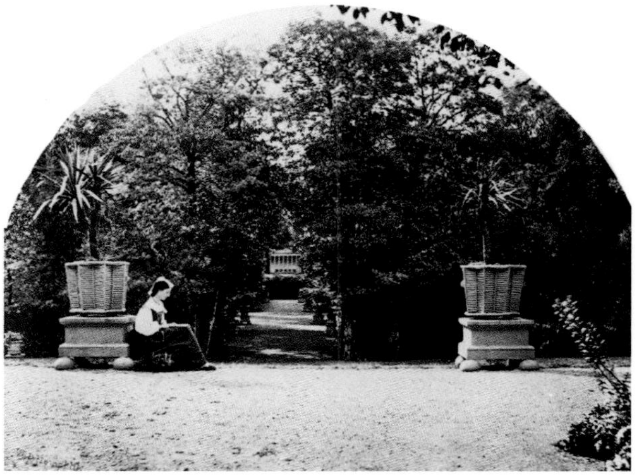

Fig. 163. The walk to Lady Osborne's summerhouse with Edith Osborne seated in the foreground on the terrace walk above the lake, 'Newtown Anner', Clonmel, Co. Tipperary. [Reproduced courtesy of the Tipperary Museum of Hidden History, Cultural Service, Clonmel, Co. Tipperary]

Frances ('Fanny') Currey, Henrietta Sophia Phipps and Anna Frances Musgrave together with Baroness Pauline Prochazka. As a schoolgirl, Frances Currey spent many long hours with Edith in the schoolroom at 'Newtown Anner', collaborating and illustrating comic envelopes (1858–1868).[5]

In February 1872, aged 26, Edith embarked on a one-year tour of Europe, which included visits to Austria, Germany, Italy, Sicily, Greece and Turkey. Accompanied by a clergyman, a maid and a cousin, she kept a diary focusing on both architecture and local culture and recorded scenes in her sketchbooks, several of which were later to be translated into lithographs and published under the title: *Twelve Months in Southern Europe* (1876).[6]

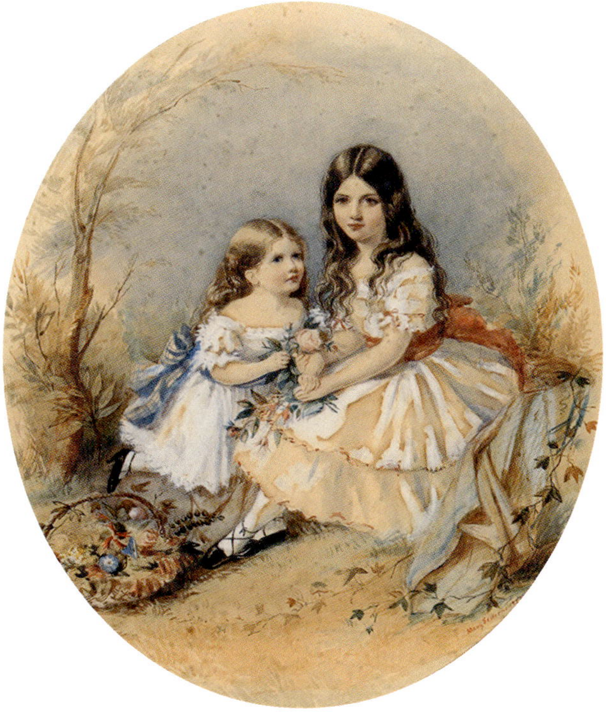

Fig. 164. Edith Osborne aged six and her sister, Grace Osborne aged four, 'Newtown Anner', Clonmel, Co. Tipperary [Private collection. Reproduced by kind permission]

Despite their own marital differences, Edith's parents were anxious for their eldest daughter to make a 'successful' marriage, just as her sister, Grace had done by marrying and becoming the second wife of the 10th Duke of St Albans. However, Edith would appear to have had other ideas.

In 1874, she eloped with, and married, Captain Henry Arthur Blake (1840–1918), a county inspector for the Irish Constabulary. Appalled at Blake's lower social status, the family immediately disinherited their eldest daughter, although both sisters kept in touch throughout their lives.

Edith's husband, a widower,[7] was the son of Peter Blake, Corbally Castle, Co. Galway, also a county inspector for the Irish Constabulary, and Jane Lane, the daughter of John Lane, Lanespark, Co. Tipperary. Henry Blake had begun his career as a clerk in a bank but after 18 months resigned and enrolled as a cadet in the Irish Constabulary (1857). Following his marriage to Edith, the Blakes moved to Belfast and began to find themselves short of money. Two years later, Edith's husband was appointed Resident Magistrate, Tuam, Co. Galway, and in 1881 he was promoted to Special Resident Magistrate.

These were difficult times in Ireland, with the Land Wars at their height, and Gladstone's Coercion Act being passed into law in 1881. As a result, Henry found himself in a dangerous position and was constantly under threat of assassination. In order to protect her husband, Edith frequently carried a cocked revolver under a blanket in the pony and trap in which they were travelling. His life was:

> *saved on several occasions by his wife's fearlessness. Lady Blake was a fine revolver shot and insisted in accompanying him wherever he went, sitting by him on his jaunting car with her revolver ready cocked in her hand below the rug and similarly armed she sat by him on the bench when he was presiding in court.*[8]

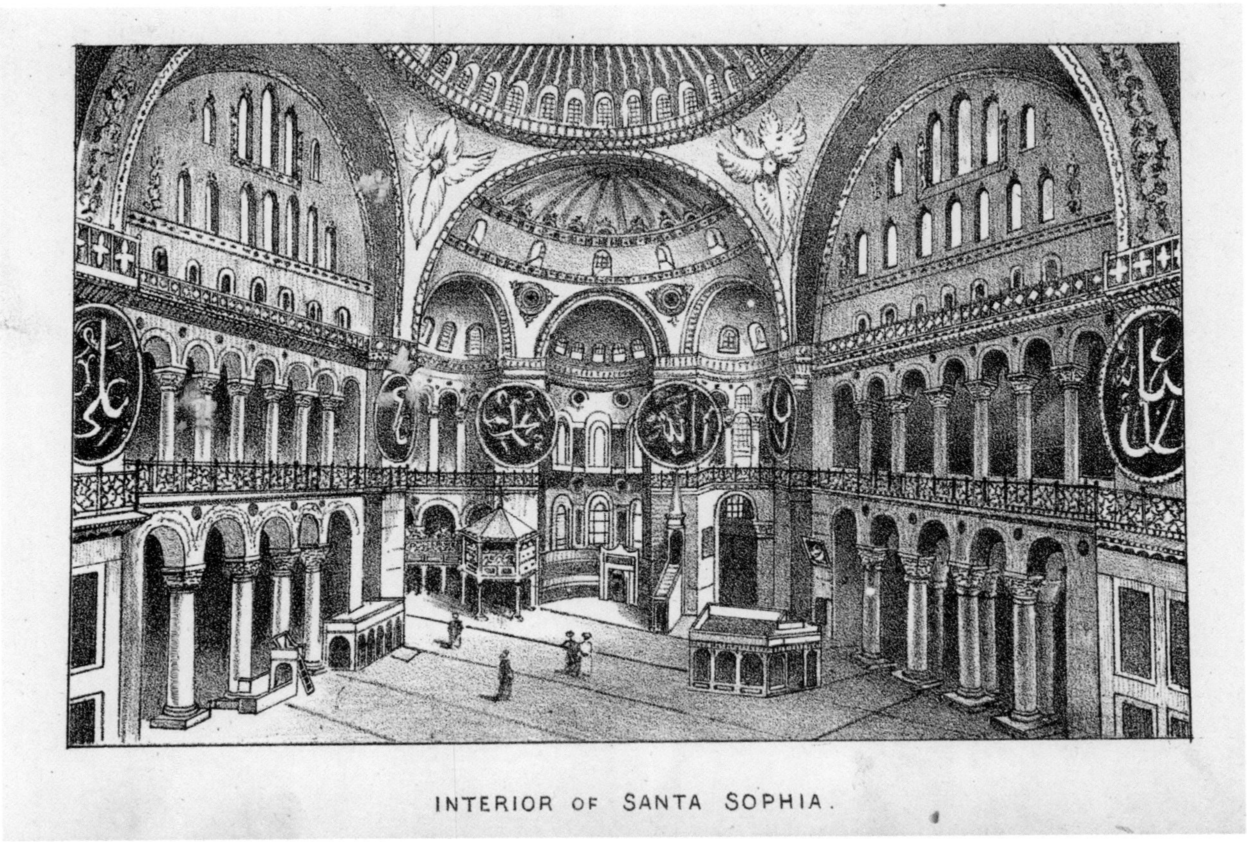


Fig. 165. Interior of Santa Sophia
Original drawing by Edith Osborne, lithograph from *Twelve Months in Southern Europe*
[Courtesy, National Library of Ireland]

Despite her husband's difficult, often dangerous, work and his unionist affiliations, Edith remained interested and sympathetic towards nationalism. She was a friend of Anna Parnell (1852–1911), sister of Charles Stewart Parnell (1846–1391), a founder of the Ladies' Land League who sought to assist the already established Land League (21 October 1879) by collecting information on estates throughout Ireland. In 1879, Edith published her second book: *The Realities of Freemasonry*. The following year, her mother died at 'Newtown Anner', and her father two years later.

Following his period as 'Special Magistrate', Henry Blake applied to the colonial service and in 1884 was offered the Governorship of the Bahamas (1884–1887). His wife took a keen interest in the

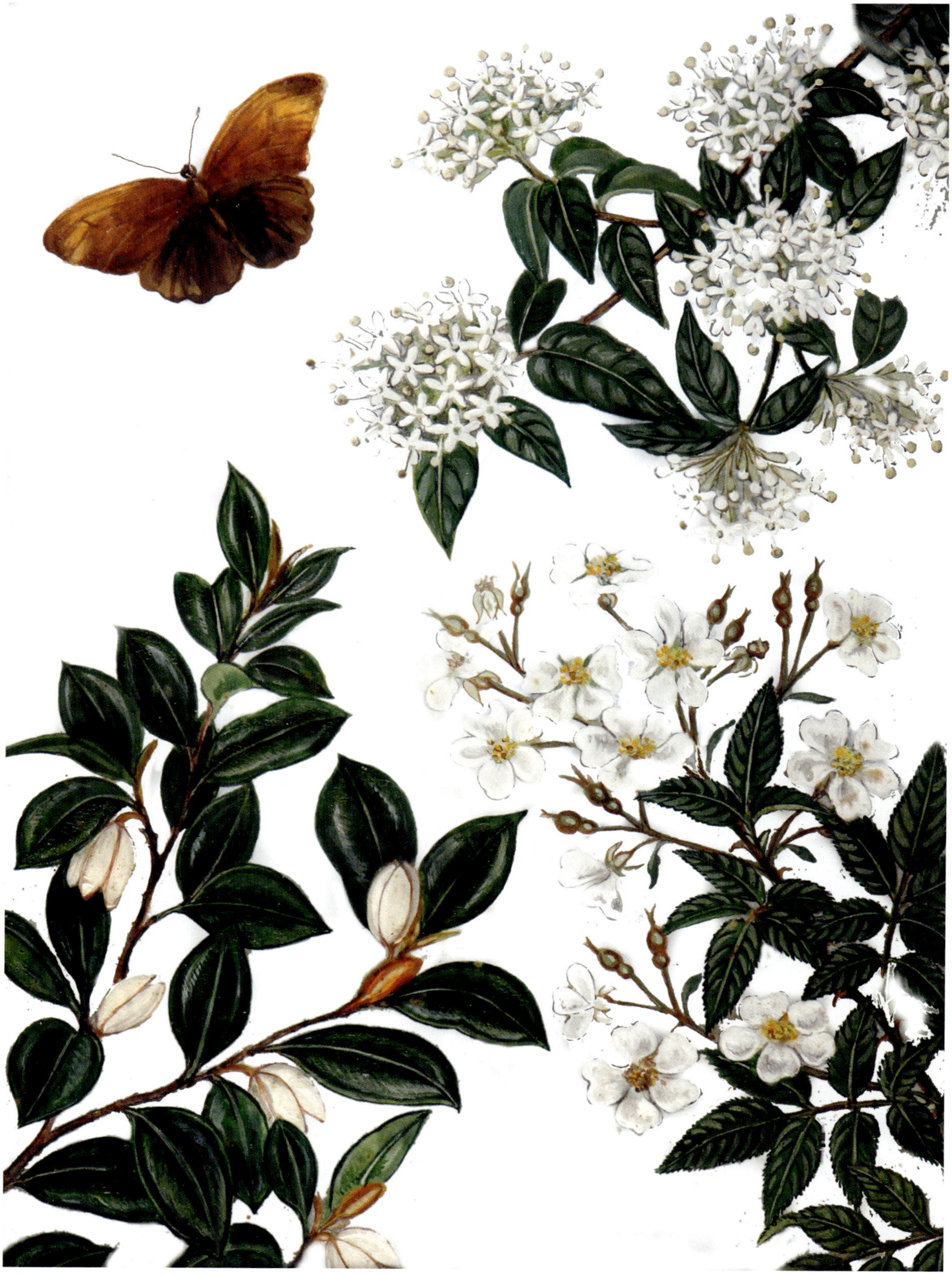

Fig. 166. *Viburnum* sp. (top right), *Michelia figo* (*Magnolia figo*) (bottom left) and *Rosa arvensis* (bottom right)
Watercolour and gouache by Edith Blake
[Private collection. Reproduced by kind permission]

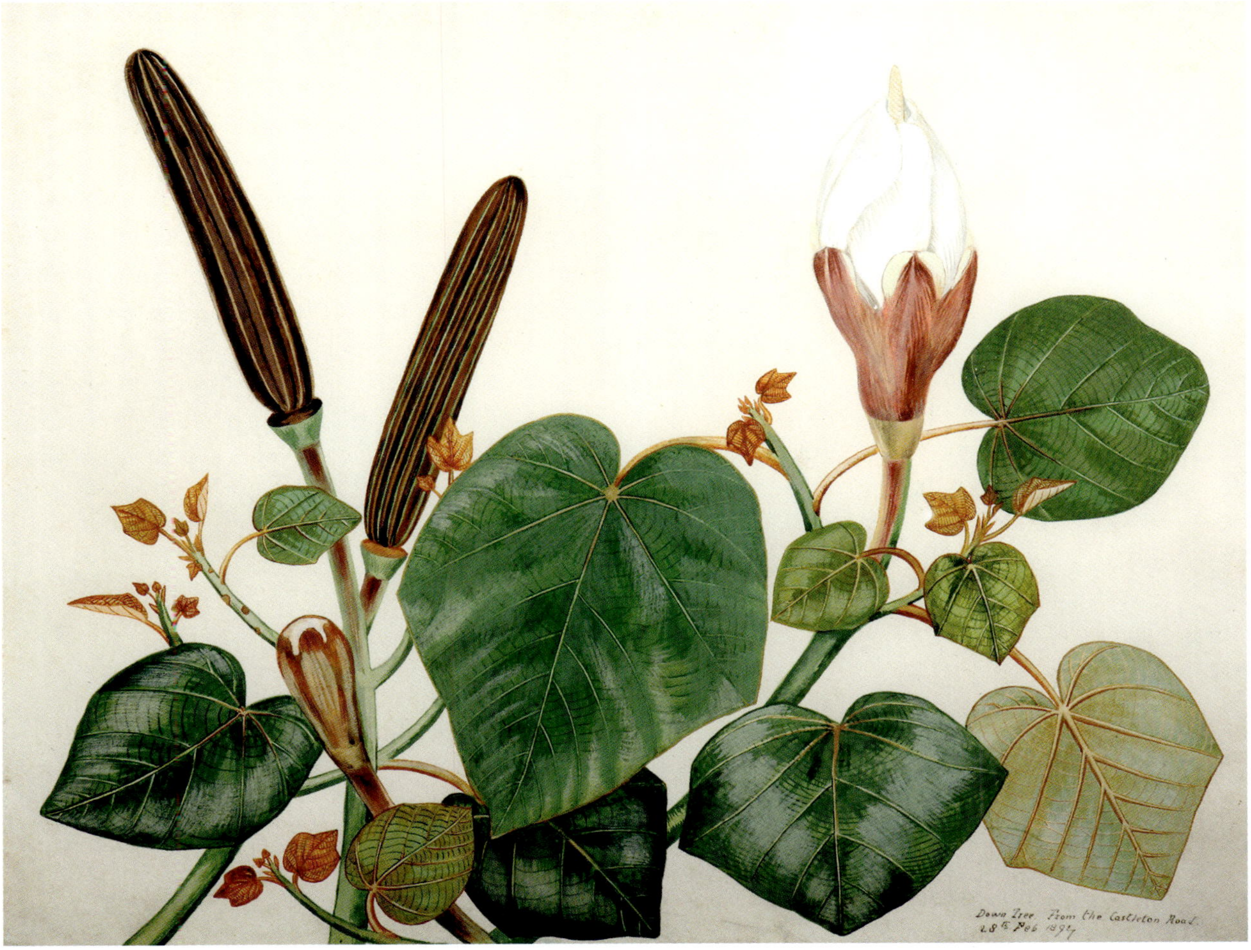


Fig. 167. *Ochroma pyramidale*, balsa wood (also known as the down tree or corkwood)
Watercolour and gouache by Edith Blake, inscribed '*Down Tree from the Castleton road 28$^{th}$ Feb 1894*'
[Private collection. Reproduced by kind permission]

country and her collection of over 100 indigenous American artefacts from the Bahamas is now in the National Museum of the American Indian in New York. This was to be the first of a number of postings which were to take the family, including their three children, Olive, Maurice and Arthur, to many countries throughout the British Empire. On each occasion, Henry Blake served as Governor:

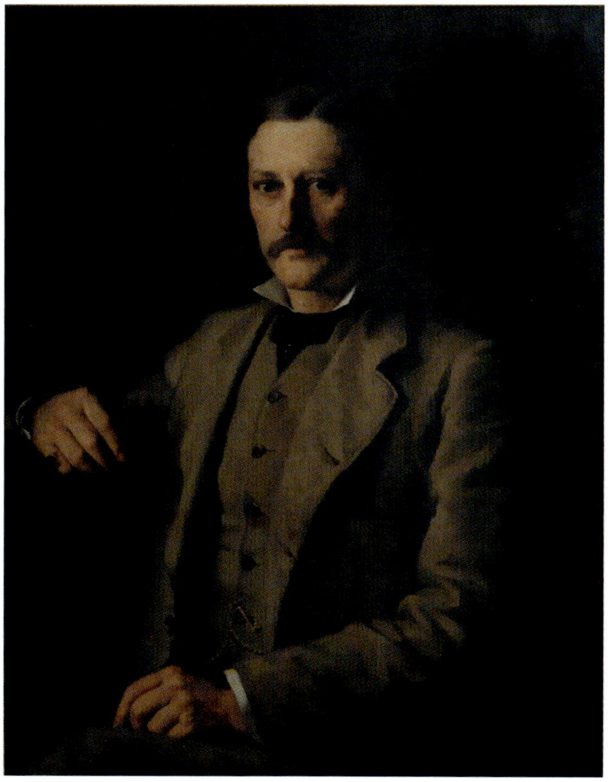

Fig. 168. Sir Henry Arthur Blake, GCMG, FRGS, FRCI (1840–1918)
[Private collection. Reproduced by kind permission]

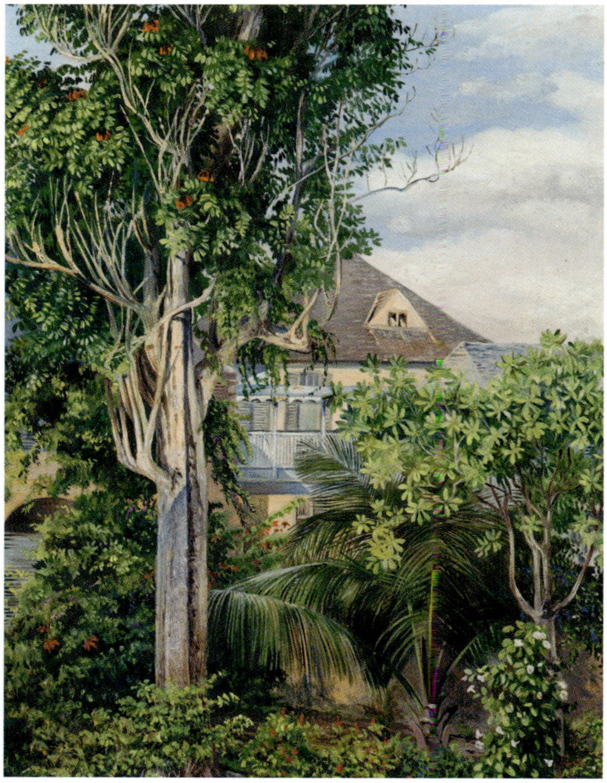

Fig. 169. The gardens of the King's House, Spanish Town, Jamaica
Watercolour by Marianne North (1830–1890), 1872
[© Royal Botanic Gardens, Kew]

Newfoundland, 1887–1888; Jamaica, 1889–1897; Hong Kong, 1898–1903; and Ceylon, 1903–1907. Henry Arthur Blake was knighted at the end of his one-year appointment as Governor of Newfoundland in November 1888, and three months later became Captain General and Governor-in-Chief of Jamaica on 9 March 1889. His term was to be extended twice, at the request of local bodies, and was to amount to a total of nine years spent in that country.

The Blakes and their children obviously loved Jamaica and worked hard to make the country well known throughout the world. They encouraged industry and development. Roads and railways were built, and hotels constructed in order to encourage tourists. On 27 January 1891, the International Exhibition, modelled on the great industrial exhibitions that had taken place in London, was opened in Kingston by George, Prince of Wales, displaying both the manufactured and natural products of the island. Edith and her husband were anxious to promote agriculture and founded the Jamaican Agricultural Society in 1895, Sir Henry Arthur becoming their first president. Edith encouraged the construction of a marine laboratory to persuade scientists to visit and study the rich flora and fauna to be found on and around the island.

Edith's interests in botany and entomology had already begun to emerge when living in Newfoundland. In a series of articles published in the *Evening Telegram* (1888–1889),[9] she attempted to trace the history of the discovery of Newfoundland and the effect on the native populations; she also revealed to the reader her interest and curiosity in natural history, describing the native mosses and lichens, together with plants and trees of the country.

In Jamaica, surrounded by the spectacular Jamaican flora and fauna, Edith began to devote more of her time to painting:

> *Lady Blake has painted from life, the caterpillars, chrysalids and adults of many of the native Lepidoptera, and her collection of over 100 watercolours of this order are a treat to the artist as well as to the entomologist.*[10]

Edith also corresponded with Daniel Morris (1844–1933), Assistant Director of the RBG, Kew. Morris had been Director of the Public Gardens, Jamaica (1879–1886) and was associated with the development of the economic resources of the West Indies. He took up his post at Kew in 1886 and, shortly after her arrival in Jamaica, Edith began to send him consignments of seeds from the island:

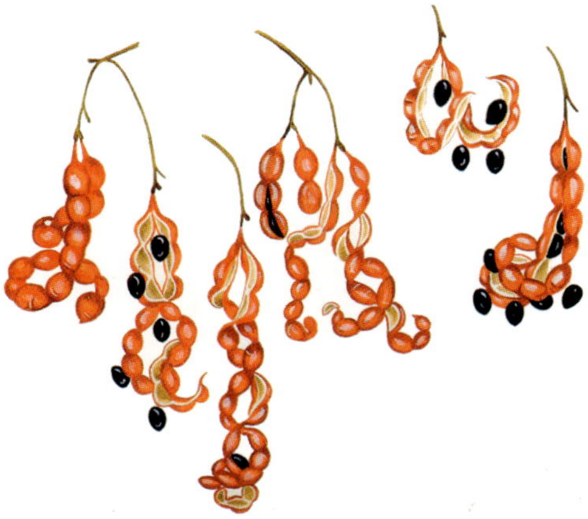

Fig. 170. *Cojoba arborea*
Watercolour by Edith Blake
[Private collection. Reproduced by kind permission]

> *I was fortunate enough the other day to [procure] some of the seeds & two roots of that magnificent white lotus which I believe was supposed to have disappeared from this island. The flowers are beautiful, as large if not larger than those of the Victoria Regia ... I send you three of the weeds in case you have not already got them ...*[11]

Living in their official residence, the King's House, the Blakes did much to improve the gardens, planting ferns, orchids and ornamental palms, which resulted in transforming it into one of the most outstanding gardens on the island. There were frequent visitors

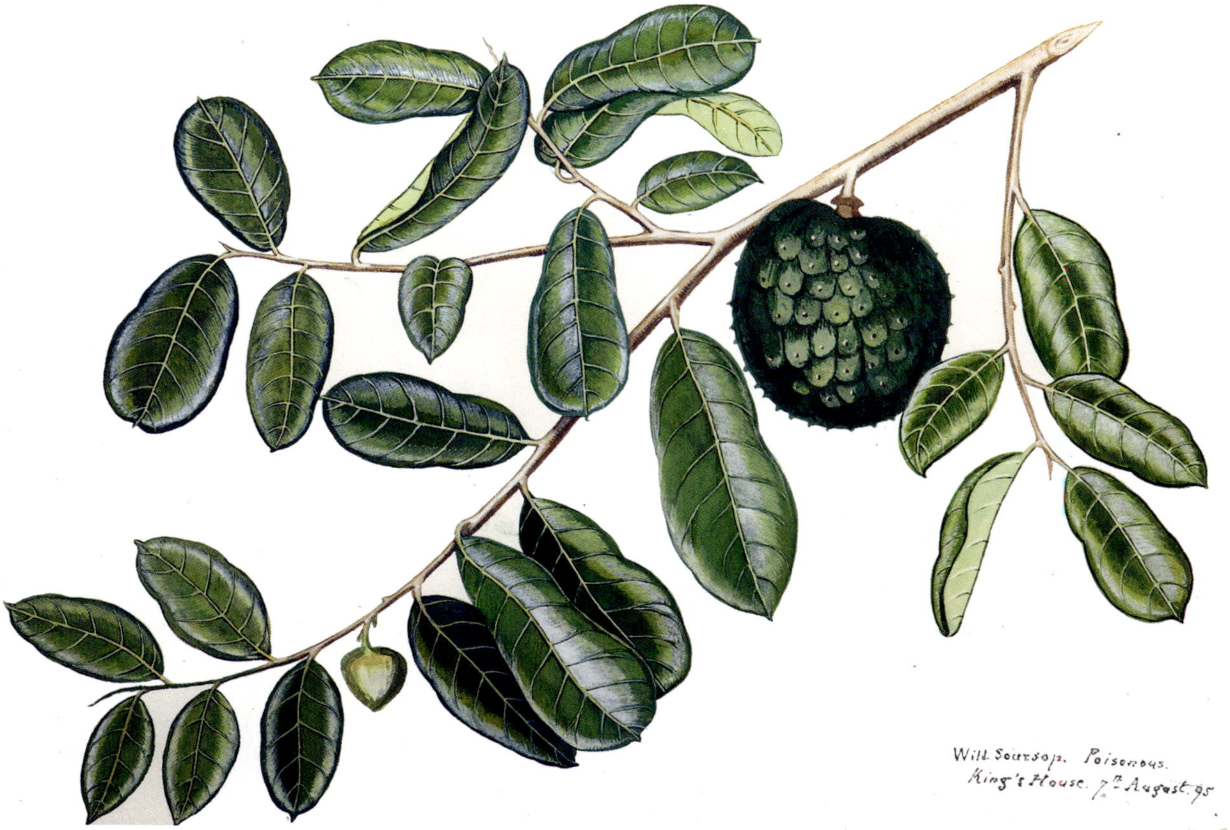


Fig. 171. *Annona muricata,* soursop
Watercolour by Edith Blake, inscribed '*Wild Soursop. Poisonous King's House 7 August '95*'
[Private collection. Reproduced by kind permission]

from Ireland to the King's House – the Villiers-Stuarts from Dromana, Co. Waterford, the Earl and Countess of Rosse, Birr Castle, Eva FitzGerald, daughter of the 4th Duke of Leinster, and a frequent exhibitor with the Water Colour Society of Ireland, together with Emily Trant (née Newton) from 'Dovea House', Co. Tipperary.[12]

The Blake Collection, consisting of drawings of Jamaican Lepidoptera and plants now in the NHM, London,[13] was executed by Edith during her stay on the island. Although the artist had no strict art academic training, these drawings are remarkable recordings. All are executed in watercolour on a wide variety of paper, and, in some areas, gouache

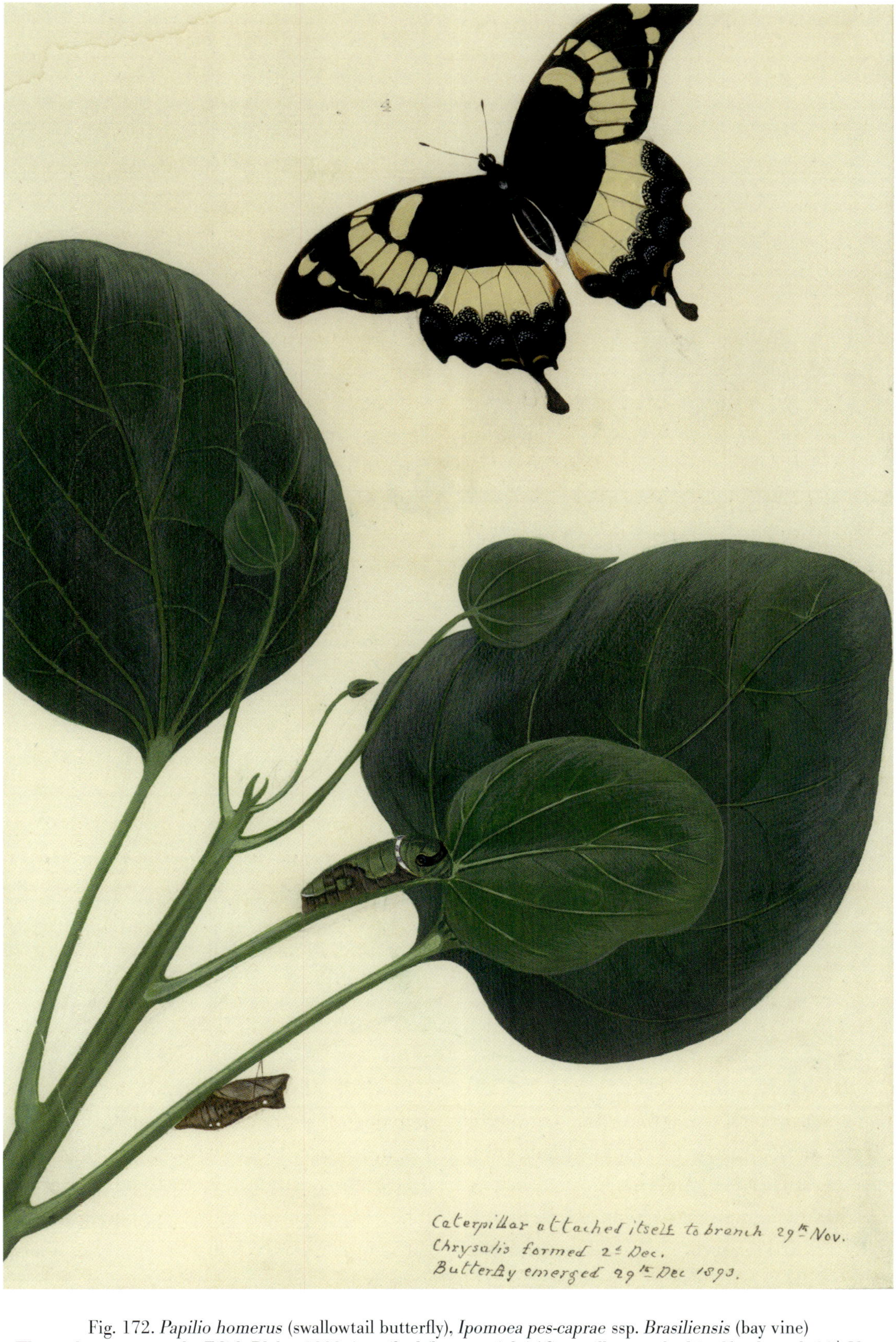


Fig. 172. *Papilio homerus* (swallowtail butterfly), *Ipomoea pes-caprae* ssp. *Brasiliensis* (bay vine)
Watercolour on paper by Edith Blake, 1893, inscribed (bottom right) '*Caterpillar attached itself to branch 29th Nov. Chrysalis formed 2d Dec. Butterfly emerged 29th Dec 1893*'
[Trustees of the Natural History Museum, London]

has been added to give a thicker consistency to the pigment.

Edith was obviously fascinated by Lepidoptera and spent a good deal of her time collecting and rearing them and making observations. Her paintings depict their life cycle, the butterfly or moth being shown together with a plant which, in the majority of cases, is the food plant of the larva. Interestingly, the artist does not record the early egg stage but, with a high degree of accuracy, illustrates the larval food plants and the damage caused to them by the larvae. Pupae are depicted attached to the plant, or drawn separately, when the larva pupates away from its food plant. The majority of the drawings are complete and vary from the vertical format coupled with delicate linearity to stark, dramatic images. In many cases, pure wash is selectively applied both to record the plant's colour and to heighten the decorative quality of the whole. Edith's amateur technique is apparent in several of the plant illustrations, which appear somewhat flat on the page.

Her watercolour of the swallowtail butterfly (*Papilio homerus*) together with the plant, the bay vine (*Ipomoea pes-caprae* ssp. *Brasiliensis*; Figure 172) records the date, 29 November, when the caterpillar attached itself to the branch, the chrysalis forming on 2 December and the butterfly emerging on the 29th of that month, 1893. This is just one painting from a collection of almost 200 that record the Jamaican butterflies, moths and plants, all unpublished, and which cover Edith's nine-year stay on the island, the first being dated a year after her arrival (1890).

Many of the artist's plant portraits depict plants grown in, or near, Castleton Botanical Gardens, Jamaica, which had been established on 19 November 1862. In the late 19th and 20th centuries, the gardens held over 4,000 species of plants, the majority being introduced from Kew. There, Edith spent long happy hours painting and recording. Her portrait of balsa wood, also known as the down tree or corkwood (*Ochroma pyramidale*; Figure 167), is inscribed: 'Down Tree from the Castleton road'. Balsa wood is among the lightest known commercial woods and before the early 20th century was used by fishermen in Jamaica for making fishing-net floats, the bark being made into ropes and rafts. *Cojoba arborea* (Figure 170), a small to very large evergreen tree with a broad, spreading crown, also formed part of her recordings; the inscription reads: 'Jamaica - Caramba from Castleton, 23rd Dec 1890'. The wood, resistant to attack by insects, is durable and ideal for heavy construction, stakes, posts, carpentry, etc. Many of Edith's plant portraits were executed from her home: 'Wild Soursop. Poisonous King's House 7 August '95' (Figure 171).

Always acutely aware of native plants and their importance to the local economy, the Blakes contributed to the first major flora of the country, *Flora of Jamaica* (1910),[14] in which both are listed as contributors.

The Jamaica International Exhibition which opened on 27 January 1891, marked Sir Henry Arthur Blake's break from typical colonial policy at the time, one that regarded the island as a place full of people previously

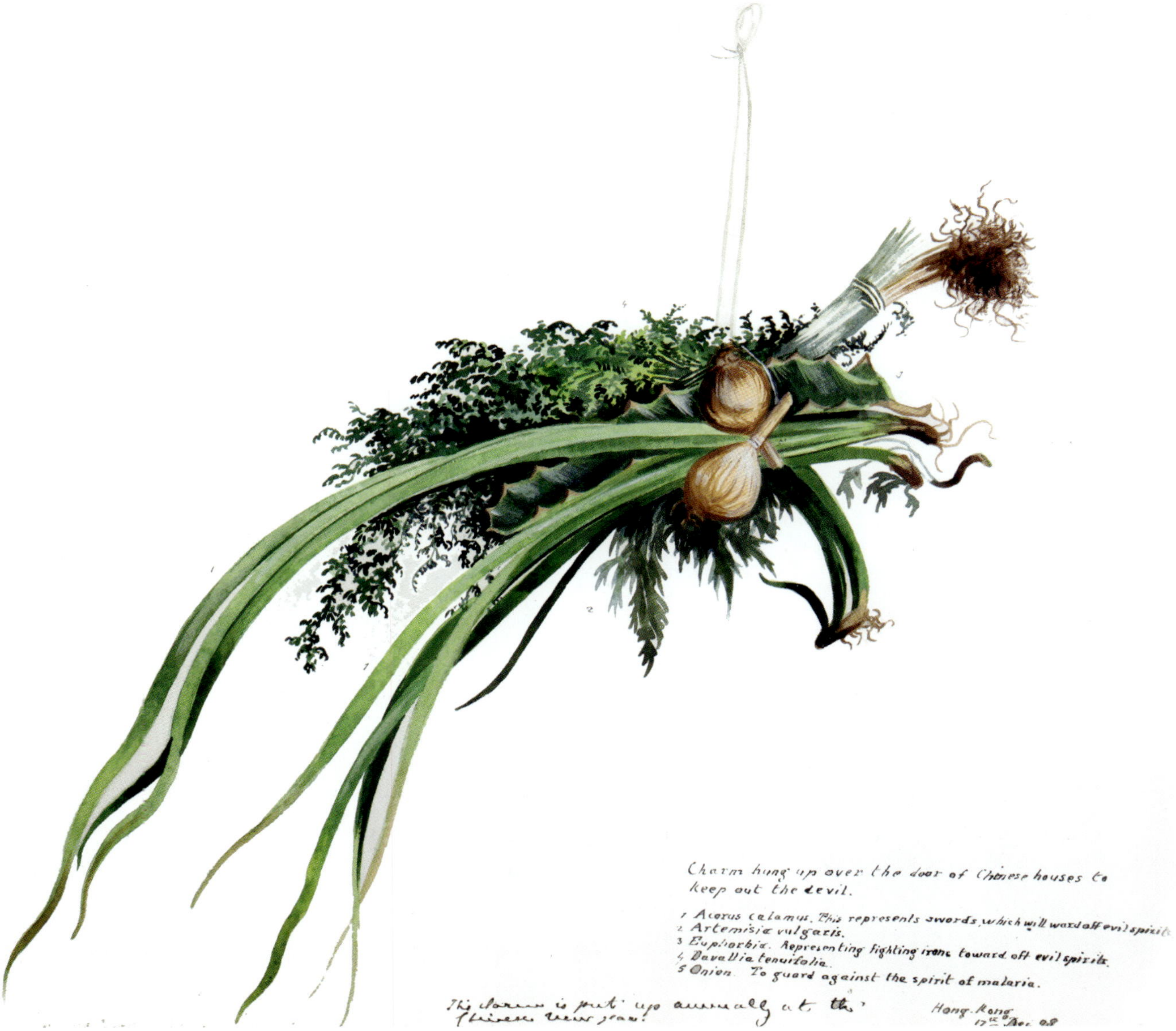


Fig. 173. 1. *Acorus calamus*, sweet flag, 2. *Artemisia vulgaris*, 3. *Euphorbia*, 4. *Davalia tenufolia* (*Odontosoria chinensis* subsp. *tenuifolia*), fern
Watercolour by Edith Blake, inscribed '*Hong-Kong 17th Dec 98*'
[Private collection. Reproduced by kind permission]

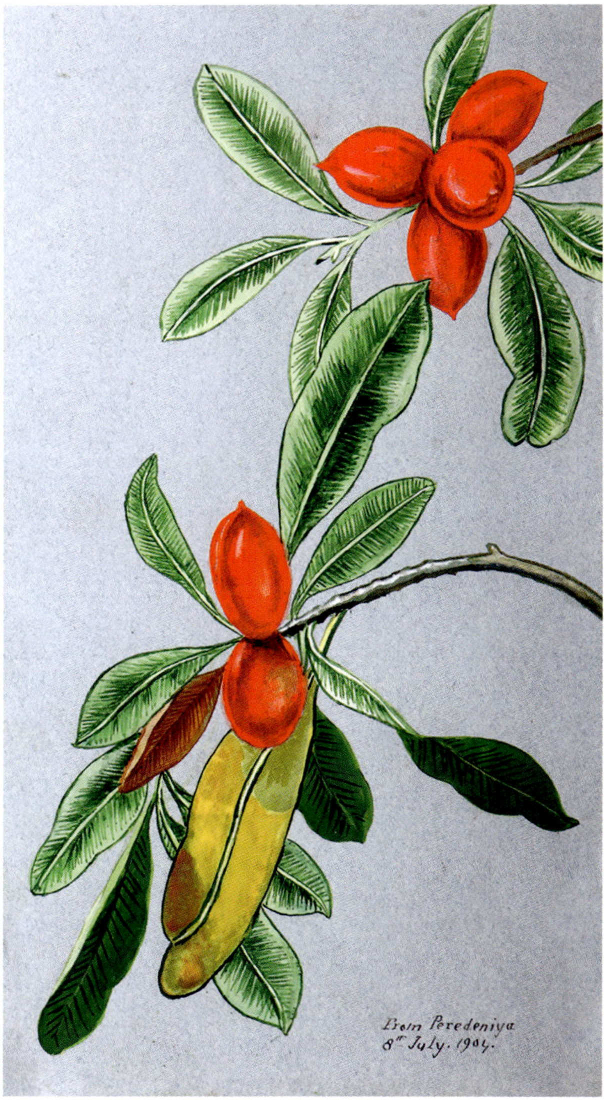

Fig. 174. *Erythroxylum* coca
Watercolour by Edith Blake, inscribed (on verso) '*From Peredeniya 9 July 1904*'
[Private collection. Reproduced by kind permission]

enslaved and considered dangerous, to one which he considered to be on the verge of a new prosperity. Always pragmatic in his views of Jamaica, Blake encouraged the local population to foster a stake in their own country. In his article 'The Awakening of Jamaica' (1890),[15] he makes clear that he believes the Jamaican Black majority to be a self-sustaining and viable community, one that was 'decidedly anxious for improvement'.[16] As part of his new approach, the international trade exhibition was launched in Kingston and written up by both husband[17] and wife. Edith remarked: 'A few months ago this delicious garden was an arid field.... The site is of unparalled magnificence'.[18] Interestingly, it was one of the very few international exhibitions to be held in a colonial city rather than in Chicago, London, Paris or New York.

Since the early 1880s, Jamaica's economy had been in decline, with both the sugar and banana exports having failed to reach their full potential; it was felt that there was a strong need to attract investment to the island. The international trade exhibition aimed to show off Jamaica's wide variety of products and to encourage trade. It received financial support from both the British and Jamaican governments, as well as from a number of private guarantors. Closing on 2 May 1891, it had succeeded in attracting over 300,000 visitors.

While living in Jamaica, Edith exhibited her botanical watercolours of the local flora and fauna at the Science and Art Museum, Dublin (1894). The exhibition was organised by the then Director, Dr Valentine Ball.[19]

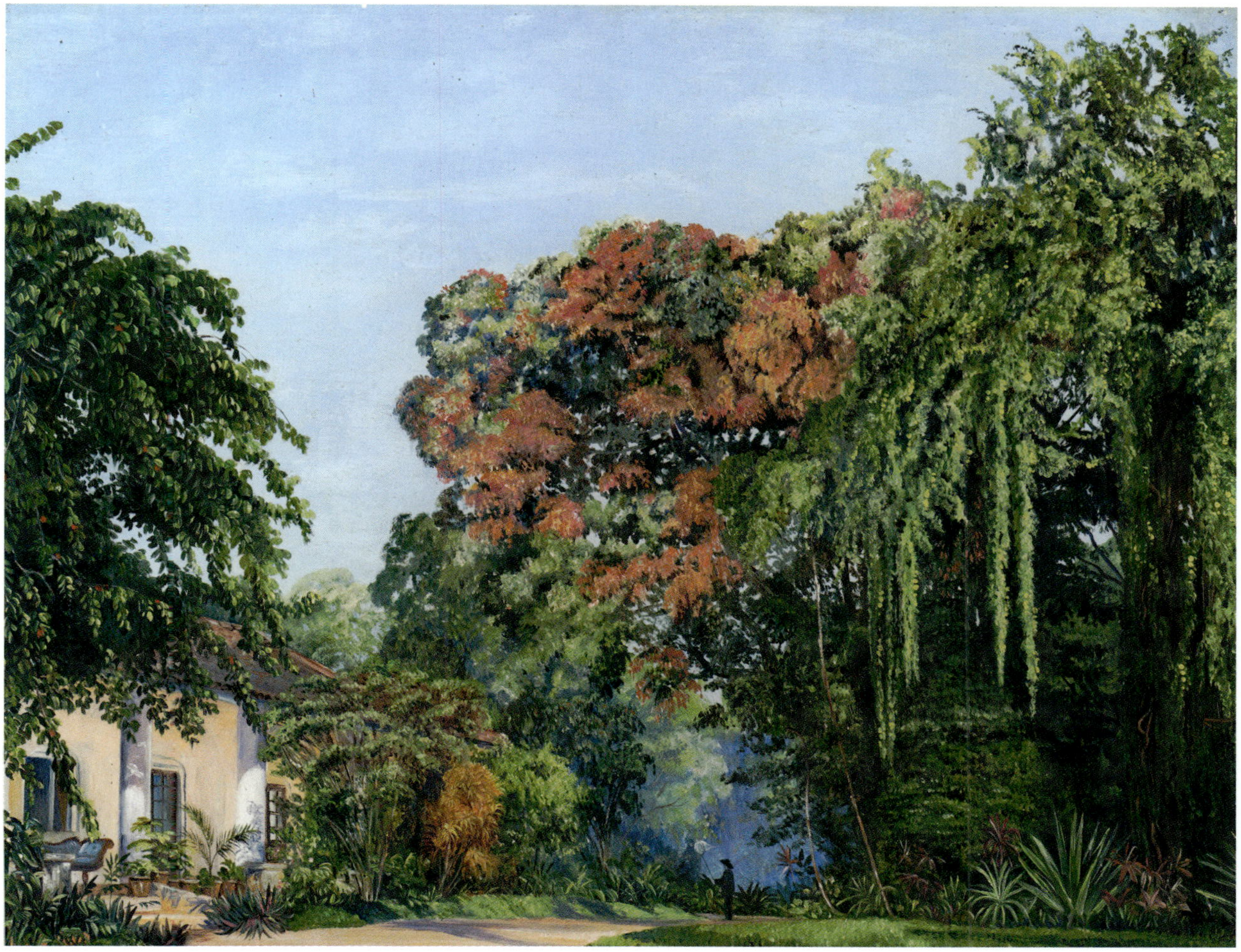

Fig. 175. A view in the Royal Botanic Gardens, Peradeniya, Ceylon
Watercolour by Marianne North (1830–1890)
[© Royal Botanic Gardens, Kew]

Under the Blakes' tenure, several programmes were implemented on the island – free primary and secondary school education (from 1893) and the Jamaica Union of Teachers, a group that would play a significant role in Jamaican political nationalism in the 1900s.[20] Both Edith and her husband were contributors to a number of English and American scientific journals.[21] Edith was always interested in the histories and folk ways of minor figures, such as the indigenous West Indian

Arawaks and Caribs, together with the Maroons of Jamaica, the latter of whom she believed to be 'courteous, loyal to their word, faithful to their friends, active and plucky'.[22] All formed the basis for a number of wide-ranging articles.

On Henry's appointment as Governor of Hong Kong in 1898, the Blakes left Jamaica, their departure being much regretted:

> *For the past nine years natural science in Jamaica has enjoyed the patronage and support in countless ways of his Excellency Sir Henry Blake, the Governor of the island and his estimable wife....*[23]

In Hong Kong, Edith's husband faced a difficult challenge, his major task being to acquire the New Territories leased by China to Great Britain in June 1898. It would appear that due to simmering political tensions, Edith had little time to devote to painting, although several examples from this period have survived. Her portrait of *Solanum wrighhtii* (commonly known as the 'potato tree'), executed in Hong Kong on 2 September 1899, was originally described by leading taxonomist and botanist George Bentham, LLD, FRS, FLS (1800–1884) in 1861, as being from Hong Kong; Bentham adding that 'no authentically wild specimens have ever been seen in China'. Edith's attractive study of 'Charm hung over the door of Chinese houses to keep out the devil' is dated 'Hong-Kong 17 Dec 98'. It consists of a collection of plants: *Acorus calamus*, representing swords to ward off evil spirits; *Artemisia vulgaris*; *Euphorbia*, representing fighting irons; *Davalia tenufolia* (now known as *Odontosoria chinensis* subsp. *tenuifolia)*; and an onion, believed to guard against the spirit of malaria (Figure 173).

While in Hong Kong, the couple continued their interest in botany. Two different species of oak, native to Hong Kong and the New Territories, were planted on the front lawn of the Governor's House and named *Quercus blakei*:

> *named after the distinguished Governor of Hong Kong, Sir Henry Blake, G.C.M.G., from whom botanical investigations in the colony have received constant support and encouragement.*[24]

The second, *Quercus edithiae*, was named after Sir Henry Arthur Blake's wife.

As a tribute to the couple for their support of the Hong Kong Botanic Gardens, the superintendent of the Botany and Forestry Department, Hong Kong, Stephen Troyte Dunn (1860–1938), named the rare Hong Kong orchid tree, *Bauhinia* x *blakeana* in their honour.[25] Since 1997, the flower has appeared on Hong Kong's coat of arms, its flag and currency.

Many wished the Blakes to continue in Hong Kong and petitions were despatched to London urging that their term of office be extended, but these proved to be unsuccessful.

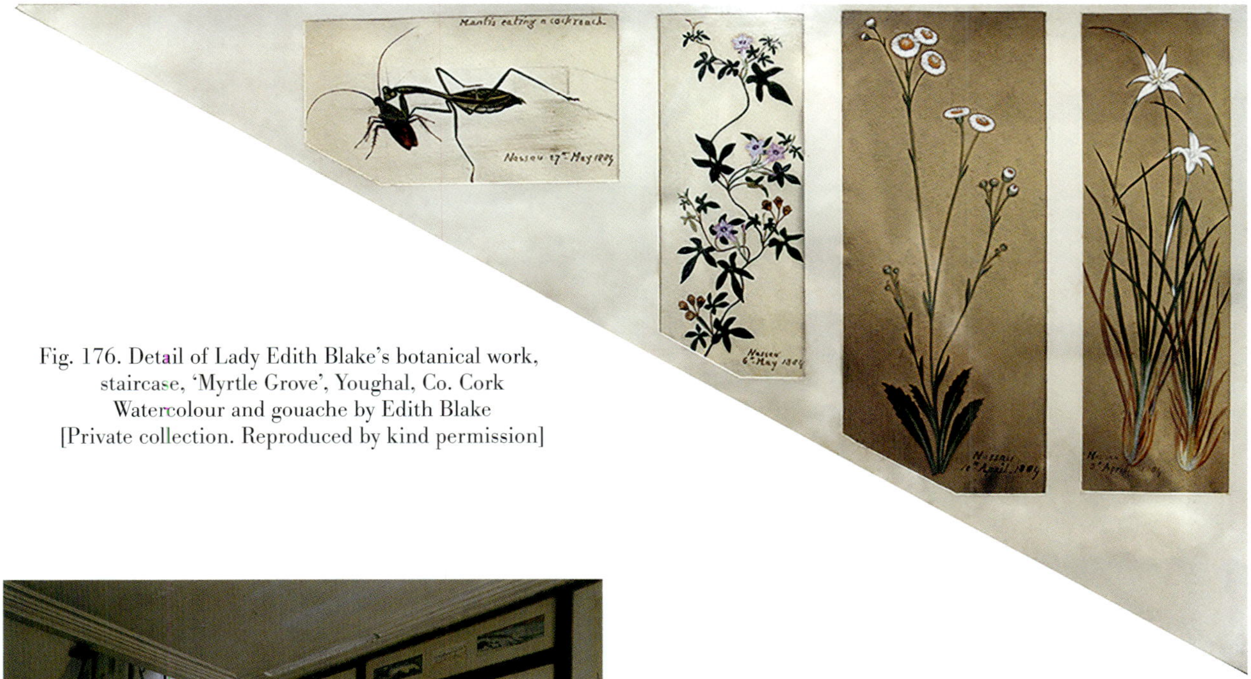

Fig. 176. Detail of Lady Edith Blake's botanical work, staircase, 'Myrtle Grove', Youghal, Co. Cork
Watercolour and gouache by Edith Blake
[Private collection. Reproduced by kind permission]

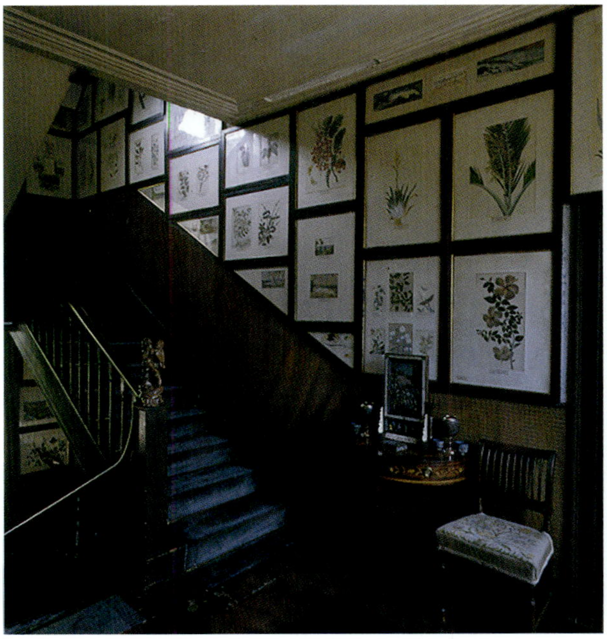

Fig. 177. 'Myrtle Grove', Youghal, Co. Cork. The staircase showing examples of Lady Edith Blake's botanical work.
[Private collection. Reproduced by kind permission]

Shortly after their arrival in Ceylon (now Sri Lanka), in November 1903, Blake established an Agricultural Society similar to that in Jamaica. It would appear to have caught the public's imagination. Writing to Sir William Turner Thiselton-Dyer (1843–1928), Director of Kew, in September 1905, Blake reported it was 'faring splendidly'.[26] His wife also continued to correspond and to despatch seeds and plants to Kew. She assisted Irish-born plant collector and director of the Public Gardens and Plantations, Jamaica, William Fawcett (1851–1926),[27] stating: 'The mango & banana plants that you wanted have been despatched to you from Peradeniya via Kew.' She also proffered advice on keeping silkworms:

*If the silk worms were kept in sheds that had net over the doors & windows to [keep] out flies, they ought to do well in Jamaica. I had some of a kind that eat castor oil plants at Kandy.*[28]

Edith obviously enjoyed spending many hours painting in the Royal Botanic Gardens, Peradeniya, which are around 5km to the west of the city of Kandy. The gardens, dating back to the 14th century, were formally established as a botanical garden in 1843 under Glasgow-born George Gardner (1812–1849), who acted as superintendent from 1844. Plants were introduced from Kew, Colombo and the Botanic Gardens of Henarathgoda, Kalutara, Ceylon. Edith's recording of the coca plant (*Erythroxylum* coca), a tropical shrub, is inscribed (on verso) 'From Peredeniya 9 July 1904' and depicts its flowers, small and disposed in small clusters on short stalks (Figure 174). The leaves, the source of the narcotic drug cocaine, are considered ready for picking when they break on being bent; the green leaves are then spread in thin layers on the ground and dried in the hot sun.

Blake retired from the colonial service and as governor of Ceylon in 1907, aged 67. On their return to Ireland, the Blakes lived at 'Myrtle Grove', Youghal, Co. Cork, a Tudor house, once the home of Sir Walter Raleigh. The Reverend S. Hayman, historiographer of Youghal, described the house in 1852 as possessing:

*Four venerable yew-trees, whose branches have grown and intermingled into a sort of summer-house thatch...[they] sheltered Rallegh when he first smoked tobacco in his Youghal garden. In that garden he also planted tobacco.*[29]

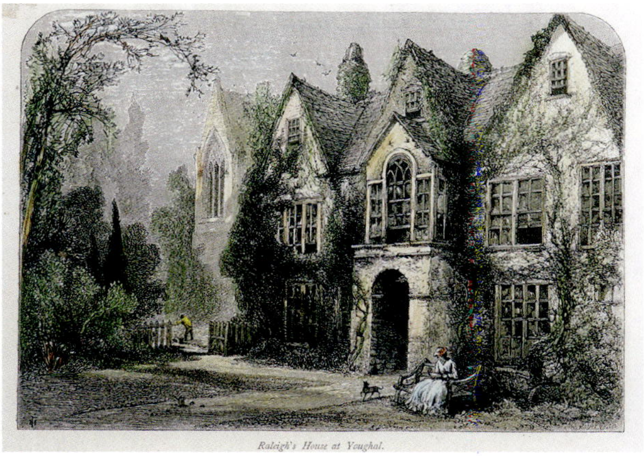


Fig. 178. *Raleigh's House at Youghal*
[Private collection. Reproduced by kind permission]

Sir Henry continued to write and contribute articles relating to Ceylon;[30] and his wife became a regular contributor to a monthly literary magazine, *Nineteenth Century* (founded 1877), with articles ranging from the position of women in China[31] to a study of Irish life and death.[32]

Sir Henry Arthur Blake died on 23 February 1918. A council member of the *Journal of the Cork Historical and Archaeological Society*, he was described as 'A man of a broad and well-cultured mind an interesting and delightful lecturer.'[33] His death was a tragic loss for his wife, who remained in mourning for the rest of her life and rarely left the house, except to sit in the garden. Lady Edith Blake died at 'Myrtle Grove' on 18 April 1926.

# Chapter 10
# Professional Botanical Artists

'The flower painter fails if a work lacks beauty, the botanical painter fails if it lacks accuracy.' These lines, written by William T. Stearn in his book *The Flower Artists of Kew*,[1] define the difference between the art of the flower painter, whose work is essentially aesthetic, and that of the botanical painter/illustrator, whose work may be aesthetic by chance, but which is principally concerned with scientifically analysing plants.

Scientific, botanical portraiture is diagnostic; the botanist's need for complete and detailed accuracy of form, shape, colour and growth must take priority over individuality of presentation. To the spectator, the botanical portrait offers an immediately accessible way of understanding and appreciating a plant.

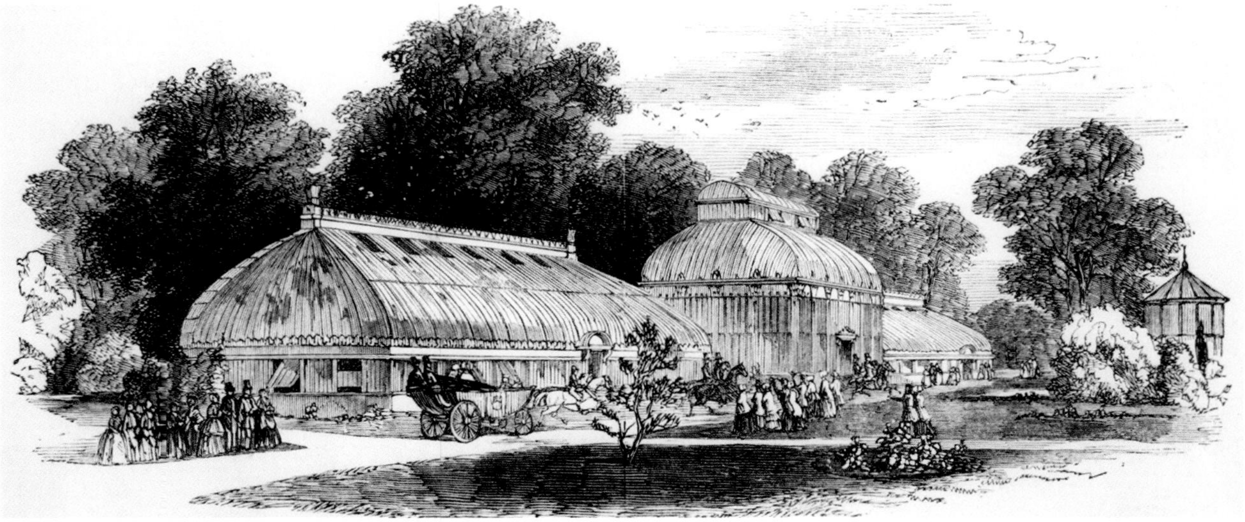

Fig. 179. The Royal (now National) Botanic Gardens, Glasnevin, Dublin, showing the completed curvilinear range
Engraving from the *Illustrated London News*, July 1849
[Private collection. Reproduced by kind permission]

# Lydia Shackleton

## (b.22 November 1828, Ballitore, Co. Kildare; d.10 December 1914, Lucan, Co. Dublin)

Botanical portraitist Lydia Shackleton more than met these requirements with energy and tenacity, being the first resident professional botanical artist to be appointed by the RBG, Glasnevin, Dublin in 1884.

She was born at 'Griesemount', Ballitore, Co. Kildare on 22 November 1828, the third child in a family of 13 children. The family's Quaker roots both in Yorkshire and at Ballitore stretch back to the early 17th century. From an early age, Shackleton devoted a good deal of her time to teaching and caring for the younger members of the family. When she moved to a house located on The Mall, Lucan, Co. Dublin, her nieces and nephews who lived in the district were sent to 'Aunt Lyd', as they affectionately called her, for instruction. She had other interests besides teaching, among them painting, writing poetry, reading and horticulture.

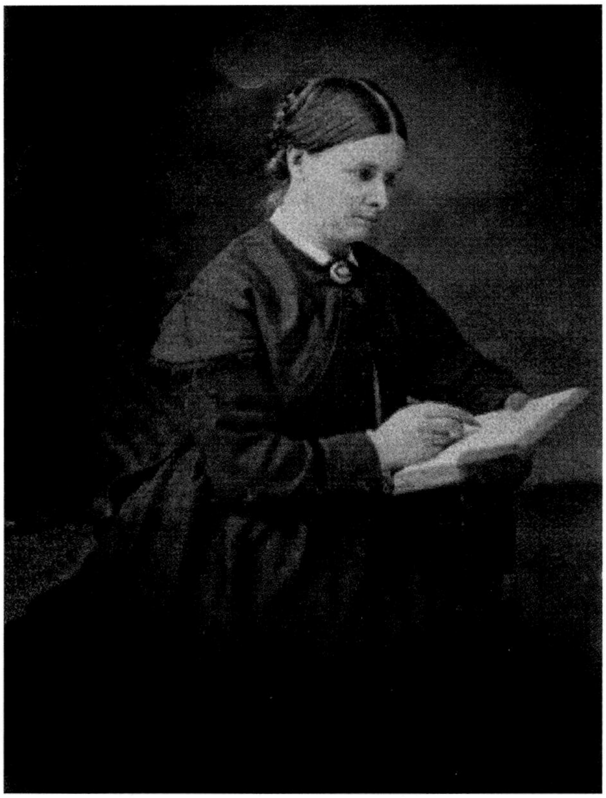

Fig. 180. Lydia Shackleton
[Private collection. Reproduced by kind permission]

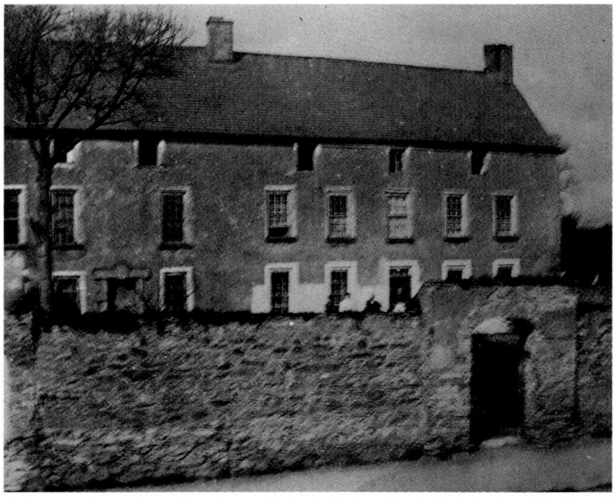

Fig. 181. Society of Friends' schoolhouse, Ballitore, Co. Kildare
[Courtesy of the Irish Architectural Archive]

In contrast with many of her contemporaries, Shackleton did not look on botanical art as being merely a fashionable and absorbing hobby. She took it seriously and studied for a period at the RDS Schools in 1850. Between 1873 and 1876, she travelled in the US. Several botanical drawings relating to the wild plants of North America have survived in a collection of her sketchbooks, now in the Garden Library, NBG, Glasnevin, Dublin.

In 1879, (Sir) Frederick Moore[2] succeeded his father, David, as Curator (re-designated Director, 1890) of the RBG Glasnevin, Dublin. Like his father, Sir Frederick Moore was a keen orchid enthusiast/grower: 'Orchids are a delightful, extraordinary and truly splendid tribe of plants.'[3] Between September 1884 and December 1907 (and in the 1890s assisted by Josephine Humphries, fl.1890s),[4] Shackleton responded to his enthusiasm by executing over 1,040 botanical portraits of orchid studies, one of which was named after the curator's wife, Phyllis Moore (née Paul, d.1974), and is illustrated here (see Figure 183). She also completed approximately 100 portraits of both introduced and native plants, including *Sarracenia*, *Lachenalia*, *Paeonia* and *Helleborus* species and hybrids.

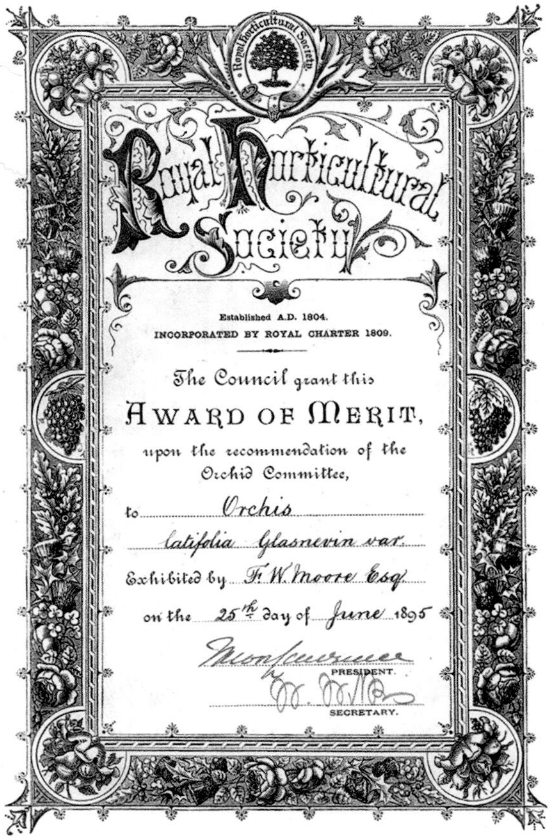


Fig. 182. Award of Merit presented to (Sir) Frederick Moore for '*Orchis latifolia* Glasnevin var.' by the Orchid Committee, RHS London
[Courtesy, National Botanic Gardens, Glasnevin, Dublin]

Shackleton's painting technique was relatively free and therefore best suited to the depiction of large flowers, as displayed in her portraits of herbaceous peonies, many of which were grown at Glasnevin in the 1890s. When painting small subjects, her technique did not adapt itself so well to the tight, concise botanical style required and therefore her work is not so successful as seen, for example, in her *Lachenalia* studies. In each case, she carefully mounted the dried specimen beside her work. Most of the orchid paintings depict individual blossoms. Moore was particularly interested in pure species of orchids rather than orchid hybrids, the latter being enthusiastically promoted by botanists such as R.A. Rolfe.[5]

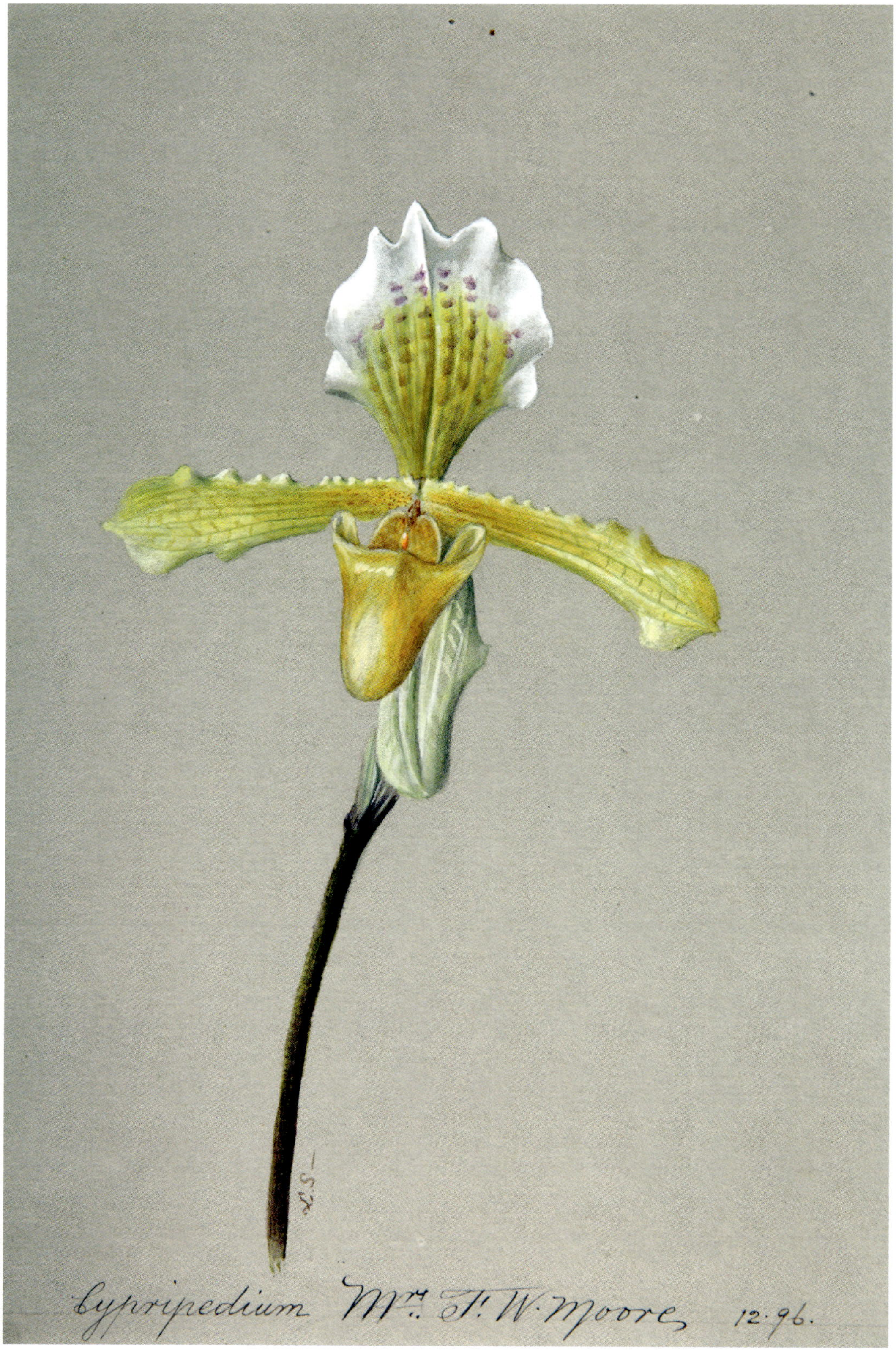


Fig. 183. *Cypripedium insigne* 'Mrs F.W. Moore' (=*Paphiopedilum* 'Mrs F.W. Moore'),
hybrid lady's slipper orchid
Watercolour heightened with white and pencil by Lydia Shackleton, December 1896
[Courtesy, National Botanic Gardens, Glasnevin, Dublin]

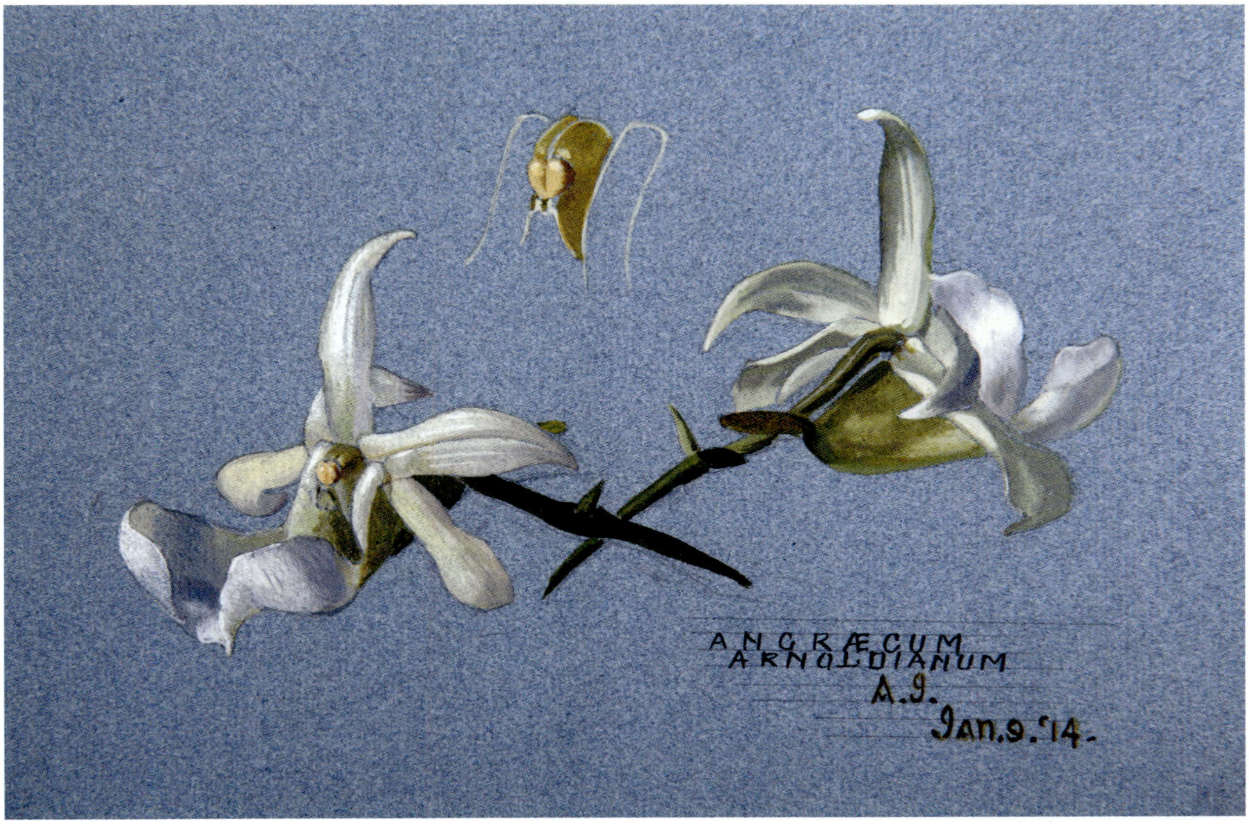


Fig. 189. *Angraecum arnoldianum* (*Angraecum eichierianum*)
Watercolour heightened with white and pencil on pale blue paper by Alice Jacob, inscribed (in watercolour) '*ANGRÆCUM ARNOLDIANUM A.J. Jan.9.'14-*'
[Courtesy, National Botanic Gardens, Glasnevin, Dublin]

for lace, floral damask, embroidery, crochetwork and painted silk.[12] By 1900, her lace designs, in particular, had become widely known and she provided designs for many of Dublin's leading linen firms (see Figure 187). A regular prize-winner at national competitions held in London, her work 'must stand at the beginning of modern design studies at the school.'[13] Her contribution was central to the improvement of the status of crafts, ensuring that 'decorative or applied art should never be looked upon as in any way an inferior branch.'[14]

## Lady Charlotte Isabel Wheeler-Cuffe (née Williams)

### (b.24 May 1867, Wimbledon; d.8 March 1967, Kilkenny)

Lady Charlotte Isabel Wheeler-Cuffe was a granddaughter of the Reverend Sir Hercules Langrishe, 3rd Baronet of Knocktopher, Co. Kilkenny. Her father, William Williams, was president of the Law Society of England and Wales. Although she was born in Wimbledon, Surrey, Charlotte's Irish connections were strengthened when, in 1897, she married Sir Otway F.L. Wheeler-Cuffe (1866–1934), a civil engineer and the heir to another Kilkenny baronetcy. Immediately after their marriage, the couple went to live for the next 24 years on the Indian subcontinent. In 1906, Sir Otway was appointed Executive Engineer and in December 1913 Superintendent Engineer in Burma.

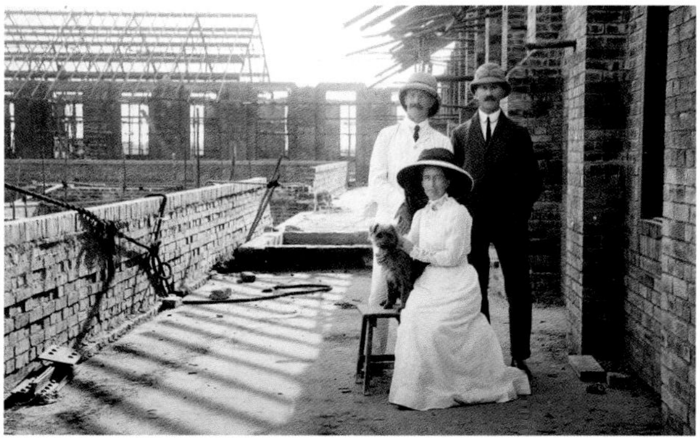

Fig. 190. Lady Charlotte Isabel Wheeler-Cuffe with her husband, Sir Otway F.L. Wheeler-Cuffe and their dog, Alanna (the figure on the right is not identified) at the new Government Press building, Rangoon, 7 March 1912 [Courtesy, National Botanic Gardens, Glasnevin, Dublin]

It was while Lady Cuffe was in Burma travelling and living in Rangoon, Mandalay, and principally in Maymyo, that she began her botanical exploration of that country. Frequently accompanied by her husband when he travelled to inspect civil engineering works and various new projects, Lady Cuffe made the journeys riding on a pony. In this way, she had an opportunity to explore many parts of south-eastern Asia, which had hitherto been undiscovered by botanists. Descriptions of many of her expeditions are to be found in the correspondence between herself and Sir Frederick Moore (1857–1949), Director of the RBG Glasnevin, Dublin, particularly with reference to her exciting botanical finds.

Full of enthusiasm and energy, she thought nothing of marching 84 miles to spend April 1912 in the mountains. She described the exciting discoveries that she and her friend Mrs Winifred McNabb had made in letters to her cousin, Baroness Pauline Prochazka (1842–1930),[15] who lived at Leyrath (or Lyrath), the Cuffe family seat in Co. Kilkenny. On the slopes of Mount Victoria, western Burma, Lady Cuffe found a white-flowered species of rhododendron, *Rhododendron cuffeanum*, whose name proclaims the fact that she was the first person to record and collect the species.

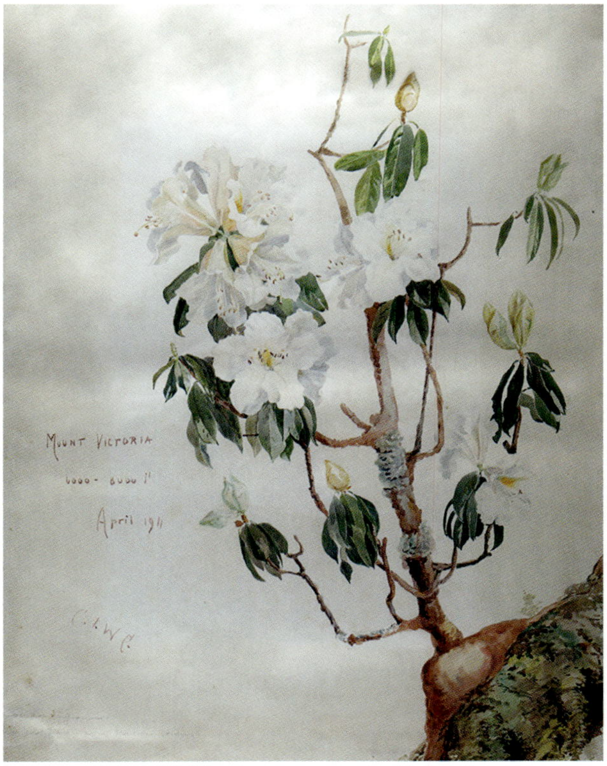


Fig. 191. *Rhododendron cuffeanum* (Burma)
Watercolour by Lady Charlotte Wheeler-Cuffe (née Williams)
Inscription: *Mount Victoria 1911*
[Courtesy, National Botanic Gardens, Glasnevin, Dublin]

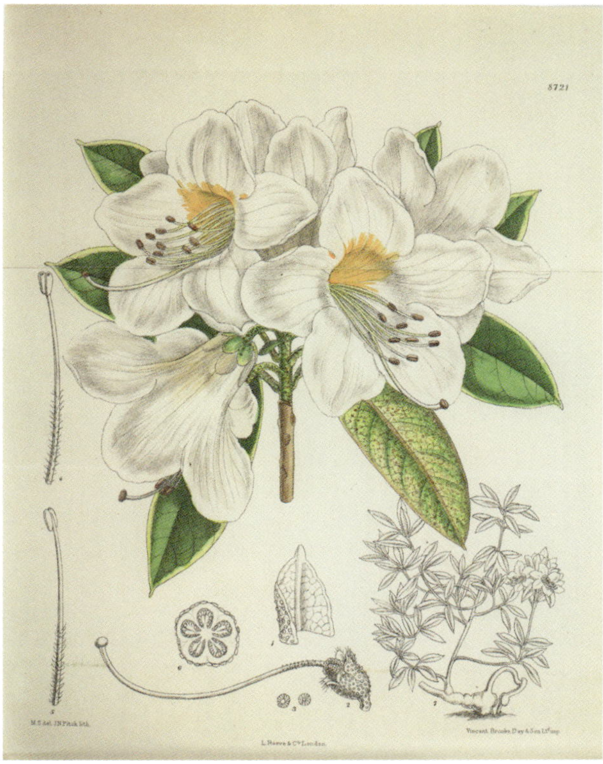


Fig. 192. *Rhododendron cuffeanum*
Lithograph by Lilian Snelling and John Nugent Fitch
From *Curtis's Botanical Magazine*, tab. 8721, vol. 13, August 1917
[© Royal Botanic Gardens, Kew]

> *This most exquisite white, sweet scented rhododendron which grows epiphytically on other trees like an orchid, never on the ground a yellow rhododendron, & whole forest of the crimson tree one.*[16]

*Rhododendron cuffeanum* was recorded by Lady Cuffe on her return to Mount Victoria, in April 1912 (Figure 191). Seeds, dried and living specimens were frequently sent back to Sir Frederick Moore at Glasnevin by Lady Cuffe for cultivation. For example, in the case of the white rhododendron, specimens were sent to the RBG Kew, London, from Glasnevin, for naming and appeared (*Rhododendron cuffeanum*) in *Curtis's Botanical Magazine* (1917) (Figure 192).[17]

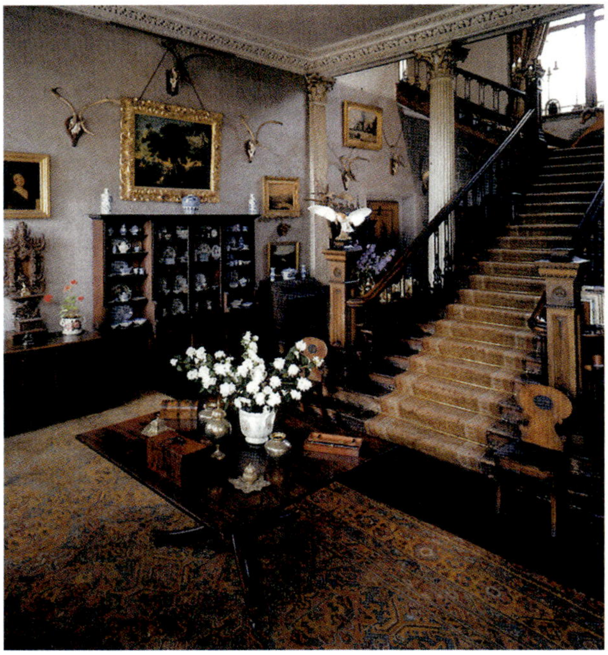

Fig. 193. The entrance hall and staircase, 'Leyrath', Co. Kilkenny, home of Sir Otway and Lady Charlotte Wheeler-Cuffe
[Private collection. Reproduced by kind permission]

On its highest slopes, Mount Victoria possesses an alpine flora. Lady Cuffe was the earliest-known botanical explorer to reach and record plants found in this area, painting in watercolour such specimens as *Anemone obtusilova* f. *patula* (named shadow's buttercup, after her own pet's name, Shadow), *Potentilla montisvictoriae,* and two unidentified species of *Primula*.

In April 1914, the artist journeyed northwards with her husband along the N'Mai Hka river, the eastern tributary of the Irrawaddy, to the Chinese frontier. This was unknown country. Lady Cuffe wrote to Sir Frederick Moore describing the trip:

> *... All up the 'Nmaikha the rocks are a sheet of vivid scarlet azaelea, often accompanied by a white briar rose ... Further up, on the main Irrawaddy-Salween Divide at Hpimaw the country is rather more open & the gorges less precipitous ... The grazing grounds above are full of primulas & gentians; above them forests of oak & pine (Pinus Khassia I believe) & higher again are rhododendrons, alder & a large white magnolia, & a host of others.*[18]

In November 1917, while living at Maymyo, Lady Cuffe was approached by Charles Gilbert Rogers (1864–1937), the head of the Forestry Department, and William Keith, the Burmese Secretary, to undertake the design, construction and initial management of a botanical garden at Maymyo. In a letter to Baroness Prochazka, she wrote

> *Can you imagine a more charming piece of work? The idea is to have a garden of all the beautiful indigenous flowers, trees & shrubs, with just a few imported things, but very few. There are a lot of beautiful wild things in the area now, including a small patch of primeval forest, a marsh, some rocks, a little lake, & a wide stretch of open valley covered with bracken fern, wild raspberries – & weeds!*[19]

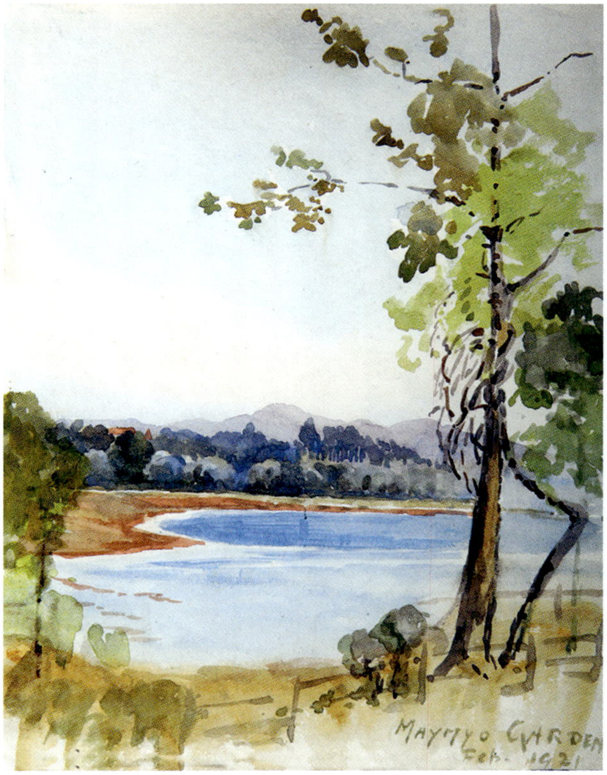


Fig. 194. '*Maymyo Garden*'
Watercolour by Lady Charlotte Wheeler-Cuffe, February 1921, inscribed (in watercolour) '*MAYMYO GARDEN Feb 1921*'
[Courtesy, National Botanic Gardens, Glasnevin, Dublin]

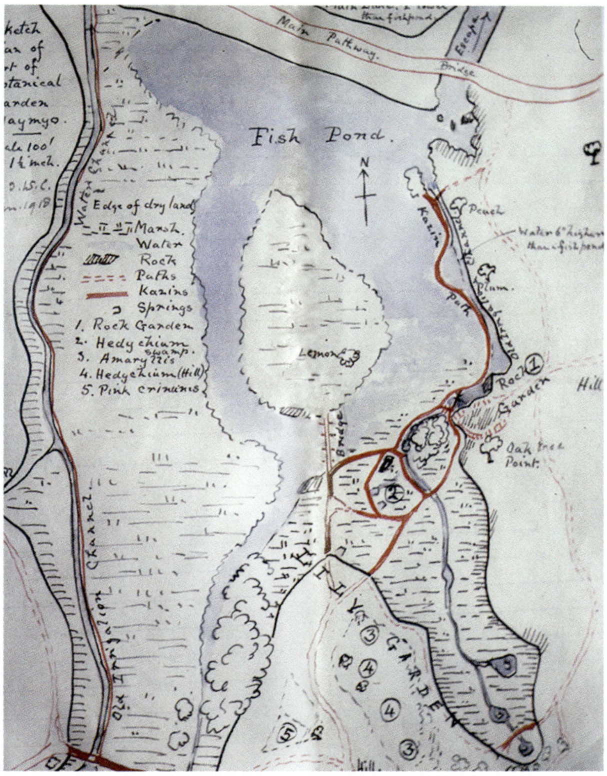


Fig. 195. Sketch-map indicating Lady Wheeler-Cuffe's proposals for laying out the Maymyo Botanic Garden, Burma (now known as the National Kandawgyi Botanical Gardens, Myanmar)
Ink and watercolour by Lady Charlotte Wheeler-Cuffe, 3 January 1918
[Courtesy, National Botanic Gardens, Glasnevin, Dublin]

The main aim in the gardens was to concentrate on the indigenous flora of Burma, and within a few months Lady Cuffe was beginning to mould, manage and shape 150 acres into a botanical garden.[20]

While in India and Burma, Lady Cuffe completed several hundred botanical paintings that were presented to the NBG Glasnevin, Dublin, in 1926, five years after she and her husband retired to live at Leyrath, Co. Kilkenny. The main collection relates to Burmese orchids dating from 1902 to 1921. There are also botanical portraits of rhododendron and Burmese native plants, together with landscapes of both Burma and Ireland.

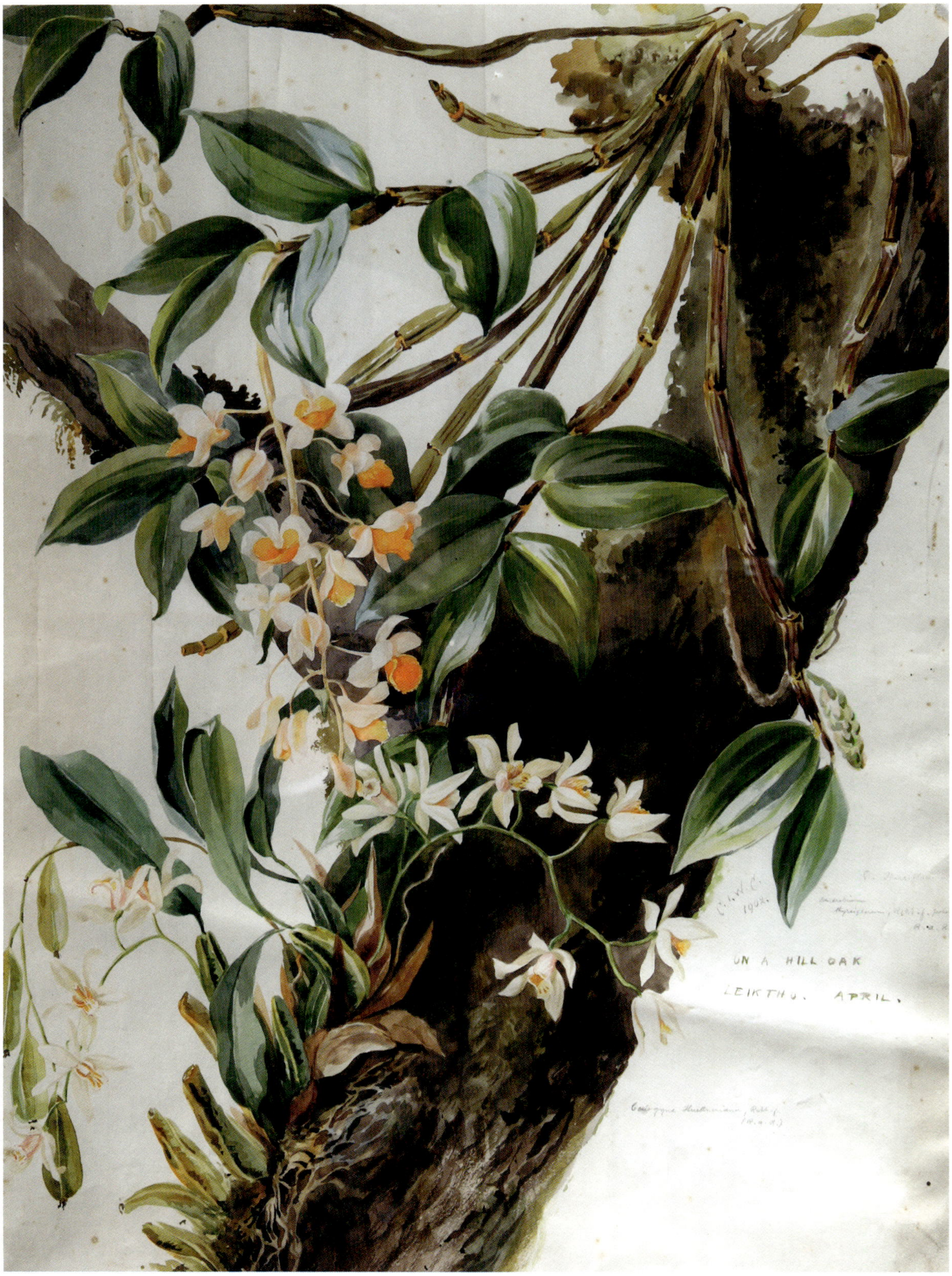


Fig. 196. *Dendrobium thyrsiflorum* and *Coelogyne huettneriana*
Watercolour by Lady Charlotte Wheeler-Cuffe, inscribed (in watercolour) '*ON HILL OAK LEIKTHO APRIL*'
[Courtesy, National Botanic Gardens, Glasnevin, Dublin]

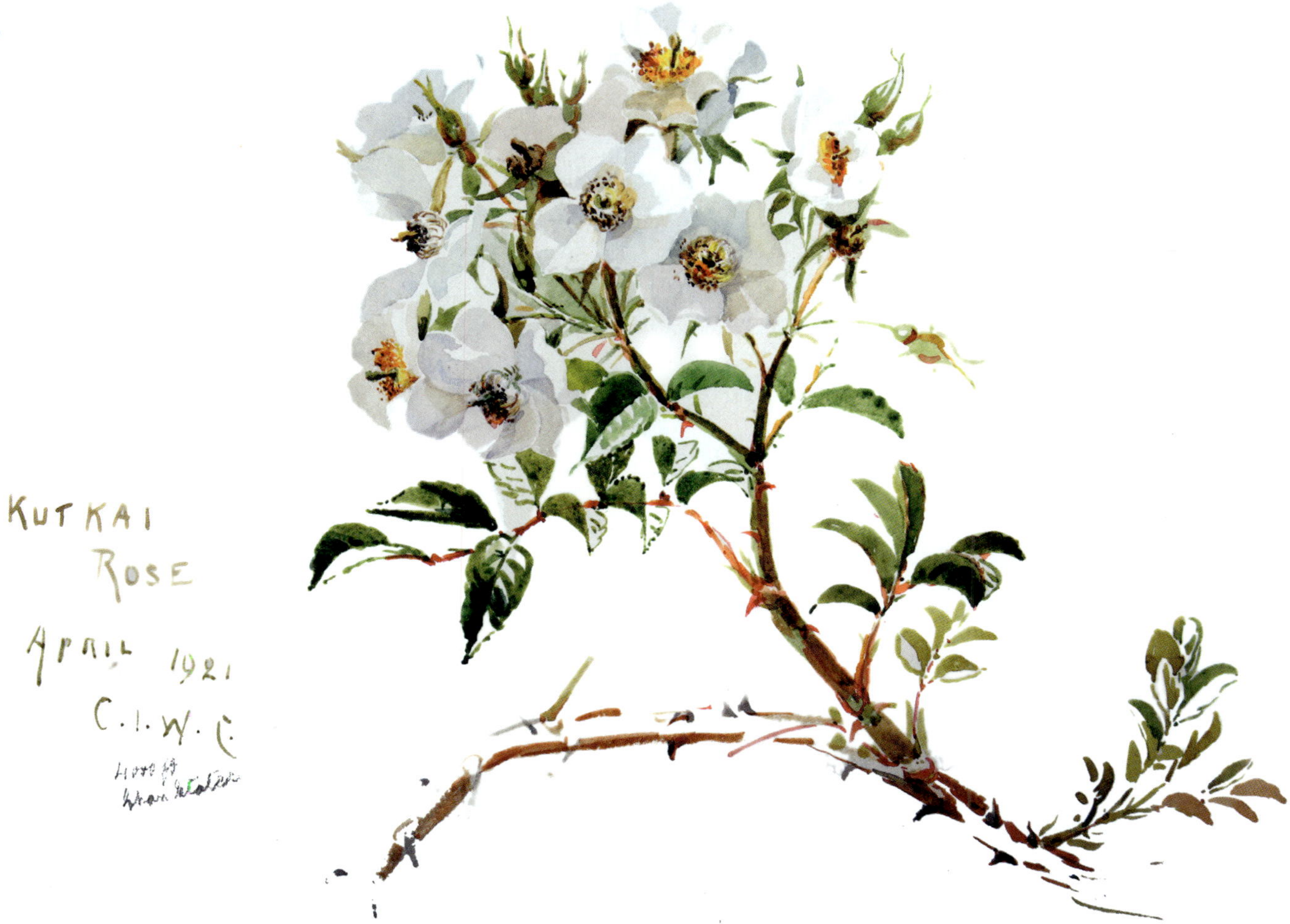


Fig. 197. 'Kutkai rose'
Watercolour by Lady Charlotte Wheeler-Cuffe, inscribed (in watercolour) '*KUTKAI ROSE APRIL 1921 C.I.W.C.*', (in pencil) '*4000 ft Shan States*'
[Courtesy, National Botanic Gardens, Glasnevin, Dublin]

The artist's botanical drawings are executed in watercolour (see Figure 197). She rarely used pencil, but instead appears to have painted direct from nature. Her orchid studies are shown in their natural habitats growing as epiphytes on the branches of trees. In several paintings, the artist chose not to emphasise the structure but rather concentrated on the graceful movement of the plant defined by leaves and stems, as they stretched, turned, overlapped and touched. The elegant outlines are carefully infilled with light, modulated washes of colour seen, for example, in Lady Cuffe's botanical portrait of orchids *Dendrobia thyrsiflorum* and *Coelogyne huettneriana* supported by an oak and painted between Leiktho and Nancho in the Karen hills, April 1902. In many cases, she did not record the full tonal complexities of the flower head but simplified these, as seen in her rendering of the Kutkai rose (Figure 197) found in Shan States at a height of 1,219.2 m (4,000 ft) and dated April 1921.

Lady Cuffe survived her husband by 33 years and died in Kilkenny, in 1967, 11 weeks short of her 100th birthday.

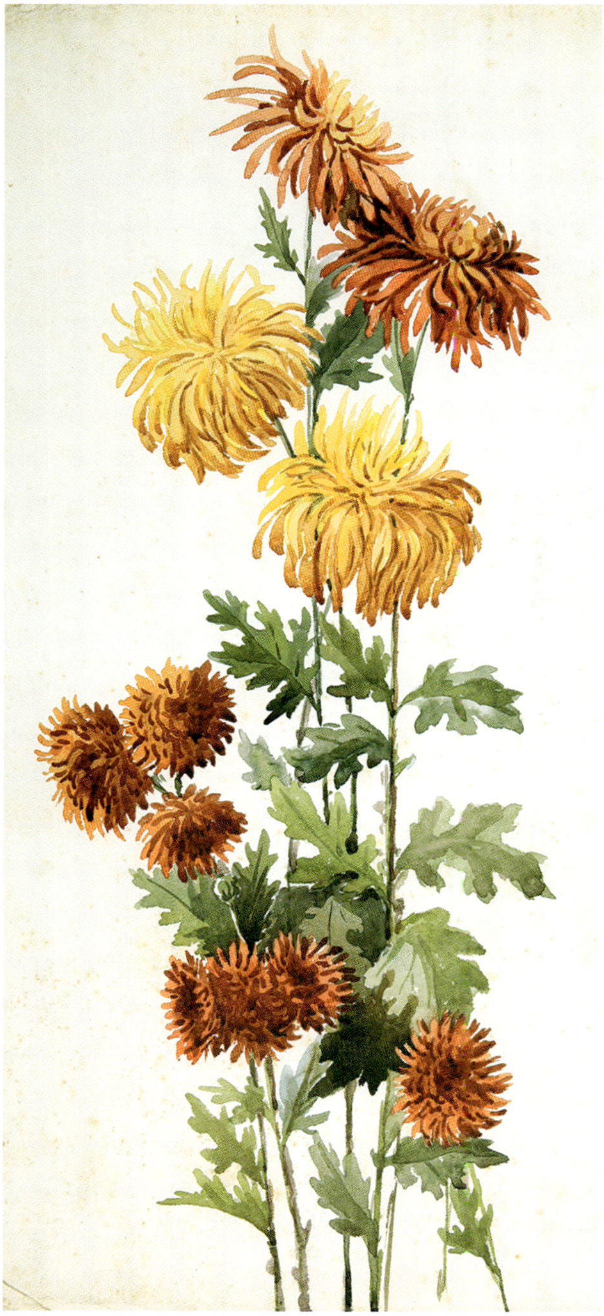

Fig. 198. '*Chrysanthemums*'
Watercolour by Charlotte Isabel Williams (later Lady Charlotte Wheeler-Cuffe), 25 November 1890, signed '*C.I. Williams*' and inscribed by Edmund A. Dobson (on verso, in pen) '*Very clever, a little grey worked into some of the shadows of the yellow flowers would much improve them*'
[Courtesy, National Botanic Gardens, Glasnevin, Dublin]

## Raymond Piper, FLS, RUA, UWS, (Hon.) HRHA

**(b.4 April 1923, London; d.13 July 2007)**

*'Eventually he led me on pilgrimages to some of the most beautiful places in Ireland. It has been my privilege to trail along behind him through hedges, over walls, across bogs and up mountains. Every year, we try to visit the Burren in May. There we have quartered a field for hours in order to track down a single fly orchid, and then been rewarded with a scatter of bee orchids flourishing unremarked by the roadside...'*

So wrote the poet, Michael Longley, in October 1994 in a note of appreciation relating to the botanical work of Raymond Piper.[21] The artist spent more than 20 years painting Ireland's wild orchids, travelling many thousands of miles in order to pay homage to them, one of his main aims being to promote the conservation of at least 30 or so wild orchid species. Fascinated by their nuances of form and colour, Piper's superb botanical portraits must serve both as scientific and historical records. Self-taught, the artist studied the complexities of their lifestyle and the microscopic intricacies of their reproductive systems, together with the parameters of the environmental requirements. As he once remarked, he could have made his peace with orchids years ago but remained obsessed throughout his life.

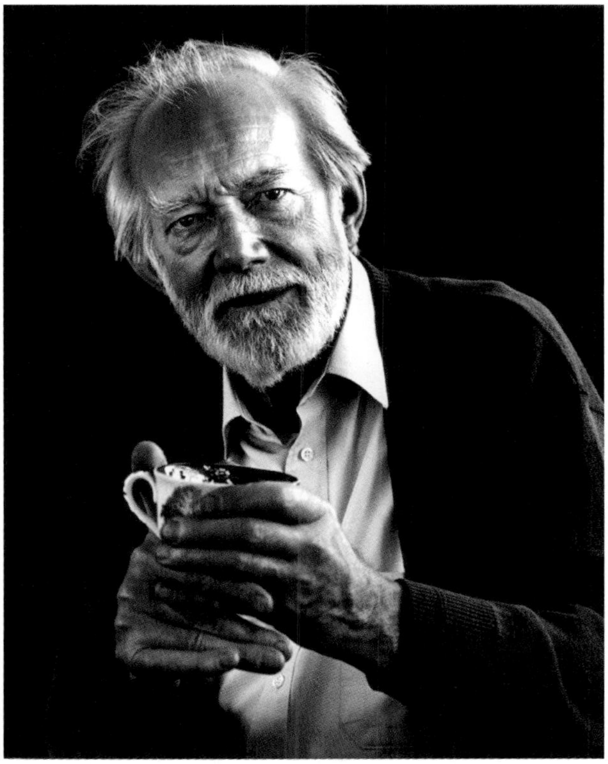

Fig. 199. Raymond Piper
[Private collection. Reproduced courtesy of Bobbie Hanvey]

Born in London, Raymond Piper and his parents arrived in Belfast when the boy was six years old. He attended Skegoniel Primary School before becoming a student at Mercantile College (now Belfast High School). His early life was spent working for six years in the shipyards of Harland & Wolff, [22] where, as he once remarked: 'I learned tolerance'. He also learned how to develop his artist's eye:

> *When I had a moment or two to spare between jobs, I would draw someone. I drew everything in those days. I carried drawing books in my pocket. I never drew ships. I drew the Cavehill from the shipyard.*[23]

In the evenings, he attended classes at the Belfast School of Art, where he was taught by Cornish artist Newton Penprase.[24] Piper also taught at the Royal School, Dungannon, Co. Tyrone.[25]

In 1948, he decided to become a full-time artist and began earning his living as a professional portrait painter. He held his first one-man show in 1953. Piper became well known in the field of portraiture throughout Northern Ireland. He was the recipient of the Gold Medal for Portraiture from the Royal Ulster Academy of Arts, 1992 and a prize from the RHA, Dublin, 1993.[26] Portraits included lord mayors of London and Belfast and other leading 'personalities' of the day. In the 1950s, Piper collaborated with Irish writer Richard Hayward (1892–1964) to illustrate a series of travel books relating to Ireland. Travelling many hundreds of miles throughout the country, the partnership produced five books in a regional series entitled *This Is Ireland*.[27] While working with Hayward on the final book, *Munster and the City of Cork* (1964),[28] Piper became drawn to botanical art and in particular to orchids. For the next 40 years, the artist was to study and interpret them in his own unique way. Piper's portraits of Irish wild orchids earned him an international reputation. Poet, Michael Longley wrote:

> *Painstaking and passionate, documentary and at the same time visionary, these marvellous pictures open the doors of perception for both the artist and the scientist in each of us, relating the one to the other at some primordial level. The precise details add up in the end to mysterious, poetic images. These are flowers in a dream, an ideal reality. In the words of Christopher Smart: 'There is a language of flowers.*[29]

The artist's orchid studies (see, for example, Figure 201) were exhibited in the NH section of the BM in 1974 and, in the same year, Piper was awarded the John Lindley Medal by the RHS for his watercolours relating to Irish orchids. This was the first time the medal had been awarded to Ireland. A Fellow of the Linnean Society, as well as an Academician of both the RUA and the RIA, the Ulster Museum and the RDS have both exhibited Piper's botanical work. In 1987, the Blackstaff Press produced *Piper's Flowers*,[30] a limited edition that included five of his Irish orchid paintings, followed, in 1994, by *Three Irish Orchids*, limited to 125 portfolios of three prints of watercolours, each signed and numbered by the artist. The following year, the artist was awarded the Beck's Bier Bursary by the Institute of Contemporary Arts, London, for outstanding services to botanical illustration.

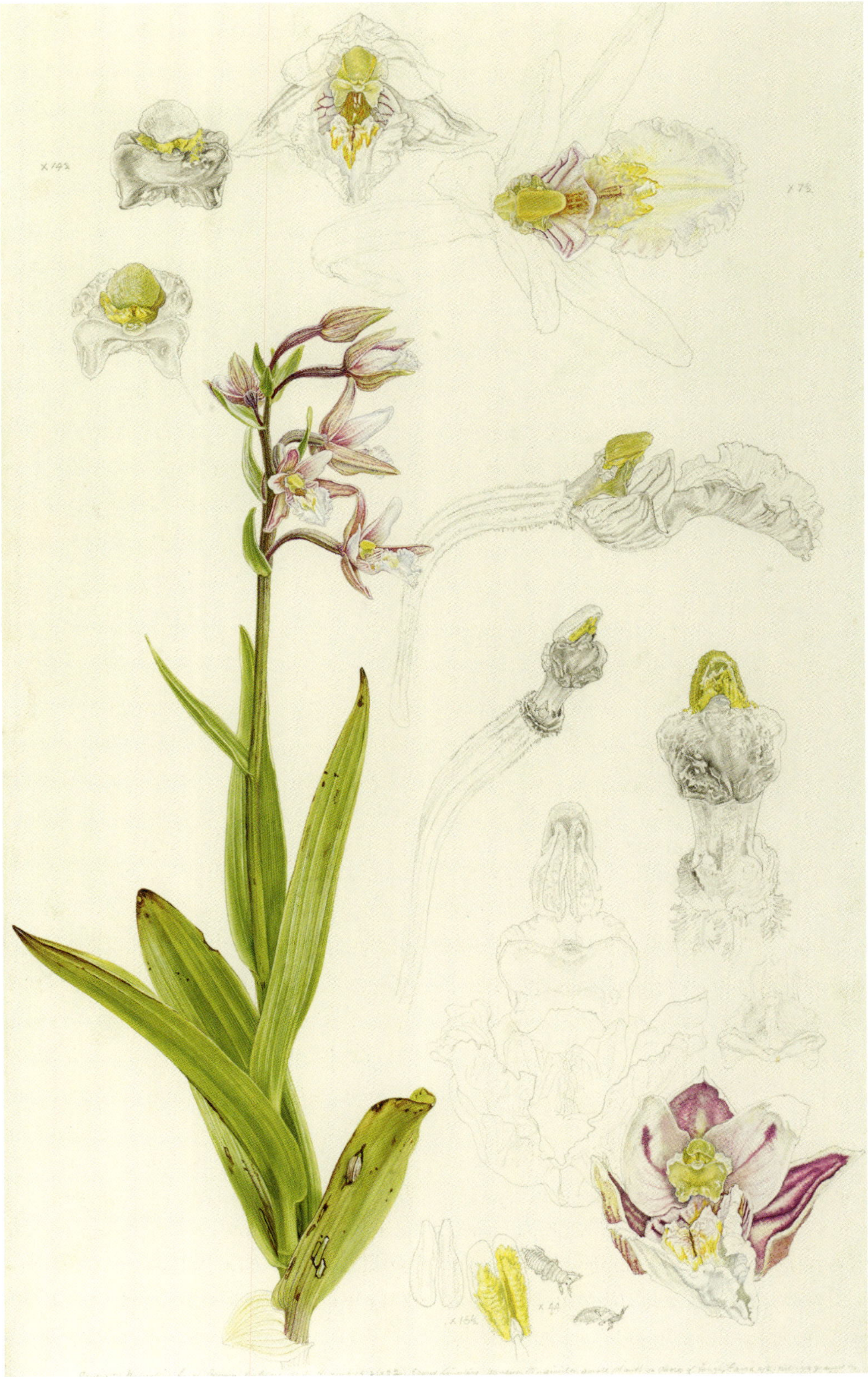

Fig. 200. *Epipactis palustris*, marsh helleborine
Watercolour and pencil by Raymond Piper
[© The artist's estate. Reproduced by kind permission. Ulster Museum]

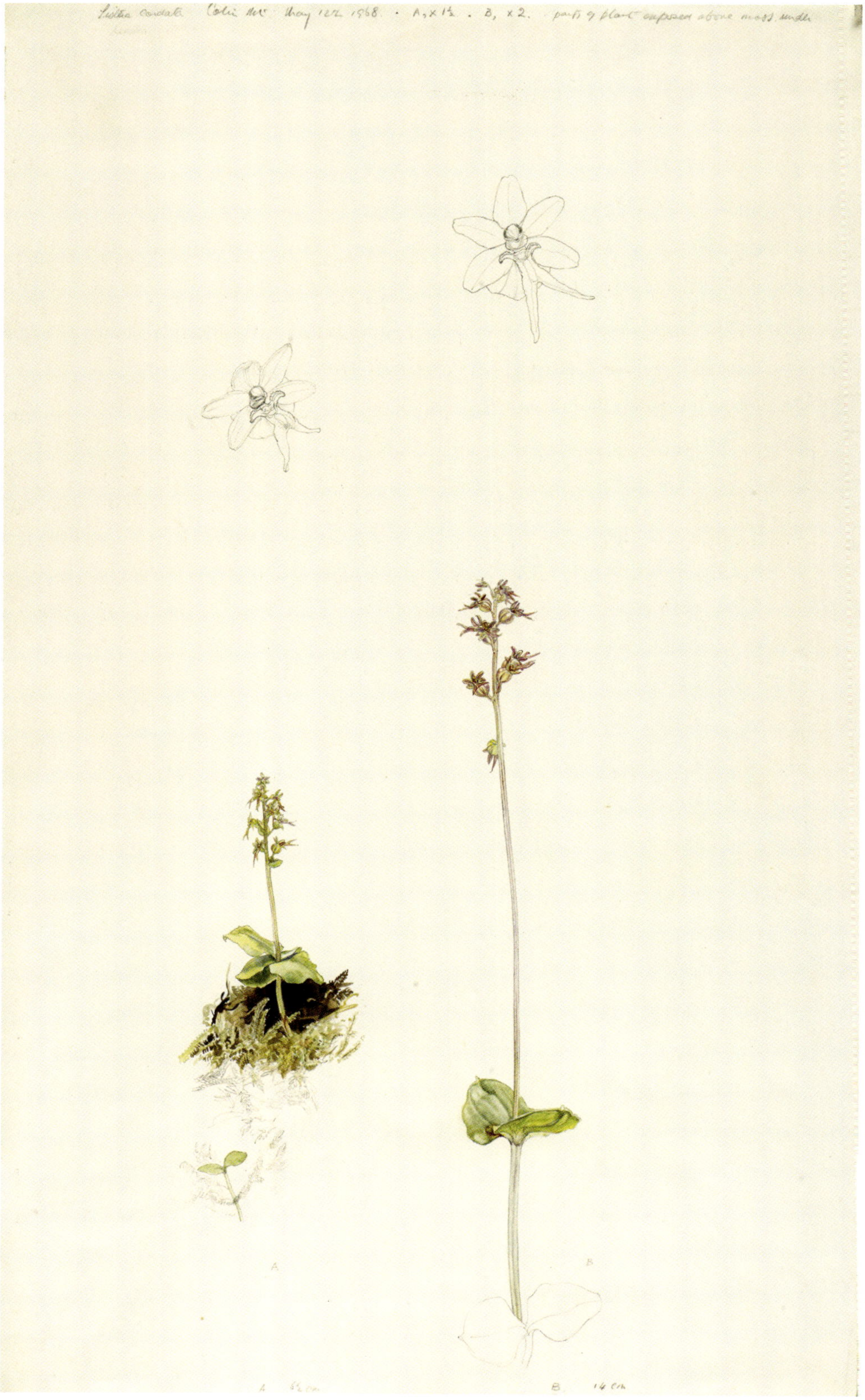


Fig. 201. *Neottia cordata* (lesser twayblade)
Watercolour and pencil by Raymond Piper

*Setting out to paint all the Irish orchids, he is tantalised by nuances of form and colour that seem to break the rules of species and sub-spcies, hybrids and races ... As an artist, he might have made his peace with orchids years ago; as a botanist, he is still obsessed.*[31]

Piper played an active part in the cultural life of Northern Ireland and had a wide circle of friends in the artistic world; his interests covered a wide area ranging from ballet to reading. Warm, approachable and gregarious, and possessing a sharp sense of humour, he was known to some of his friends as 'the orchid man'. Raymond Piper died on 13 July 2007. Many years prior to his death, Michael Viney commented in the *Irish Times*:

*How extraordinary it is, in the age of photography, that precision of this sort should still have such power. 'Boy!' commanded Piper's night-school teacher, 'make the line live. Give it shape, thick to thin to suggest shape and volume. Give it vitality – make it speak!*[32]

The Irish Society of Botanical Artists (ISBA) was established on 1 March 2014. Six years later, the following professional botanical artists, all members, participated in the NGI exhibition entitled *Drawn from Nature. Irish Botanical Art* (7 March–21 June 2020). In their own words, they describe their work:

**Mary Dillon**

*I'm fascinated by the notion of temporal change in the plant world. Every moment in the life cycle of a plant is just that, a moment in time, even when it seems that all life has left the plant, change continues to occur. The dynamism of growth, from the sprouting of a seed to the last moment of change in colour and form captivates me. Capturing the essence of a plant with its sensuality and fragility defines my work. I prefer to work in a large format, colour, light and form permeating my work and giving it a contemporary dynamism. I am a founding Chairperson, ISBA my work is represented in the Shirley Sherwood Collections/Gallery, Richmond, London, the Hunt Institute of Botanical Documentation, Pittsburgh, USA, etc.*

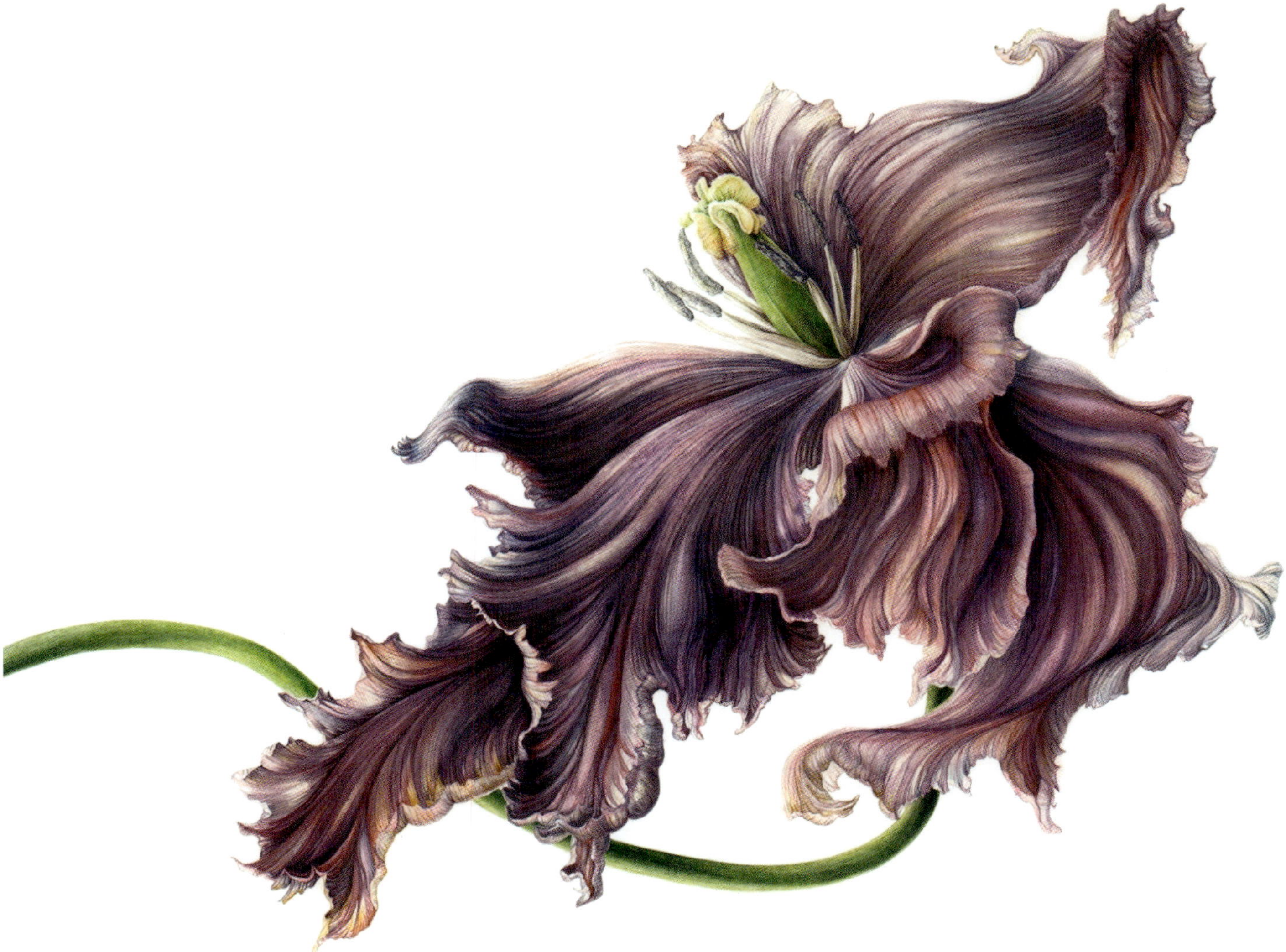

Fig. 202. *Tulipa* 'Black Parrot'
Watercolour by Mary Dillon, 2015
[© Mary Dillon. Courtesy, Shirley Sherwood Collection]

**Shevaun Doherty**

*I am an Irish botanical and natural history artist painting in watercolour on paper and vellum and currently I am President of the Society of Botanical Artists.*

*An award-winning artist, I regularly exhibit in Ireland and abroad, the highlight being the National Gallery of Ireland's exhibition, Drawn from Nature (2020). My work is represented in the Crawford Art Gallery, Cork and I have designed three sets of Flora and Fauna National postage stamps for An Post.*

*I consider myself to be a visual story-teller and I use my skills to raise awareness about endangered species and conservation. My depiction of the bumblebee is the cover image for the All-Ireland Pollinator Plan.*

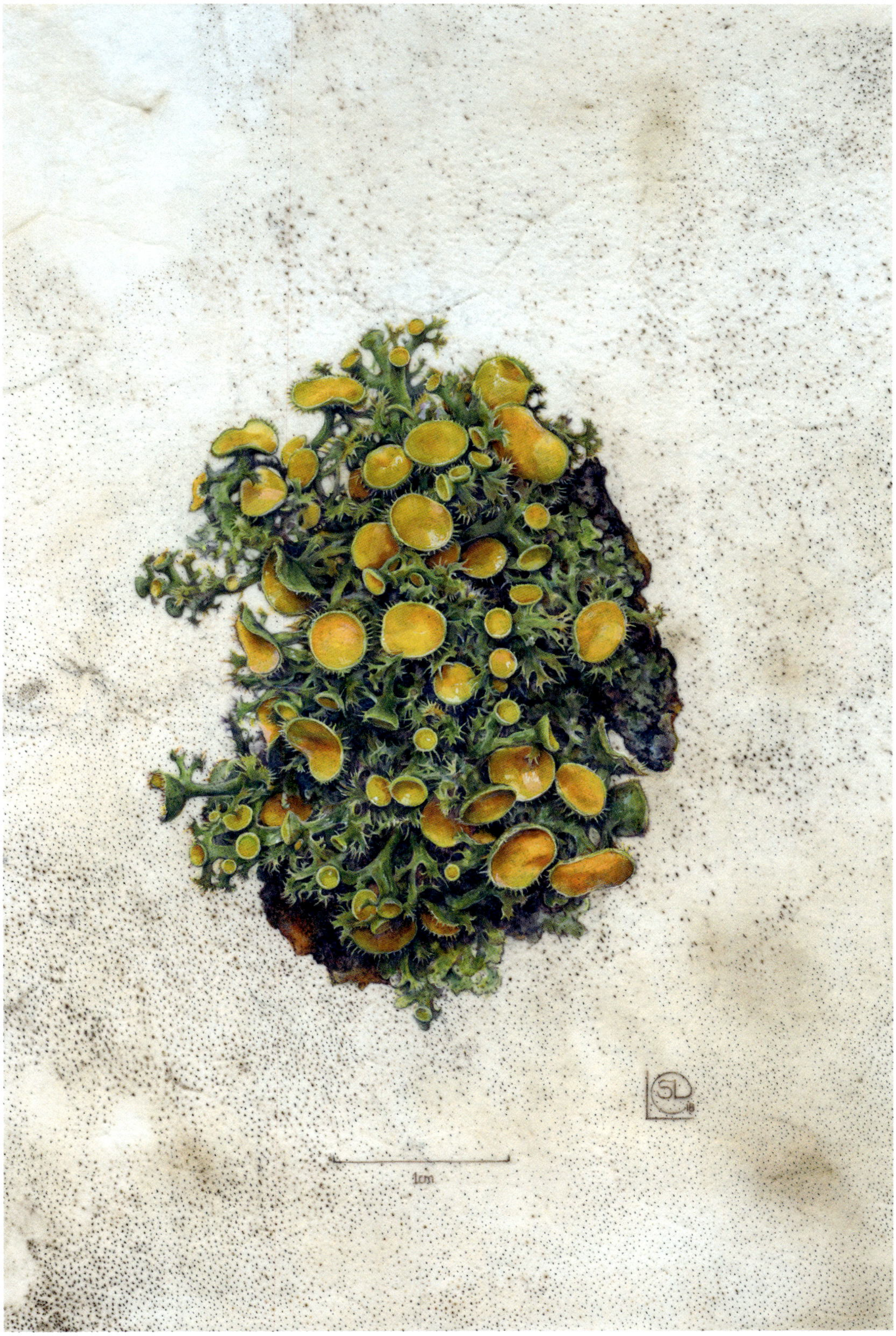


Fig. 203. *Teloschistes chrysophthalmus*, golden-eye lichen
Watercolour with body colour on calfskin vellum mounted on panel by Shevaun Doherty, 2018
[© Shevaun Doherty. Private collection]

**Siobhan Larkin**

*I am a Dublin-based artist working primarily in colour pencil. After 20 years in film animation, a career change to horticulture resulted in a love of botanical art. I am a member of The Water Colour Society of Ireland winning two awards of distinction, 2013 and 2016. I am also a member of the ISBA and regularly exhibit at the annual Bord Bia Bloom Art Exhibition winning four gold medals. I have had my artwork included in the triennial International Exhibition of Botanical Art, Hunt Institute of Botanical Documentation, Pittsburgh, Penn., US. 2016 being the first Irish artist to achieve this. I believe that observing and connecting with the natural world is now more important than ever.*

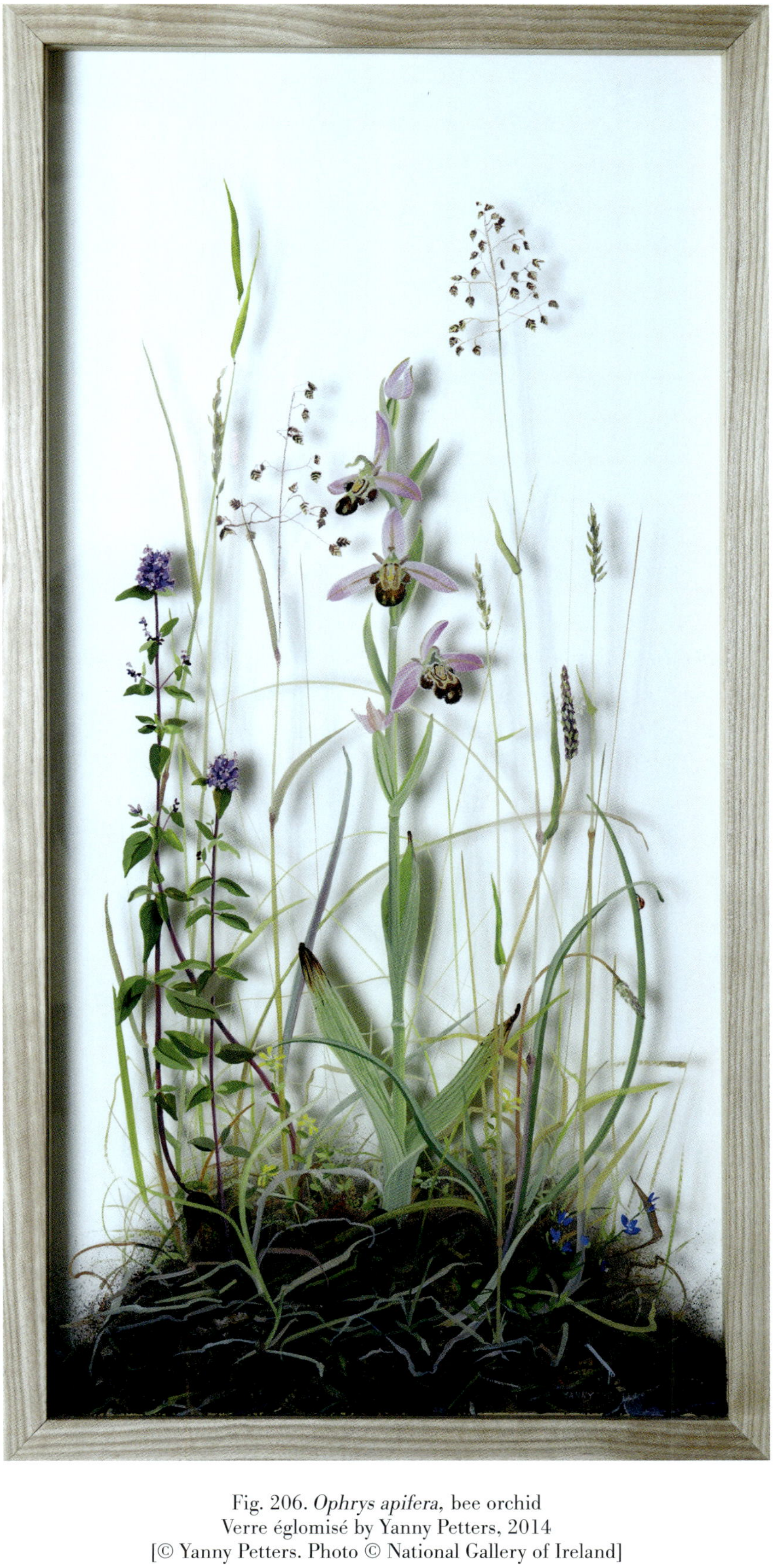

Fig. 206. *Ophrys apifera*, bee orchid
Verre églomisé by Yanny Petters, 2014
[© Yanny Petters. Photo © National Gallery of Ireland]

**Holly Somerville**

*I am an Irish artist and designer working in Enniskerry, Co. Wicklow. I read botany at Oxford University and illustration, Edinburgh College of Art. I have exhibited widely, including the RHA Dublin and RUA Belfast. I am an RHS medal winner, a member, WCSI and a founding member, ISBA. I paint highly detailed watercolours using botanical subjects drawn from both my garden and the beach.*

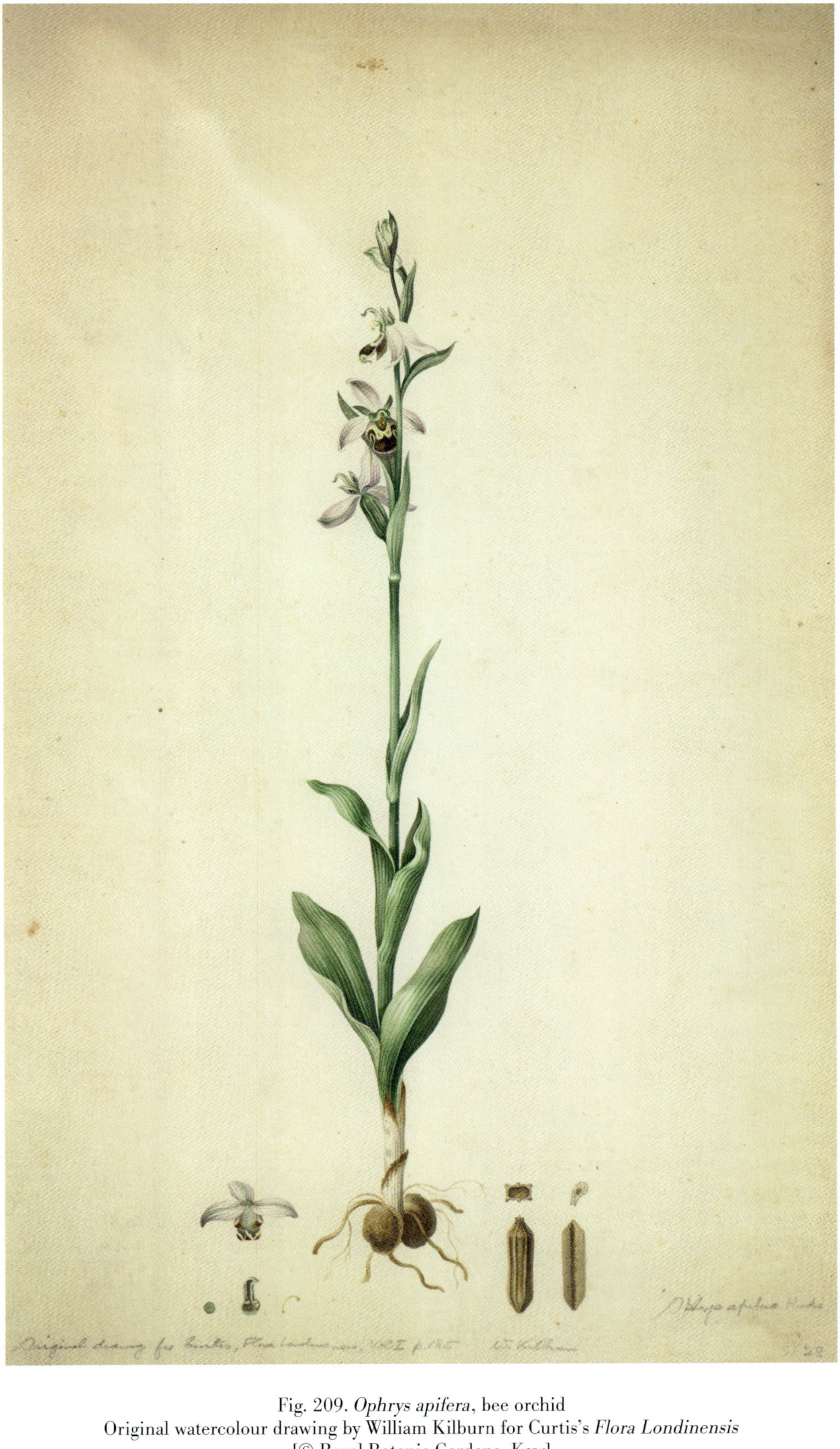

Fig. 209. *Ophrys apifera*, bee orchid
Original watercolour drawing by William Kilburn for Curtis's *Flora Londinensis*
[© Royal Botanic Gardens, Kew]

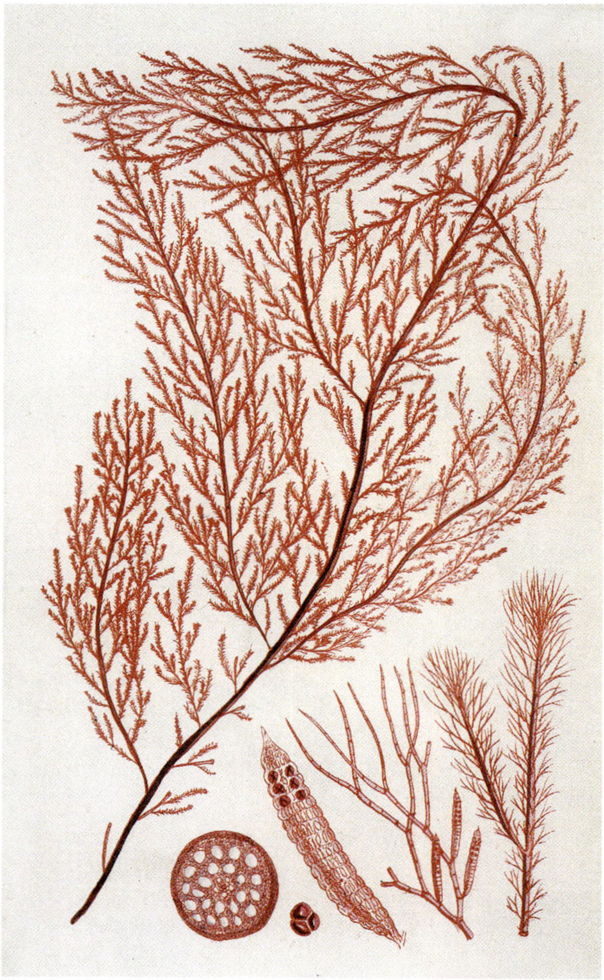

Fig. 210. *Dasya feredayae (Micropeuce feredayae)*
Lithograph from William Henry Harvey, *Phycologia Australica; or, A History of Australian Seaweeds*, vol. 3, plate 172
[Collection: Garden Library, N.B.G]

surface except for the drawn lines. These lines were all that remained at surface level to receive the ink, which was then transferred to paper in the print process. Text combined with a 'type-high' block could be printed together, saving considerable time and cost. This form of 'relief' printing produced simple outlines that were ideal for colouring by hand. For the greater part of the 16th century, woodcut illustration prevailed, with block-cutting skills becoming more refined, although subtlety was still a problem.

Towards the end of the 16th century, metal-plate engraving and etching were beginning to overtake the woodcut. This intaglio process was to remain fundamental to all linear printmaking methods for another four centuries. By using these intaglio processes, a greater delicacy and richness of form was achieved.

In etching on copper, the surface of a polished copper plate was covered with a ground composed largely of wax. A needle traced the design through the ground to the metal. A wall of wax was then raised around the edges of the copper plate and diluted nitric acid was poured over the prepared plate. The design was attacked by the acid and the lines below the surface of the metal. The acid was poured off and the surface was rinsed with clean water. The wax walls and ground were removed, the printer's ink was rubbed into the lines by a roll of canvas and the surplus ink was removed from the flat surface. A damped sheet of paper was then placed on this surface. Strong pressure was applied by a roller and the paper was pressed into the ink lines, which took up the prepared design.

With copperplate engraving, the engraver cut the design into the plate with a graver. The actual printing method was the same as for an etched plate, with the ink being confined to the incised lines or stipple and was conveyed to the plate by a high-pressure press.

For botanical illustration, stipple engraving (where small, closely spaced dots replaced lines) was the most significant and most successful development. However, copperplate did not entirely supersede the

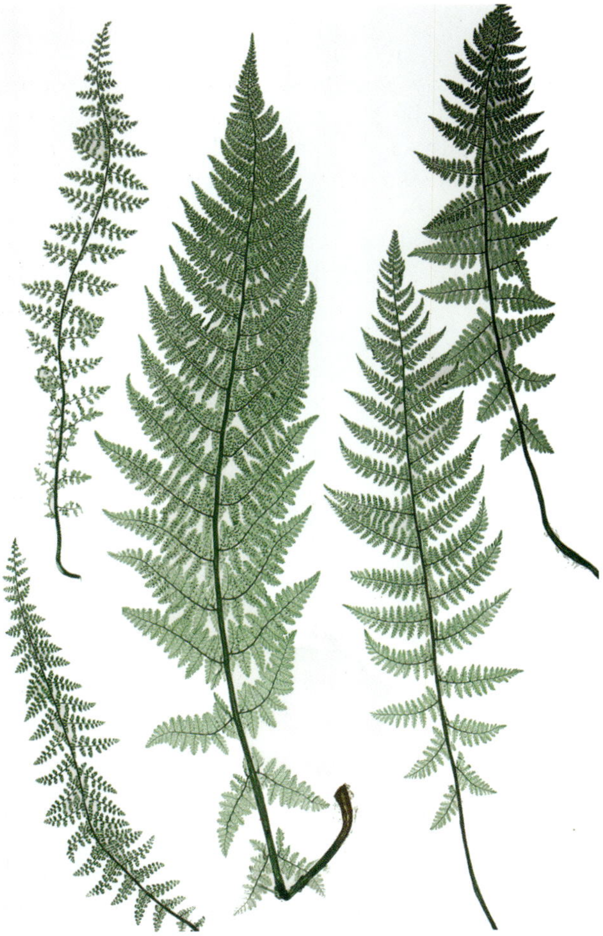

Fig. 211. *Asplenium fontanum* and *Asplenium lanceolatum*, smooth rock spleenworts
Nature-print from Thomas Moore, *The Ferns of Great Britain and Ireland* (London: Bradbury & Evans, 1855)
[Collection: Garden Library, N.B.G.]

woodblock. The latter method continued to flourish for some time, as it was cheaper to print and could easily be included on the same page as the text. William Kilburn's *Geranium robertianum* (herb Robert, see Chapter 3, Figure 39) is a superb example of an 18th-century outline copperplate engraving that has been hand-coloured, a process which was to continue well into the 19th century.

*Curtis's Botanical Magazine* (see Chapter 6, pp. 90–120), founded by William Curtis (qv) in 1787 and still in progress, began by producing copperplate outlines that were, in turn, coloured by hand. In the middle of the 19th century, lithographic outlines were introduced. A colour lithograph (one of many Irish contributions) by William Gumbleton (1840–1911) of an herbaceous peony from the Caucasus grown in the gardens at Belgrove (known as Queenstown, 1849–1922), Co. Cork, appeared in 1908 (plate 8173) and is an outstanding example.

This new printing process, known as lithography, had been introduced into botanical illustration as far back as c.1811, and was to serve science well for the rest of the century. To carry out the process, the image was drawn with ink or greasy crayon on a smooth, porous limestone. The stone was then wetted, and the greasy drawing repelled the water. The printing ink was applied and adhered only to the greasy drawing, not to the wet stone. By using a printing press, the character of the botanical artist's drawing was faithfully reproduced on paper. Eliminating the intermediate step of etching or engraving rendered the process economical, faster, efficient, and more direct. Lithographic stones were cumbersome and heavy and prepared plates of metal (aluminium or zinc) were frequently substituted when the work was comparatively straightforward.

Alternative methods of printing besides those outlined above were also in use. In the early 18th century, mezzotint had begun to be introduced into botanical printing. A tool termed a 'rocker', with a curved surface and possessing sharp teeth, was employed; and when pressed onto the soft copper, made many points in the metal, producing a velvet-

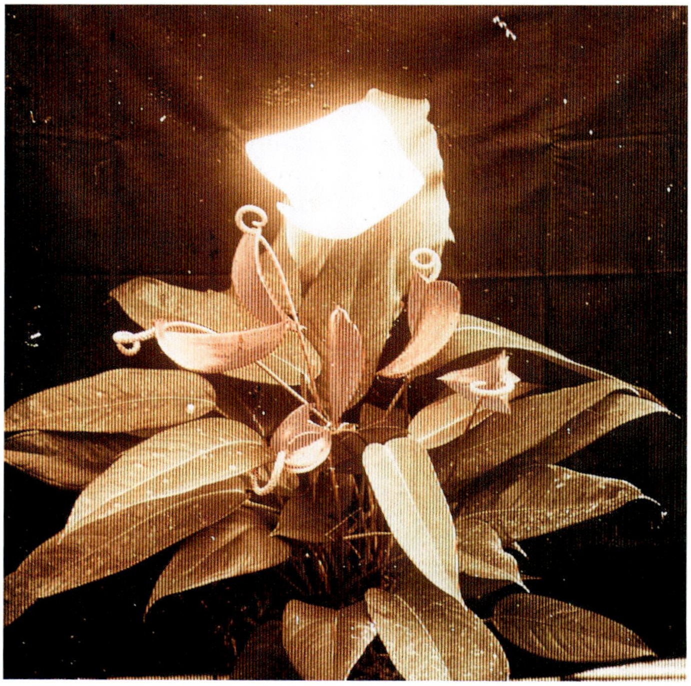

Fig. 212. Colour experimentation in a still life of *Arum* and *Anthuriums*
[Courtesy, National Library of Ireland]

like surface to the final print. The engraver then scraped and burnished each part where they wished to represent light and gradually worked it up towards the finished surface.

Another method was the use of 'drypoint'. In this process, the needle was used directly upon the plate without a ground, scratching the design by pressure and dragging, the process raising a burr beside the furrow. This method produced comparatively few copies before showing signs of deterioration.

In the aquatint process, the plate was covered with a number of coats of resin dissolved in spirit which, while drying, created numerous cracks that were, in turn, bitten into by the acid. Highlights were first stopped out by varnishing and the lighter sections treated in the same way until the last biting produced the deepest tint. A famous example of aquatint and coloured-in watercolour can be found in Robert J. Thornton's (1768–1837) folio, *The Temple of Flora* (1799–1807).

The fascination with printing objects of botanical history continued down through the centuries. 'Nature-printing' was and is a byway of printing, with the so-called nature-print creating its own image. The origins of this simple, straightforward printing technique appeared as early as the 1500s, with Leonardo da Vinci being among its earliest practitioners. The process employed objects from the world of nature which, in turn, became 'printing plates'. Leaves, grass, seeds were inked and then printed onto paper or cloth. The process was simple. To pull a print, the plant was placed on glass. Ink was then applied to both sides of the plant with a small brush. The inked plant was carefully removed from the glass with tweezers and then placed on one side of a sheet of paper that had been creased in half. The other side of the paper was folded over the top of the inked plant and rubbed firmly with the fingers. The paper was unfolded, and the plant removed. The image was represented on both the front and back of the paper.

A more sophisticated method of nature-printing was introduced by Henry Bradbury (1831–1860) in the mid-19th century. His method consisted of placing the plant to be copied between a plate of steel and a sheet of lead and applying hydraulic pressure. The result was that the plant was pressed into the lead. The object was then picked out, the lead plate was electrotyped, and the lettering and other details were engraved on the copper and printed in the colour of the original plant. Bradbury patented his method in Vienna in 1852. Examples can be seen in Thomas Moore's *The Ferns of Great Britain and Ireland*, with the nature-printing process carried out by Bradbury. In the illustration shown in Figure 211, the distinctive features of the fern, such as the central spine, have been deeply recessed in this process, while the fern's delicate traceries have left their fragile lines in the copper. The disadvantage of this method was that many specimens were destroyed in making the plates and it could only be employed for plants which could withstand heavy pressure.

The modern processes have superseded the older methods and are dependent upon photography. Any print process involving photography was derived from the discovery that certain chemical substances, when exposed to light, became sensitive, hardening when light fell on them and remaining soft elsewhere. The combination of light and chemistry could now replace hard work in the preparation of printing surfaces. These photochemical techniques could create relief, intaglio and planographic printing surfaces. Photochemical printing played a vital role in reproducing botanical art from the 1880s.

Photography could be applied to the making of intaglio plates, with the idea of reproducing tonal images. This began to be introduced commercially in the 1880s and was able to provide reproductions of an artist's botanical works with a depth of tone and accuracy of detail far superior to those made through other processes to date.

Aquatint photogravure provided the normal appearance of a photograph combined with the added richness of an aquatint and was used extensively in books and for illustrating catalogues of paintings until about the 1930s.

A process used extensively in the printing industry, and discovered as early as 1839, was electrotyping or the use of a metal facsimile through the deposition of copper by electrolysis. Electrotypes were used from the 1840s for the duplication of existing intaglio plates, avoiding wear and making it possible to print to the same standard each time.

Today, botanical artists have at their disposal an array of media and manners that can be exploited on all levels. As yet, the competent illustrator has no serious competition from photography. Their work remains in constant demand to depict well-known or new species. Botanical art and illustration seem as healthy and vigorous as in the past, this being one of the few remaining disciplines that can offer both the professional and amateur an opportunity to convey an accurate, methodical and scientific recording.

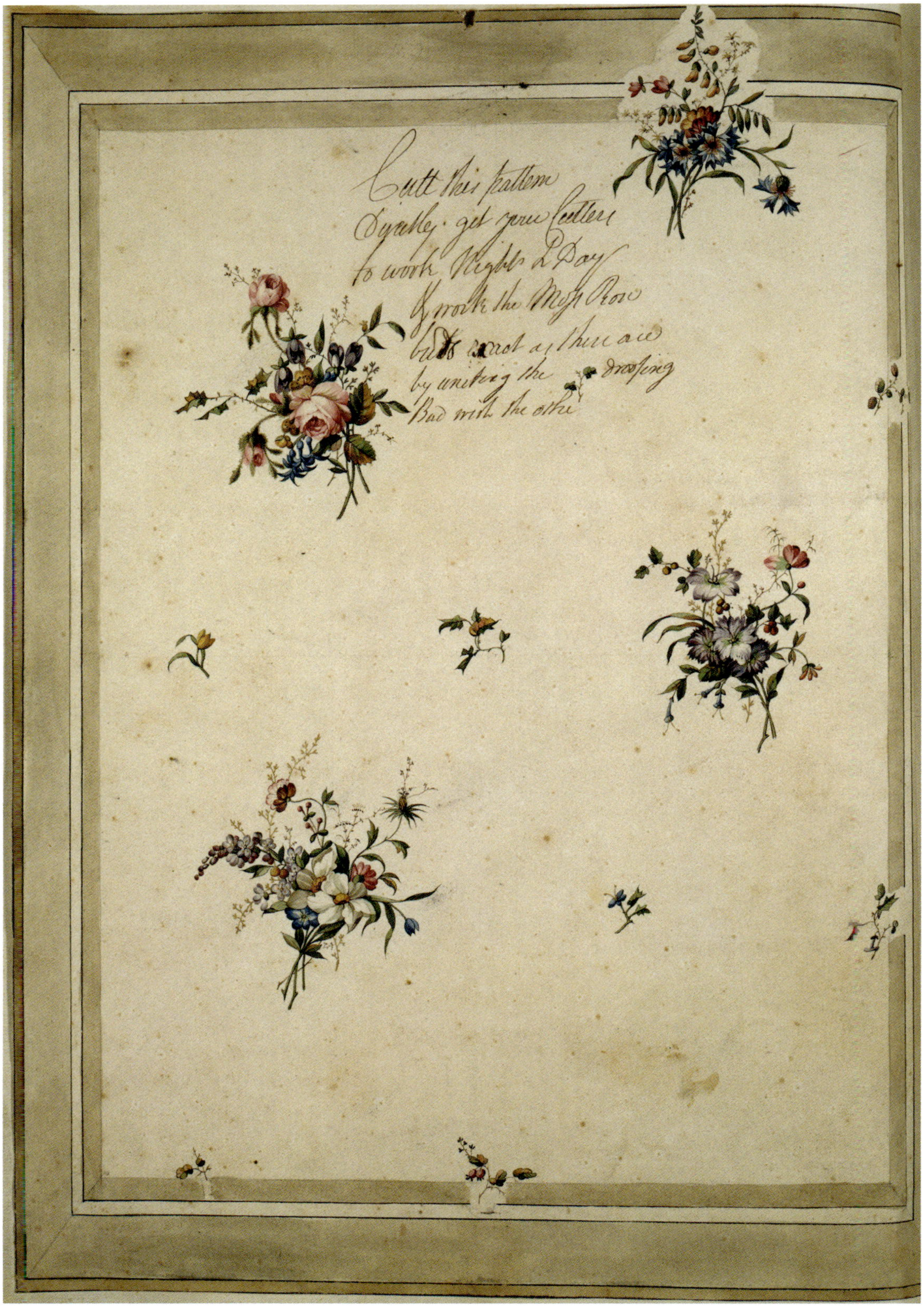

Fig. 213. Design for a printed textile
Watercolour by William Kilburn, c.1791. Inscription: '*Cutt this pattern directly-get your Cutters to work Night and Day And work the Moss Rose buds exact as these are by uniting the droopin Bud with the other*'
[© Victoria and Albert Museum, London]

# Notes

**Chapter 1: Botanical Exploration in Ireland c.1600–c.1800**

1. M.E. Mitchell, 'Irish Botany in the Seventeenth Century', *Proceedings of the RIA* 75 (1974), pp. 275–84. Katherine Baily Kane, *The Irish Flora: Comprising the Phaenogamous Plants and Ferns* (Dublin: Hodges and Smith, 1833), p. v.
2. *Zoilomastix* ('A Whip for the Detractor'). The autographed Latin manuscript consists of 353 folios and is believed to have been written by Philip O'Sullivan Beare around 1625–26, while in exile in Spain. The manuscript, thought by Irish scholars to have been lost for more than 300 years, was rediscovered in 1932 in the library at the University of Uppsala, Sweden (MS.248). A translation was recently published by Cork University Press, see Note 4, below.
3. E. Charles Nelson, 'Recollecting Ireland's Flora: Botanical Information in the 'Zoilomastix' (c.1626) of Philip O'Sullivan Beare', in *Botany and Gardens in Early Modern Ireland*, eds Elizabethanne Boran, E. Charles Nelson and Emer Lawlor (Dublin: Four Courts Press, 2022), pp. 25–44.
4. Philip O'Sullivan Beare, 'Flowers', in *The Natural History of Ireland*, trans. and ed. Denis C. O'Sullivan (Cork: Cork University Press, 2009), p. 225. For a detailed account see Nelson 2022, pp. 25–44.
5. *Lloydia serotina* (or the Snowdon lily) was discovered c.1688 by Llwyd and first appeared in Edmund Gibson's edition of William Camden's *Britannia* (first published 1586). The name of this rare alpine was changed to *Gagea serotina* in 2010; see Clive A. Stace, *New Flora of the British Isles*, 3rd ed. (Cambridge University Press, 2010).
6. On his death, William Sherard left to the University of Oxford the sum of £3,000 for the endowment of the Professorship of Botany with the proviso that his assistant, Johann Jacob Dillenius (1684–1747) was to be the first Sherardian Professor of Botany at Oxford (1734–1747).
7. Sir Arthur Rawdon (1662–1695), 2nd baronet, soldier, keen horticulturist, was the only surviving son of Sir George Rawdon and his second wife, Dorothy, eldest daughter of 2nd Viscount Conway. He succeeded to the baronetcy and estate, Moira, Co. Down, on his father's death, 1684. Rawdon shared a mutual love of plants with his friend and correspondent Sir Hans Sloane; some of his plant specimens are preserved in *The Sloane Herbarium*, BM (NH), London, and relate to 'Severall plants gathered in Ireeland by Sir Arthur Rawdon and Dr. Sherard...' (J.E. Dandy, Sloane Herbarium, London, 1958, p. 189). A large collection of tropical plants (probably acquired by the plant collector James Harlow on his Jamaican expedition) was raised and cultivated at Moira by Rawdon.
8. William Sherard's Irish plant records appeared in the second and third editions (1696, 1724) of John Ray's *Synopsis Methodica Stirpium Britanicarum*, ed. Johann Jacob Dillenius, 3rd ed. (1724), pp. 237–39.
9. Reverend Richard Heaton, born Hooton Pagnell, Yorkshire. Chaplain to Sir Thomas Wentworth's Troop of Horse in Ireland, 1633, Rector, Birr, 1633; Kilkeel, Co. Down, 1634; Dean of Clonfert, 1638. Returned to England, 1641. Following the Restoration of Charles II, returned to Ireland, 1660. Appointed Dean of Clonfert, 1660; conferred with DD, TCD, 1661.
10. John Parkinson, *Theatrum Botanicum: The Theater of Plantes* (London, 1640). The majority of the illustrations found in his herbal are woodcuts, apart from the title pages and portraits, which carry copperplate engravings, the latter becoming increasingly popular after c.1590.
11. Heaton collected *Drosera anglica*, the great sundew, from the Bog of Allen and forwarded it to Dublin apothecary Zanchie Silliard (Sylliard) (fl.1640s). The latter forwarded the specimen to English botanist John Parkinson (qv). In his *Theatrum Botanicum* (1640), Parkinson incorrectly attributed the discovery to Silliard. This was later corrected by an annoyed Heaton.
12. William How's plant records for *Phytologia Britannica* (1650) were furnished by several of his friends – George Bowle (Bowles), Walter Stonehouse and the Reverend Richard Heaton. Eight Irish plant records appeared and included *Dryas octopetala*, *Gentiana verna*, *Pyrola rotundifolia*, *Scilla verna*.
13. William How (1620–1656), *Phytologia Britannica, Natales Exhibens Indigenarum Stirpium Sponte Emergentium* (London: Richard Cotes for Octavian Pulleyn, 1650).
14. G.L.H. Davies, 'The Making of Irish Geography IV: The Physico-Historical Society of Ireland, 1744–1752', *Irish Geography* 12 (1): 92–98.
15. Isaac Butler, botanist, antiquary, bookseller, publisher, Patrick Street, Dublin; published first index of Dublin streets and public buildings (*Gentleman and Dealer's Almanack*, Dublin, 1756).
16. Dr John Rutty, historian of Irish Quakers, physician, diarist, writer. Completed education at Leiden University under distinguished physician and botanist Professor Herman Boerhaave, who was responsible for assembling over 5,000 species of plants for Leiden's botanic gardens. Rutty promoted establishment of the Dublin Medico-Philosophical Society (1756). Among his general medical publications were: *The Analysis of Milk* (1762) and *A Chronological History of the Weather and Seasons and of the Prevailing Diseases in Dublin for Forty Years* (1770). Died Dublin, 26 April 1775.
17. John Rutty, *An Essay Towards a Natural History of the County of Dublin, Accommodated to the Noble Designs of the Dublin Society*, 2 vols (Dublin: 1772).
18. Rutty, John, et al. *Indigenous Plants Used in Dying and Painting: From the Observations of Authors, the Practices of the Irish, and Some New Experiments* (Bristol: Dept. for Continuing Education, University of Bristol, 1990).

19. The Reverend Caleb Threlkeld, botanist, doctor, minister of religion, born 31 May 1676, Keiberg (or Keybergh), Kirk Oswald, Cumberland. Settled in Dublin with his large family in 1713; established a thriving medical practice. Interested since student days (Edinburgh) in botany. After approx. 12 years of collecting specimens in Dublin area, published a list of some 530 plant names – *Synopsis Stirpium Hibernicarum* (1726). Died Dublin, 28 April 1728. The genus *Threlkeldia* is named in his honour. For further information relating to Caleb Threlkeld, see Emer Lawlor, 'Caleb Threlkeld: Dissenting Minister, Physician and Botanist' in *Botany and Gardens in Early Modern Ireland*, eds Elizabethanne Boran, E. Charles Nelson and Emer Lawlor (Dublin: Four Courts Press, 2022), pp. 80–99; Declan Doogue, 'Caleb Threlkeld's Plant Records' in *Botany and Gardens in Early Modern Ireland*, eds Elizabethanne Boran, E. Charles Nelson and Emer Lawlor (Dublin: Four Courts Press, 2022), pp. 100–115.
20. Caleb Threlkeld, *Synopsis Stirpium Hibernicarum* (1726; reprint, Kilkenny: Boethius Press, 1988).
21. Nathaniel Colgan, *Flora of the County Dublin: Flowering Plants, Higher Cryptogams and Characeae* (Dublin, 1904).
22. The majority of Sherard's Irish plant records appeared in the 2nd and 3rd editions of Ray's *Synopsis* (see Note 8).
23. For further information on the sources of Threlkeld's *Synopsis Stirpium Hibernicarum*, see M.E. Mitchell, 'The Sources of Threlkeld's *Synopsis Stirpium Hibernicarum*'. *Proceedings of the RIA* 75 (1974), pp. 1–6.
24. Robert Lloyd Praeger, son of a Dutch linen merchant settled in north of Ireland, born Holywood, Co. Down, 25 August 1865, died Craigavad, Co. Down, 5 May 1953. BA Belfast, 1885, ALS, 1949. Civil engineer, 1866–1893; assistant librarian, NLI, 1898; librarian, 1920–24; President RIA, 1931–34. He has been described as '... an engineer by qualification, a librarian by profession and a naturalist by inclination'.
25. Robert Lloyd Praeger, *Some Irish Naturalists: A Biographical Note-book* (Dundalk: W. Tempest, 1949), p. 55.
26. E. Charles Nelson, 'Patrick Browne (c.1720–1790), Irish Physician, Historian and Caribbean Botanist: A Brief Biography with an Account of his Lost Medical Dissertations', *Huntia* 11(1), 5–16, p. 6. Hunt Institute for Botanical Documentation, Carnegie Mellon University, Pittsburgh, USA.
27. Patrick Browne, *The Civil and Natural History of Jamaica. In Three parts. Containing ... the Whole Illustrated with Fifty Copper-plates; ... by Georg Dionysius Ehret* (London, c.1756).
28. Georg Dionysius Ehret, botanist, entomologist, born Germany, began as gardener's apprentice near Heidelberg. Earliest illustrations (1735–36) were in collaboration with Carl Linnaeus (qv) and keen botanist, banker and owner of a rich botanical garden (Hartekamp) George Clifford III (1685–1760); together they produced *Hortus Cliffortianus* (1738). Moved to England where he was in great demand (Blunt), illustrated many of the more spectacular plants in cultivation, Chelsea Physic Garden. In 1768 he began recording botanical specimens for Joseph Banks, recently returned from Labrador and Newfoundland. The genus *Ehretia* is named in his honour.
29. Carl Linnaeus (1707–1778), Swedish botanist, zoologist, taxonomist, physician who formalised binomial nomenclature, the modern system of naming organisms. He drew up rules for assigning names to plants and animals and was the first to use binomial nomenclature consistently (1758). Introduced and provided workable keys, making it possible to identify plants and animals from his own books and is known today as 'the father of modern taxonomy'.
30. See Note 28.
31. Patrick Browne, *Fasciculus Plantarum Hiberniae* (1788). Browne's handwritten manuscript has survived and is preserved in the library, LS, London.
32. John K'Eogh (Keogh), naturalist and clergyman, born Strokestown, Co. Roscommon, TCD, 1705, graduated BA (Dublin), 1711. Following ordination, served as chaplain to 4th Baron Kingston (1693–1761), Mitchelstown, Co. Cork, and while there compiled *Botanalogia Universalis Hibernica, or, a General Irish Herbal* (Cork, 1735), an alphabetical list of plants based largely on plants grown in Kingston's garden. The work is of historical significance, as it provides evidence of plants cultivated at that time in Ireland, including lemons and oranges.
33. The RBG was established at Glasnevin, Dublin, 1795, under the aegis of the DS, with financial support from the Irish Parliament. For a history of the gardens, see: E. Charles Nelson and Eileen M. McCracken, *The Brightest Jewel: A History of the National Botanic Gardens, Glasnevin, Dublin*, Kilkenny: Boethius Press, 1987. Original watercolours by Wendy F. Walsh.
34. Walter Wade, MD, FRS (1811), ALS (1792). Professor of Botany, the DS had established its garden (then known as the RBG, Glasnevin, Dublin) 1796 (see Note 33). For further information relating to Wade, see Chapter 2.
35. Walter Wade, *Catalogus Systematicus Plantarium Indigenarum in Comitatu Dublinensi Inventarum*, published by the Dublin Society (Sleater) (Dublin, 1794). Wade lists approx. 422 County Dublin species, of which at least 132 are additions to those previously recorded. See Colgan, *Flora of the County Dublin* (1904), p. xxiv.

**Chapter 2: Botanical Illustration c.1720–1820**

1. William Maple, *A Method of Tanning without Bark* (Dublin: A. Rhames, 1732). William Maple (d.1762) was one of the 14 men who came together to form the DS. Maple was elected Curator and Registrar.
2. Walter G. Strickland, *A Dictionary of Irish Artists*, vol. 1 (Dublin and London, 1913; Shannon, 1968. Introduction by Theo Snoddy), p. 421.
3. James Gwim's mezzotint portrait of actor, Spranger Barry (1719–1777) in *Macbeth*, act 2, scene iii, is particularly fine and forms part of the NGI Prints & Drawings collection, cat. no. 10,134.
4. Sir John Gilbert, *History of the City of Dublin*, 3 vols (Dublin, 1854–1859), pp. 21.
5. Irishman, John Brooks (fl.1730–1756) is accredited as being the inventor of transfer-printing on 'Enamel, China, Glass, Delft

and other Wares'. See Bernard Watney, *English Ceramic Circle Transactions* 6(1): 62.

6. The process of transfer-printing was already being used for printing linen at a factory in Dublin. Mrs Delany, writing in December 1752 from 'Delville', Glasnevin, Dublin, refers to a visit to 'Drumcondra, half a mile off, to see a new manufactory that is set up there, of printed linen done by copper-plates; they are excessive pretty...'
7. Simon François Ravenet (1706–1774), born Paris, a pupil of French engraver, Jacques-Philippe Le Bas (1707–1773). Achieved considerable reputation before arriving, London c.1744. Employed, Battersea Enamel works. Awarded Society of Arts premium, 1761. In 1766, became member of Incorporated Society of Artists. Employed by Hogarth and various booksellers. Elected associate, RA (1770). Died Hampstead, London, 1774. Engravings remarkable for their colouring, brilliancy and careful drawing.
8. T. Hughes, 'English Painted Enamels', *Country Life* (1951), p. 51.
9. Professor of Botany, The Dublin Society, Dr Walter Wade was one of the founders of the Royal (later National) Botanic Gardens, Glasnevin, Dublin. In 1802, he gave the first public lecture to both men and women in the Director's House, Royal Botanic Gardens, Glasnevin, Dublin; he also held practical classes. For further information relating to Dr Walter Wade, see Chapter 3 pp. 37–54.
10. Walter Wade, *Catalogus Systematicus Plantarum Indigenarum in Comitatu Dublinensi Inventarum* (Dublin: DS, Sleater, 1794).
11. Walter Wade, *Sketch of Lectures on Meadow and Pasture Grasses, Delivered in the Dublin Society's Botanical Garden, Glasnevin* (Dublin: Graisberry & Campbell, 1808).
12. Walter Wade, *Salices: Or an Essay towards a General History of Sallows, Willows & Osiers. Their Uses and Best Methods of Propagating and Cultivating Them* (Dublin: Graisberry & Campbell, 1811).
13. Walter G. Strickland, *A Dictionary of Irish Artists* (1913; reprint, Shannon: Irish University Press, 1968), vol. 2, pp. 277, 278.
14. Ibid., p. 366.
15. James Ford, (1) *The Grand Hotel, Portobello, Dublin*, c.1811. NGI, 11624; (2) *The New Stamp Office*, c.1811, NGI, 11625; (3) *The Royal Infirmary from the Salute Battery, Phoenix Park*, c.1811, NGI, 11,694.
16. John White, *An Essay on the Indigenous Grasses of Ireland* (Dublin: Graisberry & Campbell for the DS, 1808).
17. James Mannin (d.June 1779). French artist, landscape and flower painter employed by the DS, 1746 as teacher of ornamental and landscape drawing in their drawing school, Shaw's Court, Dublin. Successful teacher, many well-known artists, such as Thomas Roberts, J.J. Barralet, George Barret were his pupils.
18. For further information relating to the Brocas family, see Patricia Butler, *The Brocas Collection. An Illustrated Selective Catalogue of Original Watercolours, Prints and Drawings in the National Library of Ireland with an Account of the Brocas Family and Their Contribution to the [Royal] Dublin Society's School of Landscape and Ornament Drawing* (Dublin: NLI, 1997).
19. *An Account of Saffron; The Manner of Its Culture and Saving for Use, with the Advantages It Will Be of to This Kingdom* (Dublin: printed by A. Rhames for the Dublin Society, 1732).
20. Ibid., p. 11.
21. Henry F. Berry, 'Dr. Madden's and the Society's Premium Systems', in *A History of the Royal Dublin Society* (London: Longmans, Green & Co., 1915), pp. 52–74.
22. S.H. [Samuel Hayes], *A Practical Treatise on Planting: And the Management of Woods and Coppices* (Dublin: printed by Sleater for the Dublin Society, 1794).
23. William Esdall (c.1750–1795), born Dublin, artist, engraver, one of four sons of James Esdall (d.1755), printer, publisher, bookseller and his wife, Anne (née Middleton) (c.1718–c.1795). Exhibited Society of Artists in Ireland, 1772. Esdall's work ranged from a portrait medallion (Goldsmith, 1777) to Minerva introducing music, poetry and design to Hibernia (*Hibernian Magazine*, 1755), prize certificates for schools, tickets (concerts) etc. Married, 1775, Elizabeth (née Levinge). Died Dublin, March 1795.
24. Edward Donovan's publications include: (1) *The Natural History of British Insects: Explaining Them in Their Several States etc.* Printed for the author and F. & C. Rivington, 16 vols, 576 plates, 568 coloured (London, 1792–1813); (2) *The Natural History of British birds: Or a Selection of the Most Rare, Beautiful and Interesting Birds Which Inhabit This Country*, 10 vols, 244 (total) plates (London, 1794–1819).
25. The Wernerian Natural History Society (the Wernerian Society), operating 12 January 1808–16 April 1858, an offshoot of the RS Edinburgh. Interested in presenting papers on natural history – plants, insects, mineralogy. The Society was named after the German geologist Abraham Gottlob Werner and founded by Robert Jameson, Regius Professor of Natural History, University of Edinburgh.
26. Edward Donovan, *An Epitome of the Natural History of the Insects of China Comprising Figures and Descriptions of Upwards of One Hundred New, Singular, and Beautiful Species; Together with Some That Are of Importance in Medicine, Domestic Economy* (London: printed for the author by T. Bensley, 1798). (Note: several plates are dated, 1799.)
27. Grimwood and Wykes was founded by Daniel Grimwood (c.1725–1796), a nurseryman, Kensington, London, in partnership with Samuel Hudson and Peter Barritt; the business was successor to the nursery of John Williamson & Co., 1783.
28. In 1807, Edward Donovan founded his own London Museum and Institute of Natural History, Catherine Street, the Strand, in which he exhibited cases of mammals, reptiles, fish, birds, molluscs, insects, corals and botanical specimens. Despite charging 6 pence per head (admission), his museum closed to the public early in 1817. In Donovan's opinion, he had spent around £15,000 on his museum.

**Chapter 3: Early Illustrated Floras**

1. Walter Wade, *Catalogus Systematicus Plantarum Indigenarum in Comitatu Dublinensi Inventarum* (Dublin: DS, Sleater, 1794). See Chapter 2, Note 10.

2. For further biographical information relating to William Kilburn, see Chapter 5 pp. 76–89.
3. William Kilburn contributed around 27 plates to *Flora Londinensis*: Fasc. 1: pls 2, 6–8, 11, 12, 14, 17, 19, 22, 29–32, 34, 38, 44, 53, 55, 56, 60, 70–72; Fasc. 1: pls 26, 71; Fasc. 3: pl. 67.
4. William Kilburn contributed a small number of plates, possibly two or three, to the second volume, Curtis's *Flora Londinensis*.
5. *Flora Londinensis*, vol. 1. Each number contained six plates with accompanying text. Every 12th number completed a fascicle, and three fascicles were bound in one volume.
6. It is believed that James Sowerby drew and engraved around 50 plates found in the fifth fascicle, *Flora Londinensis*. Sydenham Teast Edwards, botanical artist and close friend of William Curtis, is believed to have contributed 21 plates for the sixth fascicle, *Flora Londinensis*.
7. William Curtis employed around 30 colourists to hand-colour the copperplate engravings, among whom was colourist for the *Botanical Magazine*, William Graves (c.1754–post 1827). His son George (1784–c.1839) was later to become the editor of a further enlarged edition of *Flora Londinensis* begun in 1817 and which continued until 1828.
8. An advertisement for Walter Wade's *Floræ Dublinensis* began to appear in the *Dublin Chronicle* beginning Thursday 13 December 1787.
9. E. Charles Nelson, 'Walter Wade's Flora Dublinensis. An Enigmatic Irish Botanical Publication', *Long Room Bulletin of the Friends of the Library* (1980) 20–21, pp. 16–20.
10. E. Charles Nelson and Eileen M. McCracken, *The Brightest Jewel. A History of the National Botanic Gardens, Glasnevin, Dublin* (Kilkenny, Ireland: Boethius Press, 1987). See Chapter 3, 'Botany and Politics: Walter Wade and John Foster 1790–'95' and Chapter 5, 'The Formation and Early Years of the Botanic Gardens, 1795–1818'.
11. Walter Wade, *Plantae Rariores in Hibernia Inventae or Habitats of Some Plants, Rather Scarce and Valuable, Found in Ireland: With Concise Remarks on the Properties and Uses of Many of Them* (Dublin: np, 1804). This catalogue included lichens, bryophytes, marine algae and flowering plants.
12. *Flora Hibernica* comprises five volumes. Four are in the Ulster Museum (Department of Botany), Belfast; the fifth volume in the BM (NH), London.
13. James Townsend Mackay, born Kirkcaldy, Fife, 29 January 1775. Assistant, Professor of Botany, TCD 1804–1806. Responsible for a number of gardens on campus, TCD, including Physic Garden. Mackay also assisted the recently appointed Professor of Botany, Dr Robert Scott. Appointed Curator of newly acquired three-acre site (leased to TCD, 5 July 1806), the College Botanic Garden, Ballsbridge, Dublin, 1806, where he succeeded in establishing a distinguished reputation and fine collection of plants. Travelled widely in Ireland collecting and studying native plants, culminating in *Flora Hibernica* (Dublin: printed by W. Curray, 1836). Other contributors: Thomas Taylor (bryophytes, lichens), William Henry Harvey (algae) (qv), Member, Botanical Society of London, LLD Dublin, 1850, ALS, 1806. Died Dublin, 25 February 1862.
14. A letter dated 1896 (inside front cover) from Frances M. More to Dr Wright, Secretary, RIA states that the manuscript entitled: 'Catalogue of the Native Plants of Ireland Observed by John Templeton. A.L.S.' was drawn up between 1794 and 1810 by John Templeton. It was loaned by his son to Alexander Goodman More, when he was preparing second edition, *Cybele Hibernica*, on condition it would be placed in the library, RIA. Three drawings of Irish cryptogams with manuscript notes by John Templeton, presented by Miss A.L. Smith, 1931, form part of the collection, Botany Library, BM, London.
15. In 1803, the DS published Templeton's description of a new hybrid rose, *Rosa Hibernica* (the Irish rose), *Rosa canina* x *pimpinellifolia* (*R.* x *hibernica*) Templeton-Rose-Rosaceae, one of his many contributions of new species relating to Irish plant records.
16. Patricia Pyne, photographer, 'Out of the Shadows: Capturing the World of the Forgotten Naturalist John Templeton (1766–1825)', Ulster Museum. September–November 2016.
17. The Reverend Thomas Martyn (1735–1825) edited Philip Miller's (1691–1771) *Gardeners and Florists Dictionary* (1st edition 1724), 1795–1807.
18. The Belfast Natural History Society became the Belfast Natural History and Philosophical Society, 1842.
19. For further information relating to John Templeton, see John Killen 'John Templeton – The Gilbert White of Ireland, the Friend of Everyman', *Linen Hall Review* 9: 3/4, 4–8.
20. William Henry Harvey's knowledge of algae became so extensive that he was invited to write up the group for J.T. Mackay's *Flora Hibernica* (1836), the first comprehensive Irish flora.
21. The next volume in the series was not published until the end of the 19th century and the final volume appeared in 1925.
22. During William Henry Harvey's 22-year tenure at TCD, it is believed that he prepared and published almost nine hundred lithographic plates, on average producing almost one lithographic plate per week.
23. William Henry Harvey, *A Manual of the British Algae* (London: J. Van Voorst, 1841).
24. William Henry Harvey, *Phycologia Britannica, or, a History of British Sea-weeds*, 4 vols (London: Reeve Brothers, 1846–1851).
25. William Henry Harvey applied for the Chair of Botany, TCD as early as 1844. The Senate awarded him an Hon. MD, in order to make him eligible for the post. His application was not successful.
26. It is believed that William Henry Harvey contributed at least one hundred thousand specimens to the collections, Herbarium, TCD.
27. D.A. Webb, 'William Henry Harvey, 1811–1866 and the Tradition of Systematic Botany', *Hermathena* no.103 (1966), 44.

**Chapter 4: Early Amateur Botanists and Floras**

1. Lady Rosemary Fitzgerald, independent botanist, collector, author, conservationist and recipient of the Marsh Christian Trust Award, RBG Kew, London, 2001.
2. See Chapter 8: 'The Fair Discoverers' – Women Botanical Illustrators and Naturalists pp.135–164.

3. In her diaries, Mrs Delany records that she 'decorated shell grottoes in the authentic manner at Killala, Co. Mayo (1731), at the palace of the Bishop of Clogher, Co. Cavan and at Delville, Glasnevin, Dublin.'
4. *The Autobiography and Correspondence of Mary Granville, Mrs Delany* ..., ed. Lady Llanover, vols 1–3 (London: Richard Bentley, 1861); second series vols 1–3, (London, 1862). Vol. 3, p. 572.
5. Ruth Hayden, *Mrs Delany, Her Life and Flowers* (London: British Museum, 1980). Ruth Hayden, *Mrs Delany and Her Flower Collages* (London: British Museum, 1992).
6. Ruth Hayden, 'Chapter 7: Flower Collage: a New Art' in *Mrs Delany and Her Flower Collages* (London: British Museum, 1992), p. 131.
7. Ruth Hayden, 'Chapter 7: Flower Collage: a New Art' in *Mrs Delany and Her Flower Collages* (London: British Museum, 1992), p. 158.
8. *Ireland, Civil and Ecclesiastical*, which was accompanied by a quarto: *Memoir of a Map of Ireland Illustrating the Topography of That Kingdom and Containing a Short Account of Its Present State Civil and Ecclesiastical with a Complete Index to the Map* (London, 1792).
9. Other members of the Beaufort family: William Louis (b.1771), first son, rector of Glanmire and prebendary, Rathcooney, Cork; Rear-Admiral Sir Francis, KCB, FRS, whose work as Admiralty Hydrographer began, 1829. He, like his sister Frances, became closely connected to the Edgeworth family and helped Richard Lovell Edgeworth establish a telegraph system linking Galway and Dublin. They were able to send signals in as short a time as eight minutes. Frances's two younger sisters, Henrietta (Harriet, b.1778) and Louisa Catherine (b.1781), both wrote books for children under noms de plume. In 1827, Louisa, helped by her two brothers, produced 'An Essay upon the State of Architecture and Antiquities, Previous to the Landing of the Anglo-Normans in Ireland' (read 22 October 1827), see *Proceedings of the RIA* 15 (1828).
10. Maria Edgeworth, *The Parent's Assistant. Or, Stories for Children*, vols 1–3 (1800; reprint, Dublin: np, 1829). The 1800 edition carried three illustrations signed 'FAB' and 'FB'.
11. Frances helped to edit Maria Edgeworth's letters for *A Memoir of Maria Edgeworth*, published privately by her daughters (1867).
12. The Plunket Album, entitled: 'Wild Flowers, Painted from Nature', contains 1,200 plant portraits ranging from 1886 to 1894. Collection: The Garden Library, NBG Glasnevin, Dublin.
13. *Irish Times* (15 October 1932).
14. Ann C. Colley, *Victorians in the Mountains: Sinking the Sublime* (London: Routledge, 2016), p. 240.
15. The Hon. Frederica Plunket, *Here and There Among the Alps* (London: Longmans, Green & Co., 1875).
16. 'I remember meeting several times in Chester Square, the Hon. Frederica Plunket, famous then as the first woman to climb the Matterhorn.' Lady Rathdonnell's diary, 1879. See Turtle Bunbury, *The Life & Times of Thomas Kane McClintock Bunbury, 2nd Baron Rathdonnell, of Lisnavagh, County Carlow – Part 1 (1848–1878)*. See also 'Diary of Hon. Frederica Plunket 1866–1886', NLI, MS 42,410.
17. Letter from Hon. Katharine Plunket, 64 Eaton Place, London to Professor Thomas Johnson, professor of botany, Royal College of Science (also Keeper of Botany, Museum of Science and Art, now known as the National Museum of Ireland) dated 21 May 1893. Collection: The Garden Library, NBG Glasnevin, Dublin.
18. In 1970, the Plunket album was transferred to the Garden Library, NBG Glasnevin, Dublin.
19. George Bentham and Joseph Dalton Hooker, *Handbook of the British Flora: A Description of the Flowering Plants and Ferns Indigenous to, or Naturalized in, the British Isles. For the Use of Beginners and Amateurs* (London: L. Reeve & Co., 1920). Preface dated 1892. 6th ed., revised by Sir Joseph Dalton Hooker.
20. Mary J.P. Scannell and Christine I. Houston, 'Wild Flowers from Nature painted by Katharine Plunket (1820–1932) and Frederica Plunket (d.1886) at the National Botanic Gardens, Glasnevin', NBG, *Occasional Papers*, no. 2 (1985), p. 4.
21. *Proceedings of the RDS*, 3 November 1836–6 July 1837, vol. 73 (Dublin: RDS, 1837).
22. Moses Harris, artist, engraver and important pioneer of entomological painting in England. Became Secretary, Aurelian Society, 1762–1766 and author of *The Aurelian* (or *Natural History of English Insects*, 1766), with illustrations designed and engraved by himself, which included not only insects but also host plants. Reprinted by Country Life Books. Introduction by Robert Mays, London, 1986. Wrote on colour theory.
23. John Abbot, artist, executed natural-history drawings with plant background specialising in Lepidoptera. Published his *The Natural History of the Rarer Lepidopterous Insects of Georgia ... Collected from Observations ...* (London: J. Edwards et al., 1797). Formula used by both Harris and Abbot showed adult insects with larva and pupa (Latin: *aurelia*, 'a chrysalis') and the food-plant all placed on the same page with careful attention being paid to design and layout.
24. Éimear O'Connor, 'Miss Battersby: A Case study', in *Irish Women Artists, 1800–2009. Familiar but Unknown* (Dublin: Four Courts, 2010), pp. 37–57.
25. Ibid., p. 57.
26. Ibid., p. 49.
27. For a list of John Samuel Belay Monsell's better-known hymns, see J.D. Julian's *A Dictionary of Hymnology*, 2 vols (London & New York: John Murray, 1892), p. 762, which lists 72.
28. *NGI Illustrated Summary Catalogue of Drawings, Watercolours, and Miniatures*, compiled by Adrian Le Harivel. Intro. by Director of NGI, Homan Potterton, p. 553, cat. No. 2712. 'An Album with 68 Flower Groups; Including a Posy' (all pre-1885). Watercolour on paper. The album was presented by Miss D. Ellis, 1918.
29. Mrs Gage, *A History of the Island of Rathlin: with illustrations and maps* (Rathlin, 1851). A copy is held at the Linen Hall Library, Belfast. Original manuscript versions are in the possession of the family.
30. Catherine Gage (née Boyd) produced at least one album of flower paintings, currently in private ownership.
31. Three bound albums comprise 316

paintings. The inscription on the first album (181 paintings) reads: 'Barbara Frances Stuart: A legacy from her Aunt Adelaide Gage, 1920 – These flowers were painted by the Misses Catherine and Barbara Gage, about 1840–50 – They represent the flora etc., of Rathlin Island – The Rev. Robert Gage (father of these ladies) was Rector and owner of Rathlin'. The second album (59 paintings) reads: 'Hand-painted greenhouse and garden flowers – not necessarily grown on Rathlin Island – but painted by Miss Catherine Gage and her sister, Miss Barbara Gage – late of Rathlin Island – This book given to me by Mrs Alan Campbell (Mamie Grove) and highly prized – Barbara Frances Stuart, Mountearl, 1920'. The third album, marine subjects (76 paintings) is not inscribed. All three albums were acquired by the Linen Hall Library, Belfast, 1997.

32. *Natural History Review* (1870).
33. *The Irish Naturalist. A Monthly Journal of General Irish Natural History ...*, eds George H. Carpenter, Robert Lloyd Praeger and Robert Patterson, vol. 16 (1907), p. 53.
34. David Moore and Alexander Goodman More, *Contributions Towards a Cybele Hibernica: Being Outlines of the Geographical Distribution of Plants in Ireland* (Dublin: Hodges, Smith & Co. & London: John van Voorst, 1866). Susanna Grubb's plant records/contributions included *Pseudorchis albida, Asparagus officinalis* subsp. *prostratus*, and *Ballota nigra*.
35. Susanna Grubb (1820–1911), NBG, Registration No. 18: 1989. Herbarium, NBG Glasnevin, Dublin.
36. Maura J.P. Scannell, 'Susanna Grubb, Botanist and Artist. Biographical Notes and Historical Background', *Glasra* 4 (2008): 86.

### Chapter 5: A Designer of Distinction – William Kilburn

1. Charles O'Brien, *The British Manufacturers' Companion, and Calico Printers Assistant*, vol. 1 (London: printed by Hamilton & Co., 1789), vol. 2 (1792; reprint, London, 1795).
2. The author would like to thank the Kilburn family, in particular Alistair and Jennifer Kilburn, Corinne Ironside (née Kilburn) and Isabel Sharp, Bute Museum. Author, historian and TV presenter, Turtle Bunbury also provided generous information relating to the origins of the Kilburn (or Kelburne) family.
3. Samuel Kilburn (Kilburne, Kelburne) had one known brother, the Reverend Ebenezer Kelburne (d.27 October 1776), ordained presbyterian minister (1749) living – Dublin, 1754, Glasgow, 1755. Married Martha Strahan (née Sinclare) c.1750, widow. They had three children. Revd Ebenezer Kelburne succeeded the Revd William Patten as minister of Plunket Street Meeting House (1692), Dublin, 1749, a post he held until his death, 1773. His son, Revd Sinclair Kelburne was a well-known member of the United Irishmen.
4. Memoir of Mr William Kilburn, *The Gentleman's Magazine*, vol. 102 (March 1832), p. 222.
5. Samuel Kilburn's surname was misspelt on the patent as 'Kilburn'. He adopted this spelling and his descendants have continued to use it. For further information relating to Samuel, see P.K. Kilbourne, *The History and Antiquities of the Name and Family Kilbourn (in its varied orthography)* (New Haven: Durrie & Peck, 1856), p. 54.
6. During this period, the concentration of factories or 'printing grounds' along the banks of the River Liffey and its tributaries was high and ranged from Milltown (southside) to Drumcondra (northside).
7. Journals of the House of Commons of the Kingdom of Ireland (7, 8 and 11 November 1757), pp. 104, 108 and 124.
8. William, Jonathan and Jacob Sissons ran the factory from c.1756–1800. During this period, Sissons's linen-printing establishment, Lucan, Co. Dublin, specialised in work from woodblocks. For further information, see Ada K. Longfield, 'History of the Irish Linen and Cotton Printing Industry in the 18th Century' [read 26 January 1937], *JRSAI*, 7th Series, vol. 7, no.1 (30 June 1937), pp. 26–56.
9. *The Dublin Penny Journal*, vol. 1, no. 23 (December 1832), p. 183.
10. Martin Hopkinson, 'Shorter Notice Gardeners' Trade Cards by William Kilburn and Francois Vivares', *Print Quarterly* 35(4): 420–426.
11. William Curtis's botanic gardens were located 'about the present Crimscott-street, Grange-road'. See John Ardagh, *Chronica Botanica* vol. 9, pl. 9. John Ardagh (1885–1949) was in charge of the Botanical Library, 1922–1947, BM (NH).
12. See Chapter 2: Botanical Illustration c.1720–1820 pp. 22–36
13. See Chapter 3, Note 3.
14. Curtis (W.H.), *William Curtis, 1746–1799* (1941), p. 37.
15. Guildhall Library, MS 11936/280, no. 422584.
16. James Edwards, *A Companion from London to Brighthelmston, in Sussex* (London, 1801): part 1L, pp. 21–22.
17. Memoir of Mr William Kilburn, *The Gentleman's Magazine* 102: 223.
18. William Kilburn had married Elizabeth Brooks, a widow, on 1 January 1777 at St Luke's Church, Finsbury, Islington, London.
19. William Kilburn then married Elizabeth Brown (1765–1828), eldest daughter of Thomas Brown, 10 May 1785, at St Mary's Church, Leyton, Essex. They had six children: Thomas (1786–1830), Hannah (1798–1834), Sophia (1802–1841), William (1803–1864), Robert (1805–1821) and Benjamin (1807–1856).
20. See Chapter 8: 'The Fair Discoverers' – Women Botanical Illustrators and Naturalists, pp. 135–164.
21. Book of Designs for Printed Textiles. Title (on spine): *'Kilburn's Designs'*. Date: c.1787/1792, V&A.
22. William Kilburn's brightly coloured patterns arranged in geometric structures in neoclassical style were translated on to a woodblock by a craftsman. Outlines for each separate colour were created by the human eye on the woodblocks; several blocks were required in order to complete the pattern, which was then repeated across the surface of the fabric.
23. *Journals of the House of Commons of the Kingdom of Ireland* (17 March 1787).
24. Charles O'Brien, *The British Manufacturers Companion and Calico Printers Assistant* , vol. 1 (London: printed by Hamilton & Co., 1789), vol. 2 (1792; reprint, London, 1795).
25. See Chapter 8: 'The Fair Discoverers' – Women Botanical Illustrators and Naturalists pp. 135–164.

26. Memoir of Mr William Kilburn, *The Gentleman's Magazine* 102: 223.
27. Ibid., p. 223.
28. When seeking copyright protection for calico designs in 1787, Kilburn described himself as one of six 'Master-Printers' living in and around London who were responsible for their own designs.
29. Robert Peel and William Yates established their calico-printing firm at Burrs, near Bury, Lancashire, 1792. By 1800, profits had reached £7,000,000, which allowed Robert Peel to donate £10,000 to government, 1797, in return for which he was granted a baronetcy.
30. *Journals of the House of Commons of the Kingdom of Ireland* (17 March 1787), pp. 584–85.
31. Act of 34, George III. For further information, see *Journals of the House of Commons of the Kingdom of Ireland* (15 March 1787).
32. *Manchester Mercury*, 19 April 1802.
33. *Times*, 17 April 1802.
34. James Malcolm, *A Compendium of Modern Husbandry...*, vol. 1 (London: printed by C. and R. Baldwin, 1805), p. 6.
35. *Times*, 20 November 1819.
36. Charles O'Brien, *The British Manufacturers Companion, and Calico Printers Assistant*, vol. 1 (London: printed by Hamilton & Co., 1789), vol. 2 (1792; reprint, London, 1795).

**Chapter 6: Contributions from Ireland to *Curtis's Botanical Magazine***

1. *The Botanical magazine, or, Flower garden displayed*, (later known as *Curtis's Botanical Magazine*) was published in monthly numbers, each number consisting, at first, of three plates accompanied by descriptive letterpress. The price of each number was 1*s* and during William Curtis's lifetime 2,000 copies of every number were sold.
2. *Curtis's Botanical Magazine*, 1 (1787), Preface.
3. *Leptospermum laevigatum*, Australian coast tea-tree, *Curtis's Botanical Magazine*, vol. 32, tab. 1304.
4. John Sims studied at Leiden, settled, London, 1779. Editor, *Curtis's Botanical Magazine* 1801–1816.
5. Sydenham Teast Edwards, born, Usk, Monmouthshire, Wales, contributed over 1,200 plates to *Curtis's Botanical Magazine* (1787–1814). Illustrated William Curtis's *Lectures in Botany* (1805) 3 vols, and R.W. Dickson's *Complete Dictionary of Practical Gardening* (1805–1807) 2 vols. Severed his connection with *Curtis's Botanical Magazine* 1815 and worked for a periodical entitled *The Botanical Register*, which he helped to found.
6. The Gardens opened 1828 as the private Royal Belfast Botanical Gardens and continued as a private park (open to the public on Sundays only) until 1895, when the Belfast Corporation purchased the gardens from the Belfast Botanical and Horticultural Society. The present owner is Belfast City Council.
7. *Rodriguezia planifolia*. See *Curtis's Botanical Magazine*, vol. 10 (July 1836), tab. 3504.
8. Plant specimens collected in Argentina by Scottish plant collector, John Tweedie and based on drawings by Curator, [Royal] / Botanic Gardens, Glasnevin, Ninian Niven were published from 1836 – *Verbena tweediana*. Niven ex Hook [tab. 3541], (1836). *Tweedia versicolor* Hook. [tab. 3630], (1839).
9. Ninian Niven was born at Kelvin Grove, near Glasgow, son of Scottish gardener (also Ninian Niven), gardener, Phoenix Park, Dublin, 1827. Curator, [Royal] Botanic Gardens, Glasnevin, Dublin (1834–1838). Designed gardens, for example, Monkstown Public Park, Dublin, Santry Court, Dublin, and part of Dublin International Exhibition (see Patricia Butler and Pat O'Kelly, *The National Hall at Earlsfort Terrace. A History*, Dublin: Wolfhound Press, 2000, pp. 19, 22, 26).
10. (1) E. Charles Nelson '*In Honour of Ireland' the Hibernian Contribution to Curtis's Botanical Magazine*, vol. 4, part 1 (February 1987), edited by Christopher Grey Wilson, pp. 39–50. (2) E. Charles Nelson and Eileen McCracken, *The Brightest Jewel. A History of the National Botanic Gardens, Glasnevin, Dublin* (Kilkenny: Boethius Press, 1987).
11. David Moore, PhD Zurich. Trainee gardener on estate of Earl of Camperdown, later foreman. Foreman, Trinity College Botanic Garden (1829–1834). Botanist, Ordnance Survey of Ireland (q.v.) (1834–1838). Curator, [Royal] Botanic Gardens, Glasnevin, Dublin, 1838.
12. *Curtis's Botanical Magazine*, vol. 99. (1873).
13. Sir Frederick William Moore, born Dublin, 3 September 1857. Knighted, 1911. Curator, Trinity College Garden, Dublin 1877–1879. Succeeded his father, David Moore as Curator, (re-designated Director, 1890), [Royal] later National Botanic Gardens, Glasnevin, Dublin.
14. Sir Frederick William Moore, *Curtis's Botanical Magazine*, vol. 135, vol. 147.
15. Quotation, *Curtis's Botanical Magazine*, vol. 36 of Series 3, tab. 6489.
16. Modern rules stipulate that all original paintings have to be 21 x 12.5cm, in portrait format, and the plant is to be painted life-size.
17. *Iris kolpakowskiana*, *Curtis's Botanical Magazine*, vol. 36 of Series 3, tab. 6489.
18. Frederick William Burbidge, *The Narcissus: Its History and Culture: With Coloured plates and descriptions of All Known Species and Principal Varieties* (London: L. Reeve & Co., 1875).
19. Frederick William Burbidge, *Cultivated Plants, Their Propagation and Improvement* (Edinburgh: William Blackwood & Sons, 1877).
20. Frederick William Burbidge, *The Gardens of the Sun: or a Naturalist's Journal on the Mountains and in the Forests and Swamps of Borneo and the Sulu Archipelago* (London: John Murray, 1880).
21. John Hutchinson FRS 1947, FLS 1918, Victoria Medal of Honour 1944, Victoria Memorial Medal 1945. Author of *The Families of Flowering Plants* 1926–1934, 2 vols, 3rd ed. (London: Clarendon Press, 1973). Illustrations by W.E. Trevithick and the author.
22. John Hutchinson, 'W.E. Trevithick', *Journal of the Kew Guild*, vol. 7, no. 63 (1958), pp. 592–593.
23. William Edward Roberts Trevithick born Helston, approx. 12 miles from Penzance, Cornwall. Employed as gardener, Trevarno House, Cornwall, Canford House, Dorset, Gaunt's House, Wimborne, Dorset, and various other gardens before going to Ireland, 1912. Established arboretum, Headfort, Kells, Co. Meath.

24. For list of plates drawn and/or lithographed by William Edward Trevithick for *Curtis's Botanical Magazine*, see E. Charles Nelson and Eileen M. McCracken, *The Brightest Jewel. A History of the National Botanic Gardens, Glasnevin, Dublin* (Kilkenny: Boethius Press, 1987), Appendix 2, pp. 245–249.
25. *Curtis's Botanical Magazine*, vol. 153, tab. 9179. Artist: William Edward Trevithick. Lithographer: Lilian Snelling.
26. John Hutchinson, *Flora of West Tropical Africa* (with J.M. Dalziel), 2 vols (1927–1936) (Crown Agents for the Colonies).
27. *Brunnera macrophylla* Perennial forget-me-not. Drawn and lithographed by William Edward Trevithick (1899–1958), *Curtis's Botanical Magazine* (16 May 1924), tab. 9110.
28. The artist, Dr Wendy F. Walsh in conversation with the author, November, 2000.
29. *An Irish Florilegium: Wild and Garden Plants of Ireland*. Forty-eight watercolour paintings by Wendy F. Walsh. Introduction by Ruth Isabel Ross. Notes on the plates by E. Charles Nelson (London: Thames & Hudson, 1983). *An Irish Florilegium 11. Wild and Garden Plants of Ireland*. Forty-eight watercolour paintings by Wendy F. Walsh. Introduction and notes on the plates by E. Charles Nelson (London: Thames & Hudson, 1987).
30. *An Irish Flower Garden Replanted: The Histories of Some of Our Garden Plants*. E. Charles Nelson with illustrations by Wendy F. Walsh (1st edition Kilkenny, 1984). Reprinted and published by Eamon de Burca (Edmund Burke) (Kilkenny: Boethius Press, 1997, 2nd ed.).
31. (a) *A Prospect of Irish Flowers*. Ten watercolour paintings by Wendy F. Walsh. Foreword by Grenville Lucas. Introduction and notes by E. Charles Nelson (Belfast: Blackstaff, 1990). (b) *The Burren, Companion to the Wildflowers of an Irish Limestone Wilderness*. E. Charles Nelson and Wendy F. Walsh (Kilkenny: Boethius Press, 1991) (c) *Trees of Ireland, Native and Naturalized*. E. Charles Nelson and Wendy F. Walsh (Dublin: Lilliput Press, 1993). (d) *Flowers of Mayo, Dr Patrick Browne's Fasciculus Plantarum Hiberniae, 1788*. Edited by E. Charles Nelson, with watercolours by Wendy F. Walsh (Dublin: Edmund Burke, 1995).
32. Contributions by Dr W.F. Walsh to *The Kew Magazine (Curtis's Botanical Magazine*) included: (1) vol. 6, part 3 (August 1989), plate: 130. *Rhododendron burttii Ericaceae*. (2) vol. 7, part 3 (August 1990), plate: 152. *Nesocodon mauritianus* Campanulaceae, (3) vol. 8 (1991), plate: 166. *Tulbaghia leucantha* Alliaceae.
33. *The Kew Magazine*, vol. 10, Part 4 (November 1993), plate: 234 *Deutzia purpurascens* 'Alpine Magician', pp. 174–175.
34. Professor Grenville Lucas, recipient the Linnean Gold Medal, 2007.
35. Susan Sex. *Platystele ovatilabia, Curtis's Botanical Magazine*, vol. 33, Part 4 (December 2016), plate: 849. Further contributions included: vol. 32, no. 1, plate 802, *Dactylorhiza viridis*.
36. Jane Powers, 'Painted Petals – Deborah Lambkin, Botanical Painter', *Plant People, The Irish Garden* (November 1998), p. 18.
37. 'Vireya rhododendrons, with over three hundred species comprise almost one third of the genus Rhododendron. They occur mainly in S.E. Asia and grow as epiphytes or terrestrials in a variety of habitats from sea level to mountain tops. They were first introduced into cultivation by Thomas Lobb in 1845 for the Veitch nursery. Recent significant introductions have been made by the staff of the Royal Botanic Garden, Edinburgh where research on the taxonomy of the group is ongoing.' Donal Synnott, Director, NBG Glasnevin, 1997. Extract from exhibition of *Vireya* rhododendron paintings by D. Lambkin, Herbarium Library, NBG Glasnevin, Dublin, 16–24 May 1998. An extensive collection of *vireyas* was gifted to NBG by RBG Edinburgh and planted out with related plants near west wing of restored Turner curvilinear range, Glasnevin, 1996.
38. The curvilinear range of glasshouses, NBG Dublin were built by Richard Turner (c.1798–1881) between 1845 and 1846, restored by OPW, 1997. Richard Turner, iron master (Hammersmith Iron Works, Ballsbridge, Dublin), erected glasshouses on many Irish estates, including Colebrook, Co. Fermanagh c.1833–1837, Belfast Botanic Garden, 1839–1840, Middleton Park, Co. Westmeath, c.1850. Turner collaborated with Decimus Burton (1800–1881) FRS, FRSA, FSA, FRIBA, in erecting the Palm House, Kew (1844–1848) and the conservatory, Regent's Park, London, 1845.
39. Exhibition of *Vireya* rhododendron paintings by Deborah Lambkin, Herbarium Library, NBG Glasnevin, Dublin (16–24 May 1998).
40. The Linnean Society of London is the world's oldest active biological society, founded in 1788 by Sir James Smith (1759–1828), first President. The Society takes its name from Swedish naturalist, Carl Linnaeus (1707–1778), whose botanical, zoological and library collections have been in its keeping since 1829. The Society aims to promote the study of all aspects of the biological sciences, with particular emphasis on evolution, taxonomy, biodiversity and sustainability.
41. *Gastrodia agnicellus*. Deborah Lambkin, *Curtis's Botanical Magazine*, vol. 37, no. 3, pp. 385–395. Other contributions by D. Lambkin include: *Helichrysum arwae*. To celebrate Kew's Alpine Unit Special Part. vol. 24, Part 1 (February 2007), plate 576; *Franklinia altamaha*. vol. 24, Part 3. (August, 2,000), plate 595; *Saxifraga granulata*, Kew's 250 Anniversary Special, vol. 26, parts 1 & 2 (April, 2009), plate 642.
42. Jane Powers, 'Painted Petals', p. 19.
43. Jane Powers, 'People', *The Irish Garden* (July 2014), pp. 56–58.
44. Ibid., p. 57.
45. *Curtis's Botanical Magazine*, *Aextoxicon punctatum*, vol. 29, no.2 (June 2012), plate 737.
46. Seamus O'Brien, *Curtis's Botanical Magagine*. vol. 29, part 2 (June 2012), plate 373, pp. 182, 190, 191.
47. Lynn Stringer's contributions to *Curtis's Botanical Magazine* include: *Aextoxicon punctatum*, vol. 29. no. 2; *Patrinia villosa*, vol. 30, no. 2; *Patrinia heterophylla*, vol. 30, no. 2; *Myrceugenia leptospermoides*, vol. 33, no. 4; *Myrceugenia lanceolata*, vol. 33, no. 4; *Rhododendron barbatum*, vol. 37, no. 2; and *Rhododendron magnificum*, vol. 38, no. 2.

**Chapter 7: 'A Recorder of Life' – George Victor Du Noyer, MRIA**

1. See (1) Petra Coffey, 'George Victor Du Noyer – A Recorder of Life', in Fionnuala Croke (ed.), *George Victor Du Noyer, 1817–1869. Hidden Landscapes of Ireland* (Dublin: NGI, 1995), pp. 45–476; (2) Fionnuala Croke, ibid.; (3) Peter Murray, *Stones, Slabs and Seascapes: George Victor Du Noyer's Images of Ireland* (Cork, 2017); and (4) Gillian M. Doherty, *The Irish Ordnance Survey: History, Culture and Memory* (Dublin, 2004).
2. George Petrie, artist, archaeologist, musician, man of letters; first watercolour painter to become full member of the RHA, 1828. Among the manuscripts he secured for the RIA were *Annals of the Four Masters* and *Book of the Dun Cow*. Collected valuable material relating to antiquities, placenames and local history of various counties in Ireland. Petrie possessed a deep interest in Irish music and gathered a large collection of Irish airs, some of which were published in *The Petrie Collection of the Native Music in Ireland* (1855). For further information, see Patricia Butler, *Three Hundred Years of Irish Watercolours and Drawings*, Chapter 2, 'The Pleasing Prospect: The Topographical Tradition' (London: Weidenfeld & Nicolson, 1990), p. 43.
3. G.M. Doherty, *The Irish Ordnance Survey*, Chapter 3, 'Surveying the Surveyors; Topographical Department, Staff and Activities', (Dublin: Four Courts Press, 2006), pp. 60–61.
4. Major Thomas Colby, born Rochester St Margaret. Attended Royal Military Academy, Woolwich. Involved in the Scottish Survey, 1814. Appointed Head, OS, 1820. Founder and Fellow of the Royal Astronomical Society. In 1824, was placed in charge of Surveying in Ireland. In 1838, moved from Dublin to London. Attained rank, Major General (1846). Retired from Survey. Died, New Brighton, 1852.
5. William Wakeman, antiquary, artist, draftsman, topographical section, OS. Assistant to John O'Donovan 1839–1842. Book illustrator. Produced wood cuts for George Petrie's publications, Sir William Wilde etc. Illustrator, travel guides. 'A Survey of the Antiquarian Remains on the Island of Inismurray', *JRSAI* (1893).
6. John O'Donovan (Sean Ó Donnabháin) (1806–1861). Distinguished Irish scholar. Born, Atateemore, Co. Kilkenny, educated Hunt's Academy, Waterford. Worked for James Hardiman, Irish scholar, Commissioner Office of Public Records. Engaged to give Irish lessons to Lt Thomas Larcom, OS Ireland. 1830 applied to Larcom for position in the OS. Employed as orthographer, etymologist to assist in establishing, by reference to authoritative sources, a standard of orthography in English for Irish place names. Called to Bar, 1847, but did not practice. Contributions to linguistics recognised by RIA. Awarded Cunningham Medal (1848). Professor of Celtic Languages, Queen's University, Belfast (1849). Committee Member, Royal Academy of Prussia (1856). Awarded Hon. LLD. Dublin University (1859). Died, Dublin, 10 December 1861.
7. NAI, OS/1/12 monthly return of civil assistants employed on the OSI.
8. George Henry Kinahan. Obituary – 'G.V. Du Noyer', *Geological Magazine* (1869), p. 94.
9. Captain Joseph Ellison Portlock, geologist, engineer, soldier, born Gosport, Hampshire. Entered Royal Military Academy, Woolwich. 1813 first commission, Royal Engineers. Appointed to the OS, 1822, by Colby. 1824 became involved in the Irish OS. From 1827 in charge of IOS. 1837 opened Geological Survey Office, Belfast. 1843 published *Geology of Londonderry, Tyrone and Fermanagh ...*, which contained more than 100 fossil species. Posted to Corfu, 1843 with Royal Engineers. 1851 returned to England, inspector of studies, Royal Military Academy, Woolwich, later commander, Royal Engineers, south-east district, Dover (1856). Hon. Major-general on retirement (1857). President, Geological Society (1857–1858). Elected FRS and MRIA (1830). Contributed to Proceedings RIA on zoology, geology, ornithology. Founder member, Geological Society (1831) and Dublin Zoological Society.
10. Du Noyer's drawing skills so impressed Captain J.E. Portlock that he named a fossil after him: Lucina *Du Noyeri*. See Portlock, *Geology of Londonderry etc.*, p. 572.
11. NAI OS/1/14 (December 1837), Progress Report of the Geological Department, OSI commanded by Captain J.E. Portlock.
12. NAI OS/1/14 (November 1837), Progress Report of the Geological Department, OSI commanded by Captain J.E. Portlock.
13. Kew correspondence. DC/13/89 David Moore to Sir W.J.Hooker dated 18 October, 1837.
14. Kew Correspondence.DC/13/89. 9 October 1837 between David Moore and Sir W.J. Hooker
15. M.J.P. Scannell and C.I Houston, 'George V. Du Noyer (1817–1869). A Catalogue of Plant Paintings at the National Botanic Gardens, Glasnevin, with Aspects of His Scientific Life', *Life Sciences Journal of the Royal Dublin Society*, Vol. 2 (1980), pp. 1–13.
16. *First Public Memoir of the City and N.W. Liberties of London Derry, Parish of Templemore* (1837).
17. Joseph E. Portlock, *Report on the Geology of the County of Londonderry ... under the Authority of the Master General and Board of Ordnance* (Dublin, 1843).
18. The colour plates depict animal fossils (three plates), a grass, a sedge, two marine algae. Plant species are: *Calamagrostis lapponica, Carex busbaumii, Vertebrata fucoides* and *Vertebrata fucoides*.
19. J.E. Portlock, *Report on the Geology of the County of Londonderry*, 27 pages of ink and wash drawings together with a bound set of proofs of lithographs and 5 states of proofs for 3 plates relating to this publication are held in the GSI archives.
20. NAI OS/1/17, Monthly Returns of the Civil Assistants in the Geological Department (July1840).
21. Cahir Castle, Co. Tipperary, *Irish Penny Journal*, 33 (13 February 1841); Holy Cross Abbey, Co. Tipperary, *Irish Penny Journal*, 38 (20 March 1841).
22. Samuel Carter Hall and Anna M. Hall, *Ireland: Its Scenery and Character*. Vols 1–3 (London: How and Parsons, 1841–1843).
23. John Savage (ed.), *Picturesque Ireland – A Literary and Artistic Delineation of Its*

*Scenery, Antiquities, Buildings, Abbeys etc.* (New York: T. Kelly, 1878).

24. NAI OS/1/19 Monthly Return of Civil Assistants (February 1842).
25. On George Victor Du Noyer's Certificate of Candidature, his qualifications are listed as: 'Author of papers in the Journal of Geological Society of Dublin and in the Journal of Archaeological Institute of Great Britain'. RIA. MRIAC/413. RIA Certificate of Candidature.
26. 'Appendix No: 11: Account of the Royal Irish Academy from 1st April, 1841 to 31st March, 1842'. PRIA (1836–1869), 2 (1840), xii.
27. The RSAI purchased, by subscription, 12 folios of George Victor Du Noyer's work.
28. The Du Noyer's address on their marriage certificate was given as 114 Upper Leeson Street, Dublin.
29. Joseph Beete Jukes, geologist. Born, Summerhill, Birmingham. Educated King Edward VI school, Birmingham, St John's College, Cambridge. 1839 Geological Survey, Newfoundland. 1842 Naturalist for Survey, north-east coast, Australia. 1846 joined staff Geological Survey, North Wales. 1850 appointed Director, GSI and remained in this position for 19 years. 1866 appointed member of the Royal Commission to inquire into coal fields, England. Died, Dublin, 29 July 1869.
30. J.B. Jukes to Andrew Ramsay, 31 May 1851 (The Ramsay Papers, archives of Imperial College of Science and Technology, London) as quoted in Gordon L. Herries Davies, *Sheets of Many Colours. The Mapping of Ireland's Rocks 1750 – 1890* (RDS, Dublin, 1983). See Chapter 6, 'Years of Great Achievement 1850 – 1869. Conflict over Scales', especially p. 160.
31. Petra Coffey 'George Victor Du Noyer 1817–1869: Artist, Geologist and Antiquary', *JRSAI*, Vol. 123 (1993), p.116.

**Chapter 8: 'The Fair Discoverers' – Women Botanical Illustrators and Naturalists**

1. (a) Whitney Chadwick, 'Sex, Class and Power in Victorian England', in *Women, Art and Society*, 4th ed. (London: Thames and Hudson, 2007), pp. 175–204; (b) Deborah Cherry, 'Art Training for Women' in *Painting Women. Victorian Women Artists* (London & New York: Routledge, 1993); and (c) Patricia Butler, 'The Status and Training of Women Artists in 19th Century Ireland' in *The Silent Companion. An Illustrated History of the Water Colour Society of Ireland* (Woodbridge: ACC Art Books, 2010), pp. 62–78.
2. (a) Ruth Brandon, *Other People's Daughters. The Life and Times of the Governess* (London: Orion, 2008); and (b) Patricia Butler, 'The Status and Training of Women Artists in 19th Century Ireland' in *The Silent Companion. An Illustrated History of the Water Colour Society of Ireland* (Woodbridge: ACC Art Books, 2010), pp. 62–78.
3. The first undergraduate female student, Isabel Marion Weir Johnston (1883–1969), known as Marion Kelleher (née Johnston), entered TCD Friday, 22 January 1904 to read English and French.
4. Between 1791 and 1876, five women were elected to honorary membership, RIA, Dublin: Maria Edgeworth (1768–1849), Princess Ekaterina Dashkova (1743–1810), Mary Somerville (1780–1872), Caroline Herschel (1750–1848) and Margaret Stokes (1832–1900).
5. *The Irish Flora: Comprising the Phaenogamous Plants and Ferns* (Dublin: Hodges and Smith, 1833, reissued, 1845); published anonymously and assisted by John White, under gardener, RDS's BG Glasnevin, Dublin. Some copies have an additional title page, tipped in; this reads, within the decorative surround of a fine hand-coloured engraving of *Daboecia cantabricia*, 'The Irish Flora, Comprising the Flowering Plants and Ferns', with the publisher's address given as '104 Grafton Street', to which they had moved from '21 College Green', their address on the original title page. See M.E. Mitchell, Department of Botany, NUIG 'The Irish Floras: A Checklist of Non-serial Publications', *Glasra* vol. 4, pp. 47–57.
6. Lady Katherine Sophia Kane (née Baily) (1811–1886), born 11 March, only child of Henry Baily and Bridget Baily (née O'Kelly). Parents died young, childhood spent Rochestown House, Killiney, Co. Dublin. Married distinguished international Irish chemist, Sir Robert John Kane (1809–1890), 23 August 1838; they had nine children. Toured Italy, 1873; her garden, 'Wickham', Dundrum, Co. Dublin, was said to be magnificent. Died 25 February 1886. As Miss Baily, elected the first woman member, Botanical Society of Edinburgh, 1836. Wrote on conifer cultivation in Ireland in *Irish Farmer's and Gardener's Magazine* (1834) pp. 262–267, 591–603. Also see E. Charles Nelson, Katherine Sophia Baily (Lady Kane) and The Irish Flora (1833), *Edinburgh University Press Journals*, vol. 46, no. 1.
7. 'She could find almost anything' – Sir James Edward Smith, MD, FS (1759–1828), one of the founders of the LS (1788), London. President (1788–1828).
8. Among Ellen Hutchins's contributions were: (a) Lewis Weston Dillwyn, *British Confervae, or, Coloured Figures and Descriptions of the British plants referred by Botanists to the Genus Conferva*. (London: W. Phillips, 1802); (b) Dawson Turner, *Historia Fuci, sive ... Plantarumfucorum ... et Historia*, 4 vols, Latin and English (London, 1808–1819); (c) J. Sowerby and J.E. Smith *English Botany...* 36 vols (London, 1790–1814); (d) Sir William Jackson Hooker, *British Jungermanniae: being a history and description, with coloured figures, of each species of the genus, and microscopical analyses of the parts.* London. [1812]–1816; (e) Introduction to *Flora Hibernica*, p. x, dated Dublin, 10 May 1836. The second part of this work *(Musci, Hepaticae, Lichens)* was by Doctors Harvey and Taylor. James Townsend Mackay acknowledges Hutchins's contribution. In the section devoted to liverworts, an entry reads: 'Jungermannia hutchinsiae on wet faces of rocks especially of waterfalls in wood near Bantry. Miss Hutchins'.
9. Alicia Hutchins, 'Ellen Hutchins: A Botanist', RCB, Dublin, MS47.
10. The Irish branch of the Hutchins family descended from two cousins who arrived in the south of Ireland from Dorset and settled in the early 17th century. Richard Hutchins served under the Earl of Orrery, 1666 and became one of the commissioners of poll tax. Owned property, Blackrock, near

Bantry, Co. Cork, during the 18th century. Ellen Hutchins's father, Thomas Hutchins, Ballylickey House, Bantry, Co. Cork, married Elinor, only daughter of Arthur Hutchins, Cregane Castle, Co. Limerick, 1759, thus uniting two branches of the family.

11. (a) M.E. Mitchell, *Early Observations on the Flora of Southwest Ireland. Selected Letters of Ellen Hutchins and Dawson Turner. 1807–1814*, Occasional Papers 12 (Dublin, 1999), p. 73, n. 13; (b) Madeline Hutchins, *Ellen Hutchins (1785–1815) Botanist of Bantry Bay*, published by The Ellen Hutchins Festival, in association with Bantry Historical and Archaeological Society (Bantry, Ireland, 2019).
12. Dr Whitley Stokes, Senior Fellow, TCD, 1805. Appointed lecturer, Natural History, 1816 and Regius Professor Medicine (1798–1811), Donegal Lecturer in Mathematics (1807–1819). Resigned to take Chair of Medicine, RCSI, Dublin (1819–1828). Returned to TCD as Regius Professor Physic (1830–1840). Contributed a number of rare mosses to J. Sowerby and J.E. Smiths' *English Botany* and to Dawson Turner's *Muscologiae Hibernicae Spicilegium* (1804). Lived for most of his life, Harcourt Street, Dublin, where Ellen Hutchins went to live with his family c.1802.
13. See Note 8 above.
14. Dawson Turner, MA, FRS, FLS, FSA (1775–1858). Antiquarian, banker, collector, patron and botanist. Born Yarmouth, father was a banker, educated Pembroke College, Cambridge; intended to take Holy Orders but in 1796, following his father's death, was obliged to take on the family business. Spare time devoted to botany, with other main interest being the study of antiquities of Norfolk. Publications include: *Synopsis of British Fuci* (1802), *Museologiae Hibernicae Spicilegium* (1804), *Botanist's Guide through England and Wales* (with L.Weston Dillwyn) (Yarmouth & London, 1805).
15. *Historia Fuci*.
16. William Henry Harvey, MD, FRS (1811–1866). Appointed Professor of Botany, RDS. 1848. See Chapter 2: Botanical Illustration c.1720–1820 pp. 22–36.
17. *Fucus tomentosus*, now called *Codium tomentosus*, from Dawson Turner's *Fuci*, vol. 3.
18. Madeline Hutchins, *Ellen Hutchins (1785–1815)*, p. 16.
19. (a) 'Celebrating Ellen Hutchins', exhibition of Ellen Hutchins's letters, drawings and botanical publications. Library, Royal Botanic Gardens, Kew, London (September–November 2019); (b) 'Celebrating Ellen Hutchins (1785–1815) Ireland's First Female Botanist', School of Natural Sciences, TCD, held Foyer, Old Anatomy Building (Part One, 9 February–30 March 2017, Part Two, 30 March–28 April 2017); (c) the Ellen Hutchins Festival (Bantry Bay, West Cork, 2015).
20. Today, the majority of Ellen Hutchins's herbarium specimens are held in the NHM London, over 200 drawings, archives, RBK Kew, Sheffield Museum (46 drawings), algae section, herbarium, UCC. Specimens also form part of the collection, herbarium, Botany Department, TCD, Smith Herbarium, Linnean Society, London and the William and Lynda Steere Herbarium, New York Botanical Gardens, New York, USA.
21. Robert Braithwaite, *The British Moss-Flora*, 3 vols (London, 1887–1905). Several mosses are recorded as being collected by Hutchins at 'Belfast' and in the 'North of Ireland', 1801.
22. James Edward Smith, *English Botany*, 36 vols (London, 1790–1814), with 2,592 colour plates by James Sowerby.
23. Ibid., no. 2523, vol. 46. Taylor, in Mackay's *Flora Hibernica* (see above) also acknowledges Hutchins as the collector of 11 rare mosses in Ireland.
24. The author of *Muscologiae Hibernicae Spicilegium* (1804) described 231 species of Irish mosses, the majority of which he had seen growing in Ireland or were sent to him by naturalists such as Dr Whitley Stokes, Robert Scott, John Templeton (qv) and Ellen Hutchins.
25. Ref: Eng. Letters. Archives – Kew.
26. Lichens named in honour of Ellen Hutchins – *Lecania hutchinsiae*, *Pertusaria hutchinsiae* and *Enterographa hutchinsiae*.
27. Sir William Jackson Hooker, born Norwich, Norfolk, 1785, died Kew, Surrey, 1865. Professor of Botany, Glasgow, 1820. Director, Royal Botanic Gardens, Kew, London, 1841–1865.
28. Kew correspondence. DC/157/291. Ellen Hutchins to Sir W.J. Hooker.
29. Madeline Hutchins, great-great-grandniece of Ellen Hutchins in correspondence with the author.
30. Ellen Hutchins to Dawson Turner, 30 November 1814. Dawson Turner correspondence, Wren Library, Trinity College, Cambridge University.
31. Letter from Ballylickey House dated 1 February 1807 from Ellen Hutchins to James Townsend Mackay. Original collection of letters from Ellen Hutchins to James Townsend Mackay, Herbarium, TCD.
32. A century after Ellen Hutchins's death, a field at Ballylickey House, Co. Cork was still referred to as 'Miss Ellen's Garden'.
33. Ardnagashel House, Bantry, Co. Cork, was purchased by Arthur Hutchins (1770–1838) for £1,000 (freehold) in 1800 and comprised approx. 300 acres.
34. See R. Lloyd Praeger, *Some Irish Naturalists – A Biographical Note-book* (Dundalk: W. Tempest, Dundalgan Press, 1949), p. 107.
35. Examples of plants named in honour of Ellen Hutchins include: marine algae, e.g. *Dary hutchinsiae*, bryophytes e.g. *Jubula hutchinsia* common name Hutchins hollywort, lichens, e.g. *Pertusaria hutchinsiae*.
36. Anne Elizabeth Ball (1808–1872) supplied a number of records for William Henry Harvey (qv), which were used by him in his algological part of Mackay's *Flora Hibernica* (1836) (see Note 13) and later in his *Phycologia Britannica* (Harvey, 1846–1851).
37. Naturalist Mary Ball (1812–1898) is recognised as first recorder (c.1840) of stridulation (that is production of a harsh grating noise) in Corixidae water bugs. Her collection of insects and shells was considered to be one of the most notable of early 19th-century Irish collections. She also studied a wide range of marine invertebrates, e.g. starfish, jellyfish, sea urchins.
38. Robert Ball, LLD Dublin, 1850. His personal research included a number of zoological papers largely relating to seals, on records of cephalopods from the Irish coast and on the larger sub fossil mammals found in Ireland. He was also 'The Inventor

or Improver of the Naturalist's dredge'.

39. Robert Brown studied medicine, Edinburgh DCL Oxon. 1832, FRS 1811, ALS 1798, FLS 1822. Naturalist on Flinder's Australasian expedition, 1801–1805. Librarian to Sir Joseph Banks. Keeper, Banksian Botanical Collection, BM: Keeper of Botanical Branch. President, LS, London, 1845–1853.
40. Letter from Harvey dated 20 December 1839 to N.B. Ward.
41. Harvey (1871), plate 356.
42. See H.M. Parkes, 'Some Notes on the Herbarium University College, Cork', *The Irish Naturalists' Journal* (Old Series), vol. 11 (1953), pp. 102–106.
43. Two bound volumes of specimens of seaweeds collected by algologist, Anne Elizabeth Ball are held in the Herbarium, NBG Dublin. The volumes were presented as a gift to her sister-in-law, Amelia G. Helliocar, who married Robert Ball, 1837. The collection comprises 97 marine and 2 freshwater algae, all drawn from localities largely in vicinity of Youghal, Co. Cork. See H.M. Parkes and M.J.P. Scannell, 'Anne E. Ball, Two Volumes of Algae in Herbarium, National Botanic Gardens, Dublin', *The Irish Naturalists' Journal*, vol. 16, no. 11, p. 349.
44. Anne Elizabeth Ball, examples of fungi in NBG Glasnevin, Dublin collections: (a) *Lycoperdon pyriforme*. Stump puffball, pen and ink on paper; (b) *Clavaria rugosa*; and (c) Wrinkled coral fungus.
45. Anne Elizabeth Ball also contributed records, vol. 4 (London, 1856).
46. *Sketches with the Microscope*. Signed: '*M.W.* 18576'. 250 copies were published privately by Sheilds, printer and proprietor, *King's County Chronicle*, Parsonstown (Birr). Reprinted, 2019 by Brosna Press, Ferbane, Co. Offaly with new introductory essays by Michael Byrne and John Feehan. Published by Offaly Historical and Archaeological Society, Bury Quay, Tullamore, Ireland.
47. George L. Leclerc Buffon, *Buffon's Natural History: Containing a Theory of the Earth. A General History of Man* ..., 10 vols (London: T. Gillet, 1797 and 1807).
48. Hariette King's sister was the wife of the 2nd Earl of Rosse. Their son, William, became 3rd Earl of Rosse and a distinguished astronomer.
49. Scottish physicist, Sir David Brewster is remembered as the inventor of the kaleidoscope.
50. Sir David Brewster, *The Life of Sir Isaac Newton* (London, 1831).
51. Ward prepared samples of decomposed glass recovered from Layard's excavations of the Assyrian city of Upper Mesopotamia, Nineveh, located on the outskirts of Mosul, 1849. She drew and painted the specimens for Sir David Brewster, 1864, and the coloured plates may be seen in the Royal Society of Edinburgh *Transactions* published in the same year.
52. Ward's illustration of the natterjack toad was printed in *The Intellectual Observer* (1864).
53. Sir Richard Owen, a leading palaeontologist and comparative anatomist. Campaigned for a museum of natural history, first superintendent of BM (NH) later became NHM, London. Contemporary of Charles Darwin and known for his strong opposition to Darwin's theory of natural selection.
54. Microscope Teachings: A description of various objects of especial interest and beauty adapted for microscopic observation. Illustrated by author's original drawings. The Hon. Mary Ward. London, 1855. Chapter 111, Collection and Mounting of Objects. p. 24.
55. For details, see Note 43.
56. As quoted in Owen G. Harry, 'The Hon. Mrs Ward (1827–1869). Artist, Naturalist, Astronomer and Ireland's First Lady of the Microscope', *The Irish Naturalists' Journal*, vol. 21, no. 5, p. 199.
57. Owen G. Harry, 'The Hon. Mrs Ward (1827–1869). Artist, Naturalist, Astronomer and Ireland's First Lady of the Microscope', *The Irish Naturalists' Journal*, vol. 21, no. 5, pp. 193–200.
58. Ibid., p. 199.
59. Maura J.P. Scannell, 'A Work of Special Value', in Mary Mulvihall (ed.), *Stars, Shells and Bluebells. Women Scientists and Pioneers* (Blackrock, Co. Dublin: Samton, 1997), p. 165.
60. The author would like to thank Dr James ('Jim') White, retired of UCD School of Biology & Environmental Science, for this information.
61. Matilda Cullen Knowles, b. Galgorm, near Ballymena, Co. Antrim, 31 January 1864. Employed in the Botanical Section, Science and Art Museum, Dublin. Appointed temporary post as assistant, April 1907, placed in charge of herbarium and botanical collections from c.1923. Co-authored (with Professor T. Johnson) *Hand List of Irish Flowering Plants and Ferns* (1910) (2 editions, with a third appearing in Irish after her death). Assisted A. Lorrain Smith in studying lichens for RIA *Survey of Clare Island*. Knowles's 'The Lichens of Ireland' (RIA *Proceedings*, 1929) added over 100 species to the Irish flora. Died Dublin, 27 April 1933.
62. M.C. Knowles, 'On the Irish *Spiranthes romanzoffiana*', *Irish Naturalists' Journal*, vol. 11, pp. 2–6.
63. Cephalopod – member of the Molluscar class *cephalopoloda*, e.g.. squid, octopus, cuttlefish.
64. (1) Jane Stephens, 'Atlantic Sponges Collected by the Scottish National Antarctic Expedition', *Transactions of the Royal Society of Edinburgh*, vol. 50, no. 2, pp. 423–467; (2) Jane Stephens, 'Alcyonarian and Madreporarian Corals of the Irish Coasts. With Descriptions of a New Species of Stachyodes by Professor S.J. Hickson, F.R.S.', in *Scientific Investigations*, 1907, No. V (HM Stationary Office, Dublin, 1907), pp. 1–28.
65. The plates usually stated: 'E. Barnes del.', 'Eileen Barnes, del.' or 'Eileen E. Barnes, del.'
66. Robert Lloyd Praeger, 'An Account of the Genus Sedum, as Found in Cultivation', *Journal of the Royal Horticultural Society*, vol. 46, pp. 1–314. Plant monograph reprints, J. Cramer (New York: Lehre, 1967). This contained 185 line drawings executed by Eileen Barnes.
67. The majority of Barnes's original line drawings executed in pen and ink are in the RIA, Dublin. For details, see E. Charles Nelson, 'Catalogue of Original Drawings of Sedums by Eileen Barnes in R.I.A. Dublin', Appendix 1, in Nelson (ed ), *Robert Lloyd Praeger's Crassulaceae: A Commentary on Possible Type Specimens in the National Botanic Gardens, Dublin, and on Illustrations in the Royal Irish Academy,*

*Dublin*. *Bradleya*, vol. 11, pp. 91–106. (List contained Appendix 1, pp. 95–99.)
68. Robert Lloyd Praeger, 'An Account of the Sempervivum Group' (London, 1932), 'Sources of material', p. 32.
69. Robert Lloyd Praeger: 'An Account of the Sempervivum Group', *Journal of the Royal Horticultural Society*, pp. 1–265. Plant monograph reprints, J. Cramer (New York: Lehre, 1967).
70. Robert Lloyd Praeger, 'Some Asiatic Sedums in the Edinburgh Herbarium: with Supplementary Notes from Kew and the British Museum', *Notes from the Royal Botanic Gardens, Edinburgh*, vol. 13, pp. 67–101, plus plate 179.
71. Maura J.P. Scannell, 'A Work of Special Value', p. 165.

**Chapter 9: 'A Woman of Substance' – Lady Edith Blake**

1. Thomas Humphry Ward (ed.), *Men of the Reign*, vol. 4 (London: G. Routledge & Sons, 1885), p. 102.
2. Anon., *False Positions: Or Sketches of Character*, 2 vols (London, 1863).
3. Patricia Cockburn, 'My birth and background' in *Figure of Eight* (London: Chatto & Windus, 1985), p. 11.
4. Patricia Butler, 'Every Lady Her Own Drawing Master' in *The Silent Companion, An Illustrated History of the Water Colour Society of Ireland* (Woodbridge: ACC Art Books, 2010), pp. 89–117.
5. Mark Girouard, 'Stamped, Addressed and Illustrated. Irish Decorated Envelopes of the Victorian Era', *Country Life*, 30 July 1970, pp. 290, 291.
6. Edith Blake, *Twelve Months in Southern Europe* (London: Chapman & Hall, 1876).
7. Henry Arthur Blake's first wife was Mary Jeannie Irwin, Boyle, Co. Roscommon, whom he married, New Orleans, Louisiana, USA, and who died in childbirth (1866).
8. Anon. (1927).
9. Edith Blake, 'Beothuks of Newfoundland', *Evening Telegram*, 26 December 1888–17 January 1889.
10. H.L. Clark, 'Zoological Jamaica', *Natural Science* (September 1898), pp. 161–171.
11. Kew correspondence. DC/210/8. Lady E. Blake to Daniel Morris, Director, Public Gardens, Jamaica (1879–1886).
12. Emily G. Trant (née Newton) exhibited with both the Water Colour Society of Ireland, known then as the Irish Amateur Drawing Society (beginning 1872) and the Dublin Sketching Club (from 1904). See (1) Ann M. Stewart, *Irish Art Societies and Sketching Clubs: Index of Exhibitors 1870–1980*, vol. 2 (Dublin, 1997); and (2) Patricia Butler, 'Early Exhibitions (1871–1878)' in *The Silent Companion* (Woodbridge: ACC Art Books, 2010), p. 133.
13. Lady Edith Blake, 'Watercolours of Jamaican Lepidoptera', NHM, London, Entomology Special Collections (Call Number: SB ff BLA).
14. William Fawcett with A.B. Rendle, *Flora of Jamaica* (London: Trustees of the BM, 1910–1936).
15. Henry Arthur Blake, 'The Awakening of Jamaica', *Nineteenth Century*, vol. 28, no. 164, pp. 534–544.
16. Blake, 'The Awakening of Jamaica', p. 540.
17. Henry Arthur Blake, 'The Jamaica Exhibition', *North American Review*, vol. 152, no. 411, p. 186.
18. Lady Edith Blake, ILN (1891), p. 111.
19. Patrick N. Wyse-Jackson, 'Ball, Valentine', *Dictionary of Irish Biography* (Dublin: RIA, 2009).
20. Patrick Bryan, *The Jamaican People 1880–1902: Race, Class and Social Control* (London: Macmillan Caribbean, 1991). Also see Joy Lumsden, *Jamaican Constitutional* (University of West Indies Press, 2001).
21. Articles by Lady Edith Blake include: (1) 'In the Bahamas', *Nineteenth Century*, vol. 23, pp. 682–692; (2) 'Highlands of Jamaica', *North American Review*, vol. 154, pp. 343–352; (3) 'The Triad Society and the Restoration of the Ming Dynasty', *Nineteenth Century*, vol. 71, pp. 667–687; and (4) 'The Sacred Bo Tree', *Nineteenth Century*, vol. 76, pp. 660–673.
22. Lady Edith Blake 'The Maroons of Jamaica', *North American Review*, vol. 1676, no. 504, p. 568.
23. Clarke, 'Zoological Jamaica', pp. 161–171.
24. S.A. Skan, *Quercus edithae*. *Hooker's Icones Plantarum*, 1901, 4th series, vol. 7, pl. 2661; *Quercus blakei* Skan. *Hooker's Icones Plantarum*, 1901, 4th series, vol. 7, pl. 2662.
25. Stephen Troyte Dunn, Superintendent Botany and Forestry Department, Hong Kong (1903–1910), published the first scientific description of the tree, 1908: 'New Chinese Plants', *Journal of Botany, British and Foreign*, vol. 46, no. 550, p. 325.
26. Kew correspondence. D6/164/179. Sir Arthur Blake writing to Sir William T. Thiselton-Dyer, September 1905.
27. William Fawcett born Arklow, Co. Wicklow, 13 February 1851. Died, Blackheath, London, 14 August 1926. BSc, FLS. Assistant Department of Botany, BM, 1880–1886, Director, Public Gardens and Plantations, Jamaica, 1886–1908. Collected plants, Cayman Islands, 1888, Jamaica, 1887–1908. Published his *Guide to the Botanic Gardens, Castleton, Jamaica* (Kingston, 1904).
28. Kew correspondence. DC/208/379. Letter from Lady E. Blake to [William] Fawcett, from the Queen's Cottage, Nuwara Eliya, [Sri Lanka], 17 April 1905.
29. Sir John Pope-Hennessy, *Sir Walter Ralegh in Ireland* (London: Kegan Paul, Trench & Co., 1883), pp. 140/141.
30. Sir Henry Arthur Blake, *Progress of the Colony of Ceylon 1904–1907* (Colombo, 1907).
31. Lady Edith Blake, 'The Position of Women in China', *Nineteenth Century*, vol. 72, pp. 1040–1051.
32. Lady Edith Blake, '"Tir na Bes". A Study of Irish Life and Death', *Nineteenth Century*, vol. 74, pp. 130–135.
33. Philip G. Lee. 'Necrology: The Late Sir Henry Arthur Blake G.C.M.G.', *Journal of the Cork Historical and Archaeological Society*, vol. 24, no. 117.

**Chapter 10: Professional Botanical Artists**

1. William T. Stearn, *Flower Artists of Kew* (London: The Herbert Press in Association with the Royal Botanical Gardens, 1990).
2. Sir Frederick William Moore, ALS (1893), FLS (1911) (1857–1949). Awarded Victoria Medal of Honour (1897), Veitch Memorial Medal (1932). Curator, TCD Botanic Garden (1877–1879). Curator [Director] RBG Glasnevin, Dublin (1879–1922), knighted (1911).

3. John Charles Lyons, *Remarks on Management of Orchidaceous Plants with a Catalogue of Those in the Collection of J.C. Lyons* (London: Press, 1843), 'Remarks on Orchidaceae', p. 1. Author, J.C. Lyons (1792/3–1874) born Ladiston, near Mullingar, Co. Westmeath, enthusiastic grower and importer of orchids, published first manual relating to growing of tropical species (see above). Also contributed to W.J. Hooker's *Century of Orchidaceous Plants* (London, 1849).
4. Josephine Humphries (fl.1890s) was related to Lydia Shackleton; both were Quakers. Josephine Humphries was employed by Frederick Moore during the 1890s at Glasnevin, where she assisted Lydia Shackleton. Ninety-three orchid portraits carry the monogram 'H' or initials '*J.H.*' and are dated between June 1894 and April 1895. See E. Charles Nelson and Brendan Sayers, *Orchids of Glasnevin. An Illustrated History of Orchids in Ireland* (Dublin: Strawberry Tree, 2002).
5. Robert Allen Rolfe, ALS (1885), Victoria Medal of Honour (1921) (1855–1921). Born Ruddington, Nottinghamshire, 12 May 1855. Gardener, Welbeck Abbey, Nottinghamshire. Assistant, Kew Herbarium (1880). Founder/editor, *Orchid Review* (1893–1920). Accounts of orchids in *Flora Tropical Africa* and *Flora Capensis*, orchid study book (with C.C. Hurst) (1909). Died Kew, Surrey, 13 April 1921.
6. Lydia Shackleton's sketchbooks. See Patricia Butler and Mary Davies, *Wicklow Through the Artist's Eye. An Exploration of County Wicklow's Historic Gardens, c.1660-c.1960* (Dublin: Wordwell, 2014), Kilmacurragh, p. 168, Mount Usher, p. 284.
7. Sir Frederick Moore, Director, RBG Glasnevin, Dublin, was permitted to spend no more than £3 per year commissioning Alice Jacob's work. It had to be completed in the artist's own time.
8. The Kyrle Society, through its 4 committees provided art, music, books and open spaces for the working-class poor, based around the slogan: 'Bring Beauty Home to the Poor'. This included decoration of hospitals, schools, libraries and working class pubs'.
9. The Reverend F.C. Hayes, *A Handy Book of Horticulture. An Introduction to the Theory and Practice of Gardening* (London: John Murray, 1900).
10. Alice Jacob's botanical portraits were frequently inscribed in Celtic script. See, Patricia Butler, *Irish Botanical Illustrators & Flower Painters* (Woodbridge: ACC Art Books, 2000), pp. 30, 31.
11. Sarah Finnegan, 'Alice Jacob (1862–1921) as part of the Arts and Crafts Movement, 1898–1921', MPhil Dissertation, History of Art, TCD.
12. Alice Jacob's designs for lace were illustrated in James Brenan's *The Modern Irish Lace Industry*, in W.P. Coyne (ed.), *Ireland: Industrial and Agricultural* (Dublin: Brown & Nolan, 1902).
13. John Turpin, 'Stained Glass, Enamelling, Life Painting and Teacher Training', in *A School of Art in Dublin Since the Eighteenth Century. A History of the National College of Design and Art, Dublin* (Dublin: Gill & Macmillan, 1995), p. 210.
14. G.T. Plunkett, Dublin Metropolitan School of Art, Headmaster's Report (1901/1902). Prize Giving, 13 February 1903. NLI.
15. Baroness Pauline (Polly) Harriet Prochazka (1842–1930), daughter of Baron Ottocar Prochazka, Field Marshall Lieutenant, Austrian army, granddaughter of Lady Stuart de Decies, Dromana, Co. Waterford. Born, Prague, went to Ireland aged five, lived at Dromana and towards the end of her life lived at Leyrath (Lyrath), Co. Kilkenny. A founder member, Amateur Drawing Society and in 1872 began exhibiting work with the Society and later exhibited with WSCI until 1927. For further information, see Patricia Butler, 'Every Lady Her Own Drawing Master' in *The Silent Companion. An Illustrated History of the Water Colour Society of Ireland* (Woodbridge: ACC Art Books, 2010), pp. 97–103.
16. Letter from Lady Charlotte Wheeler-Cuffe to Baronessa Pauline (Polly) Prochazka (no date) as quoted in E. Charles Nelson, '*Mount Victoria. Spring, 1911*' in *Shadow Among Splendours. Lady Charlotte Wheeler-Cuffe's Adventures Among the Flowers of Burma, 1897–1921* (Dublin: NBG Glasnevin, 2013), p.110.
17. *Rhododendron cuffeanum* (Burma). Lithograph: Matilda Smith and John Nugent Fitch, from *Curtis's Botanical Magazine*, vol. 13, tab. 8721.
18. *Irish Gardening*, vol. 9, no. 101, p. 106.
19. Ibid. See E.C. Nelson, p.152.
20. When the Cuffes left Burma, April 1921, the India Office (on recommendation from Kew) appointed botanist, R.E. Cooper (1890–1962) as Superintendent of Maymyo Botanic Garden (now known as National Kandawgyi Botanical Gardens).
21. Michael Longley, 'Raymond Piper: An Appreciation' in *Three Irish Orchids* (Belfast: Blackstaff Press, 1994), p. 4.
22. Raymond Piper's father secured for his son a tobacco-sorting job at Gallahers, Belfast. Raymond Piper was then awarded a Junior Trade Scholarship at Harland & Wolff.
23. Raymond Piper 'Artist and botanist who was a bright light in NI' Obituary, *Irish Times*, 21 July 2007, p. 14.
24. Newton Penprase (1888–1978), figure, landscape painter, sculptor. Born, Redruth, Cornwall, son of Newton Herbert Penprase, an interior decorator. 1903, admitted to Redruth School of Mines and Art. 1911, began teaching at Belfast School of Art and remained there for 42 years. 1915, elected member of the Belfast Art Society.
25. John Hunter, Chief Inspector of Art for Schools found Piper a place teaching art at the Royal School, Dungannon, Co. Tyrone.
26. Raymond Piper was awarded the James Kennedy Award for Portraiture from the RHA, 1993.
27. Richard Hayward and Raymond Piper, *This Is Ireland: Mayo, Sligo, Leitrim and Roscommon* (London: Arthur Barker, 1955).
28. Richard Hayward and Raymond Piper, *Munster and the City of Cork* (London: Phoenix House, 1964).
29. Michael Longley, *Irish Times Magazine* (11 January 2003), 'The Orchid Man', pp. 10–12.
30. E. Charles Nelson (introduction and notes) and Wendy Dunbar (design), *Piper's Flowers Painted by Raymond Piper* (Belfast: Blackstaff Press, 1987).
31. Michael Viney, 'Another Life', *Irish Times* (15 October 1988).
32. Ibid.

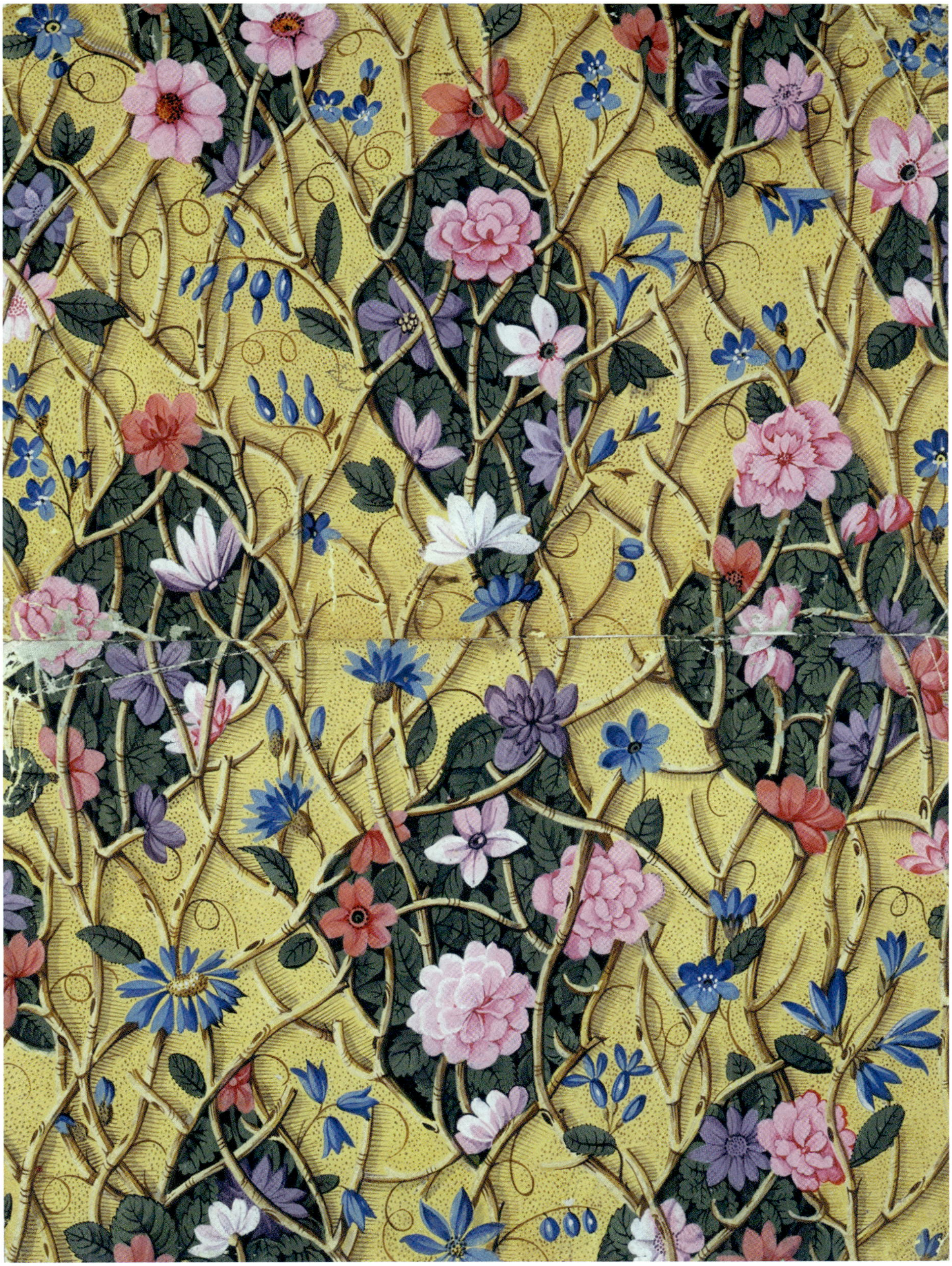

Fig. 214. Design for cotton; naturalistic flowers in a floral lattice
Watercolour by William Kilburn, made c.1788–1792
[© Victoria and Albert Museum, London]

# Select Bibliography


## BOOKS

Abbot, John. *The Natural History of the Rarer Lepidopterous Insects of Georgia ... Collected from Observations* ... London: J. Edwards et al., 1797.

Alexander, David. *A Biographical Dictionary of British and Irish Engravers, 1714–1820*. New Haven & London: Yale University Press, 2021.

*An Account of Saffron; the Manner of Its Culture and Saving for Use, with the Advantages It Will Be of to This Kingdom.* Dublin: printed by the Dublin Society by A. Rhames, 1732.

Anon. *False Positions: Or Sketches of Character*, 2 vols. London, 1863.

Baily Kane, Katherine. *The Irish Flora: Comprising the Phaenogamous Plants and Ferns*. Dublin: Hodges and Smith, 1833.

Bentham, George and Joseph Dalton Hooker. *Handbook of the British Flora: A Description of the Flowering Plants and Ferns Indigenous to, or Naturalized in, the British Isles. For the use of beginners and amateurs.* 6th ed. London: L. Reeve & Co., 1920.

Berry, Henry Fitzpatrick. *A History of the Royal Dublin Society*. London, 1915.

Blake, Edith Osborne. *The Realities of Freemasonry.* London, 1879.

Blake, Edith Osborne. *Twelve Months in Southern Europe*. London: Chapman & Hall, 1876.

Blunt, Wilfred, with the assistance of William T. Stearn. *The Art of Botanical Illustration*. 1950. Reprint, Woodbridge: ACC Art Books, 2015.

Braithwaite, Robert. *The British Moss-Flora*. 3 vols. London, 1887–1905.

Brewster, Sir David. *The Life of Sir Isaac Newton*. London, 1831.

Browne, Patrick. *The Civil and Natural History of Jamaica. In Three parts. Containing...the Whole Illustrated with Fifty Copper-plates; ... by Georg Dionysius Ehret*. London, c.1756.

Bryan, Patrick E. *The Jamaican People, 1880–1902: Race, Class and Social Control.* London: Macmillan Caribbean, 1991.

Burbidge, Frederick William. *Cultivated Plants, Their Propagation and Improvement.* Edinburgh: William Blackwood & Sons, 1877.

Burbidge, William F. *Art of Botanical Drawing*. 1873.

Butler, Patricia. *Irish Botanical Illustrators & Flower Painters.* Woodbridge: ACC Art Books, 2000.

Butler, Patricia. *The Silent Companion. An Illustrated History of the Water Colour Society of Ireland.* Woodbridge: ACC Art Books, 2010.

Butler, Patricia. *Three Hundred Years of Irish Watercolours and Drawings.* 1990. Reprint, London: Weidenfeld & Nicolson, 1990

## PERIODICALS, JOURNALS, NEWSPAPERS, UNPUBLISHED MATERIAL


Blake, Edith. 'Beothuks of Newfoundland'. *Evening Telegram*, 26 December 1888–17 January 1889.

Blake, Edith. 'In the Bahamas'. *Nineteenth Century*, vol. 23, pp. 682–692.

Blake, Edith. 'The Maroons of Jamaica'. *North American Review*, vol. 1676, no. 504, p. 568.

Edith Blake. 'The Position of Women in China'. *Nineteenth Century*, vol. 72, pp. 1040–1051.

Blake, Henry Arthur. 'The Awakening of Jamaica'. *Nineteenth Century*, vol. 28, no. 164, pp. 534–544.

Blake, Henry Arthur. 'The Jamaica Exhibition'. *North American Review*, vol. 152, no. 411, p. 186.

*The Botanical magazine, or, Flower-garden displayed* (later known as *Curtis's Botanical Magazine*) founded 1 February 1787.

Browne, Patrick. Fasciculus Plantarum Hiberniae (1788) [handwritten plant list]

Bunbury, Turtle. *The Life & Times of Thomas Kane McClintock Bunbury, 2nd Baron Rathdonnell, of Lisnavagh, County Carlow – Part 1 (1848–1878).*

Butler, Patricia. 'A Rare Flower – Susan Sex'. *Irish Arts Review*. Summer 2021, pp. 98–101.

Butler, Patricia. 'Designers of Distinction – William Kilburn (1745–1818) and Samuel Dixon (fl.1745-1769)'. *The GPA Irish Arts Review Year Book 1990–91*, pp. 153–163.

Butler, Patricia. 'Nature's Draw-Botanical Illustration'. *Irish Arts Review*, Spring 2020, pp. 105–109.

Butler, Patricia. 'Painting the Plant – Floras from the Garden Library, National Botanic Gardens, Glasnevin, Dublin'. *Irish Arts Review*, Summer 2007, pp. 100–105.

Butler, Patricia. 'Wild Flowers from Nature, Irish Botanical Watercolourists'. *Ireland of the Welcomes*, vol. 40, no. 4, pp. 25–29.

Butler, Patricia. 'William Kilburn (1745–1818)'. *Magazine of the Friends of the Royal Society of Water Colours, Drawings and Prints*, vol. 4, no. 2.

Carpenter, George H., Robert Lloyd Praeger and Robert Patterson (eds). *The Irish Naturalist. A Monthly Journal of General Irish Natural History*, vol. 16, 1907.

Coffey, Petra. 'George Victor Du Noyer 1817–1869'. *Journal of the Royal Society of Antiquaries of Ireland*, vol. 123, pp. 102–119.

*Curtis's Botanical Magazine*, London 1787–2020; C. as: *Kew Magazine* 1984–.

Davies, G.L.H. 'The Making of Irish Geography IV: The Physico-Historical Society of Ireland, 1744–1752'. *Irish Geography*, vol. 12, no. 1, pp. 92–98.

*The Dublin Penny Journal*, vol. 1, no. 23 (December 1832), p. 183.

Ellwood, C.V. and J.M.V. Harvey. 'The Lady Blake Collection: Catalogue of Lady Edith Blake's Collection of Jamaican Lepidoptera and Plants'. *Bulletin of the British Museum (Natural History)*, Historical Series, vol. 18, no. 2, pp. 145–202.

*The Gentleman's Magazine*, vol. 102, pp. 222–224.

Harry, Owen G. 'The Hon. Mrs Ward (1827–1869). Artist, Naturalist, Astronomer and Ireland's First Lady of the Microscope'. *The Irish Naturalists' Journal*, vol. 21, no. 5, pp. 193–200.

Hincks, T.D. 'Memoir of the late John Templeton Esq.' *Magazine of Natural History*, 1, pp. 403–406; 2, pp. 305–310.

Hutchinson, John. 'W.E. Trevithick'. *Journal of the Kew Guild*, vol. 7, no. 63, pp. 592–593.

*Irish Gardening*, vol. 9, no. Lady Charlotte Wheeler-Cuffe to Sir Frederick Moore.

*The Kew Magazine*, vol. 10, part 4.

Killen, John. 'John Templeton - The Gilbert White of Ireland, the Friend of Everyman'. *Linen Hall Review*, vol. 9, nos 3/4, pp. 4–8.

Kinahan, George Henry. Obituary 'G.V. Du Noyer'. *Geological Magazine*, (1869), p. 94.

Longley, Michael. 'The Orchid Man'. *Irish Times*, 11 January 2003, pp. 10–12.

*Manchester Mercury*, 19 April 1802.

Mitchell, M.E. 'Irish Botany in the Seventeenth Century'. *Proceedings of the Royal Irish Academy*, 75, pp. 275–84.

Mitchell, M.E. 'The Sources of Threlkeld's *Synopsis Stirpium Hibernicarum*'. *Proceedings of the Royal Irish Academy*, 75, pp. 1–6.

Nelson, E. Charles. 'Catalogue of Original Drawings of Sedums by Eileen Barnes in R.I.A. Dublin' Appenix 1, in Nelson (ed.), Robert Lloyd Praeger's Crassulaceae: A commentary on possible type specimens in the National Botanic Gardens, Dublin and on illustrations in the Royal Irish Academy, Dublin'. *Bradleya*, vol. 11, pp. 91–106.

Nelson, E. Charles. 'Patrick Browne (c.1720–1790). Irish Physician, Historian and Caribbean Botanist: A Brief Biography with an Account of his Lost Medical Dissertations. *Huntia*, vol. 11, no. 1, pp. 5–16.

Nelson, E. Charles. 'Walter Wade's *Flora Dublinensis*. An enigmatic Irish botanical publication'. *Long Room Bulletin of the Friends of the Library, TCD*, nos 20–21 (Spring–Autumn 1989), pp. 16–20.

O'Brien, Seamus. *Curtis's Botanical Magazine*, vol. 29, part 2, June 2012, plate 373, pp. 182, 190, 191.

Parkes, H.M. 'Some Notes on the Herbarium University College, Cork'. *The Irish Naturalists' Journal* (old series), vol. 11, pp. 102–106.

Parkes, H.M. and M.J.P. Scannell. 'Anne E. Ball. Two Volumes of Algae in the Herbarium, National Botanic Gardens, Dublin'. *The Irish Naturalists' Journal*, vol. 16, no. 11.

Powers, Jane. 'Plant People. Painted Petals – Deborah Lambkin, Botanical Painter'. *The Irish Garden*, November 1998, p. 18.

Praeger, Robert Loyd. 'An Account of the Sempervivum Group'. *Journal of the Royal Horticultural Society, London* (1932), pp. 1-265.

Praeger, Robert Lloyd. 'Some Asiatic Sedums in the Edinburgh Herbarium: With Supplementary Notes from Kew and the British Museum'. *Notes from the Royal Botanic Garden, Edinburgh*, vol. 13, pp. 67–101.

Scannell, Maura J.P. 'Susanna Grubb, Botanist and Artist. Biographical Notes and Historical Background'. *Glasra*, vol. 4, pp. 85–95.

Stephens, Jane. Sponges of the Coasts of Ireland – 2. Department of Agriculture and Technical Instruction for Ireland: Fisheries Branch: Scientific investigations, 1920.

Viney, Michael. 'Another Life'. *Irish Times*, 15 October 1988.

Webb, D.A. 'William Henry Harvey, 1811–1866 and the Tradition of Systematic Botany'. *Hermathena*, no. 103 (Autumn 1966), pp. 32–45.

*Garden*. See *Journal of Royal Horticultural Society*
*Gardening Illustrated*
*Gardeners' Chronicle*, London 1841–74
*Gentleman's Magazine*, London 1731–1907
*Glasra,* Dublin 1976–
*Huntia*, Pittsburgh 1964–
*The Irish Garden*
*Irish Naturalist. A monthly journal of General Irish Natural History*
*Irish Naturalist's Journal*, Belfast 1928–
*Irish Times*
*Journal of Kew Guild*, Kew 1893–
*Journal of Royal Horticultural Society*, London, 1846–1975; C as: *Garden*, 1975
*Kew Bulletin*, Kew 1898–
*Moorea, Journal of the Irish Garden Plant Society,* Dublin 1982–
Royal Dublin Society, *Proceedings* 1740–

## CATALOGUES

Butler, Patricia. The Brocas Collection. An Illustrated Selective Catalogue of Original Watercolours, Prints and Drawings in the National Library of Ireland with an Account of the Brocas Family and Their Contribution to the [Royal] Dublin Society's School of Landscape and Ornament Drawing. NLI Dublin, 1997.

Catalogues of the International Exhibition of Botanical Art & Illustration from Hunt Institute, California, 1968.

National Botanic Gardens, Glasnevin. Exhibition of *Vireya* rhododendron paintings by Deborah Lambkin. Introduction by Director, Donal Synott. Herbarium Library, NBG Glasnevin, Dublin 16–24 May, 1998.

National Gallery of Ireland. Illustrated Summary Catalogue of Drawings, Watercolours and Miniatures. Introduction by Homan Potterton, Director, N.G.I. Compiled by Adrian Le Harivel. 1983.

National Gallery of Ireland. Illustrated Summary Catalogue of Prints and Sculpture. Catalogue compiled Catalogues of the International Exhibition of Botanical Art & Illustration from 1968. Hunt Institute, California.

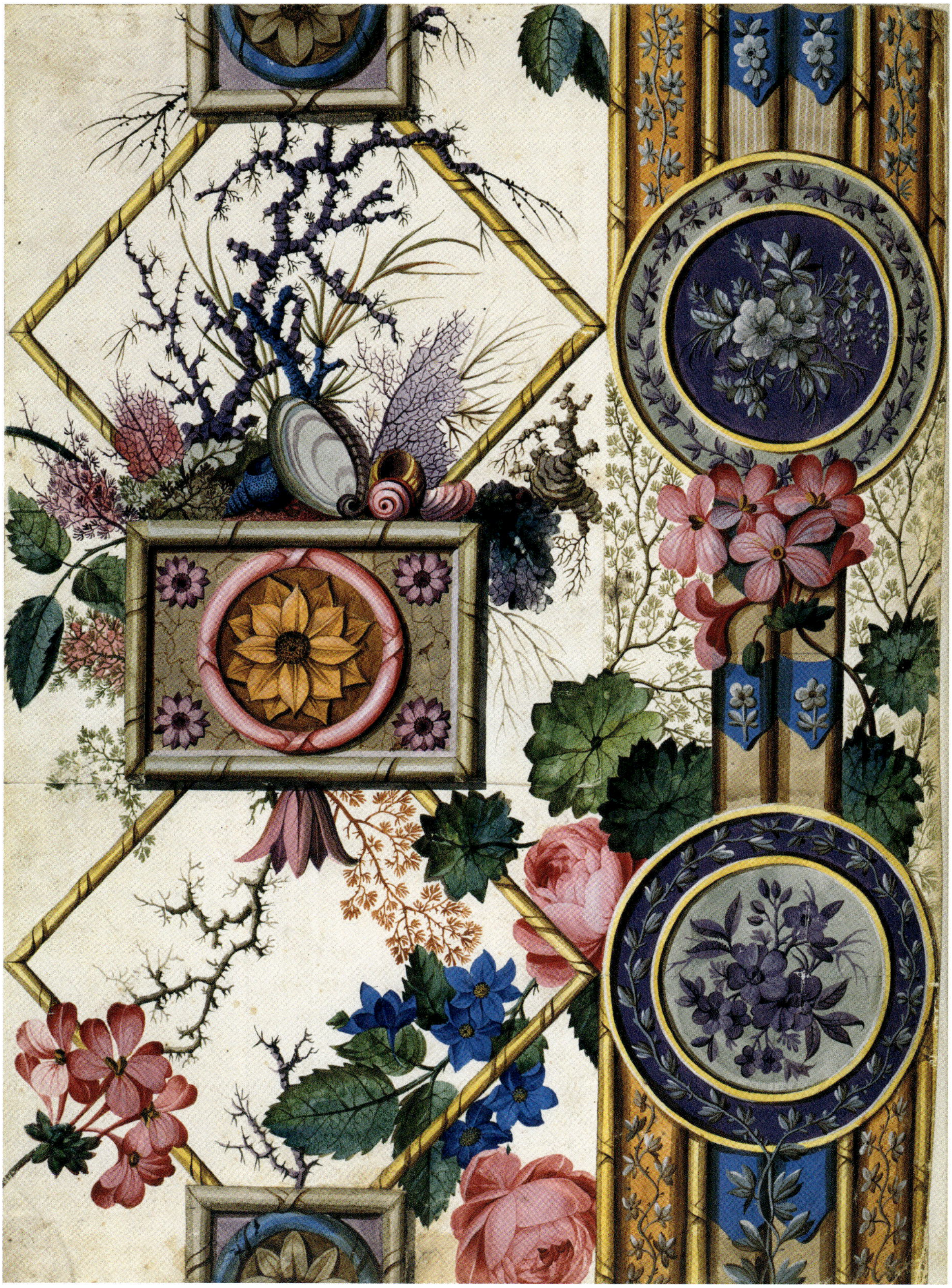

Fig. 215. Design for a printed cotton for furnishing; shells, flowers and coral
Watercolour by William Kilburn, made c.1788–1792
[© Victoria and Albert Museum, London]

# Acknowledgements

This book has been a collaborative project bringing together different strands from many countries, and without the superb and generous co-operation of individuals and institutions, it simply would not have been possible. In particular, the author would like to express her warm thanks to professional photographer, Mark Boland who photographed the majority of the images found in this publication, supplied and sustained a superb standard of photography throughout and was always more than generous with his time. At the National Gallery of Ireland, the author would like to express her appreciation to Sean Rainbird (Director, now retired), Dr Caroline Campbell (Director), Janet McLean (Curator of European Art, 1850–1950) and all the staff for their encouragement and outstanding support not only for this book but also for the NGI exhibition *Drawn from Nature: Irish Botanical Art* (2020) on which this publication is based. Invaluable assistance was received from Dr Matthew Jebb (Director) and staff of the National Botanic Gardens, Glasnevin, Dublin. Seamus O'Brien (Head Gardener), National Botanic Gardens, Kilmacurragh, Co. Wicklow provided vital specialist knowledge in relation to plant names for which the author is deeply grateful. Many kind individuals also supported and provided generous encouragement in numerous ways and to them the author offers her grateful and heartfelt thanks: Sir David Davies; Dr Shirley Sherwood, OBE; editors: Sue Bennett, Dr Rachel Finnegan; designers: Steven Farrow, Ann Kutzer; botanical artists: Mary Dillon, Shevaun Doherty, Deborah Lambkin, Siobhan M. Larkin, Margareta Pertl, Yanny Petters, the late Raymond Piper, Susan M. Sex, Holly Somerville, Jane Stark, Lynn Stringer, the late Dr Wendy F. Walsh. **Institutions: Ireland** – the Edward Worth Library; the Irish Architectural Archive; the Linen Hall Library (NI); the trustees of Muckross House, Co. Kerry; the assistant director and staff, National Library of Ireland; the National Trust (NI); the Royal Dublin Society; Ulster Museum; the Royal Irish Academy; the Royal Society of Antiquaries of Ireland; the president and committee, Society of Irish Botanical Artists; the Tipperary Museum of Hidden History, Cultural Services; Ulster Museum Picture Library; Westport House, Westport Estate, Co. Mayo. **UK** – the British Library; the British Museum; Bute Museum; the Guildhall Library, Corporation of London; the Linnean Society; the National Galleries of Scotland; the National Portrait Gallery; the Natural History Museum; the Royal Botanic Gardens, Kew; the Royal Collections, Buckingham Palace; the Shirley Sherwood Gallery; the Society of Botanical Artists; Trinity College, the University of Cambridge; the Victoria and Albert Museum. **Worldwide** – the Huntington Library, California, USA; the National Museum of the American Indian, Smithsonian Institution, New York, USA; Rhode Island School of Design Museum, Providence RI, USA; Uppsala University Library, Sweden. **Commercial Galleries/Fine Art Auctioneers**: the Martyn Gregory Gallery, London; the Olivier Cornet Gallery, Dublin; Whytes Fine Art, Dublin. **Private Collections/Collectors and Others**: Alistair D. Cargill, Turtle Bunbury, Brendan Burgess, Olwyn Burke, Christine Davies, the Earl of Derby, Shevaun Doherty, Penelope Durell, Fionnuala Fallon, Lesley Fennell and family, Bobbie Hanvey, Jesmond M. Harding, Kieran Heffernan, Biddy Hughes, Madeline Hutchins, Corinne Ironside, Kristin and Andrea Jameson, Richard Johnston, Alistair and Jennifer

Kilburn, Dominic Kilburn, Dr William Laffan, Tara Lannigan-O'Keefe, the late Melo Lenox Conyngham, Dr Stephen Lloyd, Elizabeth Mackeown, Elaine Moore Mackey, Iona and Simon Murray, Dr Peter Murray, Yanny Petters, the late Dr Daphne Pochin Mould, the Earl and Countess of Rosse, Vincent Sex, Jonathan Shackleton, FRGS, Donal Synott, the late Anne Tupper, Katherine Tyrell, the late Dr James White. **Professional Staff**: Bodleian Libraries, University of Oxford, Department of Plant Sciences, Sherardian Library: Sophie Wilcox (Alexander & Sherardian Librarian). Birr Castle Archives, Birr, Co. Offaly: Lisa Shortall (Archivist). British Museum, National Portrait Gallery, Bute Museum, Rothesay, Isle of Bute, Scotland: Isabel Sharp (Genealogist). Castle Ward, Co. Down, (NI): Dr Neil Watt (Collections and House Manager), Niamh Hanlon (House Steward). The Edward Worth Library: Dr Elizabethanne Boran (Librarian). The Huntington Library, Art Museum and Botanical Gardens, San Marino, California, USA: Anne Blecksmith (Head of Reader Services). Irish Architectural Archive: Colum O'Riordan (CEO) and staff. Irish Georgian Society: Donough Cahill (Executive Director). The Linnean Society, London: Lynda Brooks (Librarian). National Botanic Gardens, Dublin: Dr Mathew Jebb (Director), Alexandra Caccamo (Librarian, now retired, the Garden Library). Library Assistants: Colette Edward (retired) and Anna Teahan, Dr Noeleen Smyth (Conservation Botanist), Brendan Sayers (Glasshouse Foreman). National Gallery of Ireland: Sean Rainbird (Director, now retired), Dr Caroline Campbell (Director), Janet McLean (Curator of European Art, 1850–1950), Kim Smit (Head of Collections and Research), Marie McFeely (Images & Licensing Officer), image editors: Brendan Maher and Niamph O'Brien, Sinead Leahy (Events Administrator). National Library of Ireland: Dr Audrey Whitty (Director), Berni Metcalfe (Reprographics Published Collections), James Harte (Library Assistant). National Museum of Ireland's Collection Resource Centre, Natural History Division, Co. Dublin: Dr Aidan O'Hanlon (Curator of Entomology). National Museums (NI): Dr Michael Simms (Director, Science Museum), Anne Stewart (Senior Curator of Art), Angela Ross (Curator of Vertebrates). Natural History Museum: Andrea Hart (Head of Library Special Collections). Rhode Island School of Design (RISD), Museum of Art. Royal Botanic Gardens, Kew: Lynn Parker (Curator, Illustrations & Artefact Collections), Lydia White (Head of Publishing), Alice Nelson (Library & Archives), Angela Bond (Fungarium Collections Manager). The Royal Dublin Society: Natasha Serne (Archivist and Records Manager). Royal Horticultural Society: Charlotte Brooks (RHS Art Curator, Lindley Library Collections). Royal Irish Academy: Dr Barbara McCormack (Academy Librarian), Méadhbh Murphy (Deputy Librarian). The Royal Society of Antiquaries of Ireland: President and Members of Council, Marysia Wieckiewicz-Carroll (Director). Victoria and Albert Museum, London: Dr Sarah Grant (Curator, Prints, Word & Image Department), Dr Olivia Horsfall Turner (Senior Curator of Designs), Dr Ella F. Kilgallon (Assistant Curator of Designs).

The author is especially grateful to her daughter, Vanessa for all her superb support in unravelling the mysteries of the computer and for helping to make this book possible.

*To my grandchildren – Lydia, Hubert, Hedley, Patrick, Ralph and Sam, with love*

# General Index

Page numbers in **bold** refer to illustrations and/or captions

# Index of Plants

Page numbers in **bold** refer to illustrations and/or captions